I have two dedications. First, to my Dad, John Alison – who has always recognized the wisdom that keeping happy by being silly and daft is utterly critical in the journey through life! ('Never stay up on the barren heights of cleverness, but come down into the green valleys of silliness' – Wittgenstein).

The second is to my current cohort of PhD students who have recently completed or who are near completion. They are an inspiring and joyful bundle of folk to be around.

Laurence

I dedicate this book to my beautiful daughters, Daisy and Phoebe, who whilst still too young to fully understand why daddy is always at work, will never truly appreciate the light they shine in my life.

Lee

Contributors

Laurence Alison is Director of The Centre for Critical and Major Incident Psychology at The Institute of Psychology, Society and Health (University of Liverpool). He is a Chair of Investigative and Forensic Psychology and has been publishing in the field of profiling and investigative advice for over 15 years. He was at the forefront of early developments and challenges in Investigative Psychology and has a track record of providing psychological solutions for criminal investigation. His work was critical in the professionalization of profiling in the mid 1990s, especially in the aftermath of his defence report for the R-V-Stagg case, in which he provided a critique of Paul Britton's work. He has provided advice to the police and courts in over 100 cases in the UK as well as cases in Russia, Israel, Germany and Singapore. He has served as key psychological advisor on nearly 100 critical and major incident debriefs and with Prof. Jonathan Crego he co-directs the newly formed 'HYDRA Foundation', a research/practitioner organization that contributes to critical incident decision making in the public and private sector.

Louise Almond is a Lecturer at The Institute of Psychology, Society and Health at The University of Liverpool. In 2006 she worked on a project funded by the Leverhulme Trust, which examined the content of offender profiles and behavioural investigative advice in addition to how such advice is interpreted and used. She graduated with a PhD in Investigative Psychology in 2006. Her PhD thesis investigated the characteristics and behaviour of youths who sexually harm. In 2001, Dr. Almond carried out a project commissioned by the Home Office into arson and arsonists.

Jennifer Brown was awarded a Chair in Forensic Psychology from the University of Surrey where she was Director of the Crime and Justice Initiative. She is currently Deputy Director of the Mannheim Centre for Criminology at the London School of Economics. Her research interests span police occupational culture particularly in reference to diversity issues and stress, and psychological aspects of police investigative practice.

Terri Cole is a Senior Behavioural Investigative Adviser working at the National Policing Improvement Agency. She has worked in the field of serious crime investigation since 1997 as an assistant analyst in the Serious Crime Analysis Section of NPIA, and as a BIA since 2002. She was accepted on the ACPO Approved list of BIAs in 2005 and has provided over 100 written reports for serious crime investigations throughout the UK in relation to behavioural offence linkage, crime scene assessment, offender profiling and prioritization of persons of interest. She has recently gained a PhD from the University of Surrey, exploring a pragmatic psychological approach to the provision of behavioural investigative advice for difficult to detect murder investigations in the UK.

Alasdair Goodwill is a Lecturer at Ryerson University. His main research interests are in offender profiling research, in particular developing, analysing and delivering pragmatic multi-phasic methods for suspect prioritization in serious and violent criminal investigations. He is a chartered forensic psychologist (Health Professions Council, UK) a chartered scientist (CSci – British Psychological Society) and a fellow of the Royal Statistical Society (UK).

Adam Gregory is the Deputy Head of Profession for Behavioural Investigative Advice within the NPIA. After gaining a BSc (Hons) in Psychology in 1994, he subsequently spent five years in the Behavioural Science Section of Surrey Police, an operational research unit dedicated to furthering the behavioural understanding of sexual offences and homicide. Adam was accepted on the ACPO Approved list of BIAs in 1998, joined the NCOF (now the NPIA) in 1999, and to date has provided more than 150 written reports in support of major crime investigations. He has played a leading role in the development of innovative investigative support techniques, including the prioritization of familial DNA search results.

Susanne Knabe-Nicol is a PhD candidate at the Centre for Critical and Major Incident Psychology at The Institute of Psychology, Society and Health (University of Liverpool). She spent a considerable amount of time with Geographic Profilers from the UK, and Behavioural Investigative Advisers in the UK and Germany, observing and shadowing their work and conducting extensive interviews with them with regards to their operational practice. She is currently working in the major crime team of Suffolk Constabulary.

Matthew L. Long is the Violent and Sexual Offender Manager for Kent Police and the force lead for the investigation into the sexual abuse of children online. He is also responsible for the countywide community management of the highest risk sex offenders through Multi-Agency Public Protection Arrangements (MAPPA). He leads the Public Protection Crime Unit (PPCU), which is the force's response to organized crime groups of sexual abuse online. He is currently undertaking a PhD studying sexual offences and risk at the Centre for Critical and Major Incident Psychology (University of Liverpool).

Michelle McManus is a PhD candidate at the Centre for Critical and Major Incident Psychology at the Institute of Psychology, Society and Health (University of Liverpool). Her MSc work and current PhD thesis focuses on the possession of indecent images of children and risk of contact sexual abuse. She has been working closely with Kent Public Protection Crime Unit in examining this in the context of policing. This work has led to presentations to forces across Europe.

Benjamin Marshall is a Forensic Psychologist specializing in research design and methodology. He graduated from Liverpool University with a distinction in Investigative Psychology before working for several years at UCL's Jill Dando Institute of Crime Science where he conducted projects commissioned by the Home Office, Metropolitan Police, Defra and DVLA amongst others. More recently, Ben left academia to focus full-time on public sector research, which has included spells at the Ministry of Justice and the Home Office.

Louise Porter is a Research Fellow with the Australian Research Council Centre of Excellence in Policing and Security, Griffith University (Brisbane, Australia). Formerly, from 2004–2008, Louise was employed as a lecturer in forensic psychology at the University of Liverpool, where she also completed her Masters degree in Investigative Psychology and an ESRC funded PhD focusing on group crime (applying social psychological theories of group behaviour and leadership to offending contexts). Louise's research interests centre on interpersonal processes, specifically leadership and peer influence in forensic contexts, and has explored social and organizational features of group crime, specifically with regard to rape and robbery groups and, more recently, police corruption.

Lee Rainbow is the Head of Profession for Behavioural Investigative Advice within the NPIA and secretary of the ACPO Sub-Committee for Behavioural Science. After gaining an MSc in Investigative Psychology in 1996, he subsequently worked within Cleveland Constabulary as a criminal intelligence analyst and Surrey Police as a behavioural science consultant before being employed by the NCF (now NPIA) as the first ever full-time Behavioural Investigative Adviser. He has produced over 250 written reports in support of serious crime enquiries and has supported many of the most high-profile cases in the UK, as well as cases in Europe and the Caribbean. He has played a leading role in the national co-ordination of behavioural investigative advice within the UK, and has contributed significantly to the enhanced professionalization of the discipline from both a tactical and strategic perspective.

Gaëlle Villejoubert is a Senior Lecturer in Psychology at Kingston University London. She lectures on cognitive processes and research methods. She sits on the executive committee of the European Association for Decision Making and she is the newsletter editor of the EADM Bulletin and the website administrator of the EADM website. Her research focuses on the study of the cognitive processes and pragmatic inferences underlying reasoning, judgment and decision making. She publishes her research in international journals such as *Applied Cognitive Psychology, Cognition, Memory and Cognition, Psychological Science* and *Thinking and Reasoning*.

Claudia van den Heuvel is a PhD candidate at The Centre for Critical and Major Incident Psychology at The Institute of Psychology, Society and Health (University of Liverpool). Her research focuses on police and terrorist decision making in counter-terrorist (suicide bombing) operations. She holds a BA in Social Sciences from University College Utrecht, an MSc in Social and Organisational Psychology from Leiden University, and an MSc in Investigative and Forensic Psychology from the University of Liverpool.

Jan Winter completed his MSc in Clinical Psychology at the Vrije Universiteit Brussels (VUB; Belgium), and his MSc in Investigative Psychology at the University of Liverpool. His studies focus on novel sequence analysis methods to disentangle the intricate offender–victim interaction in stranger rapes. In collaboration with the Belgian and Dutch police, and the British Serious Crime Analysis Section (SCAS), he investigates the cross-situational stability of offence behaviours to better inform efforts regarding comparative case analysis.

Preface

Laurence Alison and Lee Rainbow

Sections of this chapter have been published previously. Reproduced here with kind permission from the authors, Laurence Alison and Marie Eyre, and Pennant Books.

On the 15 July 1992, a young woman was murdered on Wimbledon Common in London. Although the tragic circumstances of this crime were sufficient for widespread reporting in the media, set amongst the background of almost 700 homicides recorded in England and Wales that year, it may have seemed unlikely that it could have a lasting effect on anyone unconnected to the victim. As a couple of undergraduate psychology students, we had no idea that the murder of Rachel Nickell in 1992 was destined to become a critical event in shaping our professional lives and would come to represent one of the most significant landmarks in 'offender profiling' in the UK. With the recent successful prosecution of the offender responsible for taking Rachel's life (Robert Napper – see Alison and Eyre, 2009), the case provides a suitable backdrop against which to reflect on the mistakes made, the lessons learnt and the legacies left after almost two decades.

The murder of Rachel Nickell occurred at a time of much excitement about the potential for psychologists and behavioural experts to generate 'profiles' of offenders from the 'latent behavioural traces' left at a crime scene. At that time, *Silence of the Lambs*, *Cracker* and a plethora of TV shows and movies were actively perpetuating the myth that profilers had some special insight enabling them to sweep through a crime scene and see what the police could not. The myth was that these categorizations into 'types' of offenders then enabled the profiler to derive a pen portrait, including living circumstances, previous criminal history, psychiatric history and sexual fantasies.

So powerful was this narrative of the maverick profiler that even in recent years it has been hard for professionals to distance this 'invented truth' from the contemporary reality, and as such, certain naive assumptions about what profilers do remain.

Back in 1992, whilst the majority of such activity was focused within the Behavioural Science Unit of the FBI, a growing interest within UK policing circles saw the emergence of a select number of individuals offering such services to British investigations. Paul Britton, at the time the Regional Head of Forensic Psychology in Leicestershire, was thus engaged in the Rachel Nickell murder investigation.

In 2002, eight years after his initial involvement, Paul Britton appeared before the British Psychological Society (BPS) accused of professional misconduct over his role in the Rachel Nickell investigation. The complaint was brought by Colin Stagg; the man who had been prioritized as a suspect largely on the basis of the offender profile produced by Britton. By the time of the BPS' disciplinary hearing (which was dismissed on the grounds that the eight-year delay made a fair hearing impossible), Stagg's life was in ruins as a result of the failed investigation and felt that the intervening years had done little to eradicate its impact on his life. He was, understandably, less than satisfied at the outcome of the BPS' decision.

Stagg had argued that Britton had not conducted his duties in a proper and scientific manner. Britton's lawyers commented that Stagg's allegations against their client were 'scandalous' because they were 'wholly misconceived'.

The essence of the difficulties in Britton's involvement in the hunt for Rachel Nickell's killer is summarized in Alison and Eyre's book, *Killer in the Shadows*, but in short the failings included the fact that he worked in relative isolation across a very broad range of areas (from interview advice, to profiling, to under cover work) and that it appeared, at least in terms of his relationship with the enquiry team, that his advice was closely and inextricably tied in with the decision making – with little consideration of the more appropriate view that the central decision making should always have rested within the domain of the senior investigating officer.

> 'Whilst Mr. Britton clearly had areas of significant expertise and substantial experience there were no limits set clearly to prevent a creeping slow-but-sure slippage between professional standards and methods of practice that were less than reliable. For example he claimed that, given knowledge of a suspect's sexuality, he would 'know immediately that he [the offender] was likely to have killed Rachel Nickell, without him mentioning it.'
>
> (p. 165)

The suspect, Britton asserted, would merely need to walk into his consulting room for this thaumaturgy to occur. As Alison and Eyre (2009) pointed out, 'It needs saying – in the plainest terms – that such a claim is unscientific' (p. 126).

The claim that one can identify a murderer reliably simply by having them walk into a room borders on notions of telepathy and not clinical expertise.

Paul Britton furnished the Rachel Nickell team with two offender profiles, one detailing 17 different points to which he expected the offender to conform. He covered, among other things, age, education, type of employment, lifestyle, location, likely pre-convictions and (lack of) car ownership. These days a profiler would not offer such advice without indicating the evidence base for their claims. In other words, they would detail exactly why they had inferred the offender was, for example, in his twenties, supported by a sound rationale.

Britton also provided 'information' on the rarity (or otherwise) of particular sexual fantasies, interview techniques for the Colin Stagg interviews and advice on the undercover operation that was initiated. He also diagnosed the man with a personality 'disturbance' and this 'information' on Stagg's supposed personality disturbance was all in the public domain, pored over by national tabloids and TV news reports.

Scientists are entrusted with finding the truth. In that endeavour, scientists cannot rely on faith, intuition or hunches, just proof. Then this work is published for the rest of the academic community to see if others can disprove it (in fact even prior to publication such research – at least in journals – is peer reviewed and very frequently revised based on other expert opinion). The peer review system is predicated on establishing what you have done, how you have done it, and seeing if someone can replicate it or disprove: it is important.

It is as important as quality control in a general practitioner's office, a dentist or a meteorologist; after all, who would deny the usefulness of having a second person test what the first one has done? In any walk of life, if it matters and is likely to have real and high-risk consequences, we need to double check. Scientists are as human as anyone else. They may simply make honest mistakes or, worse, may not be trusted to do the honourable thing, which is why it's so important to have a system where other academics try to find the flaws in others' arguments as well as provide alternative solutions to important problems.

As such, advisers have a responsibility not to break the trust placed in them and a duty to uphold the reputation of their profession. Most importantly, they have a duty to the public to make sure that when they are remotely unsure, to say so. Expert testimony is known to have swayed juries and caused miscarriages of justice in cases as serious as murder, so there is a real professional requirement to caveat and make clear any claims made in criminal cases.

Britton does not appear to have any systematic basis for, and of his, assertions and claims to rely mainly on clinical experience (cf. *The Jigsaw Man*, Britton, 1997) and the concerns with these exclusively intuitive methods became one of the central features of the case when the enquiry team tried to get the case prepared for a court hearing.

In fairness to Britton he does correctly state that profiling is a matter of probabilities, not absolute certainty. The criminal justice system demands a threshold set at proving 'beyond reasonable doubt' that the defendant standing before them is the person who committed the crime. At that threshold, profiling would make an extremely unworthy opponent in the overwhelming majority of cases, because profiles predict things that are not yet known for sure so it cannot prove *anything* beyond reasonable doubt. This doesn't mean profiling is a redundant activity: merely that it is not suited to court appearances. Offender profiles were designed to be used in criminal investigations to help direct police towards things that are more probable than others and, used in that environment, they can (if they are good) be useful and as operationally relevant as blood spatter analysis, ballistics advice.

In the two profiles Britton produced for the Nickell enquiry – one general profile detailing the likely characteristics of the killer and a second profile that contained information on his likely sexual preferences, fantasies and so on – he did not, as a scientist should, make reference to the evidence base he used from which he drew his conclusions. However, notwithstanding our earlier observations concerning the importance of a scientific approach, Britton's failings must also be considered against commensurate failings by the investigation. The blind acceptance of such misguided advice and the sanctioning of a 28-week 'honey trap' operation based on the assumption that Stagg would reveal 'guilty knowledge' concerning the murder quickly degenerated into a disturbing series of sexual inducements towards a confession, which was ultimately deemed inadmissible as evidence by the presiding judge.

Whilst one could be tempted to make conclusions around 'the blind leading the blind', more mature reflection may promote a more accurate interpretation of 'the unscientific but enthusiastic leading (and indeed being led by) the enthusiastic but unscientific'.

There have been many dramatic changes since the Rachel Nickell murder enquiry: the psychology of witness interviewing, suspect interviewing, decision making, leadership and motivation, stress and, of course, methods for psychologists assisting the police – including the provision of behavioural science support.

Profiling and profilers (now 'Behavioural Investigative Advisers') – have changed profoundly, with greater regulation, greater professionalism and integrity and far less personality-based media attention. These changes have been almost exclusively positive. This case should not be used to cast blame on our contemporary police service or behavioural profilers, but rather serve as a template against which to evaluate the developments outlined in this volume.

Against this backdrop of increased professionalization, an interesting phenomenon has occurred. When the mistakes of the Rachel Nickell enquiry were being made, profiling enjoyed a widespread acceptance as a valid and effective investigative technique. More recently however, the discipline has become the target for widespread suspicion and criticism, particularly from the academic community. Such an inverse relationship between professionalism and reputation is not easily explained. Reference to the vast majority of the academic criticisms demonstrate either a complete misunderstanding of the role of behavioural investigative advice or reliance on outdated popularizations of historical practice, particularly from North America. To judge contemporary practice from such sources holds as much merit as proffering an opinion about today's football premiership based on a review of George Best's autobiography.

It is therefore hoped that the academic community will embrace this volume with an open and enquiring mind and seek to develop a more constructive research agenda based on an updated understanding of contemporary practice. We are committed to the continued professionalization of this discipline and issue a challenge to researchers to trade the easy publications of lazy debunking for a more collaborative partnership in recognition of our shared goals.

The development of behavioural investigative advice in the UK has not been an easy road. Mistakes have been made and lessons learnt. It is hoped and genuinely believed that such mistakes as evidenced during the Rachel Nickell enquiry would not and could not be repeated, and that the lessons learnt have informed a contemporary practice that places the UK at the forefront of such endeavours.

How far have we come? That is for the reader to judge. How far have we yet to go? That is for practitioners, police officers, researchers, media and all interested stakeholders to recognize and address for the benefit of all.

Reference

Alison, L., & Eyre, M. (2009). *Killer in the shadows: the monstrous crimes of Robert Napper*. London: Pennant Books.

unbelievably pleasant and fun it has been – and that fact alone makes the effort so worthwhile. I'd also like to thank Marie Eyre and Lauren Mondshein, both of whom helped me organize some of the prepublished material.

Lee Rainbow acknowledgements

Like many a seemingly good idea this one started in the pub. When Laurence first approached me to co-edit this volume, my delight was completely uninformed by any knowledge of the task ahead. However, such effort has been extremely rewarding and served to remind me what a fantastic academic, researcher and most importantly good friend Laurence is. I cannot begin to imagine embarking on such a journey without such a skilled navigator, and I thank Laurence for both his support and guidance on this book and for his continued shared vision for the future of behavioural investigative advice.

I would like to thank all my colleagues (past and present) at the NPIA and all the police officers who have the courage, insight and dedication to engage with and support this emerging field of investigative support. In particular, I would like to acknowledge the positive influences and supportive hands of David Canter, Rupert Heritage, Alex Horn, Bram van der Meer, Jennifer Brown, Gisli Gudjonsson, Sam Harkness, Brian Lavery and Gary Shaw and the assistance of Kim Rossmo, Sarah Galambos and Kathleen Ambrose.

I would also like to acknowledge the remarkable contribution of my BIA colleagues, Adam Gregory, Pippa Gregory, Terri Cole and Paul Lobb, whose tireless commitment to supporting the most harrowing of crimes is largely unrecognized and unrewarded. Finally, special thanks go to Adam Gregory, who has provided the most invaluable support over the past decade. In keeping me grounded between over enthusiasm and despair, such professional support is matched only in his friendship. Thank you.

Behavioural Investigative Advicer (BIA) in the UK, making explicit the actual role, services and products, underlying investigative philosophy and working practices, whilst dispelling many of the myths still surrounding such activity within both the popular and academic literature. This deconstruction of the naive 'profiling as pen portraits' view is reinforced in Chapter 3, which highlights how assisting the decision making of Investigating Officers is a key feature of advice provision, from a traditional decision-making perspective focusing on heuristics and biases. Such discussion serves not only to further inform an accurate perception of BIA activity, but also provides a useful exemplar of the theoretical, practical and interdisciplinary mechanisms underpinning such activity.

These practitioner views from the front line are complemented by a more academic perspective in Chapter 4, exploring what can and cannot be achieved within the domain of behavioural investigative advice, with reference to the published research evidence. In this chapters the authors highlight the interdisciplinary nature of behavioural advice and consider that it lies at a possible intersection between psychology, criminology, sociology, geography, communications studies, business management and statistics amongst many others, depending upon the nature and type of advice. The authors argue that very little has been done to formally identify this range of activity and breadth of disciplines as well as failing to explore the potential tacit, experiential knowledge that may also be relevant.

Chapter 5 represents long overdue work in exploring the actual expertise of Behavioural Investigative Advisers, moving the discussion from *what* BIAs do to *how* they do it, through the synthesis of observations made by Knabe-Nicol in her ethnographic field studies and cognitive task analysis with BIAs here in the UK and in Germany. Many of the individuals in these studies have over ten years' experience working on high profile, difficult and serious cases, and yet there has been little systematic effort to capture these experiences and explore the expertise gained. The unique access to this set of experienced practitioners provides a critical insight into the cognitive processes and expertise required to work in such a demanding field. This analysis is complemented by a similar exploration of the work of Geographical Profilers in Chapter 6, allowing the reader to broaden their understanding of this related but distinct discipline and reflect on the differences in specific expertise between the two.

Building on this theme of *how* Behavioural Investigative Advisers synthesise their expertise within the investigative arena, Chapter 7 provides a detailed example of an innovative new development from Gregory and Rainbow in response to evolving forensic science techniques. Through detailed articulation of a robust scientific methodology for the prioritization of DNA analysis results, the contribution of a BIA in offender identification can be seen to be highly significant and of critical importance in complex inquiries. Such pioneering work further emphasizes both the continued scientific aspirations and achievements of the discipline as well as providing powerful evidence for the essential and successful integration of such expertise within UK serious crime investigations.

1 Taming the beast

The UK approach to the management of behavioural investigative advice

Lee Rainbow

The goal of this chapter is to reflect on the pertinent issues surrounding the effective management of behavioural investigative advice, by making explicit the experiences, developments, learning and achievements of such endeavours from a UK perspective. Specifically, the issues of national regulation of professional and ethical standards, working conditions for Behavioural Investigative Advisers, audit and evaluation, strategic development, and learning and development of profiling skills are explored. Some broad observations regarding evaluation of the UK approach are discussed and consideration given to the future challenges facing the field of behavioural investigative advice provision to major crime investigations.

Introduction

In 1992 the Metropolitan Police Service commissioned research into the investigative usefulness of 'offender profiling', following concerns that despite over 200 British Police investigations utilizing such services in the preceding decade, no reliable or valid scientific assessment had been conducted to evaluate its usefulness (see Copson, 1995).

Whilst the explicit focus of the research was directed towards the methodologies employed and the resulting usefulness of profiling, it also provided important signposts towards the challenges facing this emerging discipline within the UK; most significantly in the observation that no governing body for the regulation of professional or ethical standards existed, and that there was no formally recognized programme for the training of UK practitioners in profiling techniques.

As the debate concerning both the overall usefulness of profiling and the specific approaches employed by profilers continues unabated (e.g., Ainsworth, 2001; Alison, Bennell, Mokros and Ormerod, 2002; Alison, Smith, Eastman and Rainbow, 2003a; Alison, Smith and Morgan, 2003b; Alison, West and Goodwill, 2004; Badcock, 1997; Boon, 1997; Canter, Alison, Alison and Wentnick, 2004; Hazelwood, 1995; Mokros and Alison, 2002; Pinizzotto and Finkel, 1990) within the published domain, the business of profiling continues. Whilst efforts, such as those highlighted above, demonstrate an increasing understanding by the UK Police

Service that such innovative investigative techniques must be properly underpinned through thorough research programmes, the operational demands of the senior investigating officer are far removed from such idealistic goals and protracted time-scales. Indeed, the use of Behavioural Investigative Advisers is advocated on UK senior detective training programmes and fully enshrined within national guidance manuals including the Murder Investigation Manual (ACPO, 2006).

It is this fundamental discord between the immediate practical needs of the investigator and the ultimate goals of the researcher which presents the most immediate challenge to the effective application of behavioural investigative advice to major crime investigations. Whilst the published literature is characterized by academics and practitioners continuing to debate the fundamental principles and practices, theoretical models and practical applications, the issue of how best to manage the discipline until such a 'holy grail' is achieved has received scant attention.

It is the goal of this paper to reflect on the pertinent issues surrounding the effective management of behavioural investigative advice, by making explicit the experiences, developments, learning and achievements of such endeavours from a UK perspective.

National regulation of professional and ethical standards

It was acknowledged as early as 1987, with the inception of the Association of Chief Police Officers (ACPO) Crime Committee on Offender Profiling that the practice of giving and using behavioural and psychological advice had developed in a somewhat ad hoc fashion in the absence of any strategic overview or regulation from the Police Service. Detailing the extensive and commendable efforts of this sub-committee and its subsequent guises to address these issues is beyond the scope of this paper. However, it is noteworthy that it was not until 2001 that a significant watershed in such endeavours occurred; most conspicuously evidenced by the replacement of the term 'offender profiler' with 'Behavioural Investigative Advisor' (BIA). Built upon existing foundations, including a central register of experts and a tacit agreement that investigators would only utilize the services of such 'ACPO Approved' BIAs, three critical factors were central in achieving the effective management and delivery of qualified behavioural advice to the UK Police Service that are experienced today: (1) the establishment of a set of working conditions for BIAs; (2) a process to audit and evaluate the behavioural advice provided to investigators; and (3) accurate management information to enable evidence-based strategic development, priority setting, resilience and a clear application process for new BIAs.

Working conditions

On 1 January 2001, the ACPO Sub-Committee for Behavioural Science implemented a set of working conditions to which all existing BIAs were invited to sign if they wished to retain their ACPO Approved status. These working conditions made explicit the responsibilities of the BIA, including: administrative protocols, commitment to producing written reports, agreement to have work annually audited and evaluated and acceptance that the results of such audits would determine the retention or removal of ACPO approved status. The working conditions also detail the following minimum requirements concerning report content, making explicit that such information represents some of the criteria against which reports are evaluated:

- a statement of the background and expertise of the BIA tailored to the particular case including qualifications and methodology used;
- a caveat clearly detailing the limitations of the approach used;
- an agreed timescale for the completion of the report and the date on which the report was submitted;
- a clear description of the BIA's understanding of the brief written as explicit terms of reference;
- a brief description of the crime including salient features;
- the material used, including details of verbal briefing, crime scene visits, photographs and relevant statements;
- details of any information, documents, etc. that were requested by the BIA but not made available prior to report preparation;
- details of other reference material (e.g. databases, academic publications, etc.) with suitable referencing;
- clear and understandable conclusions relevant to the brief;
- investigative suggestions/recommendations highlighted and listed in a degree of certainty/confidence;
- interpretations/investigative suggestions supported by evidence/rationale.

Attention is drawn specifically to the final requirement that supporting evidence/rationale for suggestions is included. Whilst the need to make explicit such a requirement may appear somewhat condescending to the skilled professional, reference to the historic debate over whether 'profiling' represents art or science illustrates the disregard that those purporting to be behavioural scientists had for such basic, scientific requirements. When one further considers the forensic arena in which this new discipline was being practised, notwithstanding initial legal naivety, it is almost inconceivable that such arrogance in personal opinion, in the absence of valid supporting evidence, characterized the evolving discipline. It is this requirement for making the supporting rationale explicit, which arguably represents the most significant advancement in the professionalization of behavioural investigative advice within the UK.

Audit and evaluation

As part of the BIA working conditions, all ACPO Approved BIAs agree to have their work audited annually by a suitably qualified independent panel. This panel, which constitutes the ACPO Sub-Committee for Behavioural Science, comprises prominent psychologists and senior police officers under the direction of the

ACPO lead for behavioural science. Two randomly selected pieces of written behavioural advice from every BIA who has been active in the preceding 12 months are evaluated in terms of both the appropriate application of behavioural science theory, and the effective application of research findings to the investigative needs of the enquiry. Feedback on the work of BIAs received from investigating officers is also considered by the panel. This audit panel has the responsibility and authority to either renew or revoke the BIAs ACPO approved status for the following year. Individual feedback is also sent to each BIA for the purposes of personal and professional development, and the findings of the audit are made available to all investigating officers requesting the services of a BIA. Of course, such a system of working practices is only credible and enforceable if the sanctions are as robust as the rhetoric, and as such, it is noteworthy that following the first such audit and evaluation process conducted within the UK, one BIA did in fact have his ACPO approved status revoked.

Strategic development

As highlighted above, the third critical factor recognized as central in achieving the effective management and delivery of behavioural investigative advice to the UK Police Service was the requirement for accurate management information to enable evidence-based strategic development, priority setting, resilience and a clear application process for prospective new BIAs.

Historical difficulties

In the 1980s a handful of 'pioneers' were responsible for the vast majority of early profiling efforts. This was followed in the 1990s by a rapid expansion in the number of individuals offering their services to the police. Notwithstanding the aforementioned considerations regarding professional and ethical competency at the individual level, the nature in which potential providers were entering the market without any reference to actual customer need represented a major and multi-faceted challenge to the effective management of this new discipline. The absence of any accurate management information regarding the use of behavioural advice across the UK seriously compromised attempts to understand fully the nature of this evolving discipline and the resilience required to continue to meet customer needs. Despite numerous efforts to introduce systems and protocols to ensure the capture of such information, it is disappointing to report that it was the lack of sustained cooperation from individual BIAs that ultimately characterized repeated failures.

Such an assessment of previous failings requires further qualification. Against a backdrop of: (1) ever increasing demand for the services of individual practitioners, (2) a lack of education for investigators utilizing this new development and (3) the ever present financial pressures of major investigations, an environment where the provision and acceptance of verbal advice, in the absence of a written report, became established. Whilst such working practices may have been mutually beneficial to both provider and customer (although one may wish to reflect on the interpersonal and professional dynamic which led to such customer compliance), the lack of any record of advice was a major underlying factor in the lack of tangible information available for both quality assurance and strategic business planning.

Impact of management information

The introduction of the new working practices and the annual audit and evaluation process therefore had a twofold effect. In making explicit the need to document all advice provided, and that retention of ACPO status was dependant upon the successful evaluation of such reports, not only were quality assurance issues addressed, but the true extent of behavioural science provision to UK investigations could be known for the first time.

An experiential note of caution is however required. It is difficult to effect such fundamental changes in working practices overnight, and adherence to previous established habits initially prevailed. Whether this represented inadvertent oversight, a failure in communication and understanding, or more concerted efforts to avoid the very evaluation process underpinning the need for written reports is unclear. It is noteworthy that the imposition of sanctions against non-compliance ran parallel with an increasing commitment by most practitioners to the new working conditions.

The significant impact this collation of management information had on the strategic management of behavioural advice cannot be overstated. With respect to an assessment of the scale to which behavioural advice was being utilized by investigations, an observation worthy of reflection was the marked difference between the number of cases BIAs claimed to be involved in prior to the introduction of the new systems and the figures available post implementation. Whether this is a greater reflection of the resource implications of writing professional reports in comparison to providing verbal assistance, or the changing face of the UK BIA environment with the introduction of full-time BIAs (see below), is difficult to determine. However, one wonders what effects the lack of an appropriate management and regulatory system to control the evolving competition for market share may have had on such claims, and perhaps more controversially, what contribution publishers and media sources made to the apparent clamour to be recognized as the 'UK's leading profiler'.

Resilience

Not only did this new system allow for a more accurate understanding of the frequency with which behavioural investigative advice is provided to major crime investigation, it also allowed for more detailed qualitative and quantitative analysis of all aspects of supply and demand. The previous system of accreditation was characterized by self-referrals and subjective scrutiny by a small sub-committee of the then governing body. The consequence of such evolution was an over-representation of expertise in certain specific domains and a critical shortfall in others. The availability of accurate management information following the introduction of the new systems allowed for the development of an objective, evidence-based strategy, and procedures to ensure the correct matching of expertise with need; with reference to specific expertise, geographical dispersion, succession planning and personal and professional development.

New applicants

In tandem with these developments, a new set of criteria was devised making explicit the minimum requirements for applicants wishing to be considered for inclusion on the ACPO Approved list of BIAs. Given the low numbers of individuals required to meet the identified and anticipated need, the opportunity to set the bar high was recognized and appropriate standards were set. This provided reasonable assurances concerning individuals' professional standing and governance as well as reducing the administrative burden previously encountered due to the considerable interest from graduates and professionals who were largely unqualified for the task. For reference, the following represent the minimum requirements to be considered for ACPO approved BIA status, although it is emphasized that such criteria reflect merely the minimum standard for application and not for successful selection.

Civilian:

- degree in psychology, criminology or related field;
- professional qualification and membership to professional body or institute;
- chartership and evidence of exposure to offenders and/or victims.

Police:

- degree in psychology, criminology or related field;
- relevant specialism evidenced by research and operational involvement.

Learning and development of profiling skills

Before discussing aspects relating to the UK approach to training and development of BIAs, it is necessary first to outline in more detail the underlying structure underpinning the effective delivery of behavioural advice to major crime investigations.

As alluded to in the preceding discussion, since the early 1990s, behavioural investigative advice has been provided to UK policing by a group of professionals approved by ACPO. Since 1999 however, individuals have been recruited by the National Policing Improvement Agency (NPIA – formerly the National Crime Faculty) as full-time BIAs. Where possible, provision of an ACPO Approved BIA will be made from within the NPIA and as such is provided at no of this training and development programme is a prerequisite for independent working as a full-time NPIA BIA without mentorship, and to achieve the status of ACPO Approved Behavioural Investigative Adviser (subject to ACPO approval).

Independent research commissioned by the precursor organization to NPIA identified seven areas of competency required by individuals to offer behavioural investigative advice effectively. These seven areas were identified as: (1) interpersonal and verbal communication skills; (2) personal integrity; (3) writing skills; (4) critical thinking skills; (5) managing the work; (6) familiarity with the techniques of behavioural science as applied to criminal investigations; and (7) knowledge of the investigative and legal process.

It is highlighted that although seven competency areas are identified, they do not represent completely separate domains and should be viewed as closely related and overlapping content areas (it should also be noted that the order in which the competencies have been presented does not imply any order of importance). However, for the purposes of providing a clear roadmap for development, the competencies are initially assessed individually, with a more holistic view of overall competency included in the final decision-making process regarding successful completion. Whilst the roadmap provides a flavour of the context in which such competencies apply, the assessment framework represents a detailed set of criteria against which each competency can be assessed within the role of BIA. Due to the nature of the competencies, different assessment methods are required for different competencies. As the principal method of training is mentorship, the assessment framework is designed to be as objective as possible, to provide clarity to mentor and student, and accountability to outside scrutiny. As such, for those competencies where potentially subjective mentor assessment is required, assessment guidelines are provided to ensure objectivity, reliability and transparency.

The adoption of this training and development programme provides the necessary assurances regarding the competencies of those BIAs providing the vast majority of behavioural advice within the UK. Although the investment in such systems should not be underestimated, with two years being the minimum time expected for completion of the BIA roadmap.

It is self-evident that any training programme of this kind must address and teach the fundamental methodological approach underpinning the provision of behavioural advice to major crime investigations within the UK. It is perhaps pertinent to highlight that despite all the processes, protocols and practices now fully enshrined in the management of behavioural advice within the UK, the ACPO Sub-Committee for Behavioural Science has deliberately refrained from providing guidance on the specific methodology to be employed. Whilst not wishing to engage in debate regarding methodology, for the purposes of context and re-emphasis of earlier observations regarding the need for explicit supporting rationale within BIA reports, the NPIA approach is characterized by an adherence to the principles of Toulmin's (1958) philosophy of argument, with respect to argument construction and presentation. Such an approach allows for individual differences in specific approach and background expertise, but provides a consistent framework within which to encourage the professionalism and minimum standards expected and required. For a greater understanding and critical review of this approach the reader is directed towards Alison *et al.* (2003a) and Almond, Alison and Porter (in press).

Working within this argument framework, BIAs will analyse information and intelligence – including: behavioural evidence available at crime scenes, victim statements and forensic and pathology reports – in order that testable hypotheses concerning likely events may be proposed to investigators. The generation of such hypotheses may be guided by published theory and empirical research, analysis of relevant crime databases, and experience of comparable cases. Hypotheses should be useful to investigators inasmuch as they suggest possible lines of enquiry or support pre-existing 'hunches' that investigators may have. Predictions concerning the likely characteristics of an unknown offender may be made in a similar manner. Again, suggested characteristics should be useful to investigators in terms of guiding investigative strategy (e.g. suspect prioritization, searches and suspect and witness interview strategies).

In essence, whilst 'clinical' experience will inevitably influence the approaches adopted by individual BIAs, the general approach to giving behavioural investigative advice should be 'scientific', in that: (1) it should be grounded in empirical research (e.g. concerning associations between offence characteristics and offender characteristics) and testable theory (e.g. offender typologies, victimology, theories of personality and mental disorder, pathways into criminality, etc.); (2) predictions should be qualified in terms of probabilities and are not suggested as certainties; and (3) the methods employed should be clearly described so that others may critically evaluate approaches and behavioural advice given (cf. Ainsworth, 2001; Alison, Goodwill and Alison, 2005).

Evaluation of approach

Whilst it has been made clear that individuals providing behavioural investigative advice are evaluated on an annual basis, it is recognized and acknowledged that a similar evaluation regarding the overarching approach to the management of such advice is required, and is indeed currently in progress. Although detailed results are not available at the time of writing, some broader observations are possible.

In order to evaluate the approach, however, some measure of success must be identified against which to assess the present system. Due to the evolving nature of the discipline and the lack of formalized approaches across the world against which to compare, the relative success of the UK approach outlined above is perhaps best measured by the absence of previously identified problems, rather than against any prescribed template.

Discussions with international colleagues concerning behavioural science provision in their respective countries or jurisdictions are characterized by a shared frustration and concern regarding the growing number of individuals who are offering such services, but whose competency in such endeavours is at best unknown, and more often inadequate. Since the introduction of this management approach within the UK, such concerns have been eliminated. This has the direct result of not only providing confidence and quality assurance to UK policing, but has also had a positive effect on the practitioner community by eliminating the more unsavoury challenges to one another's professional practice, which were a hallmark of the discipline within the UK previously and which appear to be an ever present issue worldwide. Under the current structure of behavioural advice provision within the UK, you are either deemed competent and proficient by an independent panel of experts, or you simply cannot engage in such activity at all. It may also be argued that this has had a corresponding positive effect on the research community, with a greater proliferation of objective, constructive research initiatives to both support the profiling process and evaluate and improve the discipline per se. This contrasts favourably with previous experiences of publications being characterized by destructive agendas, with researchers appearing more interested in potential market share as practitioners than objective science. This has been further supported by the central collation of all reports for the purposes of the annual audit and evaluation process which has provided researchers with a wealth of data that was previously unavailable.

Evaluation of the introduction of the working conditions for BIAs also compares favourably with previous experience. As noted above, it is the requirement for making explicit the supporting rationale for any inferences of recommendations proffered that may be regarded as the most significant achievement of the UK approach. Investigators now have the ability to judge for themselves the weight of evidence for each piece of behavioural advice, which is critical to their role as investigative decision makers, particularly within the context of ever increasing scrutiny of such processes. Contrast this to the plethora of 'profiles', which are offered elsewhere, where such rationale is substituted with the implicit requirement of absolute trust in individuals' opinions, and the advantages to investigating officers are self evident.

Whilst not unique to the UK approach, the employment of a nationally funded cadre of BIAs to support major crime investigations also contrasts positively with previous UK experience. In addition to the advantages of removing any financial burden from individual investigations, such a system allows for a far more rapid development of competency and skills due to the large amount of casework such a dedicated role allows. Furthermore, such exposure has encouraged a far greater understanding of the investigative process within which such behavioural advice is offered. This is further evidenced by the significant advancements in investigative techniques that have resulted from an interdisciplinary approach with experts in related disciplines (e.g. search, forensic science, investigative interviewing). Such joint research initiatives were neither recognized nor possible under the previous system characterized by limited exposure to cases, segregation from other experts, and time and resource constraints due to consultancy status.

Finally, with respect to evaluation, it is recognized that it is crucial to consider how the customer (i.e. the investigator) evaluates the service and the products produced. This reflects both a further aspect of the system and an evaluation criterion in itself. The effective use of behavioural investigative advice is established as a component of national Senior Investigating Officers training programmes, and every effort made to educate officers on how best to evaluate and use such advice. Research has been commissioned to investigate officers' interpretation of such advice and to identify what, when and in what format they find such advice to be of greatest assistance. Only through a thorough knowledge of the customer's experiences, requirements and understanding of behavioural investigative advice can the UK truly assess the current success of its approach to the management of the discipline, and continue to deliver the best possible service to its investigators.

Future challenges

The development of the current system for the effective management and delivery of behavioural investigative advice in the UK represents a significant advancement towards the aspirational goals shared by all stakeholders in this process. However, as with any profession, the constantly changing landscape in which we operate presents continual challenges.

Due to the manner in which the discipline has evolved, the aforementioned considerations relating to the management of UK BIAs suggest an implicit focus on the regulation of those consultants not directly employed by the police service. The successful changing of working practices has taken place against a supporting backdrop of greater police education, to ensure that only those consultants holding current ACPO approved status are employed to provide behavioural investigative advice. With the concept of behavioural investigative advice now fully enshrined within UK policing, previous boundaries and accepted applications are being challenged as the customer seeks to optimize every potential investigative opportunity this field may have to offer. Similarly, the expansion and availability of postgraduate forensic psychology courses, and courses more specifically focusing on some form of 'profiling', has created a misconception that such skills are readily available and are no longer restricted to the previously accepted realms of a select few specialists. This has created a situation where individuals within the police service itself are exploiting the opportunity to apply the principles of behavioural science to the investigative process, but for which the appropriate quality assurance mechanisms could be lacking. Such ambiguous provision of support must be addressed to arrest the potential dilution and undermining of the current high standards of the service.

Perhaps the most pressing of contemporary challenges to the professionalism of behavioural investigative advice in the UK results from the intense media interest in such activity. Media coverage of any major crime story in the UK is almost exclusively accompanied by a psychologist or 'profiler' waxing lyrically about the offender's likely characteristics, personality, psychopathology and the resulting recommended investigative actions. Whilst such observations are a somewhat inevitable product of both the popular fascination of 'getting inside the mind of the killer' and 24-hour news scheduling, the apparent readiness with which some individuals feel compelled to feed such appetites may be viewed as contrary to expected levels of professionalism. That is not to say that individuals should be prevented from expressing valid viewpoints within the media, or to expound views at the request and direction of investigators, but the growing number of uninformed commentaries on live ongoing enquiries is a cause for concern. These individuals should be acutely aware from experience that the information available within the public domain during investigations is a deliberately restricted subset of the known facts in the case. To base speculation on such limited information demonstrates a disregard for expected standards of scientific integrity. Similarly, with the ever-increasing sophistication of police media strategy, the uninvited musing of the seemingly credible but uninformed expert has the potential to undermine police objectives. Given that the experienced BIA is aware of these issues, it is difficult to comprehend what value the 'expert profiler' truly believes they are adding in these circumstances, and invites speculation that the enhancement of personal media profiles outweighs any detrimental impact to investigative strategy and outcome. In the absence of any formal censure for such activity it is incumbent upon BIAs to recognize their ethical and professional responsibilities to each other, the discipline and the police service, in order that the reputation and respect currently earned may be maintained, and the continued development of the profession safeguarded.

References

ACPO (2006) *Murder Investigation Manual*, Wyboston: National Centre for Policing Excellence.

Ainsworth, P.B. (2001) *Offender profiling and crime analysis*, Cullumpton: Willan Publishing.

Alison, L., West, A. and Goodwill, A. (2004) 'The academic and the practitioner: pragmatists' views of offender profiling', *Psychology, Public Policy and Law*, 10: 71–101.

Alison, L., Bennell, C., Mokros, A. and Ormerod, D. (2002) 'The personality paradox in offender profiling: a theoretical review of the processes involved in deriving background characteristics from crime scene actions', *Psychology, Public Policy and Law*, 8: 115–135.

Alison, L.J., Smith, M.D. and Morgan, K. (2003b) 'Interpreting the accuracy of offender profiles', *Psychology, Crime & Law*, 9: 185–195.

Alison, L.J., Goodwill, A.M. and Alison, E. (2005) 'Guidelines for profilers', in L.J. Alison (ed.) *A forensic psychologist's casebook: psychological profiling and criminal investigation*, Cullompton: Willan Publishing.

Alison, L.J., Smith, M.D., Eastman, O. and Rainbow, L. (2003a) 'Toulmin's philosophy of argument and its relevance to offender profiling', *Psychology, Crime and Law*, 9: 173–183.

Almond, L., Alison, L.J. and Porter, L. (2007) 'An evaluation and comparison of claims made in behavioural investigative advice reports compiled by the National Policing Improvement Agency in the United Kingdom', *Journal of Investigative Psychology and Offender Profiling*, 4(2): 71–83.

Badcock, R.J. (1997) 'Developmental and clinical issues in relation to offending in the individual', in J.L. Jackson and D.A. Bekerian (eds) *Offender profiling: Theory, research and practice,* Chichester: Wiley.

Boon, J.C.W. (1997) 'The contribution of personality theories to psychological profiling', in J.L. Jackson and D.A. Bekerian (eds) *Offender profiling: Theory, research and practice,* Chichester: Wiley.

Canter, D.V., Alison, L.J., Alison, E. and Wentink, N. (2004) 'The organized/disorganized typology of serial murder: myth or model?', *Psychology, Public Policy, and Law,* 10: 293–320.

Copson, G. (1995) *Coals to Newcastle: Part 1a study of offender profiling,* London: Home Office, Police Research Group.

Hazelwood, R.R. (1995) 'Analysing the rape and profiling the offender', in R.R. Hazelwood and A.W. Burgess (eds) *Practical aspects of rape investigation* (2nd ed), Boca Raton, FL: CRC Press.

Mokros, A. and Alison, L. (2002) 'Is profiling possible? testing the predicted homology of crime scene actions and background characteristics in a sample of rapists', *Legal and Criminological Psychology,* 7: 25–43.

Pinizzotto, A.J. and Finkel, N.J. (1990) 'Criminal personality profiling: An outcome and process study', *Law and Human Behaviour,* 14(3): 215–232.

Toulmin, S. (1958) *The Uses of Argument,* Cambridge: Cambridge University Press.

2 What Behavioural Investigative Advisers actually do

Lee Rainbow and Adam Gregory

Sections of this chapter have been published previously. Reproduced here with kind permission from *The Journal of Homicide and Major Incident Investigation.*

Introduction

Whilst it is easy to lay the blame at the feet of the popular media for their inaccurate and misleading portrayal of 'criminal profiling', such artistic license is understandable and perhaps even acceptable given the central intention to entertain rather than inform. Of greater concern is the recent proliferation within the academic literature of rather uninformed commentaries and perceptions of the contemporary role of Behavioural Investigative Advisers (BIAs), which is at best outdated, and at worst seemingly based upon misconceptions served up by crime writers, Hollywood producers and the aforementioned misconstructions of the media.

Whilst it is acknowledged that the absence of published accounts from contemporary practitioners makes reliance on misperceptions perhaps somewhat inevitable, it is still disappointing that such commentators appear exempt from the standards of scientific enquiry they demand from practitioners. That is, whilst the focus on such academic debates is directed towards theoretical models and methodological frameworks, grounded reference to the activity they purport to critique is notably absent. In particular, many of the supposedly robust and reliable 'academic' accounts present rudimentary arguments of the form 'profilers say they can derive offender characteristics from crime scene analysis but there is no evidence they can'. However, to address such criticism, we must first take a step back and ask whether such simplistic statements adequately reflect what today's BIAs actually do.

As such, before exploring more methodological issues and presenting some examples of *how* BIAs continue to aspire to the rigorous scientific standards expected (see Chapters 7 and 8), this chapter aims to make explicit *what* contemporary UK practitioners actually do, to provide an accurate context and disabuse academics, investigators and the general public many of the misperceptions still present in both the popular and academic literature. More specifically, it is hoped the critical reader will begin to appreciate the central underlying philosophy that every contribution made from a behavioural science perspective has the single goal of supporting investigative decision making, and that any 'one size fits all' notions of predicting background characteristics, without reference to the context of both the offence and the investigation, are undesirable, unrealistic and inaccurate.

It should however be highlighted at the outset, that the following experiences and working practices outlined below are UK specific and should not be generalised across different countries and policing jurisdictions. It is as naive and simplistic to believe that all BIAs operate in the same way throughout the world as it is to believe that their police colleagues follow universally accepted processes and procedures, regardless of cultural, political, legislative, scientific and experiential differences.

Popular misconceptions

Prediction of a criminal's personality

The prediction of an unknown criminal's personality is not BIA business

Perhaps the most widely held misconception regarding the role of the contemporary BIA surrounds the insistence that speculative predictions concerning the unknown criminal's *personality* are routinely made. They are not. Not only is such activity lacking scientific reliability and validity, in itself it serves very little, if any, purpose in assisting police officers to identify the offender. Despite the tabloid appeal of psychological musings over traits such as narcissism, misogyny, introversion and the like, the lack of any police database recording such facets of the criminal population makes them somewhat limited in terms of investigative utility.

Whilst criminal profiling was historically characterised by such a focus on personality prediction and underpinned by often quoted philosophies such as 'the crime scene is presumed to reflect the murderer's behaviour and personality in much the same way as furnishings reveal the homeowner's character' (Douglas *et al.*, 1992: 21), contemporary BIAs focus very firmly on those aspects of the unknown offender directly amenable to investigative doctrine. It is perhaps only in the form of investigative suggestions and interview strategy development where BIAs may on occasion consider more trait-based interpretations and their associated behavioural implications at the investigative level (see below).

Prediction of a criminal's background characteristics

The prediction of an unknown criminal's background characteristics is not the exclusive product of BIA endeavours

Whilst the prediction of those facets of an unknown criminal's background that are amenable to investigative action serve as a great asset in major crime enquiries, this does not represent the only contribution of contemporary BIAs (as detailed below). Analysis of the type and scope of report produced by the BIAs employed by the National Policing Improvement Agency (NPIA) reveals a steady decline in producing 'offender profiles', from over 60 per cent of all operational activity at the launch of the unit over a decade ago, to a little over 10 per cent in 2009. Such figures do not however imply that such inference generation regarding offenders is no longer undertaken on a routine basis, but rather that such inferences often form the basis of a more bespoke service to Senior Investigating Officers (SIOs), tailored to their specific investigative needs.

However, the implicit assumption that all the additional services provided by BIAs are dependent upon such prescriptive predictions concerning the unknown offender is also inaccurate. Many of the products and services, as outlined below, are wholly independent of any such speculative inferences regarding the type of unknown person who has committed the offence in question.

Solving crime

The aim of behavioural investigative advice is not to 'solve' the case

It is however acknowledged that many of the foundations for such misperceptions have been laid by the proliferation of published accounts by past and present practitioners. Such accounts are characterised by highly subjective and self-serving memoirs focusing on idiosyncratic personal contributions and incredible levels of insight and accuracy. The authors of such popular memoirs readily claim primary responsibility for successful resolution, in the absence of any objective measure of accuracy or indeed any qualification of their role within the overall investigative context.

As made explicit above, every contribution made from a behavioural science perspective has the single goal of supporting investigative decision making. The role of the BIA is to provide the investigating officer with an additional perspective and decision support through a serious crime investigation; an additional 'tool in the box' rather than any magical panacea.

Established science

Behavioural investigative advice is not an established science

The contribution of behavioural investigative advice to the investigative process can not be described as a well established scientific endeavour. Nor should it purport to be. This is not however a mortal blow to the activity, rather recognition of its investigative, rather than evidential, focus.

It is worth reflecting on the notion that there are many areas within the investigative arena that similarly fail to reach the elevated standards of scientific acceptance (e.g. handwriting, firearms/bullets, tool marks, footwear impressions, tyre impressions, bite marks and fingerprints: National Research Council, 2009), and reflection upon the entire investigative process would reveal a similar lack of scientific basis. However, such contributions are invaluable to an investigator, who is more concerned with intelligence and decision support than sample sizes and significance levels, and despite the prevailing view of many sceptics, can readily appreciate the difference between the two.

What behavioural investigative advice does (or certainly should) offer is methodologically rigorous, based upon observations of data, and situated within an understanding of the investigative and behavioural science contexts and limitations. Indeed, one of the underlying philosophies of such advice and support to major crime investigations is to enhance the scientific method of the investigative process through appropriate provision of hypotheses, evidence-based prioritisation of the 'most likely' and associated decision support strategies, grounded firmly in psychological principles and available empirical research findings; a process which forms a central theme throughout the rest of the volume.

It is perhaps worthy of reflection that recent developments within the discipline have produced products and services that are now as capable of withstanding scientific or methodological scrutiny to a level that would match, if not exceed, the standards achieved by the 'hard' sciences such as DNA or fingerprint evidence (see Chapter 7).

As such, the statement that behavioural investigative advice does not currently enjoy established scientific status must be understood within the context of both its underlying purpose and its continued development toward such aspirational goals. Whether such aspirations will ever reach the levels desired by academic psychologists remains a debate that is more likely to mirror wider debates concerning pragmatic psychology (e.g. Fishman, 1999) than be resolved by volumes such as these.

Expert evidence

Behavioural investigative advice is not expert evidence

Closely aligned to the above discussion regarding the scientific status of Behavioural Investigative Advice, it is made explicit within BIA reports that they do not constitute expert evidence. BIA reports deal in probabilities, not certainties, and provide the most likely 'type' of individual in order to systematically prioritise lines of enquiry. Due to the probabilistic nature of the findings, while the majority of recommendations will prove effective for the majority of cases, it is to be expected that in a minority of cases the individual responsible will demonstrate significant variance with the reported probabilities.

Even if a significant overlap exists between the 'profile' and defendant, the best that could be inferred is that the defendant has the characteristics that have been suggested as most likely from a behavioural analysis of crime scene and related information. This should be deemed insufficiently relevant and reliable, and too prejudicial to be received by the court as evidence of the defendant's guilt. It is for this very reason that it is made explicit that a BIA's report is not fit for purpose in attempting to provide evidence of an individual's involvement or guilt, or conversely as evidence that a specific individual cannot be responsible for an offence. This is not a failing, rather recognition of its investigative utility as a means of better understanding an event and informing and prioritising investigative decision making and actions. As such a 'profile' should never be attempted to be used as evidence with regards to identity. However, the wider discipline of behavioural investigative advice may, under specific circumstances, be able to contribute to the court process, although the exact parameters and process for such a contribution are at present unclear and may be found to fall foul of the same obstacles as 'profiles' if tested (for a review of the evidential obstacles facing 'offender profiling' see Ormerod and Sturman, 2005).

Crime analysis

Behavioural investigative advice is not crime analysis and crime analysts are not Behavioural Investigative Advisers

Due to the plethora of terms that have been used, often interchangeably, to describe techniques allied to those employed by BIAs (such as 'criminal profiling' (e.g. Douglas *et al.*, 1986), 'psychological profiling' (e.g. Egger, 1999), 'criminal personality profiling' (e.g. Pinizzotto and Finkel, 1990), 'offender profiling' (e.g. Jackson and Bekerian, 1997), 'investigative profiling' (e.g. Annon, 1995) and 'crime scene profiling' (e.g. Homant and Kennedy, 1998)), the distinction between BIAs and crime analysts is often overlooked and misunderstood.

Gottlieb, Arenberg and Singh state:

> crime analysis is defined as a set of systematic, analytical processes directed at providing timely and pertinent information relative to crime patterns and trend correlations to assist operational and administrative personnel in planning the deployment of resources for the prevention and suppression of criminal activities, aiding the investigative process, and increasing apprehensions and the clearance of cases. Within this context, crime analysis supports a number of department functions including patrol deployment, special operations and tactical units, investigations, planning and research, crime prevention, and administrative services (budget and program planning).

> (1994: 13)

Reference to this seminal definition of crime analysis highlights the critical difference between such activity and that performed by a BIA (see below). The overriding function of crime analysis is to find meaningful information within vast amounts of data and disseminate this information to relevant officers and investigators (Osborne and Wernicke, 2003). Such analysis is focused more upon the 'crime problem' than the individual perpetrator and requires no grounding in psychological theory, research and methodologies. It is as inappropriate for such practitioners to provide BIA services as it is for GPs to perform surgery.

The evolution of the role of the analysts within the Serious Crime Analysis Section (SCAS) of the NPIA, from their origins in the late 1990s to their current form, is perhaps an appropriate illustration of how some elements of the 'profiling' discipline in the UK have been legitimately harnessed by highly trained and competent staff, who by design have always worked very closely with

BIAs within NPIA. However, even this group of highly specialist analysts, dealing exclusively with behaviourally rich, serious crime data, have a clear remit that is distinct from that of a BIA. Their bespoke training and mentoring in 'behavioural interpretation', emerging as it has from the expertise of their BIA counterparts, provides them with enhanced skills essential for their 'comparative case analysis' role and the identification of potentially linked offences, but it does not make them 'profilers'. The strict professional ethics of both disciplines ensures that these roles remain harmoniously linked with behavioural science at their core and yet fundamentally separate in terms of their respective remits and investigative utility.

Geographic profiling

Behavioural investigative advice is not geographic profiling and
Geographic Profilers are not Behavioural Investigative Advisers

Geographic profiling is a specific technique designed to locate the offenders' residence or anchor point based on the analysis of the crimes, from a spatial and temporal perspective (for a more detailed description and analysis of geographic profiling, see Chapter 6). It is typically based on the analysis of the locations of a connected series of offences, the characteristics of the neighbourhoods in which they have occurred and, where available and relevant, the BIA's contribution.

Whilst BIAs traditionally provided advice regarding potential geographical associations of the unknown offender, such contributions are now routinely provided by Geographic Profilers, although BIAs may still provide some advice in cases that only involve one specific location. Whilst it is recognized as good practice for the two disciplines to work closely together, BIAs and Geographic Profilers are now recognized as two distinct disciplines, with differing underlying theoretical, empirical and research considerations.

Multidisciplinary approach

Behavioural Investigative Advisers are not isolated experts and
behavioural investigative advice is not a standalone service

Despite the popular characterisation of individualistic, and almost maverick, working practices, BIAs do not operate in an investigative void, with little or no support from analytical and law enforcement colleagues. The contribution from BIAs is greatly enhanced through multidisciplinary collaboration with all aspects of relevant investigative expertise, but particularly with the more closely aligned disciplines of crime analysts and Geographic Profilers. This is particularly pertinent within the NPIA where the creation of multidisciplinary support teams has greatly enhanced the sum of the individual parts and has played a major role in the effective integration of behavioural investigative advice within major crime investigations (see Case Study 1).

Case Study 1 Working together within NPIA

Circumstances

A series of nine offences of sexual assault are forwarded to the Behavioural Investigative Adviser from an investigating officer seeking guidance and advice regarding linkage.

Analysis

The nine offences are entered onto the Violent Crime Linkage Analysis System (ViCLAS) by analysts within the Serious Crime Analysis Section (SCAS). Reference to this dataset allows for validation of initial hypotheses regarding linkage, as well as providing statistics on the frequency of individual behaviours, and more significantly, combinations of behaviours. This is supplemented by reference to research conducted on this dataset, which provides a greater understanding of consistency and variability of offenders when committing a series of offences.

Results

The resulting analysis prioritises seven of the offences as being likely to have been committed by the same person.

Additional support

Further contributions from the Behavioural Investigative Adviser can now proceed on the basis of the linkage analysis, which can also inform additional SCAS products and services. The removal of two potentially unlinked cases will enhance the contribution from geographic profiling, with their analysis based only on those cases which have been prioritised as relevant to a single offender.

Working practice and process

All behavioural investigative advice within the UK is provided upon request, and although advocated on senior detective training programmes and within national guidance manuals, does not represent a procedural requirement, but rather a carefully considered investigative decision.

Once a BIA has been engaged by the Investigating Officer, a meeting takes place where an exchange of information and views leads to the agreement of explicit terms of reference. These terms are established in writing and clearly articulate what is expected of both parties. This is particularly important with regard to ownership of any material and confidentiality, which is expected in instances where a BIA might have privileged access to sensitive information about crime scenes and/or victims. This should, for example, inhibit disclosure of certain information to the media without the SIO's permission. Terms of reference should also provide similar assurances to the BIA that all relevant case materials will be made available, and any developments which may support, refute or refine the advice proffered, be communicated as soon as reasonably possible.

It is at this stage that the precise nature of any behavioural science support will be discussed and agreed. As will be made explicit below, the potential products and services from contemporary BIAs are far broader and more diverse than either the media or naive academics would proffer, and should not be regarded as the exclusive generation of inferred offender characteristics, either as a product in its own right or as the necessary foundation to other contributions.

In order for the BIA to undertake their behavioural analysis and provide timely advice, a variety of case materials will be required from the investigation. The provision of these assist the BIA to commence their analysis and return a detailed report to the investigation within a time frame that maximises the utility of the advice (i.e. as soon as practically possible, but with cognisance to the investigation's overall strategy and resourcing and competing BIA demands from other cases). Although by no means exhaustive, and with cognisance that different enquiries will generate different information and different products and services require different source material, the following represents a summative overview of the material required and utilized.

- full verbal case briefing and access to the SIO/investigation team;
- all relevant statements;
- crime report;
- any officers' reports/status reports;
- pathology and forensic reports/findings;
- full set of crime scene and post-mortem photographs (where applicable);
- available analysis (e.g. telephony, palynology, entomology, etc.);
- relevant maps;
- visit to all relevant scenes.

It is worth highlighting that the scene visit represents a critical component of the process, as it allows the BIA to gain a fuller understanding of the decision-making process of the offender. Such information is not routinely available from crime reports, statements or photographs, where often the evidential focus is too restrictive to provide the necessary 'behavioural' perspective (see Case Study 2).

In addition, the scene visit is typically complemented by a visit to the incident room/enquiry team, allowing the BIA to ask questions concerning the demographics and crime profile (i.e. the type, frequency, patterns and interpretation of previous criminal activity) of the area, as well as to get a full briefing from the

Case Study 2 The importance of a crime scene visit

Circumstances

A female was raped whilst out walking during the hours of daylight. As she walked along a canal towpath, the offender emerged from the adjacent woodland, grabbed her and pulled her into the wooded area. The victim reported the offender was out of breath and smelt heavily of cigarettes.

Supplied crime scene material

Photographic recording of the scene illustrated the area of woodland in which the offence took place, with corresponding views back towards the canal.

Investigative consideration

Requested analysis of other people using the same stretch of towpath prior to the attack revealed a large number of potential alternative victims. Closer examination revealed that these persons, although alone, were in relatively close temporal and spatial proximity to one another, increasing the chance of witness interruption for the offender. The victim was distinct in the fact that she was neither preceded nor followed closely by other people. This led to the inference that the offender may have consciously chosen the victim based upon reduced risk.

Crime scene visit

Personal visit to the crime scene revealed the location at which the victim was attacked was such that surveillance of the towpath in both directions was impossible due to the topography. Further observation at the scene exposed a nearby bridge over the canal, which upon investigation revealed a vantage point affording unobstructed views over and beyond the crime scene. By standing in the middle of this bridge, potential victims could be identified and the presence or absence of potential witnesses confirmed over a considerable distance. The possibility of reaching the crime scene location after viewing a potential victim and confirming a lack of potential witnesses was confirmed, albeit at a running pace.

Impact

A possible understanding of the offender's pre-offence behaviour and movement was established. This led to the widening of forensic considerations to the bridge and the identification and recovery of a pile of same brand cigarette butts at the point on the bridge where such inferred surveillance was optimised.

regularly reminded by BIAs to ensure any advice proffered achieves the highest possible standards of quality and effectiveness.

It is of utmost importance that any behavioural advice provided to an investigation is utilised in the manner in which it was intended. In particular, it should be remembered that advice is typically offered on the basis of what is most likely or what should be prioritised. Behavioural investigative advice does not deal in absolutes, and as such advice from a BIA should always be evaluated carefully by the SIO to ensure that its impact on the investigation is proportionate.

Investigative contribution

Behavioural investigative advice has the potential to contribute to many aspects of the investigative process and may take many forms throughout the life of the enquiry. Whilst all of the products and services available offer tactical or strategic solutions in their own right, as highlighted above, all are underpinned by a broader philosophy of adding value to the decision making of the SIO, through an enhanced understanding of the offence and offender from a perspective different from that routinely employed within major crime investigation teams. Such differences in perspective can be broadly characterised as evidence (SIO) versus understanding (BIA), although both are directed at supporting the single goal of case resolution. It is this additional perspective and associated expertise that should be recognized as the critical success factor of behavioural investigative advice.

Crime scene assessment and hypothesis generation

Critical to the provision of many BIA products and services is a fundamental understanding of the offence, and hence the offender(s), from a behavioural perspective. This is achieved through crime scene assessment (CSA) and hypothesis generation. This involves a thorough examination of the criminal event and generating hypotheses based upon the available information. Support for or against each of the possible hypotheses is then forwarded with reference to psychological theory, relevant research findings and experiential knowledge, with information gaps identified that will further enhance the process. The benefits of such an approach are that specific hypotheses regarding the offence can be tested in a systematic, reasoned and objective fashion, based upon sound supporting rationale (see Chapter 3 for an illustrative example of this approach). Such a methodology is consistent with, and provides a tangible product of, the investigative philosophy promoted within national policing guidance. Recent practice advice advocates the application of scientific principles and methods as core investigative doctrine to be adopted across the UK police service (ACPO, 2005).

Offence linkage analysis

In the absence of any physical evidence linking a number of crimes, the contribution of a behavioural analysis may be significant. Research into behaviour exhibited by offenders during the commission of their crimes has led to a greater understanding in consistency and variability of offenders when committing a series of offences. The Serious Crime Analysis Section (SCAS) of the NPIA, through their mandate to collect and analyse a range of sexually motivated offences throughout the UK, now has more than 16,500 offences on the ViCLAS (Violent Crime Linkage Analysis System) database (the collection criteria cover homicide, serious sexual assault and abduction offences, including attempts). The creation of such large data sets allows for validation of initial hypotheses regarding linkage, as well as providing statistics with regards to the frequency of individual behaviours, and more significantly, combinations of behaviours. Typically, a behavioural linkage analysis will be undertaken by a BIA in consultation with an analyst or senior analyst from within SCAS.

Predictive profiling

Drawing inferences in relation to a particular offender on the basis of a comprehensive crime scene assessment is a process commonly referred to as predictive (or offender) profiling. However, it is important to recognize that in contrast to its media portrayal, the focus of modern day predictive profiling is very much on investigative utility rather than psychological interest. A BIA will endeavour to make accurate assessments in relation to objective and verifiable elements of an offender's background. Consideration will be given to the likely age of the offender, whether he is likely to have previous police convictions and if so what these may be, and where he may reside or be based. Where possible, a BIA will work in collaboration with a Geographic Profiler in order that the utility of predictions regarding offender residence are maximised. The goal of the BIA in this process is to allow the SIO and the enquiry team to focus on areas of investigation most likely to identify the offender.

Nominal generation

An extension to predictive profiling, suspect generation may be undertaken by the investigation under the guidance of a BIA. By taking the predictions made in relation to an offender's likely background characteristics, it is possible to utilise local crime and intelligence databases as well as the Police National Computer (PNC) in order to generate pools of potential suspects. Increasingly, this type of work is being undertaken by experienced analysts within SCAS utilising, for example, the PNC. Outside of the criminal arena, in some cases it may also be possible to highlight additional potential suspect pools on the basis of advice offered by a BIA, such as those from housing lists, voters register, employment records and so on. This will always be evaluated by the BIA on a case by case basis.

Prioritization matrices

Again an extension of the predictive profiling process, a prioritisation matrix simply takes the individual predictions made in relation to the proposed background of the unknown offender and integrates them in the form of a matrix. Each facet of a potential suspect will be given a numerical value such that nominals within an enquiry can be objectively scored and ranked in terms of how well their background characteristics fit with those proposed for the unknown offender. This process is of particular utility if an investigation wishes to undertake an intelligence-led DNA screen, or is seeking to prioritise many hundreds potential suspects from a cold case enquiry or mass media appeal. Where possible, a suspect prioritisation matrix will be developed so as to integrate the behavioural predictions (in relation to an offender's background) with a geographic profile in relation to their most likely area of residence.

Investigative suggestions

In line with the BIA's intention to make their report as investigative-focused as possible, it is normal practice now for BIAs to offer direct investigative suggestions on the basis of the information supplied to them. It should be recognized that whilst the BIA role is very much an 'advisory' one, they do typically possess significant experience of major criminal investigations (e.g. the BIAs at the NPIA have an accumulated experience of over 1,000 cases). This experience combined with their ability to draw logical inferences on the basis of an offender's behaviour means that they will offer investigative suggestions to the SIO as a routine part of their report. Suggestions are made strictly on a case by case basis and should always be accompanied by a clear supporting rationale.

Veracity assessment

By combining a comprehensive understanding of the relevant research literature with their own behavioural and investigative knowledge and experience, a BIA may be able to assist in cases of sexual assault where there are believed to be issues with regards to the veracity of a victim's account. It is not for the BIA to provide a definitive judgement as to the truthfulness of an alleged victim but rather to offer some interpretation and advice in relation to what is said to have occurred. Additional lines of enquiry or areas of particular investigative interest will be highlighted in order that the allegation can be handled in the most appropriate and sensitive manner. This work frequently brings the BIA into a close working relationship with the NPIA's National Interview Adviser, and often promotes liaison and consultation with psychologists and other experts specialising in issues such as memory and organic brain damage.

Risk assessment

Analysis of an offender's background history and offence behaviour can provide information that may assist in specifying the social, environmental and interpersonal circumstances in which that person might be considered to be at an increased risk of offending. This information combined with local intelligence can help determine strategies for managing such offenders in the community. This service is typically undertaken by an external (i.e. non-NPIA) forensic clinical psychology or forensic psychiatry consultant, and as such is likely to come at a financial cost to an investigation.

Interview advice

Contributions from a behavioural perspective can provide a significant enhancement to the development of interview strategies. Such contributions can be classified as either interviewee-specific advice or crime scene-specific advice. With respect to the former, more traditionally recognized interviewee-specific advice, an identification of salient behavioural characteristics of the individual to be interviewed can inform strategies to maximise interaction and the quantity and quality of information disclosed, and minimise confabulation and fabrication. The more contemporary contribution from a crime scene-specific perspective provides additional guidance to interviewing officers in understanding the offence, will identify any gaps, inconsistencies and ambiguities in the information and provide a template against which investigative hypotheses can be systematically tested during interview. It is however essential that interview advice gained from a BIA is complemented with advice from the NPIA's National Interview Adviser or appropriate in-force or ACPO Approved Interview Adviser, in order to ensure compliance with relevant legislation and support of the overall investigative aims, objectives and strategies.

Media advice

In certain circumstances it may be advisable to seek opinions from a BIA in relation to utilising the media in major investigations. This advice is intended to maximise the use of the media when, for example, making appeals to the public or releasing information about an offence, but also to enable SIOs to better understand the potential effects of the media on the behaviour of an offender.

Familial DNA prioritization

Familial DNA (fDNA) searching works on the general principle that people who are related are likely to have more DNA in common than those who are not, and thereby seeks to identify individuals on the National DNA Database (NDNAD) who have a greater genetic similarity to the unknown offender and hence a greater potential to be related. The BIAs in collaboration with SCAS can utilise a sophisticated process (see Chapter 7) that allows the resulting lists from forensic science providers to be reprioritised with respect to age and geographic association. By adjusting the genetic prioritisation to take into account an individual's age and geographic association, those individuals who are more likely to be relatives of the offender should become more readily identifiable from the more general backdrop of the lists, whilst still preserving the appropriate weight assigned to them through their genetic similarity.

Search advice

BIAs may also be able to contribute to any search activity within an investigation. An enhanced understanding of the offence and/or likely offender can inform search parameters for forensic evidence, witnesses, CCTV, etc., and in combination with relevant research findings assist in prioritising potential body deposition sites. Additionally, an enhanced knowledge of specific psychological or criminal dispositions may assist in broader search considerations, such as briefing search officers as to the potential significance (from an intelligence perspective) of items that may be observed within the course of more evidential searches (see Case Study 3).

Case Study 3 Search advice

Circumstances

A young female has been reported missing and suspected of being abducted by a sexually motivated offender.

Aims and objectives of advice

To brief and advise search personnel conducting house searches within identified areas of interest to highlight potential indicators of a sexual interest in children that may be evident when conducting searches of nominals' premises, but whose potential significance may not be appropriately recognized.

Briefing provided

Attention was drawn to the presence of both 'attractors' and 'interactors'.

'Attractors' were highlighted as those items that could be used to attract and interest children that appear out of place in the context; particularly with reference to males living alone. Examples of pets, DVDs, toys, posters, sweets, bathroom accessories, etc. were provided to illustrate the concept, but emphasis was made that the examples were by no means exhaustive and that the intention was to promote general awareness rather than the provision of a definitive, prescriptive list.

Similarly, 'interactors' were highlighted as those items that may represent sexually arousing stimuli but potentially appear innocuous due to the absence of overt sexual or child abuse content. Examples of clothing catalogues, medical books, reference books, advertising literature, DVDs

---

(e.g. 'Home Alone'), photographs, artwork, etc. were provided, but again the emphasis was on providing a greater awareness and understanding of child erotica as distinct from child pornography.

In addition to these considerations outlined during the briefings, attention was also drawn to the potential significance of individuals who proactively seek opportunities to bring them into contact with children. These include occupation, hobbies, voluntary work, leisure activities, intimate relationships, etc. Again the intention was to highlight the potential investigative significance of such intelligence rather than the production of a definitive list.

Conclusion

The role of the Behavioural Investigative Adviser has undergone a significant evolution in recent times. Contemporary BIAs are no longer isolated experts restricted to generating inferences about offenders in an investigative void. Rather they have become a more professional group of individuals with a vast experience of serious crime and how best to integrate their behavioural advice into the modern day major investigation.

BIAs can offer SIOs an additional perspective and decision support throughout a serious crime investigation through the pragmatic application of behavioural science theory, research and experience.

The behavioural analysis of information gathered by the investigation team can assist in prioritising lines of enquiry, potential suspects and DNA sampling processes as well as helping to identify other critical pieces of information to progress investigative efforts. Advice surrounding nominal generation, risk and investigative interviewing can all enhance existing efforts and contributions, and the overall philosophy of providing an enhanced understanding of the criminal event and investigative decision making offers significant value to even the most experienced SIOs.

In this chapter, we have presented an accurate and up-to-date description of the role of a BIA in major crime investigations to enable the academic community and all interested parties to achieve a greater understanding of contemporary practice. Through the deconstruction of many popular myths and the explicit articulation of the diverse range of potential contributions the evolving responsiveness and agility of this developing discipline has been revealed. It is hoped that this enhanced understanding will encourage a more constructive and balanced research agenda, and encourage academics to move away from naive problem-oriented arguments to a more psychologically relevant and solution-focused findings and recommendations.

References

ACPO (2005) *Practice Advice on Core Investigative Doctrine*, Wyboston: NCPE.

Annon, J.S. (1995) 'Investigative profiling: A behavioural analysis of the crime scene', *American Journal of Forensic Psychology*, 13 (4): 67–75.

Douglas, J.E., Burgess, A.W., Burgess, A.G. and Ressler, R.K. (1992) *Crime Classification Manual: a standard system for investigating and classifying violent crime*, New York: Simon and Schuster.

Douglas, J.E., Ressler, R.K., Burgess, A.W. and Hartman, C.R. (1986) 'Criminal profiling from crime scene analysis', *Behavioural Sciences and the Law*, 4: 410–421.

Egger, S.A. (1999) 'Psychological Profiling, Past, Present and Future', *Journal of Contemporary Criminal Justice*, 15 (3): 242–261.

Fishman, D.B. (1999) *The Case for Pragmatic Psychology*, New York: New York University Press.

Gottlieb, S.L., Arenburg, S., and Singh, R. (1994) *Crime Analysis: from first report to final arrest*, Montclair, CA: Alpha Publishing.

Homant, R.J. and Kennedy, D.B. (1998) 'Psychological Aspects of Crime Scene Profiling: validity research', *Criminal Justice and Behaviour*, 25: 319–343.

Jackson, J.L. and Bekerian, D.A. (eds) (1997) *Offender Profiling: theory, research and practice*, Chichester: Wiley.

National Research Council (2009) *Strengthening Forensic Science in the United States: a path forward*, Washington, DC: National Academies Press.

Omerod, D. and Sturman, J. (2005) 'Working with the courts: advice for expert witnesses', in Alison, L. (ed.) *The Forensic Psychologist's Casebook: psychological profiling and criminal investigation*, Cullompton: Willan.

Osborne, D.A. and Wernicke, S.C. (2003) *Introduction to Crime Analysis: basic resources for criminal justice practice*, New York: The Haworth Press.

Pinizzotto, A.J. and Finkel, N.J. (1990) 'Criminal personality profiling: an outcome and process study', *Law and Human Behaviour*, 14: pp. 215–233.

3 BIA support to investigative decision making

Lee Rainbow, Louise Almond and Laurence Alison

Sections of this chapter have been published previously. Reproduced here with kind permission from the editors, Laurence Alison and Jonathan Crego and Willan Books.

Introduction

As highlighted in Chapter 2, every contribution to the investigation of serious crime from a behavioural science perspective has the single underlying goal of supporting investigative decision making. Whilst a more prescriptive summary of the individual products and services that offer explicit tactical and strategic solutions in their own right have already been highlighted, this chapter aims to shed light on the less obvious but nevertheless critical and underlying contribution of Behavioural Investigative Advisers (BIAs) on the decision-making process.

The field of decision making is well established within the psychological literature and offers a multitude of well established influences on decision making. The focus of this chapter however will be directed towards those factors that are commonly encountered by BIAs within major crime investigations, namely heuristics and biases. It is cognisance of these factors within an investigative environment that underpins an implicit but often overlooked contribution from BIAs.

It is acknowledged that such a focus does not do justice to the multitude of decision-making theories and research findings that will undoubtedly interact with the principles of traditional decision-making theory (Bernoulli, 1738; Savage, 1954) adopted here. Similarly, no attention has been directed towards the decision-making processes of the BIAs themselves (which is addressed within a more naturalistic decision making paradigm [Klein *et al.*, 1993] in Chapter 5). Such deliberations are far too large to address in a single chapter; they would detract from the central intention to expand on the discussion in Chapter 2 and provide a practitioner-focused account of BIA's contribution to investigative decision making.

This chapter illustrates these contributions by reference to practical, real-life examples to demonstrate the potential impact of these factors on investigative decision making. We also illustrate the value of a psychologically informed perspective to both recognize and overcome such cognitive fallibilities.

Before discussing some of the most empirically well established and relevant heuristics and biases that affect investigative decision making, it is first necessary to provide an appropriate foundation with an understanding of base rates and probability.

Base rates fallacy

Base rate information refers to reliable, broad-based information that is available to us, such as statistical information. Within an investigative setting, for example, BIAs have access to large datasets that provide base rate information regarding the frequency of certain behaviours within sexual offences, or the number of rapists who have previous convictions prior to their index offence. However, Kahneman and Tversky (1973) reported a series of studies, which showed that when people make judgements, they often ignore or misuse base rate information; they termed this phenomenon the base rate fallacy. The best known example of this is the 'cabs' problem (Kahneman and Tversky, 1973) where participants are told that there are two cab companies in the city: the Blue Cab Company which has 85 per cent of the city cabs, and the Green Cab Company which has 15 per cent. A cab is involved in a hit and run accident and a witness later identified the cab as a green one. Under tests the witness was shown to be able to identify the colour of a cab correctly 80 per cent of the time but would confuse it with the other colour 20 per cent of the time. The participants are then asked whether it is more likely that the cab is green or blue. The majority of participants think the correct answer is green when in fact it is blue, due to the high percentage (larger base rate) of cabs in the town being blue.

In another study Kahneman and Tversky (1973) presented participants with a series of short personality sketches. Participants were given descriptions of several individuals said to be taken from a random sample of 100 professionals – engineers and lawyers. Participants were either told that there were 70 engineers and 30 lawyers or they were told that there were 30 engineers and 70 lawyers. The participants were asked to assess the probability that the description belonged to an engineer rather than to a lawyer. The participants have different base rate information and should have been guided by it – the probability that any description belongs to an engineer should be higher in the first condition and lower in the latter. However, participants did not use the given probabilities to evaluate the likelihood of someone being an engineer; instead, they formed their judgements based on the degree to which the description was representative of a 'stereotypical' lawyer or a 'stereotypical' engineer (the so called representativeness heuristic, see below). When they had no other information, the participants used prior probabilities correctly but this was effectively ignored when a description was introduced. Numerous studies involving similar tasks have shown that, generally, when participants make probability judgements, they will ignore or severely neglect base rate information. This lack of reference to appropriate base rates is probably the most commonly experienced fallacy and it is the one that is most frequently addressed by BIAs.

The consideration of whether a number of offences represent a linked series (i.e. the actions of a single offender) is a critical decision within major crime enquiries; the resulting opinion has a significant impact on overall investigative strategy and resourcing. Typically, some form of comparative case analysis will be performed, whereby the number of commonalities between the offences is identified and used to guide judgements regarding linkage. Those offences sharing multiple factors (i.e. high correlation) may strengthen the belief of linkage, but the typical base rate pattern of those factors is often overlooked by investigating officers. As an example, consider a number of sexual offences, all committed within six months of each other and all reported within the same policing district with the following commonalities; assault site in open air, surprise approach, weapon used and the offender makes sexual comments towards the victim. Without knowledge of base rates we might be tempted to consider these linked due to the presence of four independent factors across all the offences. Even an investigator with some grasp of the fallacy of such conclusions may proffer that whilst an assault site in open air and surprise approach are relatively common, the use of a weapon and the offender making sexual comments towards the victim are rare enough to suggest linkage. However, such base rates are often reliant on the investigators' own experiences (see the representativeness heuristic below) and, as such, have not been formed by appropriate reference to actual base rate frequencies. If we now suppose that the base rate frequencies of these behaviours are 80 per cent, 65 per cent, 55 per cent and 52 per cent respectively, we can readily appreciate the error in linkage. To put it another way, if we ignore the temporal and geographic proximity of the offences, across a dataset containing 10,000 sexual offences (a conservative estimate for the databases available within the UK), there could be as many 1,500 other crimes which share these similarities and hence could be 'linked' in the same manner.

It is a critical role of a BIA to understand, communicate and perhaps most importantly to overcome such fallacious practice through their access to appropriate national datasets and other relevant base rate data.

As alluded to in the previous example, Tversky and Kahneman argue that it is the use of the representativeness heuristic that causes people to ignore base rate information.

The representativeness heuristic

The representativeness heuristic (Tversky and Kahneman, 1974) is a heuristic wherein we assume commonality between things that are similar to a prototype. An individual then assesses the probability of an event by judging the degree to which that event corresponds to an appropriate prototypical model, such as sample and a population or an act to an actor (Payne, Bettman and Luce, 1998). Of course, it is extremely helpful to be able to make a fast judgement when we encounter something novel by saying, 'Oh, this is similar to a typical case of X' and proceed with a decision accordingly. The unfortunate downside is that problems can occur when there is no commonality between the two things we are comparing, they are merely superficially similar, and/or when the prototype we have as a mental representation is awry.

As a concrete example, a Senior Investigating Officer (SIO) investigating the murder of a homosexual male in a known cottaging (a British gay slang term referring to anonymous sex between men in a public place) area judged the event to correspond to a prototypical 'gay-bashing', which informed his decision making accordingly. In fact, closer examination of the known facts by a BIA suggested a significant difference from such an interpretation. The circumstances were at odds with any prototypical homophobic motivation; such a prototype in itself only discernible from numerous research studies with large samples and statistically significant results to which the SIO had understandably no knowledge or access. The reprioritized scenario of a theft-motivated offence, with the potential of the (unknown) offender's home as an additional scene, had a significant impact on future decision making and negated the initial errors arising from the representativeness heuristic.

The representativeness heuristic is similar to the idea that correlation does not assume causation; that is, the fact that two things are (apparently) similar does not necessarily mean that one has any bearing on the other. This can lead to what is termed an illusory correlation (Chapman, 1967) and can often be misleading when base rates are not considered.

If we consider the investigation into a potentially linked series of prostitute murders, a typical initial investigative action would be the interviewing of individuals who last had contact with the victims. However, whilst an identified individual who had recently had contact with all the victims (i.e. high correlation) may be deemed of greater interest to the investigation and hence represent a potential suspect, reference to the typical base rate pattern of men who frequent prostitutes would reveal that they do so with numerous different prostitutes. As such, the seemingly high correlation of recent suspect–victim interaction is potentially no greater than the norm, and carries reduced significance from an investigative sense.

Not everybody agrees that the representativeness heuristic is responsible for people's tendency to ignore base rate information when they make judgements. Nisbett *et al.* (1976) offer another explanation; they suggest that base rate information is ignored in favour of individuating information because the former is remote, pallid and abstract while the latter is vivid, salient and concrete. Bar-Hillel (1980) has argued that the notion of relevance is central to why people ignore base rate information. He argued that participants ignore base rate information because they feel that it is irrelevant to the judgement they are making. One determinant of perceived relevance is causality; that is, we *will* take notice of information if it fits in as one of our links in a causal chain of who, what, why. For example, performance on the 'cabs' problem has been found to improve greatly if participants are told that there are equal numbers of blue and green cabs but that 85 per cent of the cabs involved in accidents are blue cabs. This provides participants with a causal connection between blue cabs and accidents, which facilitates utilization of the base rate – it's now deemed relevant.

Despite differences in opinion on what causes people to ignore base rate information, we can at least agree that we necessarily select what information we will make use of. As social beings, we are always making sense of the world, processing it and inferring meaning from what goes on around us as we make decisions. As we strive to make sense of it, it is perhaps a natural human tendency to endeavour to seek patterns. The trouble is we will do this even where none actually exists. This is known as the clustering illusion (Gilovich *et al.* 1985). If a data set is large enough, patterns will inevitably appear. For investigative decision makers who, par excellence, are faced with having to make sense of incomplete information, it is important to be wary of the clustering illusion. There are, of course, many potential benefits in looking for patterns, especially in serial crime, but problems can occur if it is not acknowledged that patterns are not always meaningful.

The most common demonstration of investigators falling foul of this clustering illusion is when making judgements regarding potential linkage and the highlighting of a number of similarities between offences which have no bearing on the likelihood of linkage. As an example, one Senior Officer had linked a number of rapes due to the following similarities; prostitute victim, 'confidence' approach (specifically soliciting for sex), vehicle used, victim transported to another location and victim only partially undressed. Irrespective of the base rate fallacy outlined above concerning the relative rarity or otherwise of these features, the selection of these behaviours as discrete variables is methodologically flawed on the basis of independence. Closer examination of the variables reveals that they are all highly correlated to the victim being a prostitute, describing the nature of (consensual) prostitution within which an offence is likely to take place. The decision to link the offences across five seemingly separate commonalities has failed to account for the clustering illusion, inferring a pattern within the data which is nothing more than an artefact of one of the variables.

Similarly, even once this source of reasoning error has been addressed, many investigators may still focus attention of the perceived pattern of victimology (i.e. all prostitutes) and infer further meaning. Such a pattern may or may not be meaningful; danger also lies in attributing the wrong meaning to a pattern, extrapolating from it and speculating, say, that the offender has a particular sexual motive – especially if lines of enquiry shift as a result. There may be no need for an explanation any more complicated than this one: people who work as prostitutes are more easily accessible; hence, they are available as, and therefore more vulnerable to, becoming victims. Even simpler, the pattern is meaningless.

With the development of 'suspect prioritization matrices' (see Chapter 2) now becoming an accepted investigative technique, the potential errors of clustering illusions have an even greater potential detrimental effect on an enquiry, with officers attempting to construct their own without cognisance of such biases. Such efforts are typified by the inclusion of categories such as 'VISOR nominal', 'registered sex offender', 'previous convictions for a sexual offence', 'committed offence with similar MO', etc., listed as separate criteria when attempting to prioritize potential suspects for a sexual offence. However, such clustering of factors ignores the fact that they are actually all points along a continuum of 'similar sex offender', and any such individual will therefore be disproportionately heightened in terms of investigative interest as a result.

It is in guiding the Investigating Officers around these issues, with the appropriate theoretical, methodological and empirical expertise that represents one of the central roles of a BIA.

Availability heuristic

Unlike representativeness, which involves comparing events to a particular model, availability as defined by Kahneman and Tversky (1973) involves evaluating events according to the ease by which they can be imagined or retrieved from memory. People tend to assume that if a number of instances can be readily recalled, then that instance occurs frequently and it is predicted with a high probability to happen again in the future; on the other hand, instances that are harder to recall are regarded as less frequent and less probable. We find it easier to retrieve the memory of the times the bus sailed past just as we reached the bus stop than we do to remember the times we caught the bus without bother; hence, we are likely to overestimate the probability of buses that arrive 30 seconds too early and even consider such an event typical when it is almost certainly not. Schwartz *et al.* (1991) suggested that it is not the number of instances recalled that is the most important determinant but the ease of recall. Therefore, availability relates primarily to feelings of effort or effortlessness of mental productions (Keren and Tiegen, 2004).

Lifelong experience teaches us that, in general, we can recall instances of large frequencies better and faster than instances of less frequency; we know that likely occurrences are easier to imagine than unlikely ones, and that the association connection between events are strengthened when the events frequently co-occur. As a result, availability is a useful clue for assessing frequency or probability by the ease with which they are retrieved from memory. Like other heuristics, it is useful in forming judgements with minimal effort, but the availability heuristic is also affected by a number of additional factors that can affect retrievability.

If some information is more readily retrievable than other information, it follows that there is a possibility of systematic biases. There are different influencing factors, which are a result of cognitive constraints – for example, in the way human memory is organized (Evans, 1989). One such cognitive constraint is familiarity, so a sample whose instances are easily retrieved will appear more numerous than a sample of equal frequency whose instances are less retrievable. This bias is due to the selective storage of the more memorable instances. Tversky and Kahneman (1974) carried out an experiment, which demonstrated that people judge words with K as the initial letter to occur more frequently in the English language than those with K as the third letter. Objectively, the answer is incorrect. The problem, they argue, is not that people do not know more words with K in the third position, but rather retrieval by initial letter is much easier. After all, nobody ever played 'I spy with my little eye, something with "K" in the middle'; the familiarity of retrieval by the first letter allows a greater number of words to come to mind and so they seem more frequent.

Another influencing factor is salience, which refers to distinctive stimuli that disproportionately engage attention; for example, actually seeing an event occur will have a greater impact on the subjective probability of such an event occurring than reading about the same event in, say, a journal article. Biases in availability can also arise from events that have been retrieved accurately from memory but the events being recalled constitute a biased set of examples. This may be brought about by media coverage, which produces heavily distorted perceptions of risk. Evans (1989) argued that people radically overestimate the likelihood of dying from accidents compared with illnesses, due to the media providing highly selective coverage of violent and spectacular deaths but very little coverage of deaths by routine causes. Timing is also an influencing factor; recent occurrences are more likely to be available than earlier occurrences. For example, it is common for individuals' subjective probability of traffic accidents to rise after seeing a car overturned by the side of the road.

The availability heuristic is most commonly encountered in rape investigations, where an officer who has previously dealt with a false allegation assigns a greater probability to the next allegation also being fabricated. Such salient exposure to the previous investigation has negated any objective appreciation of base rate frequencies concerning the true prevalence of fabricated allegations (estimated at approximately 2 per cent; Katz and Mazur, 1979). The role of a BIA is to both recognize this potential reasoning error and objectively assess the allegation with reference to empirical research findings and large data sets, in order to provide an appropriate safeguard against such biases.

Anchoring and adjustment

When people have to make judgements about uncertain quantities, they are often influenced by initial values and the initial values are usually suggested by an external source. These initial values serve as a salient comparison value or 'anchor' from which upwards or downwards adjustments are made. This process of anchoring and adjustment creates estimates that tend to be biased or assimilated in the direction of the anchor. For example, when asked to estimate the length of the Mississippi River, people will give a higher estimate after they have been asked whether it is longer or shorter than 5,000 miles than when they have considered whether it is longer or shorter than 200 miles (Jacowitz and Kahneman, 1995). In other words, you are likely to be anchored by 5,000 or 200, depending on which one was set as the initial value.

When the anchor is informative and relevant then, despite the inbuilt bias, anchoring and adjustment is clearly an adaptive heuristic. However, when people are uncertain they can be influenced by an irrelevant or completely implausible anchor value. For example, Tversky and Kahneman (1982) asked participants to spin a wheel of fortune to generate a starting number point between zero and 100. The participants were asked whether the percentage of African countries in the United Nations was higher or lower than the starting number point they had just generated. They were then asked to give an absolute estimate value.

These starting number points had a marked effect on estimates even though they were completely arbitrary. For example, the median estimate for participants who spun 10 as a starting point was 25 (African countries in the UN) whilst participants whose starting point was 65 gave a median estimate of 45.

In the investigative domain anchoring is most often observed as a tendency to rely too heavily – or 'anchor' – on one piece of information or aspect of a case when making decisions. Studies have shown that investigators are more sceptical of information that disconfirms their prior beliefs than information that confirms it, so-called asymmetric scepticism (Ask and Granhag, 2007). In a recent case involving a series of sexual offences committed against elderly victims, the investigation team were heavily influenced by the term 'gerontophile' as an explanatory description of the likely offender as well as the underlying motivation for his offending. This anchored much of the subsequent investigative and media strategy, to the exclusion of alternative interpretations. Even as evidence of a potentially vast number of non-contact offences emerged, and more subtle behavioural interpretations were highlighted within the offender's behaviour and speech, this anchoring effect became difficult to shift, effectively causing the investigation to reject, or at least deprioritize information that went against this initial position. It is the role of the BIA in these circumstances to first recognize the presence of such 'anchoring' and then to mitigate against its impact through the thorough explanation of alternative interpretations with objective theoretical and empirical evidence.

It is worth repeating that although factors are necessarily discussed sequentially here, it should be borne in mind that, in practice, heuristics may overlap or operate in conjunction or through causal links with each other. In particular, heuristics are seen to derive from biases. For example, if investigators 'anchor' on a piece of information or a particular suspect, they may then tend to fail to look for or ignore evidence against that which they have already favoured or anchored to. This is known specifically as a confirmation bias and we shall discuss this and other biases in the next section.

Biases

Biases are used to describe deviations from the norm or as an inclination to disproportionately favour one judgement over another. Although biases do not in themselves indicate errors in judgement they are often regarded as systematic, suboptimal judgement. Biases can be the result of cognitive limitations, processing strategies, specific motivations and cognitive styles. They are traditionally regarded as being the by-product of heuristics (Keren and Tiegen, 2004).

Belief persistence

Once a belief or opinion has been formed, it can be very resistant to change and this has been described, unsurprisingly enough, as belief persistence. Early work on this issue investigated the extent to which first impressions persevere when new information appears to disconfirm people's initial beliefs. Asch's (1946) study of impression formation suggested that, when adjectives were presented in sequence, the first adjectives in the list had more of an impact on people's impressions than the adjectives that were presented later. Asch gave participants a list of adjectives describing someone's personality, and when adjectives with positive connotations were presented first (e.g. intelligent, industrious) and the words with negative connotations were shown afterwards (e.g. stubborn, critical), the participants rated the person positively; but when the adjectives were presented the other way around, participants had a less positive view of the person described. Hence, subsequently introducing new (negative) evidence after the initial belief had been formed did not change the participants' initial belief about that person.

Later researchers investigated people's responses to the discreditation or invalidation of the 'old' evidence on which they had based their initial beliefs. Logically, the negation of the original evidence should result in the eradication of the belief. However, numerous studies have found that people stick to their beliefs even when the original evidential basis for those beliefs is shown to be flimsy or even downright fictitious. Ross *et al.* (1975) presented participants with a task requiring them to discriminate between genuine and fictitious suicide notes. They then supplied the participants with fabricated feedback on their performance so that they were led to believe that they had done either much better or much worse than average. Following the task, they told participants that the feedback had been fabricated. Despite this total invalidation of their apparent performance at the task, participants who had been given 'success' feedback still believed that they had performed better than the average, whilst participants exposed to fabricated 'failure' feedback continued to believe that they had done much worse. Tversky and Kahneman explained this finding thus: they argued that people generate causal explanations to account for observed events. These causal explanations, scripts or schemas provide an effective way of organizing and understanding social phenomena and, just like heuristics, they can be an efficient means of reducing processing time but once a causal explanation has been created, it becomes functionally independent of the original evidence so that if this evidence is discredited, the explanation remains intact to sustain the belief (Tversky and Kahneman, 1974).

Davies (1997) examined whether belief persistence after evidential discrediting was related to the source of the explanations. In other words, did it make a difference whether participants generated their own explanations for an event as opposed to being provided with an explanation by the experimenter? He found that belief persistence was significantly greater for explanations that the participants themselves had generated. The elaboration likelihood model of persuasion (Petty and Cacioppo, 1986) can be used to explain this finding. This model proposes that individuals who think about issues and evaluate arguments engage in central processing, whereas people who devote little thought to the issues and arguments engage in peripheral processing. Petty and Cacioppo (1986) argued that central processing leads to beliefs that are stronger, more persistent and more resistant to counter persuasion than beliefs produced by peripheral processing. An important factor in belief persistence is the tendency for people to retrieve or generate evidence that confirms their initial belief (Ross and Anderson, 1982).

Within an investigative context, belief persistence effects often arise during the course of an investigation due to investigating officers generating story-like narratives in order to make sense of the information they gather (Ormerod *et al.* 2005). This cognitive elaboration is needed to help determine who did what to whom and why; in turn, these causal explanations are required to convince jury members of the validity of the police account (Innes, 2002). In this respect, it is a beneficial mechanism but cognitive elaboration has been shown to result in attitudes that are stronger, more persistent and more resistant to counter persuasion than attitudes produced by peripheral processing, so belief persistence is a potential danger.

When one considers that the majority of serious crime investigations are characterized by missing or ambiguous information, decision making is often complex, which can often encourage complicated theories. A danger here is that an investigative team can easily be drawn into developing *overly* complex theories and strategies to explain offending, that isn't necessarily warranted, causing errors in decision making and judgement. The principle of Occam's razor can help to minimize this danger. Based on the idea that one should 'shave off' any unnecessary elaborations, it states that the most valid and reliable methods, theories or strategies are those that make the fewest assumptions and postulate the fewest hypothetical arguments. It perhaps makes more sense to look for complex solutions to complex problems but the best solution is often the simplest.

To illustrate the point, consider the following case example. A 90-year-old female was found dead in her own home. Crime scene examination revealed that her heart had been removed and laid on a silver platter, blood had been drained from her body into a vessel, upon the rim of which traces of lip marks were discovered. A candlestick had been arranged next to her body, the red candle from within having been placed upright on the mantelpiece, whilst two pokers positioned in the shape of a crucifix had been positioned at her feet. Of additional interest was the location of the murder on a small island off the coast of Wales dotted with ancient Druid ruins, characterized by relatively isolated rural communities. Narratives of ritualistic sacrifice, vampires and the occult are easy to generate from such lurid and strange details but are of limited investigative value when compared with what else could be reasonably determined from an objective behavioural analysis of the crime scene.

In terms of probabilities, it was extremely unlikely that there was an organized vampiric cult – or anybody else for that matter – travelling purposely to a small island to commit murder, and yet within the first week officers were deployed to the other side of the UK to liaise with another case 'bearing some similarity'. In terms of prioritizing suspects, base rate information from research into elderly homicide together with a logical crime scene interpretation strongly indicated that the offender was likely to have some association to the victim and probably live in close proximity.

The offender had left a shoeprint when he broke into the victim's home. That and other forensic evidence were used to identify the 17-year-old from the same village who delivered newspapers to her door for the previous three years. Applying Occam's razor here would suggest: prioritize suspects nearby, especially if they are known to have had knowledge of the victim at her property, and use the available evidence. Whilst some may wish to spend numerous hours speculating on the potential motives of such an offence, for the purposes of solving the crime, complex and elaborate explanations were largely irrelevant.

There may be other features of the broader context that overlay individual biases. A key element to consider in major enquiries is that of organizational inertia or momentum. Organizational momentum, in investigative terms, refers to the ability to change direction in the midst of a major enquiry. Amidst intense media, public and organizational scrutiny, it can be particularly difficult to change direction from an established theory or suspect and admit that the original direction was wrong. However, the inability to recognize organizational momentum/inertia as a factor, favouring stability over responsiveness, say, can have catastrophic results. Therefore, it is essential to strike a balance between investigative stability (e.g. setting goals and hypothesizing outcomes) and responsiveness to new information and priorities.

A tendency to stick with an established theory or suspect, then, is a factor that may operate at the organizational or individual level, so in the next section, we shall discuss confirmation bias.

Confirmation bias

Confirmation bias is a phenomenon whereby decision makers have been shown to actively seek out and assign more weight to evidence that confirms their hypothesis, and ignore or underweigh evidence that could disconfirm their hypothesis. This bias can result from belief persistence. Nickerson (1998: 175) noted that, 'If one were to attempt to identify the single problematic aspect of human reasoning that deserves attention above all others, the confirmation bias would have to be among the candidates for consideration'. Confirmation bias can be said to operate by two mechanisms – selective information search and biased interpretation of available information.

Selective information search

Watson (1960) was the first to demonstrate confirmation bias by devising the two, four, six concept attainment task. In this task, participants are told that the experimenter has a rule of thumb in mind that produces a series of three numbers (each series of three is referred to as a 'triple'), an example of which is two, four, six. The participants were told to produce triples of numbers in order to figure out the experimenter's rule of thumb. Every time they produced a triple, the experimenter indicated whether the triple conformed to the rule or not. The subjects were told that once they were sure of the correctness of their hypothesized rule, they should announce it. Participants seemed to only test 'positive' examples; that is, triples that would conform to their rule and thus confirm their hypothesis. What the participants did not do was attempt to falsify their hypotheses by testing triples they believed did not conform to their rule. Therefore, people tend to seek information that they consider supportive of favoured hypotheses or existing beliefs described as positive testing strategies. Conversely, they tend not to seek and perhaps even avoid information that would be considered counter-indicative with regards to those hypotheses and beliefs and supportive of alternative possibilities (Koriat, Lichtenstein and Fischoff, 1980).

Biased interpretation of available information

Studies have found that people interpret available information in ways that support their existing beliefs (Synder and Swann, 1978) so why does this biased interpretation occur? For a number of reasons: first if you entertain only a single possible explanation for an event or phenomenon, you preclude the possibility of interpreting data as supportive of any alternative explanation; in other words, you can't evaluate how data fit with other hypotheses if you have only come up with one to begin with. Second, this issue of restricted attention to a favoured hypothesis relates to the tendency to give greater weight to information that supports existing hypotheses (rather than giving weight to information that runs counter to them). This does not necessarily mean completely disregarding the counter-indicative information but it does mean that individuals are less receptive to it, and therefore either discredit or explain away the information. Third is the clustering illusion we mentioned earlier; that is, people's tendency to see patterns in information that they are looking for regardless of whether the patterns are there or not.

It is well established, then, that people are generally biased towards confirming the hypotheses and beliefs they already hold. Even if you give two different hypotheses and the same set of evidence, people will tailor it to support their own beliefs. An early study by Kelley (1950) showed that students' perceptions of the social qualities of a guest lecturer were influenced by what they were led to expect from a prior description of the individual, showing that people with initially conflicting views can examine the same evidence and each still finds reasons to support their existing opinions. Similarly, where information is ambiguous, it is more likely to be seen as confirming rather than disconfirming prior hypotheses (Ross and Anderson, 1982).

The bias also operates in a law enforcement context. Ask and Granhag's (2005) study of confirmation bias in criminal investigations has shown that participants' processing of case material was influenced by the hypothesis that had initially been presented to them (either suspect's motive or alternative culprit); further, as the participants had all been presented with a fixed amount of information, confirmation bias here was not a result of selective information searching but rather that they were interpreting the available information to be consistent with their hypotheses. In their study of investigative bias and offender profiles, Marshall and Alison (2007: Chapter 11) found evidence of the confirmation bias for participants who engaged in cognitive elaboration. These participants appeared to be more influenced by a profile that supported their judgements than a profile that was incongruous. Therefore, the influence of a profile in an investigation may depend on the degree to which the profile is consistent or inconsistent with an investigating officer's belief about a case. It is also likely that investigating officers interpret information contained within offender profiles in ways that support their existing beliefs, by giving greater weight to information that supports their hypotheses than to information that runs counter to them.

The contribution of a BIA can be highly significant in mitigating against belief persistence, confirmation bias and selective information search, with the contemporary practice of producing hypotheses trees to guide and inform decision making. As outlined in Chapter 2, behavioural crime scene assessment leads to the generation of specific hypotheses that can be supported or refuted with reference to psychological theory, relevant research findings and experiential knowledge, with information gaps made explicit, which will promote the search for additional information and further enhance the process. The use of such a methodology promotes an objective view, with each potential scenario being subjected to the same level of rigorous contemplation, and an explicit need to evaluate evidence that both supports and negates each inference. The use of such a decision-making template greatly assists in overcoming the biases outlined above and supports the principles of effective investigative decision making as presented in ACPO (2005) Practice Advice on Core Investigative Practice.

By way of a recent example, the hypothesis tree in Figure 3.1 was prepared in a missing person case, where the circumstances of a child's disappearance were unknown.

By way of context, the initial report supporting this case comprehensively detailed each and every pathway through the hypothesis tree, with reference to theoretical and empirical research findings.

It is perhaps pertinent to reflect whether such investigative frameworks and tools would have developed in the absence of BIA efforts to bring methodological rigour and a cognisance of decision-making fallibilities into the investigative arena, and to synthesize such considerations with the knowledge of and access to the appropriate research literature.

Conclusion

The ability for investigators to make rational decisions in major crime enquiries is influenced by the same heuristics and biases that affect all of our day to day judgements. Base rate fallacies, representativeness heuristics, illusory correlations, clustering illusions, availability heuristics, anchoring and adjustment, belief persistence, confirmation bias and selective information search all have the potential to undermine even the most astute of investigators' decision-making capabilities. Whilst such influences are by no means any more (or indeed less) prevalent among Senior Investigating Officers than among you or me, the

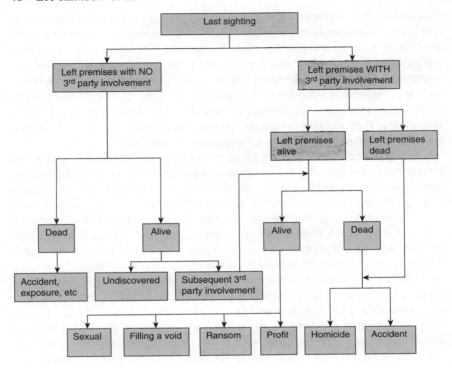

Figure 3.1 Hypothesis tree.

consequences of error within a murder enquiry are of arguably greater consequence than the majority of our daily decisions.

It is a critical role of the contemporary Behavioural Investigative Adviser to mitigate against such errors of decision making through the implicit integration of such considerations within all advice and support offered. Whilst such cognisance of these biases and heuristics does not form a 'product' or 'service' in its own right, it may be argued to represent one of the biggest contributions from BIAs, providing the foundations on which the goal of supporting investigative decision making can be soundly built.

References

ACPO (2005) *Practice Advice on Core Investigative Doctrine,* Wyboston: NCPE.
Asch, S. (1946) 'Forming impressions on personality', *Journal of Abnormal and Social Psychology,* 41: 258–290.
Ask, K. and Granhag, P. (2005) 'Motivational sources of confirmation bias in criminal investigations: the need for cognitive closure', *Journal of Investigative Psychology and Offender Profiling,* 2: 43–63.

Ask, K. and Granhag, P. (2007) 'Hot cognition in investigative judgements: the differential influence of anger and sadness', *Law and Human Behavior*, 31: 537–551.

Bar-Hillel, M. (1980) 'The base rate fallacy in probability judgements', *Acta Psychologica*, 44: 211–233.

Bernoulli, D. (1738) 'Specimen theoriae novae de mensura sortis [exposition of a new theory of the measurement of risk]', *Commentari Academiae Scientrum Imperialis Petropolitanae*, 5: 175–192.

Chapman, L.J. (1967) 'Illusory correlation in observational report', *Journal of Verbal Learning and Verbal Behavior*, 5: 151–155.

Davies, M. (1997) 'Belief persistence after evidential discrediting: the impact of generated versus proved explanations on the likelihood of discredited outcomes', *Journal of Experimental Social Psychology*, 33: 561–578.

Evans, J. (1989) *Bias in human reasoning: causes and consequences*, Hillsdale, NJ: Erlbaum.

Gilovich, T., Vallone, R. and Tversky, A. (1985) 'The hot hand in basketball: on the misperception of random sequences', *Cognitive Psychology*, 17: 295–314.

Innes, M. (2002) 'The process structures of police homicide investigations', *British Journal of Criminology*, 42: 669–688.

Jacowitz, K. and Kahneman, D. (1995) 'Measures of anchoring in estimation tasks', *Personality and Social Psychology Bulletin*, 21: 1161–1167.

Kahneman, D. and Tversky, A. (1973) 'On the psychology of prediction', *Psychological Review*, 80: 237–251.

Katz, S. and Mazur, M.A. (1979) *Understanding the rape victim: Synthesis of research findings*, New York: John Wiley.

Kelley, H. (1950) 'The warm-cold variable in first impressions of persons', *Journal of Personality*, 18: 431–439.

Keren, G. and Tiegen, K. (2004) 'Yet another look at the heuristics and biases approach', in D. Koehler and N. Harvey (eds) *Blackwell handbook of judgement and decision making*, Oxford: Blackwell Publishing.

Klein, G.A., Orasanu, J., Calderwood, R. and Zsambok, C.E. (eds) (1993) *Decision making in action: models and methods*, Norwood, CT: Ablex.

Koriat, A., Lichtenstein, S. and Fischoff, B. (1980) 'Reasons for confidence', *Journal of Experimental Psychology: Human Learning and Memory*, 6: 107–118.

Marshall, B. and Alison, L. (2007) 'Stereotyping, congruence and presentation order: interpretative biases in utilizing offender profiles', *Psychology, Crime and Law*, 13: 285–303.

Nickerson, R. (1998) 'Confirmation bias: a ubiquitous phenomenon in many guises', *Review of General Psychology*, 2: 175–220.

Nisbett, R., Borgida, E., Crandall, R. and Reed, H. (1976) 'Popular induction: information is not necessarily informative', in D. Kahneman, P. Slovic and A. Tversky (eds) *Judgement under uncertainty: heuristics and biases,* Cambridge: Cambridge University Press.

Ormerod, T.C., Barrett, E.C. and Taylor, P.J. (2005) 'Investigative sense making in criminal contexts', paper presented at Proceedings of the seventh international NDM conference on Ed. J. M. C. Schraagen in Amsterdam, June.

Payne, J., Bettman, J. and Luce, M. (1998) 'Behavioral decision research: an overview', in M. Birnbaum (ed.) *Measurement, judgment and decision making*, San Diego, CA: Academic Press.

Petty, R. and Cacioppo, J. (1986) *Communication and persuasion: central and peripheral routes to attitude change*, New York: Springer-Verlag.

Ross, L. and Anderson, C. (1982) 'Shortcomings in the attribution process: on the origins and maintenance of erroneous social assessments', in A. Tversky, D. Kahneman, and P. Slovic (eds) *Judgement under uncertainty: heuristics and biases*, Cambridge: Cambridge University Press.

Ross, L., Lepper, M. and Hubbard, M. (1975) 'Perseverance in self perception and social perception: biased attributional process in the debriefing paradigm', *Journal of Personality and Social Psychology*, 32: 880–892.

Savage, L.J. (1954) *The Foundations of Statistics*, New York: Wiley.

Schwartz, N., Strack, F., Hilton, D. and Naderer, G. (1991) 'Base rates, representativeness and the logic of conversation: the contextual relevance of "irrelevant" information', *Social Cognition*, 9: 67–84.

Synder, M. and Swann, W. (1978) 'Hypothesis-testing processes in social interaction', *Journal of Personality and Social Psychology*, 36: 1202–1212.

Tversky, A. and Kahneman, D. (1974) 'Judgement under uncertainty: heuristics and biases', *Science*, 185: 1124–1131.

Tversky, A. and Kahneman, D. (1982) 'Judgements of and by representativeness', in D. Kahneman., P. Slovic and A. Tversky (eds) *Judgement under uncertainty: heuristics and biases*, Cambridge: Cambridge University Press.

Watson, P. (1960) 'On the failure to eliminate hypotheses in a conceptual task', *Quarterly Journal of Experimental Psychology*, 12: 129–140.

4 Pragmatic solutions to offender profiling and behavioural investigative advice

Laurence Alison, Alasdair Goodwill,
Louise Almond, Claudia van den Heuvel
and Jan Winter

Several countries' police services regularly employ the assistance of psychologists in relation to the prevention, management, and investigation of crime (Alison, 2005). Although some of what they are engaged in might be described as offender profiling, the support from psychologists over the last ten years, in the UK at least, might be more accurately described as *behavioural investigative advice* (BIA; ACPO, 2006). The older term *offender profiling* has developed an almost mythic status in popular literature and drama (Herndon, 2007), although, as this paper will demonstrate, in its best understood but narrow definition, it has failed to make much operational impact. Moreover, several studies have shown that the idea of psychologists being able to generate a coherent set of offender characteristics by inferring latent patterns or 'styles' of offending from crime scene information has proven empirically and theoretically problematic (see Snook, Cullen, Bennell, Taylor, & Gendreau, 2008), although they themselves recognize some recent and notable exceptions (e.g. Goodwill & Alison, 2007; Goodwill, Alison, & Beech, 2009; Mokros, 2007; Santtila *et al.*, 2008) as the field has developed. In the last ten years, however, a broader definition of offender profiling, or *BIA*, has emerged which recognizes the range of fruitful, reliable, tested, and transparent evidence-based methods by which psychologists might provide advice to the police during investigations (Alison, McLean, & Almond, 2007).

The relatively new term BIA (ACPO, 2006) is broad in its scope, inter-disciplinary in nature, and benefits from a *tacit knowledge* (Sternberg & Horvath, 1999) of the policies, procedures, and protocols of the police service with which it engages. The type of expertise that Behavioural Investigative Advisers build up 'on the job' by working closely with investigators can be referred to as *tacit knowledge*, knowledge 'so thoroughly grounded in experience that it cannot be expressed in its fullness ... knowledge that is built-up in activity and the effort around it' (Sternberg & Horvath, 1999, p. ix). We argue that this is potentially why researchers and practitioners alike have faced many challenges in their attempts to firmly ground this new approach in empirical evidence and good practice principles. Establishing 'what works' is an applied endeavour requiring pragmatic approaches and solid partnerships between academics and their police counterparts.

This paper will outline the studies that have criticized the narrower offender profiling term, describe the ethos of the BIA approach, and recommend methods for researching it, as well as critically examining this new approach. As such, the purpose of this article is to put some distance between the old and new terms, illustrate the lack of empirical support for narrow definitions of profiling, and offer a more optimistic albeit tempered view of what may be possible within the remit of BIA.

The past

A recent thorough literature review covering the last three decades revealed that the majority of articles on offender profiling comprised discussion pieces lacking any clear theoretical framework for the process of offender profiling, with very few articles utilizing empirical multivariate research techniques (Dowden, Bennell, & Bloomneld, 2007). A meta-analysis by Snook, Eastwood, Gendreau, Goggin, and Cullen (2007) pointed to the plethora of 'common sense' (as opposed to scientifically evidenced) rationales in 130 articles on offender profiling. Consequently, the apparent lack of validity in offender profiling has warranted a healthy scepticism among law enforcement personnel (Copson, 1995; Snook, Haines, Taylor, & Bennell, 2007) and even outright apprehension among forensic mental health professionals (Torres, Boccaccini, & Miller, 2006).

Traditional approaches to offender profiling

The different approaches to traditional offender profiling can be broadly categorized into three types: a *criminal investigative* approach, a *clinical practitioner* approach, and a *scientific statistical* approach (Muller, 2000). Each approach reflects a different type of knowledge domain (usually coinciding with the background of the respective proponents) on the basis of which hypotheses are drawn in order to understand offenders' behaviour (Goodwill *et al.*, 2009). These respective knowledge domains are based on specific investigative experience (mostly in cases of sexual and violent offending), hands-on expertise from working with criminals in a clinical context, and applied scientific knowledge from broader domains, respectively. Although the approaches differ, all the three domains, at various points in their evolutionary history, have argued that it is possible to identify reliable clusters of crime scene behaviours, and, from these, infer various latent descriptors of those taxonomic classifications and, finally, work backwards to provide coherent lists or a pen portrait of the most likely type of offender. These approaches have been described elsewhere in great detail (e.g. Hicks & Sales, 2006) and will therefore only briefly be illustrated here.

The criminal investigative approach

This approach, developed by Federal Bureau of Investigation (FBI) agents in the 1970s, presents the first systematic attempt to utilize all available information on a violent offence in combination with considerable investigative knowledge to make inferences about the type of unknown offender (Douglas, Ressler, Burgess, & Hartman, 1986). Douglas *et al.* state that the technique of profiling is acquired 'through brainstorming, intuition, and educated guesswork. [Profilers'] expertise is the result of years of accumulated wisdom, extensive experience in the field, and familiarity with a large number of cases' (1986, p. 405). According to this view, it can be argued that offender profiling relies heavily on a mix of tacit and evidence-based expert knowledge. Arguably, this may make a profiler's advice more susceptible to cognitive biases and faulty decision making (Kahneman, Slovic, & Tversky, 1982). However, this charge that heuristics and biases are inherently faulty mechanisms cannot be claimed, by any means, to represent the definitive view, and – albeit beyond the scope of this paper – there is extensive work relating to the positive, adaptive aspects of heuristics (Gigerenezer, 2000). Certainly, in this applied area of offender profiling, the contribution of practitioner expertise to the evolutionary story of 'what works' should not be rejected. Reporting in favour only of academic findings would itself be a biased as well as crude conclusion. Nevertheless, subjecting practitioner findings to empirical validation was identified as being necessary.

Efforts to formalize this tacit knowledge used by profilers in the form of various typologies (e.g. organized/disorganized) have received criticism (Canter & Alison, 1999; Egger, 1999), mostly concerning the lack of scientific methodological rigor, sound theoretical underpinning, and falsification of these typologies (Muller, 2000; Wilson, Lincoln, & Kocsis, 1997). The oversimplification of complex situational behaviours into dichotomous categories, a typical strategy used within this approach, has also been empirically refuted (e.g. Canter, Alison, Alison, & Wentink, 2004). However, in recent years the FBI and several of their retired profilers have adopted a more scientific approach to behavioural investigative research, publishing empirical papers in several peer-reviewed journals (Hazelwood & Warren, 1999, 2003; Safarik & Jarvis, 2005; Safarik, Jarvis, & Nussbaum, 2000, 2002). These articles provide evidence of a new, more integrative approach between FBI profilers, clinicians, law enforcement, and academics to produce innovative and theoretically sound contributions more in line with the concept of BIA outlined herein (Burgess, Commons, Safarik, Looper, & Ross, 2007; Myers, Husted, Safarik, & O'Toole, 2006).

The clinical practitioner approach

In the same manner, individuals using the clinical practitioner approach rely on their practical experience, knowledge, and to varying degrees intuition to draw inferences from crime scene information. Clinical profiling approaches appeared to be primarily based on the expertise and knowledge of the individual profiler (Copson, Babcock, Boon, & Britton, 1997). However, as is the case with the criminal investigative approach, it is difficult to judge when and how a clinician's tacit knowledge gets translated into formalized, explicit, and falsifiable knowledge, as well as how this knowledge subsequently leads to the generation of useful offender profiles.

The statistical approach

The statistical approach is primarily based on the multivariate analysis of behavioural and other information found at the crime scene to infer an offender's characteristics and psychological processes. The pioneering work of Canter (1995, 2000) and his colleagues aimed to employ an explicit, psychological (i.e. scientific) framework to provide offender characteristics that are *directly* useful (i.e. avoiding non-falsifiable and non-pragmatic motivational and/or psychodynamic explanations) to police investigations. This approach has stimulated an increasing amount of academically peer-reviewed research into many aspects of offender profiling, including, amongst others, burglary (e.g. Bennell & Canter, 2002; Goodwill & Alison, 2006), robbery (e.g. Woodhams & Toye, 2007), homicide (e.g. Salfati, 2003; Salfati & Dupont, 2006), arson (e.g. Canter & Fritzon, 1998; Häkkänen, Puolakka, & Santtila, 2004), and sexual offending (e.g. Almond & Canter, 2007; Canter, Bennell, Alison, & Reddy, 2003; Greenall & West, 2007; Häkkänen, Lindlöf, & Santtila, 2004). The most significant critique of this approach is whether nomothetical and often inductively gathered research findings can be applied to specific idiographic cases; this is especially true when the base-rate of a behaviour is disregarded, and when studies are based on small or even unrepresentative samples.

Moving nearer to the contemporary picture, it is evident that practitioners have moved on to an eclectic, often multidisciplinary approach (i.e. BIA) that combines the apparent advantages of all three perspectives (e.g. Alison, West, & Goodwill, 2004; Rainbow, 2008). This has rendered debates over inductive versus deductive inferences somewhat redundant (Turvey, 2008) and moved the focus towards the bidirectional partnerships between academics and practitioner counterparts. Thus, in defining what works, it is more appropriate to ask to what degree behavioural investigative advisers rely on available and adequate empirical research. Another remaining challenge is to identify the contribution of tacit knowledge as a form of implicit expertise to the behavioural investigative process, and its impact on providing investigative advice professionally. Differences also exist between countries in the preferred amount of contribution from each (knowledge) domain (e.g. Germany: Federation-State Police Forces Project Group, 2003; UK: Rainbow, 2008). This translates into who is eligible to provide BIA or, in fact, be employed as a Behavioural Investigative Adviser.

In research driven by pragmatic principles (see Fishman, 1999), several studies (see Alison, 2005, for a review) have focused on the psychological mechanisms (including attention, encoding, and problem solving) that influence the ways in which the content of profiles is understood (and misunderstood), as well as the evidence upon which any given profiling claim appears to be based. For example, Alison, Smith, Eastman, and Rainbow (2003) found that 80 per cent of the approximately 4,000 claims made in the profiles they sampled were unsupported. The claims lacked appropriate *grounding* in psychological knowledge, contained no *warrants* (specific examples of supportive research), were provided with no estimation of their *veracity* (i.e. probability) and less than one third were *falsifiable* (Toulmin, 1958).

However, a contemporary UK study conducted by Almond, Alison, and Porter (2007) of behavioural investigative reports produced by the National Policing Improvement Agency (NPIA) found that these reports had clearer boundaries around the claims made within them, and presented material in a more coherent and evidence-based format than previous expert advice. This new approach is thus characterized by adherence to the abovementioned principles (Toulmin, 1958) and allows for individual differences in expertise, while providing a framework within which minimum expectations and requirements are set (Rainbow, 2008). Additionally, the NPIA has set out a new requirement for all reports to make the supportive rationale behind their advice explicit, a change that 'represents the most significant advancement in the professionalization of BIA within the UK' (Rainbow, 2008, p. 91). Although not explicitly aimed at establishing the utility of such profiles, such studies reveal the extent to which empirical findings have been incorporated into daily working practices.

Behavioural Investigative Advisers: how can they contribute?

In recent years, several countries in particular the UK, Canada, Germany, the Netherlands, and more recently, Singapore, have opted for a more integrated multidisciplinary approach to the erstwhile concept of offender profiling. Over the last couple of decades, there has been an increasing realization, particularly in the UK, that *behavioural analytic approaches* are not only paramount to the clinical understanding of offences (e.g. West, 2000) but also aid investigative efforts. Depending on their respective background and tacit knowledge of an area, BIAs may contribute to the investigative process by aiding: (1) suspect prioritization, (2) linking crimes and crime scenes, (3) geographical profiling,[1] (4) the interviewing process, and (5) risk assessment of offenders in clinical settings. Before these various contributions are discussed, it is necessary to review the evidence with regard to the initial underlying assumptions for historical offender profiling, and consequently the new assumptions underlying the provision of BIA.

Consistency and homology in offence behaviour

Alison, Bennell, Mokros, and Ormerod (2002) outlined two theoretical tenets of offender profiling relating to 'the necessary (*consistency*) and sufficient (*homology*) conditions for offender profiling to be valid and useful' (p. 122). The *consistency assumption* held that the variations in actions (i.e. behaviours) of an offender across their series must be less than the variation in actions by all other offenders. The second assumption holds that people who commit crimes in a similar style will have similar background characteristics – called the *homology assumption*.

Research has shown that offenders can behave relatively consistently in a number of ways, from their choice of crime type (Farrington & Lambert, 1997), and their behaviour across crimes in burglary (Goodwill & Alison, 2006), arson

(Santtila, Fritzon, & Tamelander, 2004), robbery (Woodhams & Toye, 2007), and sexual assault (Grubin, Kelly, & Brunsdon, 2000; Santtila, Junkkila, & Sandnabba, 2005). Thus, there does seem to be some degree of supporting evidence that offenders commit crimes in a consistent manner which, in turn, offers potential utility in respect of 'what works'.

However, the second and perhaps most notable aspect of behavioural consistency is the fact that an individual's behavioural variation must be less than others' to be *investigatively* useful. This aspect has been called *differentiation* (Bennell & Canter, 2002) or distinctiveness (Woodhams & Toye, 2007) and is an implicit necessity in proving consistency for investigative purposes. This has been explored in relation to some types of offence. Studies on burglary and robbery have shown that it is possible to discriminate between particular characteristics and consequently predict accurately whether several offences are (un) linked (Bennell & Jones, 2005; Goodwill & Alison, 2006; Woodhams & Toye, 2007).

In terms of offender homology, the findings are less encouraging, at least at the many actions-many characteristics level. Empirical tests of the homology assumption have been largely unsupported for various types of offences (Doan & Snook, 2008; Mokros & Alison, 2002; Woodhams & Toye, 2007). Rapists tend to be especially versatile, antisocial offenders (Harris, Smallbone, Dennison, & Knight, 2009); this finding challenges a simplistic homology assumption (at least in this context). Thus, Alison *et al.* (2002) suggest that a direct link between offender characteristics and offence behaviour (i.e. homology) is unlikely to prove fruitful without acknowledging the influence of the situation.

By now, a substantial amount of findings from different domains demonstrate the variability in offending behaviour under the influence of situational and contextual factors, especially for sexual offences. Rich, qualitative studies by Polaschek, Hudson, Ward, and Siegert (2001) and Ward, Hudson, and Keenan (1998) showed that a sexual offence is a highly dynamic event with regard to cognitive, behavioural, affective, and volitional aspects of the offender. Also, Ullman's (2007) review highlighted that the type of victim resistance strategy has a significant impact on the offender's behaviour and consequently on the outcome of the offence. Beauregard and colleagues (Beauregard, Proulx, Rossmo, Leclerc, & Allaire, 2007; Beauregard, Rossmo, & Proulx, 2007) have demonstrated that several aspects of serial sex offenders' modus operandi are influenced by various contextual factors (e.g. type of offence site, familiarity with the environment, etc.). They also described how a rational choice perspective can serve as an explanation for the way in which situational structure influences the offenders' decision-making process. Although an innovative study by Woodhams, Hollin, and Bull (2008) found no evidence for the temporal stability of thematic 'if... then' offender-victim interactions in rape, Goodwill and Alison (2007) confirmed that the incorporation of the context and carefully chosen variables enables the prediction of rapists' characteristics from crime scene information. Novel sequence analysis techniques (Taylor *et al.*, 2008) offer the possibility of a more realistic way of modelling offender behaviour which in turn could be used to test the homology assumption. Future research should also examine the role of psychological moderators, as Mokros (2007) recently showed that sexual offenders' psychological characteristics (e.g. extraversion, narcissism, etc.) can be predicted from scaled crime scene behaviours. This might hold the (as yet untested) promise that distinct psychological characteristics could also be linked to different socio-demographic characteristics of the offender.

Suspect prioritization

BIAs may aid the investigation by reducing the time spent on wholly irrelevant suspicions and providing an evidence-based approach for developing lines of inquiry and making investigative decisions. Marshall and Alison's (2007) study illustrated the mixed operational potential of investigative advice. By providing a similar picture to the preconceived idea an officer carries, the advice may be reinforcing, and ultimately promote confirmation bias. However, the study also showed that officers were forced to rethink and think more thoroughly about their assumptions where the profile did not match. Caution should, therefore, be exercised around likely responses from recipients of advice. Nonetheless, the key issue appears to relate to the adviser's ability to provide an evidential basis for any given claim and draw upon, where possible, the relevant databases and theoretical models.

In order to successfully prioritize possible suspects, it is necessary to predict offender characteristics that are of actual value to police investigations such as prior criminal antecedents or offender age; in other words, information that is readily accessible to the investigator. There is a fundamental dispute whether to limit the predictions to the direct associations between (an) offence behaviour(s) and (an) offender characteristic(s) (e.g. Davies, Wittebrood, & Jackson, 1997) or to try to collate crime scene actions into themes or scales of offence behaviour to predict offender characteristics (e.g. for arson, Häkkänen *et al.*, 2004; burglary, Santtila, Ritvanen, & Mokros, 2003; rape, Santtila *et al.*, 2005). However, Goodwill *et al.* (2009) made empirical comparisons between direct association techniques (e.g. multivariate regression), thematic and typological approaches, finding the more powerful multivariate direct association statistical technique significantly more predictive of offender characteristics. Yet, thematic and typological approaches which were based on a multidisciplinary approach (e.g. law enforcement, clinical, and statistical domains) were found to perform better than those that relied purely on a statistical basis. Therefore, it is still not clear whether analyses of behavioural information should constitute precise independent or multivariate predictions or comprise approaches that incorporate themes, or 'fuzzy' boundaries.

The adoption of filter-style models is another emerging approach that has direct investigative use and has had some empirically validated success (Goodwill & Alison, 2006). The particular advantage of this approach is its straightforward application for law enforcement agencies; investigators can make objective decisions at each step of the hierarchical decision-tree based model while also utilizing their experiential knowledge in those decisions. The result is a decision-making framework that is somewhat malleable to investigator experience while also providing objective and transparent investigative decision support in the form of an empirically based model.

So far, filter models for serial burglary and armed robbery have been proposed (Goodwill & Alison, 2006; Snook, Wright, House, & Alison, 2006, respectively) taking advantage of the combined information of spatial and behavioural offence characteristics in order to prioritize lists of possible suspects. These studies have illustrated that geographical information (e.g. how close an offender lives to a crime site) outperforms behavioural information (e.g. used a weapon) in accurately prioritizing potential suspects and should be employed as the first stage in filtering suspects. Models, especially those of a pragmatically useful nature (e.g. filter-style models), that have been developed based on well-researched facts (e.g. regardless of the committed offence type, offenders tend to operate in close proximity to their home (Santtila, Laukanen, Zappalà, & Bosco, 2008) are clearly the way forward for developing 'what works' in suspect prioritization techniques.

One drawback to such models is that the analyses underlying the empirically-based decision-tree or filter models seldom account for situational variability – this is left to investigators to consider. Although this may lead to potentially greater investigative success on occasion, it is a less transparent and bias free approach resulting in a less scientifically defendable outcome. A more parsimonious approach has been recently proposed that also integrates situational interactions in a decision-tree style approach. Goodwill and Alison (2007) successfully predicted offender age on the basis of the victim's age when the moderating effects of the degrees of planning and aggression were taken into account.

Yet another emerging area of research, which may potentially bridge the gaps between prediction of offender characteristics, situational aspects of the offence, and the analyses of offence behaviour, is the utilization of probabilistic research methods. Aitken, Connolly, Gammerman, Zhang, and Oldfield (1995) and more recently, Baumgartner, Ferrari, and Palermo (2008) have employed Bayesian network modelling to aid in the suspect prioritization process with (albeit as yet limited) positive results.

Nevertheless, the fact that most offenders have criminal antecedents of some kind, the future challenge lies in efficient exploitation of the nowadays vast amount of electronically stored information on previously identified offenders (Cullen, Snook, Rideout, Eastwood, & House, 2006). BIAs may assist in the construction of databases and decision support systems as well as in advising on how data might be most fruitfully collected, stored, and utilized. Additionally, psychological input can be useful in informing what data are collected and how to generate systems that can be coded reliably and efficiently. The sobering fact is that most criminals appear to be in the system already, investigators just need to know at what, and especially where, to look. Essentially, future research must encourage validation of approaches similar to the aforementioned statistical, thematic, Bayesian, and filter-style models across various crime types (e.g. sexual offences, homicide) that remain pragmatic and investigatively useful in their application.

Linking of crimes and crime scenes

BIA may also be given in regard to determining whether two (or more) cases are likely to have been committed by the same offender(s), commonly referred to as *case linkage* or *comparative case analysis*. Santtila *et al.* (2005) suggest that this may pertain to two different situations: (a) establishing whether a new offence can be attributed to a previously identified string of offences or offender(s); (b) linking a group of unidentified offences. The stepwise process of case linkage or comparative case analysis has been described elsewhere in detail (e.g. Woodhams, Bull, & Hollin, 2007).

Apart from physical evidence such as DNA (Grubin *et al.*, 2000), geospatial information appears to hold the most merit for a successful linking process. As mentioned before, serial offences do reflect some degree of behavioural consistency, although certain behaviours appear to be temporally less stable and are more susceptible to situational influence, especially in sexual offences (Bootsma & van den Eshof, 2006). The jury is still out on whether specific single behavioural similarities (e.g. rare behaviours) are more accurate for a successful linkage analysis than behavioural scales or themes. Several studies have demonstrated some linking accuracy in different crime types using a thematic approach (e.g. Santtila *et al.*, 2004; Santtila *et al.*, 2005; Santtila, Korpela, & Häkkänen, 2004; Woodhams, Grant, & Price, 2007), although linking accuracy tended to be low (e.g. 25.6–33 per cent). Most recently Santtila *et al.* (2008) found that the use of non-parametric Mokken scaling in combination with discriminant function analysis yielded a linking accuracy of 62.9 per cent in a sample of 116 Italian serial murders (chance expectation was 6.2 per cent). This already high rate was even more improved when using a full Bayesian approach with high- and low-frequency behaviours in the same sample (linking accuracy = 82.8 per cent, chance expectation = 5.3 per cent; Salo, 2008). Although more evidence is needed, it appears that certain offences, particularly serial homicide, may be successfully linked with either a thematic or probabilistic approach. Perhaps not surprisingly these studies of linking methods have provided insight into the reliability of certain aspects of crime scene information and as a result have contributed to the call for the development of an evidence-based reduction of information in decision-support systems such as ViCLAS (Violent Crime Linkage Analysis System; Goodwill *et al.*, 2009).

Investigative interviewing

The provision of an investigative interviewing strategy can also constitute an aspect of 'what works' in BIA. Advice may centre on interview strategies through the means of preparing officers or Tactical Interview Managers for what they might expect psychologically from a given offender. This issue is currently being formalized, though there are indications that having a psychologist advise on issues, additional to the way the interview itself is conducted, can only be of value if that psychologist has some understanding of what is legally admissible and procedurally correct. BIA may thus provide both tacit and experiential knowledge (as based on experience with previous cases), in the form of hypotheses, theoretical formulations, and empirical information, to the investigative interview (Alison *et al.*, 2004). Specifically, BIAs may assess the credibility of statements, evaluate interviewer performance (and assist in the structuring and planning of an interview), and advise on what aspects of the account might most fruitfully be challenged or explored in more detail (see Porter and ten Brinke, 2009), and offer empirically supported advice on how to evaluate claimed amnesia (see van Oorsouw and Merckelbach, 2009).

Clinical interviews may thus provide experiential frameworks within which crime scene data can be interpreted. Not infrequently, for example, the NPIA will refer a Senior Investigating Officer (SIO) to an expert on the advisory list (BIA) who has an understanding of, among other areas, the debates in so-called recovered and false memories, malingering, or the dynamics of interviewing vulnerable witnesses or people with learning disabilities (Alison, 2005). Specifically, studies have shown that using a cognitive interview (CI) approach with vulnerable victims or witnesses will lead to enhanced recall of correct information and a reduction in the amount of confabulations made (Milne, Clare, & Bull, 1999) resulting in more complete and accurate reports. Naturally, the full picture is not so straightforward: for example, praxis in relation to CI does not necessarily reflect the ideal with regard to theoretical knowledge (e.g. Walsh & Milne, 2008). It is a complex area beyond the scope of this paper. Notwithstanding, the central tenet of BIA (as with other areas discussed in this paper) – stating *probabilities* not *certainties* – holds good in relation to interviewing styles as well, and constitutes a standard proviso which ensures investigations are not misled (Rainbow, 2008). Nevertheless, further validity and utility studies are needed in order to expand the empirical basis on which the issue of statement credibility in particular are based.

A related controversial point involves the provision of BIA on the admissibility of *bad character evidence*. Bad character may arise in a criminal trial or investigation where a defendant has a criminal record, or in which past misconduct (irrespective of whether it resulted in a conviction or not) is introduced as evidence against the defendant (Criminal Justice Act, 2003, Section 101 [1]). Bad character evidence is only admissible if: (a) all parties to the proceedings agree to the evidence being admissible, (b) the evidence is adduced by the defendant him (or her) self or is given in answer to a question asked by him (or her) in cross-examination intended to elicit it, (c) it is important explanatory evidence, (d) it is relevant to an important matter in issue between the defendant and the prosecution, (e) it has substantial probative value in relation to an important matter in issue between the defendant and a co-defendant, (f) it is evidence to correct a false impression given by the defendant, or (g) the defendant has made an attack on another person's character (Criminal Justice Act, 2003, Section 101 [1]). If and when these criteria are met, BIA may be provided in order to advise the court on the psychology of a defendant, specifically if a person's previous misconduct has significance for determining matters in the present case. However, as is the case with advice on the veracity of witness statements, these statements should be put forward with discretion and only in terms of probabilities and not certainties, in order to not give bad character evidence undue weight and thereby distort the criminal proceedings.

Risk assessment

As a case in point, forensic risk assessment illustrates the greater breadth of the definition of BIA to offender profiling. Osterheider and Mokros (2006) explain how a thorough understanding of the actual offence behaviour and dynamics, a mainstay of behavioural investigate advice, is vital for forensic practitioners. Osterheider and Mokros (2006) argue that an objective, evidence-based, recon-struction of the offence process (as opposed to the offenders' personal perspec-tive) can contribute to more accurate risk assessments. This is especially true with regard to sexually motivated homicide offences; the degree of sexual deviance and other relevant aspects can be deduced from an objective analysis of the crime scene behaviour. Horn (2006) illustrated how assessment of pre-arrest BIA in collaboration with forensic mental health practitioners post-conviction can assist in improving BIA in future cases. He also delineated how cooperation between BIAs and forensic practitioners led to the development of the 'HEADS' (Haft-Entlassenen-Auskunfts-Datei-Sexual sträftater, trans. = Excon Information Index for Sexual Delinquents) initiative in Bavaria, Germany, in which high-risk sexual offenders are flagged in a centralized database three months prior to their release from jail, including all information that relates to that individual's risk assess-ment. When such an offender begins his or her reintegration into society, the police put into place a follow-up process in collaboration with the judiciary, pris-ons and probation services, in order to prevent the offender from committing future offences (Horn, 2006).

Implications and caveats

By taking advantage of the now more substantial knowledge of 'what works' in BIA, police forces can demonstrate a continuing commitment to intelligence-led policing and the policing of risk. This is in line with national policing initiatives in the UK. Crucially, however, if investigators do choose to embrace the contri-bution from psychologists, they should retain a healthy scepticism. As Canter and Alison (1999, p. 39) noted, 'one must check and treat with caution all opinions and not simply assume that because it is said with great conviction by someone with experience that it must be true'. Because officers should not be expected to have a full and comprehensive knowledge of the scientific methods used, it can prove difficult for any given SIO to know what qualities of the expert s/he should be looking to evaluate. In recent ACPO guidelines (Kent Police, 2008), the effective and appropriate use of BIA is made explicit. Additionally, these guidelines have been incorporated as a core component in recent national training programmes for SIOs, through which they are taught how to best evaluate and use BIA (Rainbow, 2008). However, officers are unlikely to know the range of issues that psychologists and others may assist with, since there is currently no formal checklist of the range of possible contributions. Although not all SIO courses have a training input on profiling and advice, several have now taken up contributions from psychologists and advisers regarding this contribution (D. Crompton, personal communication, 2007).

Limitations and boundaries

Rigid rules exist governing the use of expert evidence in criminal trials (Criminal Procedure and Investigations Act, 1996). The general consensus is that BIA does not amount to probative evidence that can be used in court to establish guilt (Kent Police, 2008). Additionally, due to the heterogeneous nature of profiling along with a poor conceptual understanding of a BIA's tacit knowledge, BIA currently yields poor reliability and probative value (Meyer, 2007). This has led to past profiling techniques and present-day BIA alike failing expert admissibility standards (Meyer, 2007).

If BIA were to be received by the court, it would need to satisfy the legal tests of relevance and admissibility as well as the rules concerning the reception of expert opinion evidence. The latter relate to the BIA's qualifications, the perceived helpfulness and reliability of the evidence, and, in the case of investigative advice, its potential categorization as a novel technique. Generally, the degree of difficulty that the rules will pose depends on the purpose that the profiling evidence is intended to serve. As Ormerod and Sturman (2005) point out, where the purpose is to identify the defendant, profiles are likely to be excluded (in England and Wales at least) as unreliable, prejudicial, unscientific, and insufficiently relevant; however, they may be deemed admissible if their purpose falls under one of the following categories:

(1) The profiler may be able to testify about the crime scene.
(2) Profiles may be admitted as comparative crime scene analysis.
(3) The accused seeks to establish his or her personality and its incompatibility with the police profile.
(4) A profile might be admitted where the question is whether it is more likely that defendant A rather than defendant B committed the crime with which they are both charged.

Neither the British Psychological Society nor the American Psychological Association (APA) has devoted special attention to the ethical, legal, or professional issues raised by the involvement of BIAs in criminal investigations. Rather, their codes of conduct set out general principles which all psychologists must adhere to in their professional endeavours. However, the APA statement below, illustrating boundaries of competence, gives the general overview of what is expected:

> In those emerging areas in which generally recognized standards for preparatory training do not yet exist, psychologists nevertheless [should] take reasonable steps to ensure the competence of their work and to protect clients/patients, students, supervisees, research participants, organizational clients, and others from harm (Standard 2.01, APA, 2002).

Establishing the contribution made by BIAs

There have been relatively few studies that have attempted to quantitatively evaluate the profiling profession (see Kocsis, 2006, for a review) and fewer that look at contemporary methods. Those studies that have been done are relatively inconclusive, where findings indicated that, on one hand, the majority of investigators agreed that criminal profiling does help solve cases, while many officers also believed that the application of offender profiling was limited, or even that it had the potential to mislead an investigation (see Copson, 1995; Pinizzotto & Finkel, 1990; Snook *et al.*, 2007 for details). Additionally, several studies found that self-proclaimed profilers made a greater number of correct predictions to those produced by laypersons or investigators combined, but that general investigative experience does not matter in the profiling process as much as critical thinking skills do (Gogan, 2007; Kocsis, 2006). On the other hand, a tentative study by Bennell, Corey, Taylor, and Ecker (2008) found no significant relationship between critical thinking ability and profile accuracy. Thus, there is much research ahead to determine fully the contribution made by BIAs.

Although recent studies have attempted to examine expertise in (geographical) profiling (for a review, see Bennell, Taylor, & Snook, 2007), some confusion remains as to whether the results in general can be delineated from criticisms of what support (e.g. expert computer systems) *may* be used from what *is* actually used in the provision of BIA globally. We argue that in order to begin any evaluation of BIA generally, geoprofiling specifically, or any other psychological contribution to criminal investigation, it is important to describe the range and diversity of what the advice encompasses and is based upon. In the specific case of geoprofilers, as we have indicated, these individuals appear to have a multidisciplinary, multivariate set of contributions beyond, for example, the simple idea of putting an 'x' on a map. BIAs develop this respective expertise across a vast range of areas based on both their individual tacit knowledge, as well as scientific, evidence-based knowledge that is required for the profession. In order to fully understand how BIAs put their tacit knowledge to use in aiding the investigation process, one must seek to tap into their knowledge and make it explicit. This task is yet to be comprehensively accomplished though important steps have begun.*

---

* See Chapter 5 for details of this seminal work.

The NPIA's 'BIA Roadmap' seeks to make explicit the type of knowledge and core competencies which are required for BIAs to fulfil their role successfully, and provides a framework to assess those competencies. It therefore provides a first attempt at an evidence-based framework that provides a clear, transparent, and documented system of achievement for all BIAs (Rainbow, 2008). However, beyond this 'Roadmap', there is as yet a scarcity of research attempts to tap in to the respective expertise or tacit knowledge of BIAs.

Different approaches and methodologies may be adopted to achieve this aim. For example, in terms of cognitive processing, it is known that experts, compared to novices, are able to integrate and process complex information into meaningful chunks, (Chase & Simon, 1973), ignore more information than do novices (Gigerenezer, 2000) and can more accurately and expeditiously notice missing information or inconsistencies (Militello, Hutton, Pliske, Knight, & Klein, 1997). This has also been classified as automaticity – the ability to perform a task so easily it no longer requires effortful attention, thereby greatly reducing cognitive load and increasing speed and accuracy of processing. Thus, further research would be required to unpack the component parts that constitute experts' 'rules of thumb' used in all of their daily operations.

We have found applied cognitive task analysis (ACTA, developed by Klein Associates, Inc; Militello *et al.*, 1997; Schraagen, Chipman, & Shalin, 2000) helpful in this regard. ACTA specifically focuses on the cognitive elements that are central to decision making, judgments, and goal generation (Militello & Hutton, 1998). The technique consists of three distinct parts: the *task diagram*, in which the expert is asked to break their contribution into six consecutive subtasks (and those into further sub-subtasks, respectively) the *Knowledge Audit*, in which many skills associated with expertise are probed, including the ability to detect patterns, anomalies, and opportunities, as well as identify expert strategies and potential novice errors; and the *Simulation Interview*, in which the expert is guided through a specific scenario they might encounter during their work whilst the interviewer probes the cognitive processes the expert is going through as s/he engages with the task (see Militello *et al.*, 1997 for further details).

By way of illustration, Knabe (2008) recently conducted and analysed the output of ACTA conducted with six geoprofilers and found that even experienced detectives, although relying on some basic heuristics, did not appear to have the same domain specific knowledge as geoprofilers.* Knabe established that much of a geoprofiler's work entails performing temporal and spatial analyses to provide an overview of when and where offences took place. This illustrative study went on to make explicit the elements of expertise in one particular specialism within contemporary BIA (see Knabe, 2008 for more details) and provides the first in, hopefully a line of, thick descriptive studies of the cognitive processes and the identification of domain specific knowledge of BIAs with a view to rendering their contribution more explicit.

---

* See Chapter 6 for details of this work.

Concluding comments

The aim of this article has been to draw a line under the early beginnings of an emerging field of psychology, criminological, and investigative exploration commonly referred to as offender profiling. It has been argued that the definition of offender profiling relates to a narrow view of a field which now encompasses a broad range of scientifically based yet pragmatic activities related to assisting police investigations. The current – still developing field – widens the scope from the specific (i.e. offender profiling: predicting offender characteristics from crime scene information) to the broad, namely BIA (e.g. provision of investigative recommendations), based on replicable, transparent, and valid knowledge and research. The impetus on the emerging field of BIA is to contribute to police investigative methods parsimoniously, pragmatically, and above all with scientific scrutiny and validation.

Note

1 *Geographical profiling is a substantial area of study and application in BIA, but it is beyond the scope of the current paper and will not be included as a major topic of discussion. A geoprofiling study is used below for illustrative purposes to address this gap, but see Rossmo (2000) for a review of geoprofiling techniques and related issues.*

References

ACPO (2006). *Murder investigation manual.* Wyboston: National Centre for Policing Excellence.

Aitken, C., Connolly, T., Gammerman, A., Zhang, G., & Oldfield, D. (1995). *Predicting an offender's characteristics: An evaluation of statistical modelling.* London: Home Office, (Special Interest series – Paper 4).

Alison, L. (Ed.), (2005). *The forensic psychologist's casebook: Psychological profiling and criminal investigation.* Devon: Willan.

Alison, L., McLean, C., & Almond, L. (2007). Profiling suspects. In T. Newburn, T. Williamson, & A. Wright (Eds.), *Handbook of criminal investigation* (pp. 493–516). Devon: Willan.

Alison, L., West, A., & Goodwill, A. (2004). The academic and the practitioner: Pragmatists' views of offender profiling. *Psychology, Public Policy and Law, 10,* 71–101.

Alison, L., Bennell, C., Mokros, A., & Ormerod, D. (2002). The personality paradox in offender profiling: A theoretical review of the processes involved in deriving background characteristics from crime scene actions. *Psychology,* Public Policy and Law, *8,* 115–135.

Alison, L., Smith, M. D., Eastman, O., & Rainbow, L. (2003). Toulmin's philosophy of argument and its relevance to offender profiling. *Psychology, Crime and Law, 9*(2), 173–183.

Almond, L. & Canter, D. V. (2007). Youths who sexually harm: Multivariate model of behaviour. *Journal of Sexual Aggression, 13,* 217–233.

Almond, L., Alison, L. J., & Porter, L. E. (2007). An evaluation and comparison of claims made in behavioural investigative advice reports compiled by the National Policing Improvement Agency in the United Kingdom. *Journal of Investigative Psychology and Offender Profiling, 4,* 71–83.

American Psychological Association [APA] (2002). *Ethical principles of psychologists and code of conduct*. Washington, DC: Author. Retrieved December 10, 2008, from www.apa.org/ethics/code2002.html#2_05

Baumgartner, K., Ferrari, S., & Palermo, G. (2008). Constructing Bayesian networks for criminal profiling from limited data. *Knowledge-Based Systems*, 21(7), 563–572.

Beauregard, E., Rossmo, D. K., & Proulx, J. (2007). A descriptive model of the hunting process of serial sex offenders: A rational choice perspective. *Journal of Family Violence*, 22, 449–463.

Beauregard, E., Proulx, J., Rossmo, D. K., Leclerc, B., & Allaire, J. F. (2007). Script analysis of the hunting process of serial sex offenders. *Criminal Justice and Behavior*, 34(8), 1069–1084.

Bennell, C., & Canter, D. (2002). Linking commercial burglaries by modus operandi: Tests using regression and ROC analysis. *Science and Justice*, 42, 153–164.

Bennell, C., & Jones, N. J. (2005). Between a ROC and a hard place: A method for linking serial burglaries using an offender's modus operandi. *Journal of Investigative Psychology and Offender Profiling*, 2, 23–41.

Bennell, C., Taylor, P., & Snook, B. (2007). Clinical versus actuarial geographic profiling strategies: A review of the research. *Police Practice and Research*, 8(4), 335–345.

Bennell, C., Corey, S., Taylor, A., & Ecker, J. (2008). What skills are required for effective offender profiling? An examination of the relationship between critical thinking ability and profile accuracy. *Psychology, Crime and Law*, 14(2), 143–157.

Bootsma, L., & Van dan Eshof, P. (2006). *The use of behavioural themes in identifying serial rapists*. Paper presented at the 16th annual conference of the European Association of Psychology and Law, Liverpool.

Burgess, A. W., Commons, M. L., Safarik, M. E., Looper, R. R., & Ross, S. N. (2007). Sex offenders of the elderly: Typology and predictors of severity of crime. *Aggression and Violent Behavior*, 12, 582–597.

Canter, D. V. (1995). *Criminal shadows*. London: Harper Collins.

Canter, D. V. (2000). Offender profiling and criminal differentiation. *Legal and Criminological Psychology*, 5, 23–46.

Canter, D. V., & Alison, L. J. (1999). *Profiling in policy and practice* (Vol. 2). Aldershot: Ashgate.

Canter, D. V., & Fritzon, K. (1998). Differentiating arsonists: A model of firesetting actions and characteristics. *Legal and Criminological Psychology*, 3, 73–100.

Canter, D. V., Alison, L. J., Alison, E., & Wentink, N. (2004). The organized/disorganized typology of serial murder: Myth or model? Psychology. *Public Policy and Law*, 10, 293–320.

Canter, D. V., Bennell, C., Alison, L. J., & Reddy, S. (2003). Differentiating sex offences: A behaviourally based thematic classification of stranger rapes. *Behavioral Sciences and the Law*, 21, 157–174.

Chase, W. G., & Simon, H. A. (1973). The mind's eye in chess. In W. G. Chase (Ed.), *Visual information processing* (pp. 215–281). New York: Academic Press.

Copson, G. (1995). *Coals to Newcastle? Part 1: A study of offender profiling*. London: Home Office Police Research Group, (Special Interest Series).

Copson, G., Babcock, R., Boon, J., & Britton, P. (1997). Articulating a systematic approach to clinical crime profiling. *Criminal Behavior and Mental Health*, 7, 13–17.

Criminal Justice Act (2003). (c. 44). London: The Stationery Office. Retrieved March 4, 2009, from www.opsi.gov.uk/acts/acts2003/pdf/ukpga_20030044_en.pdf

Criminal Procedure and Investigations Act (1996). London: The Stationery Office. Retrieved April 8, 2009, from www.opsi.gov.uk/acts/actsl996/ukpga_19960025_en_1

Cullen, R., Snook, B., Rideout, K., Eastwood, J., & House, J. (2006). Using local police data to inform investigative decision making: A study of commercial robbers' spatial decisions. *The Canadian Journal of Police and Security Services*, *4*(4), 193–204.

Davies, A., Wittebrood, K., & Jackson, J. L. (1997). Predicting the criminal antecedents of a stranger rapist from his offence behaviour. *Science and Justice, 37*, 161–170.

Doan, B., & Snook, B. (2008). A failure to find empirical support for the homology assumption in criminal profiling. *Journal of Police and Criminal Psychology*, *23*(2), 61–70.

Douglas, J., Ressler, R., Burgess, A., & Hartman, C. (1986). Criminal profiling from crime scene analysis. *Behavioral Sciences and the Law, 4*(4), 401–421.

Dowden, C., Bennell, C., & Bloomfield, S. (2007). Advances in offender profiling: A systematic review of the profiling literature published over the past three decades. *Journal of Police and Criminal Psychology, 22*, 44–56.

Egger, S. A. (1999). Psychological profiling: Past, present and future. *Journal of Contemporary Criminal Justice, 15*, 242–261.

Farrington, D. P., & Lambert, S. (1997). Predicting offender profiles from victim and witness descriptions. In J. L. Jackson & D. A. Bekerian (Eds.), *Offender profiling: Theory, research and practice* (pp. 133–158). Chichester: Wiley.

Federation-State Police Forces Project Group (2003). *The use of behavioural analysis by the German police-quality standards for behavioural, professional and personal quali-fications, and training courses for police behavioural analysts*. Wiesbaden: BKA. Retrieved June 13, 2005, from www.bka.de/lageberichte/weitere/behavioural.pdf

Fishman, D. B. (1999). *The case for pragmatic psychology*. New York: New York University Press.

Gigerenezer, G. (2000). *Adaptive thinking: Rationality in the real world*. New York: Oxford University Press.

Gogan, D. (2007). Investigative experience and profile accuracy: A replication study. In R. Kocsis (Ed.), *Criminal profiling: International theory, research, and practice* (pp. 383–392). Totowa, NJ: Humana Press.

Goodwill, A. M., & Alison, L. J. (2006). The development of a filter model for prioritizing suspects in burglary offences. *Psychology, Crime and Law, 12*, 395–416.

Goodwill, A. M., & Alison, L. J. (2007). When is profiling possible? Offence planning and aggression as moderators in predicting offender age from victim age in stranger rape. *Behavioral Sciences and the Law, 25*, 823–840.

Goodwill, A. M., Alison, L. J., & Beech, A. (2009). What works in offender profiling? A comparison of typological, thematic, and multivariate models. *Behavioral Sciences and the Law*. Retrieved June 28, 2009 from http://www3.interscience.wiley.com/journal/122369581/abstract

Greenall, P., & West, A. (2007). A study of stranger rapists from the English high security hospitals. *Journal of Sexual Aggression, 13*(2), 151–167.

Grubin, D., Kelly, P., & Brunsdon, C. (2000). *Linking serious sexual assaults through behaviour*. London: Home Office, Policing and Reducing Crime Unit, (Special Interest Series).

Häkkänen, H., Lindlöf, P., & Santtila, R. (2004). Crime scene actions and offender char-acteristics in a sample of Finnish stranger rapes. *Journal of Investigative Psychology and Offender Profiling, 1*, 17–32.

Häkkänen, H., Puolakka, P., & Santtila, P. (2004). Crime scene actions and offender characteristics in arsons. *Legal and Criminological Psychology, 9*, 197–214.

Harris, D., Smallbone, S., Dennison, S., & Knight, R. (2009). Specialization and versatility in sexual offenders referred for civil treatment. *Journal of Criminal Justice, 37*, 33–37.

Hazelwood, R. R., & Warren, J. I. (1999). The sexually violent offender: Impulsive or ritualistic. *Aggression and Violent Behavior: A Review Journal, 5*, 267–279.

Hazelwood, R. R., & Warren, J. I. (2003). Linkage analysis: Modus operandi (MO), ritual and signature in serial sexual crime. *Aggression and Violent Behavior, 8*, 587–598.

Herndon, J. (2007). The image of profiling: Media treatment and general impressions. In R. Kocsis (Ed.), *Criminal profiling: International theory, research, and practice*. Totowa, NJ: Humana Press.

Hicks, S., & Sales, B. (2006). *Criminal profiling: Developing an effective science and practice*. Washington, DC: American Psychological Association.

Horn, A. (2006). Die Zusammenarbeit zwischen Fallanalyse und forensischer Psychiatrie [The cooperation between case analysis and forensic psychiatry]. In C. Musolff & J. Hoffmann (Eds.), *Täterprofile bei Gewaltverbrechen: Mythos, Theorie, Praxis und forensische Anwendung des Profilings* (2nd ed., pp. 351–367). Berlin: Springer.

Kahneman, D., Slovic, P., & Tversky, A. (1982). *Judgment under uncertainty: Heuristics and biases*. New York: Cambridge University Press.

Kent Police Policy Documents (2008). *N48 Behavioural Investigation Adviser (offending profiling)*. Retrieved March 1, 2009, from www.kent.police.uk/About%20Kent%20Police/policies/n/n048.html

Knabe, S. (2008). *Geographic profiling under the microscope: A critical examination of the utility of geographic profiling and expert geographic profilers*. Unpublished master's thesis, The University of Liverpool, Liverpool.

Kocsis, R. N. (2006). Validities and abilities in criminal profiling: The dilemma for David Canter's investigative psychology. *International Journal of Offender Therapy and Comparative Criminology, 50*, 458–477.

Marshall, B. C., & Alison, L. J. (2007). Stereotyping, congruence and presentation order: Interpretative biases in utilizing offender profiles. *Psychology, Crime and Law, 13*, 285–303.

Meyer, C. B. (2007). Criminal profiling as expert evidence? An international case law perspective. In R. Kocsis (Ed.), *Criminal profiling: International theory, research, and practice* (pp. 207–247). Totowa, NJ: Humana Press.

Militello, L. G., & Hutton, R. J. B. (1998). Applied cognitive task analysis (ACTA): A practitioners' toolkit for understanding cognitive task demands. *Ergonomics, 41*, 1618–1641.

Militello, L. G., Hutton, R. J. B., Pliske, R. M., Knight, B. J., & Klein, G. (1997). *Applied cognitive task analysis (ACTA) methodology (Rep. No. NPRDCTN-98-4)*. San Diego, CA: Navy Personnel Research and Development Center.

Milne, R., Clare, I. C. H., & Bull, R. (1999). Using the cognitive interview with adults with mild learning disabilities. *Psychology, Crime and Law, 5*(1), 81–99.

Mokros, A. (2007). *Die Struktur der Zusammenhänge von Tatbegehungsmerkmalen und Persönlichkeitseigenschaften bei Sexualstraftätern [The structure of relations between crime scene actions and personality characteristics in sex offenders]*. Frankfurt: Verlag für Polizeiwissenschaft.

Mokros, A., & Alison, L. J. (2002). Is offender profiling possible? Testing the predicted homology of crime scene actions and background characteristics in a sample of rapists. *Legal and Criminological Psychology, 7*, 25–44.

Muller, D. A. (2000). Criminal profiling: Real science or just wishful thinking? *Homicide Studies*, *4*(3), 234–264.

Myers, W. C., Husted, M. D., Safarik, M. E., & O'Toole, M. E. (2006). The motivation behind serial sexual homicide: Is it sex, power and control, or anger? *Journal of Forensic Sciences*, *51*, 900–907.

Ormerod, D., & Sturman, J. (2005). Working with the courts: Advice for expert witnesses. In L. Alison (Ed.), *The forensic psychologist's casebook: Psychological profiling and criminal investigation* (pp. 170–191). Devon: Willan.

Osterheider, M., & Mokros, A. (2006). Tatortanalyse in der forensischen Psychiatrie: Die Bedeutung der Rekonstruktion des Tatgeschehens für Diagnostik, Therapieplanung und Prognose [Crime scene analysis in forensic psychiatry: The relevance of reconstructing offence behaviour for diagnostics, therapy and prognosis]. In C. Musolff & J. Hoffmann (Eds), *Täterprofle bei Gewaltverbrechen: Mythos, Theorie, Praxis und forensische Anwendung des Profilings* (2nd ed., pp. 325–338). Berlin: Springer.

Pinizzotto, A. J., & Finkel, N. J. (1990). Criminal personality profiling: An outcome and process study. *Law and Human Behavior*, *14*(5), 215–233.

Polaschek, D., Hudson, S., Ward, T., & Siegert, R. (2001). Rapists' offence processes. A preliminary descriptive model. *Journal of Interpersonal Violence*, *16*(6), 523–544.

Porter, S., & ten Brinke, L. (2009). Dangerous decisions: A theoretical framework for understanding how judges assess credibility in the courtromm. *Legal and Criminological Psychology*, *14*(1), 119–134.

Rainbow, L. (2008). Taming the beast: The UK approach to the management of behavioral investigative advice. *Journal of Police and Criminal Psychology*, *23*(2), 90–97.

Rossmo, D. K. (2000). *Geographic profiling*. Boca Raton, FL: CRC Press.

Safarik, M. E., & Jarvis, J. P. (2005). Examining attributes of homicides: Towards quantifying qualitative values of injury severity. *Journal of Homicide Studies*, *9*, 183–203.

Safarik, M. E., Jarvis, J. P., & Nussbaum, K. E. (2000). Elder female serial sexual homicide: A limited empirical test of criminal investigative analysis. *Homicide Studies*, *4*, 294–307.

Safarik, M. E., Jarvis, J. P., & Nussbaum, K. E. (2002). Sexual homicide of elderly females: Linking offender characteristics to victim and crime scene attributes. *Journal of Interpersonal Violence*, *17*, 500–525.

Salfati, C. G. (2003). Offender interaction with victims in homicide: Multidimensional analysis of frequencies in crime scene behaviors. *Journal of Interpersonal Violence*, *18*, 490–512.

Salfati, C. G., & Dupont, F. (2006). Canadian homicide, an investigation of crime-scene actions. *Homicide Studies*, *10*(2), 118–139.

Salo, B. (2008). *Crime linking in serial homicide based on single offender behaviors: A Bayesian approach*. Unpublished master's thesis, Åbo Akademi University, Turku, Finland.

Santtila, P., Fritzon, K., & Tamelander, A. L. (2004). Linking arson incidents on the basis of crime scene behavior. *Journal of Police and Criminal Psychology*, *19*, 1–16.

Santtila, P., Junkkila, J., & Sandnabba, N. (2005). Behavioural linking of stranger rapes. *Journal of Investigative Psychology and Offender Profiling*, *2*(2), 87–103.

Santtila, P., Korpela, S., & Häkkänen, H. (2004). Expertise and decision-making in the linking of car crime series. *Psychology, Crime and Law*, *10*(3), 97–112.

Santtila, P., Ritvanen, A., & Mokros, A. (2003). Predicting burglar characteristics from crime scene behaviour. *International Journal of Police Science and Management*, *6*(3), 136–154.

Santtila, P., Laukkanen, M., Zappalà, A., & Bosco, D. (2008). Distance travelled and offence characteristics in homicide, rape, and robbery against business. *Legal and Criminological Psychology*, *13*, 345–356.

Santtila, P., Pakkanen, T., Zappalà, A., Bosco, D., Valkama, M., & Mokros, A. (2008). Behavioural crime linking in serial homicide. *Psychology, Crime and Law*, *14*(3), 245–265.

Schraagen, J. M., Chipman, S. F, & Shalin, V. L. (Eds.), (2000). *Cognitive task analysis.* Mahwah, NJ: Erlbaum.

Snook, B., Haines, A., Taylor, P., & Bennell, C. (2007). Criminal profiling belief and use: A study of Canadian police officer opinion. *Canadian Journal of Police and Security Services*, *5*(3/4), 1–11.

Snook, B., Wright, M., House, J., & Alison, L. (2006). Searching for a needle in a needle stack: Combining criminal careers and journey-to-crime research for criminal suspect prioritization. *Police Practice and Research*, *7*, 217–230.

Snook, B., Cullen, R. M., Bennell, C, Taylor, P. J., & Gendreau, R. (2008). The criminal profiling illusion: What's behind the smoke and mirrors? *Criminal Justice and Behavior*, *35*, 1257–1276.

Snook, B., Eastwood, J., Gendreau, P., Goggin, C, & Cullen, R. M. (2007). Taking stock of criminal profiling: A narrative review and meta-analysis. *Criminal Justice and Behavior*, *34*, 437–453.

Sternberg, R. J., & Horvath, J. A. (1999). *Tacit knowledge in professional practice.* Mahwah, NJ: Erlbaum.

Taylor, P. J., Jacques, K., Giebels, E., Levine, M., Best, R., Winter, J., *et al.* (2008). Analysing forensic processes: Taking time into account. *Forensic Update*, *8*, 43–55.

Torres, A., Boccaccini, M., & Miller, H. (2006). Perceptions of the validity and utility of criminal profiling among forensic psychologists and psychiatrists. *Professional Psychology: Research and Practice*, *37*(1), 51–58.

Toulmin, S. (1958). *The uses of argument.* Cambridge: Cambridge University Press.

Turvey, B. (Ed.), (2008). *Criminal profiling: An introduction to behavioural evidence analysis* (3rd ed.). San Diego, CA: Academic Press.

Ullman, S. (2007). A 10-year update of 'review and critique of empirical studies of rape avoidance'. *Criminal Justice and Behavior*, *34*(3), 411–429.

Walsh, D. W., & Milne, R. (2008). Keeping the PEACE? A study of investigative interviewing practices in the public sector. *Legal and Criminological Psychology*, *13*, 39–57.

Ward, T., Hudson, S., & Keenan, T. (1998). A self-regulation model of the sexual offense process. *Sexual Abuse: A Journal of Research and Treatment*, *10*(2), 141–157.

West, A. (2000). Clinical assessment of homicide offenders – the significance of crime scene in offense and offender analysis. *Homicide Studies*, *4*(3), 219–233.

Wilson, P., Lincoln, R., & Kocsis, R. (1997). Validity, utility and ethics of profiling for serial violent and sexual offenders. *Psychiatry, Psychology and Law*, *4*(1), 1–12.

Woodhams, J., & Toye, K. (2007). An empirical test of the assumptions of case linkage and offender profiling with serial commercial robberies. *Psychology, Public Policy, and Law*, *13*(1), 59–85.

Woodhams, J., Bull, R., & Hollin, C. (2007). Case linkage-identifying crimes committed by the same offender. In R. Kocsis (Ed.), *Critical profiling: International theory, research, and practice* (pp. 117–133). Totowa, NJ: Humana Press Inc.

Woodhams, J., Grant, T., & Price, A. (2007). From marine ecology to crime analysis: Improving the detection of serial sexual offences using a taxonomic similarity measure. *Journal of Investigative Psychology and Offender Profiling, 4*, 17–27.

Woodhams, J., Hollin, C., & Bull, R. (2008). Incorporating context in linking crimes: An exploratory study of situational similarity and if-then contingencies. *Journal of Investigative Psychology and Offender Profiling, 5*, 1–2.

5 The cognitive expertise of Behavioural Investigative Advisers in the UK and Germany

Susanne Knabe-Nicol, Laurence Alison and Lee Rainbow

Introduction

As previously discussed in this volume, the somewhat glamorous mystery that surrounds profiling has given rise to an image of the utilization of psychology in police investigations as being devoid of scientific foundation. The media portray profilers as having special intuitive skills and illuminating insights that outstrip conventional wisdom and, as if in a flash of inspiration, the profiler can see patterns and cues where other law enforcement officers cannot. However, next to no effort has as yet been invested in revealing to the viewer what these insights are based on or how they actually operate. Perhaps the 'reveal' of the 'trick' would make for poor viewing or, alternatively, excessively intricate scripting.

This chapter addresses the question of expertise within the domain of psychologists assisting police investigations and seeks to ascertain whether Behavioural Investigative Advisers (BIAs in the UK and OFAs [Operative Fall Analytiker] in Germany) possess specific learnt skills, experiential learning and/or expertise built up over successive cases. We outline and define expertise, methods to establish its existence and present two exploratory studies conducted with UK-based BIAs as well as their counterparts in Germany.

We illustrate how analysis of the data obtained through Applied Cognitive Task Analysis (ACTA, Militello *et al.*, 1997) from nine professional behavioural investigative police advisers in Germany and the UK, identified a variety of analytical processes, specialized skills in linking offenders' behaviour to their psychology, specific knowledge and decision-making, all being indicative of expertise. Participants demonstrated how they utilize specific cognitive strategies to selectively focus on salient pieces of information that novices may miss, identify anomalies in cases, group large amounts of behavioural information into meaningful themes or units, whilst constantly having a meta-cognitive awareness of common mistakes and distractions. Furthermore, participants were able to identify the aetiology of various behaviours, which is not visible or apparent to non-experts in this field. These features, identified across the small sample, are consistent with psychological attributes that commonly occur through expert knowledge (Chase & Simon, 1973; Militello *et al.*, 1997; Savelsbergh *et al.* 2005;

Mislevy, 2010). These results suggest the presence of expertise in carrying out behavioural analyses for major crime investigation in the participants studied.

Background

Offender profiling has long been the target of bad press and criticism, both in the media as well as the academic field. Whilst some of the criticism is well deserved (for instance in the Rachel Nickell enquiry; the interested reader is directed towards Alison and Eyre (2009) for a detailed discussion regarding this case), the generalization and sheer misconception of the profession has tainted the reputation of this discipline regardless of whether it is carried out by a self-proclaimed profiler working on intuition and a 'hunch', or a reputable scientist operating to a strict ethical code and drawing on facts and objective crime statistics to make their inferences. A study comprising meta-analyses of how a wide variety of profilers' statements were worded found that all too often, commonsense arguments were used rather than scientific data and rationales (Snook *et al.*, 2007). Yet one needs to draw a clear line between self-proclaimed non-accredited/approved profilers on the one hand, and BIAs/OFAs on the other hand who are fully trained, accredited/approved and audited on a regular basis, using psychology and research on criminal behaviour as their scientific foundation to work on the most complex major investigations on a daily basis. The studies presented in this chapter focus on establishing whether there is something that sets BIAs, both in the UK as well as in Germany, apart from others, whether they have developed an expertise in analysing behaviour in order to support criminal investigations.

Various studies have attempted to measure the accuracy of the descriptions and predictions that profilers as well as the BIAs/OFAs have been providing in relation to perpetrators of serious offences. The results of such studies have been largely negative and often failed to show that profilers were any more accurate than lay people (e.g. Kocsis, 2004; Kocsis *et al.* 2002). Whilst on the surface of it, this may also seem to discredit the profession of providing behavioural investigative advice, one must consider what exactly these studies were actually measuring.

It is quite straightforward to extract key statements from a BIA's/OFA's comprehensive report such as the profiled offender's age range, his geography and previous convictions, for instance, which constitute the main content of the profile (i.e. the most likely parameters or characteristics and demographic attributes of the unknown offender). These extracted characteristics are then compared to the offender convicted for the offence in question, and it is measured how many of the BIA's/OFA's descriptions or predictions were correct, which, at first glance, seems to be a reasonable procedure. However, there is a flaw within such a study design, namely that a BIA's/OFA's profile parameters are based on statistical research and only represent the *most likely* characteristics of the offender, as BIAs/OFAs cannot deal with absolutes. For instance, if in the past, say 90 per cent of offences with attributes x and y were committed by male offenders of ethnicity z who are of an average age of 27, then the BIA/OFA will use that research as a scientific basis for reporting back to the investigation that the offender for this offence, which has those same certain attributes of x and y, is most likely to be of ethnicity z and to be aged between, say, 22 and 33 years. The report they submit back to the investigation will detail the statistical basis of those statements, thereby leaving an audit trail for their decision making. Unless there were behaviours apparent from the crime that would hint at lower or higher age parameters, the BIA/OFA would have no reason not to use the statistics as a basis for making their inference about the offender's most likely age range. Therefore, if it later turned out that the BIA's/OFA's prediction of the offender's age was indeed incorrect, this would simply mean that whilst most perpetrators of that offence *are* of that age, *this particular* offender was not. This fact does not reflect upon the competence of the BIA/OFA however, since they utilized a scientifically valid and accurate procedure.

A more suitable measure of the BIAs'/OFAs' utility, rather than checking if the most likely statistical parameters apply to a specific case, would be to determine how much investigative value they add to the operation, in terms of helping police prioritize lines of enquiry and suspects, as well as identifying new lines of enquiry through enhanced understanding of the offence, the motive and the offender. For instance, they might suggest that the enquiry focus on the area surrounding the encounter site, if it appears the offender has a link to that place in some way, for example if he was already at the location and a random potential victim fitting his required criteria walked past. On the other hand, if the offender appears to have been targeting a specific victim, then the area in which the offence took place may have been part of *her* routine activity rather than his, and he simply followed her there, which would mean he may have no link to the location, however he does have a link to the victim. In this case a BIA/OFA would advise the investigation to dig deeper into the victim's background, routine activity and acquaintances and anyone else she would come into contact with. Studies should therefore aim to assess the utility of the BIA's/OFA's entire input to the investigation rather than just the profile, and they should also evaluate their effect on the investigating team beyond the report. Quite often, OFAs/BIAs work closely with the team and provide ongoing support and advice beyond their report. It should be assessed if the presence of the BIA/OFA has a beneficial effect on the morale of the team, their welfare and confidence, as well as their level of understanding of the offence, motives and actions involved. The authors are not aware of any studies that have taken these core aspects of a BIA's/OFA's work as criteria against which their utility is measured.

As noted in previous chapters, the BIAs in the UK are approved by the Association of Chief Police Officers (ACPO) and employed by the National Policing Improvement Agency (NPIA). In Germany, their counterparts are Operative Fall Analytiker (OFAs, which translates to 'operational case analyst[s]') who perform the same role as the BIAs. The UK BIAs and the German OFAs have emerged through an ongoing process of professionalization which started in the 1990s (see Chapter 1 for an overview from the UK perspective). They direct specific attention at ensuring that statements in their reports are backed up by reference to the facts of the case, academic research and crime statistics, thereby creating a scientific audit trail for their inferences and hypotheses. The BIAs'/ OFAs' work is based on models and statistics acquired through the extensive analysis of previous crimes and offenders (e.g. Salfati, 2000; Canter, 2004; Keppel & Weis, 1993; Farrington & Lambert, 1997). Furthermore, as noted in preceding chapters, their remit of work is far wider reaching than the creation of a 'pen portrait' profile, i.e. specifying the most common demographic parameters of offenders who committed a similar crime previously. The authors would therefore advise against the continued use of the term 'profiler', as that would seem to minimize the various types of support they have actually been providing to police investigations for up to two decades to one single activity.

Expertise

It has long been the holy grail of expertise research to identify exactly what expertise is, how experts differ from non-experts (i.e. 'normal' people) and if the expertise of one person can be shifted or taught to another. Expertise has been described as being inherent in people who have a specific knowledge base that is not accessible and cannot be adjudicated by non-experts, and therefore constitutes a social relation where experts have a certain authority in their particular field over non-experts due to their possession of that particular knowledge (Prince, 2010). A more cognitive definition focuses on the common recurring difficulties that people new to a domain usually encounter (Salthouse, 1991). Therefore, experts are those who successfully handle these difficulties, who know which information is relevant, how to integrate that information, who know what to expect, what to do and when to do it (Mislevy, 2010). It follows that an expert is someone who, through learning, cumulative experiences and building up of effective patterns and associations, knows what to see in situations and how to think and talk about them (Mislevy, 2010). Those patterns are embedded in long-term memory and are activated when the expert encounters a similar situation; experts are not so different from novices in their general mental ability per se (de Groot, 1946), but are superior in terms of what they know, how that knowledge is organized and how it is used (Ericsson *et al.*, 2006).

Expertise has been researched in many different areas, and much of that research has focused on experts' exceptional cognitive abilities, such as the construction of mental representations, memory encoding and perception, for instance. Such work has examined experts in a variety of different domains including sports, chess, medical diagnoses, music and sciences (Ericsson, 2005; Ericsson and Kintsch, 1995; Kalakoski, 2007; Norman, 2005). Many issues have been discussed in the academic literature, including whether experts' performance is innate, whether expertise in one field facilitates superior performance in another field, and how it is that experts perform so much better than others.

It has been proposed that expertise contains two distinct categories (Shanteau, 1985): perceptual expertise, which would include making reliable judgements based on information presented (e.g. in providing medical diagnosis), and conceptual expertise, which is dependent upon a superior ability to grasp concepts, including playing chess, for instance. Expertise has also been found to be domain-specific (Gilis *et al.*, 2008), and is dependent upon the expert's acquiring a vast amount of domain-specific knowledge (Militello *et al.*, 1997). It is thought that one of the advantages an expert has as compared to a novice is the ability to perceive large amounts of information as meaningful chunks rather than numerous unrelated pieces of information (Chase and Simon, 1973); further it has been suggested that this pattern-recognition ability enables experts to perceive abnormalities in what is presented, or to notice when something is missing that should be there (Militello *et al.*, 1997). Automaticity – the ability to perform a task so easily it no longer requires much deliberate attention and a need to analyse – is also thought to be present in experts and greatly reduces cognitive load and increases speed and accuracy of the expert's performance. Such swiftness and precision is also aided by the presence of a large empirical knowledge base of similar previous tasks, situations or problems, which the expert can draw upon from memory (Militello *et al.*, 1997). This skill is further supported by the fact that experts seem to have superior memory in their domain of expertise, both in the short term and the long term, due to their skill of being able to organize information into mean-ingful chunks or themes (Chase and Ericsson, 1982).

It seems that particular core proficiencies that are the make-up of one's exper-tise are dependent on the specific role or type of work someone has (Allard *et al.* 1993). For example, such a core skill that distinguishes experts from novices can be identified in the task of predicting accurately the height and direction of a penalty kick, which is an essential skill for a football goalkeeper: Expert goal keepers spend more time than beginners fixating on the non-kicking leg of the person about to kick the ball, and take more time before initiating a response overall. Novices on the other hand, tend to react more quickly and generally fail to recognize the non-kicking leg as an indicator of where the ball is going to go (Savelsbergh *et al.* 2005). It seems then, that one crucial aspect to provid-ing expert predictions is the ability to identify the most accurate and reliable indicator hinting at the outcome, which in this case was the non-kicking leg. Experts use such predictive information, or 'advance cues', far more efficiently than do novices, and hence they are better able to guide their responses accord-ingly (Abernethy, 1987; Williams and Burwitz 1993; Abernethy *et al.*, 2001). Experts do not tend to take in more information *per se*; rather they take in infor-mation more selectively (Savelsbergh *et al.*, 2005), paying attention mainly to those cues that are of value to making an accurate prediction or inference in their field.

Expertise in providing behavioural investigative advice

Within the profession of providing behavioural investigative advice, expertise may be necessary at all stages of the process. Behavioural expertise would facili-tate the mental comparison of offenders' behaviours to a vast knowledge base of previous violent crimes to detect anomalies and examine those as to their meaning (Militello *et al.*, 1997). The analysis of case materials, victimology and offender behaviours may provide a wealth of information, and the BIA must be able to determine those bits that are the most valuable when trying to understand the offender's decision making and connection to the crime; in other words, they must identify the advance cues hidden within large amounts of information (Abernethy, 1987; Williams and Burwitz 1993; Abernethy *et al.*, 2001) and select which bits are the most useful to make inferences from (Savelsbergh *et al.* 2005). It is precisely this point that might be of particular relevance to the work of a BIA/OFA. Within an ongoing investigation, many different individuals such as investigators, BIAs/OFAs, analysts and geographical profilers might be provided with identical sets of information. However, each individual involved in the investigation may use the available information differently, depending on their particular remit, skills and task. A BIA/OFA will deal with information and data that might hint at the offender's decision-making processes and his knowledge of the victim or the crime scene. They will examine how the perpetrator came to choose that particular victim, the crime location(s), how he travelled, why he was at a particular place at a particular time, what his initial motive was, how the offence and events then unfolded, how he knew the location where he attacked the victim, how he knew the victim was going to be there and so forth. It is this aspect of the OFAs'/BIAs' work, their expertise in providing investigative advice based on such crime information, that is going to be examined in the studies presented.

Reference to the following quote serves to illustrate the current lack of understanding regarding BIA/OFA expertise:

> We contend that, in any field, an "expert" should decisively outperform non-experts (i.e., lay persons). The practical problem with designating profilers or experienced individuals as experts lies in the fact that their services are requested based on their presumed expertise, which increases the likelihood of their having considerable impact on the direction of a given investigation.
>
> (Snook *et al.*, 2007)

However, whilst dismissive of any potential expertise within BIAs, this research did not actually attempt to verify such claims. The studies presented in this chapter are aimed at doing exactly that; identifying whether expertise exists within the domain of providing behavioural investigative advice to police investigations by today's professional practitioners. A cognitive task analysis was performed on the five Behavioural Investigative Advisers in the UK working exclusively for the NPIA (Study 1), and the four senior OFAs of the Bavarian police in Germany (Study 2).

The results of these qualitative studies suggest that the profession entails precise thought processes, strands of psychological reasoning as well as logical inferences and conclusions based on scientific data on offending behaviour and psychology. These components are further embedded within a context of professional accountability, collaboration with senior officers and external experts, being sensitive to each investigation's circumstances, personalities and resources, whilst every inference is based on academic research, statistics and solid knowledge of criminal and investigative psychology as well as major crime throughout the UK and Germany. Furthermore, various features of expertise were identified in both groups. These findings may somewhat strip the profession of its glamour and mystery, yet they also seem to support its validity as a supportive and scientific tool in major crime investigations and suggest that these professionals have indeed developed an expertise in their discipline. Most previous studies in this field have looked at the output and the product provided by BIAs, OFAs or 'profilers', rather than the process that eventually produces that output. The studies presented in this chapter do not constitute an evaluation of providing behavioural investigative advice in terms of accuracy or investigative benefit. Those aspects are left to others to explore. The purpose of the current research is to identify the expertise and cognitive processes within this discipline. Unlike previous research that has examined the output of BIAs/OFAs, i.e. their inferences and reports, the current studies scrutinize how information is perceived and cognitively processed in order to generate their output, aiming to ascertain the presence or absence of an inherent expertise within the profession. To explore the cognitive processes involved in providing behavioural investigative advice, a qualitative study was carried out using Applied Cognitive Task Analysis (Militello *et al.*, 1997). The methodology involves extensive one-to-one interviews aimed at extracting the cognitive steps, mental processes, challenges and their remedies, and errors commonly made by novices, in order to make a particular profession more explicit. The procedure is explained in detail in the Appendix.

Study 1: Cognitive processes in the Behavioural Investigative Adviser (BIA) in the UK

As made explicit in Chapter 1, within the UK the NPIA employs a cadre of full-time BIAs to provide behavioural investigative advice to UK policing. Any police investigation team can contact the NPIA to request operational support. If deemed appropriate, a BIA is assigned to the case and a briefing is arranged, which is also attended by the NPIA Regional Adviser and additional relevant NPIA specialists (see Chapter 2 for a more detailed description of the multidisciplinary approach adopted within the NPIA). The BIA and the others are then briefed on the case, visit the crime scene(s), ask questions, receive the information available on the case and specify any other information they will require. They set the terms of reference with the Senior Investigating Officer (SIO) and take the information away as they work predominantly from home, to commence examining the case papers. They usually agree to provide their report to the SIO within two weeks, during which time they may contact the investigation again for further clarifications or to request more information to be gathered. The investigation should contact the BIA with any new information that might affect their analysis, and it is understood that once the BIA has submitted their report, they need to be informed of new developments and a follow-on report may be appropriate.

The results of the analysis of the cognitive processes involved in providing behavioural investigative advice are displayed in Table 5.1. This is a cognitive

Table 5.1 Cognitive demands table for providing behavioural investigative advice

	Assess the overall case
	Difficult cognitive element –Determine type, extent and utility of our involvement
	Why difficult?
	BIA involvement is not always possible or necessary, as not every case is amenable to behavioural analysis. There may be insufficient behavioural information present within the case, and it may reflect a crime type for which there are little or no relevant pieces of research or crime databases available to draw from. Alternatively, the current knowledge on the case is ambiguous or insufficient or there may already be a strong suspect.
	Common errors
	To acquiesce to an unsuitable request and produce a report that will be outside the BIA's area of competence, unsupported by valid rationale or not actionable. This might embarrass investigative colleagues through negative publicity and tarnish the reputation of behavioural investigative advice through inappropriate handling of the request.
Assess the overall case	**Strategies**
	To maintain a sensitive and constructive attitude at all times, clearly articulating the reasons as to why the BIA cannot complete the requested work. Proposing an alternative course of action for this particular case as an idea to be considered by the SIO, backing it up with appropriate arguments. Suggesting alternative sources of potential expertise.
	Difficult cognitive element –Ascertain what the SIO wants and what they need – then give them the latter.
	Why difficult?
	The negotiation of a different product or service to that initially requested may be viewed as challenging the SIO's authority and has the potential to create tensions between the BIA and the investigating team. The recognition of the most effective service provision is reliant on significant experiential knowledge of the products/services available and the investigative environment in which they are required.
	Common errors
	A lack of experience, confidence or appropriate negotiation skills may result in compliance with the initial request, through a desire to fulfil professional expectations and avoid disappointment or potential conflict. Similarly, a lack of experience of a novice BIA may prevent an objective assessment of the needs of the investigation and the most appropriate behavioural science support.

Strategies
Positively explain and confirm the utility of what they asked for in cases in which it might indeed be of use – then illustrate why this particular case might necessitate a different course of action. Back your arguments up with your previous experience, research and facts. Maintain a stance of professional, objective and scientific independence and manage expectations honestly. Confirm understanding of the negotiated terms of reference to ensure full understanding and agreement.

	Examine SIO's reasoning process and personality style
	Difficult cognitive element – Some SIOs can have a rather dominant and overbearing personality
	Why difficult?
	a) Dominant personalities are likely to hinder your initiative, and can lead you to passively follow instructions and prevent you from remaining objective to, and critical of, their ideas and expectations.
	b) Briefings can be predominated by the SIO's or the investigating team's own inferences, rather than pure fact. It can be difficult to separate the two and to remain continually conscious of such potential discrepancies in the information presented. This is particularly difficult as the SIO may be mistaken themselves regarding the provenance of the information presented.
	Common errors
	a) To become subservient to an SIO's potentially dominant personality and refrain from appropriate questioning of validity. To denigrate your own expertise and fail to challenge inappropriate investigative strategy, and eventually providing an ineffective service through compliance with inappropriate instruction. Such errors may result in the SIO questioning your expertise and credibility. If you assume a submissive status in relation to the SIO, they may not view you as credible enough to accept your advice.
	b) To accept all information as fact without questioning the provenance of each and every facet of that information.
	Strategies
	a) Earn the SIO's respect in a non-confrontational manner based on your competence and skill. It is necessary to gain the SIO's acceptance as an authority in *your field*, which will serve to support the SIO's authority in their investigation. Help them understand that your status and competence will actually help the SIO to conduct their investigation rather than threaten it. Be willing to defend your position and views, with supporting evidence to demonstrate their validity.
	b) Ask for all relevant information to be provided in its original source format rather than someone's interpretation. Be willing to challenge the presented information in a constructive manner if necessary.

The left vertical label reads: Examine SIO's reasoning process and personality style

Difficult cognitive element –You come in as the outsider and you might be greeted with scepticism
Why difficult?
It can be very demotivating and frustrating having to justify your presence, and this may lead to you not getting to be more effectively engaged in the investigation. Similarly, it may prove difficult to provide an optimal service when you perceive that the advice is unwanted or unlikely to be acted upon.
Common errors
When greeted with a level of antagonism it is easy to be dragged into a defensive and hostile communication style. You may decide to disengage from the case and be disinclined to provide an optimal service and be tempted to just 'go through the motions'.
Strategies
Prove your competence and potential value, and earn their acceptance, by showing your understanding of their case and illustrating parallels to relevant previous investigations you worked on. Emphasize that your role is purely a supportive one, bringing a different perspective to that routinely available within most incident rooms. Reiterate that any advice offered is just that – advice – and that the implementation of any recommendations provided lies entirely at the SIO's discretion. Explain that your role is focused on decision support and explain the potential benefits from a 'policy book' perspective (i.e. providing them with the rationale to support their investigative audit trail).
Difficult cognitive element –Ascertaining the SIO's level of experience, competence and openness to expert input
Why difficult?
This can be a sensitive task and attempts to tease out the required understanding of SIO's knowledge of specific investigative, forensic or BIA techniques and procedures must be balanced against creating perceptions of being patronizing or questioning their competency. Such exploration cannot be direct, but must be effectively woven within the overall contact with the SIO.
Common errors
It might seem too sensitive a task to check what they have and what they haven't done and it might seem easier not to ask those vital questions. Alternatively, if an SIO does not seem to be very supportive and appreciative of our involvement, you might be tempted not to be as astute and to keep constructive feedback to yourself. Being too direct in ascertaining the required SIO's knowledge of specific investigative, forensic or BIA techniques and procedures. Being overly directive and compromising your professional obligation to remind the SIO to remain objective and critical of any advice offered. Assuming the SIO has a greater understanding of specific aspects than they really have and hence tailoring subsequent advice inappropriately.

(Left margin, rotated:) Examine SIO's reasoning process and personality style

	Strategies
Examine SIO's reasoning process and personality style	An inexperienced SIO needs to be supported; however they should also be urged to remain objective and critical, to our input. Otherwise they might withhold information from us that counters what we suggested, simply because they have become biased. They do need to work independently at the same time as being open to our suggestions and objective towards incoming information. If the SIO appears competent, it might even be useful to disclose some early thoughts and ideas to them at the beginning of the investigation, as it would be safe to assume they apply those cautiously. On the other hand, a less experienced or more desperate SIO might be tempted to act on such early ideas too soon and with too much rigour, thereby discarding the openness they need. Ensure common understanding of all topics discussed, acknowledging the rarity or complexity of relevant aspects to minimize any potential embarrassment or perceived undermining of competence.

Difficult cognitive element –Some investigations have run out of steam and they don't know how to carry on

Why difficult?

You may feel you need to prove your status as an expert and justify your presence by coming up with early inferences and suggestions. It may be very difficult to remain firm, and refuse to make any assumptions too early, if the investigation appears to be counting on you to guide them in any further actions or offer any 'quick fix' solutions.

Common errors

Feeling obliged to provide instant ideas and making suggestions at the outset without having analysed all the available information. Committing 'competency drift' and overstepping acceptable professional/discipline-specific boundaries. Reinforcing the unrealistic expectations.

Strategies

Having the confidence to say 'I don't know'. They may already have a list of suspects, and may focus on the wrong person if what you are suggesting initially seems to fit one of their many theories. However, theories and hypotheses are usually more accurate when all the vital information has been evaluated. Be cognisant of the potential weight that may be assigned to more speculative and exploratory remarks, in order to avoid subsequent inappropriate investigative action being initiated prior to receipt of a full analytical product.

Analyse information
Analyse information
Difficult cognitive element – What police investigators might present to you as important and salient, may not be the important and salient bits we are looking for
Why difficult?
The focus of a BIA's interest is likely to be quite distinct from that of the SIO's. Whilst SIOs are often focused on evidential aspects, BIAs are interested in information that reveals the offender's knowledge, behaviour and decision-making processes. As such, when an SIO presents a briefing highlighting the important or salient information, they are likely to restrict or interpret this information from their own investigative perspective, which may be quite different to the BIA's.
Common errors
a) Not to ask for additional information, accepting the information provided as all that is available even if insufficient for behavioural analysis.
b) Focusing too narrowly on what is present with no consideration and confirmation of what was absent. Failure to expand the 'crime scene' beyond that designated for forensic retrieval purposes (e.g. the entirety of the victim's intended route).
Strategies
a) Identifying and clearly articulating the information you require and providing a sound rationale for why that information is of value to any behavioural analysis, which the officers may not have gathered, e.g. information on the victim's routine behaviours, habits, etc. This may be vital in order to spot anything that was different either at her home (if that is where the crime occurred or where she is thought to have disappeared from), or in something she was doing (e.g. she was walking a route which she wouldn't usually have taken). This kind of information may not be of evidential value, but it may help the behavioural analysis in determining how a third party may have become involved with the victim. Request information you need and work closely with the Family Liaison Officers (police officers who are assigned to be a point of contact to the family of the victim) in order to collect that information from those who were closest to the victim.
b) Also look at the area surrounding the body, what are the circumstances of the crime scene, what is missing, what is unusual? Think more holistically about the convergence of the victim and offender at that particular point in time and space. What happened just before the crime, what are the antecedents, what are the consequences? What is the level of risk the offender was willing to take? What was brought to the scene and what was taken from it? Establish the absence of behaviour and/or evidence, and make explicit to the SIO and relevant investigators why such aspects are critical to behavioural analysis.

	Difficult cognitive element – Getting an understanding of the case
	Why difficult?
	In line with the above considerations, the gaining of an accurate understanding of the case is often hampered by inaccuracies in information, inaccuracies in interpretation of the information and incomplete information, all of which needs to be evaluated from a quality assurance perspective.
	Common errors
	Assuming that the information provided is correct without checking its accuracy. Inability to recognize the potential of inaccuracies and why they are likely to occur.
	Strategies
	Order all information in sequence and establish a timeline. Check if timings and other information can be corroborated by more exact sources, such as call data, CCTV footage, etc. Identify information gaps and inconsistencies and ask the investigation to remedy those. Identify information gaps and seek clarification, always making explicit the potential value of requested information.
	Difficult cognitive element – Get an understanding of the victim
	Why difficult?
	A thorough 'victimology' analysis is not routinely available with the detail desired by a BIA. Aspects such as routine behaviours, attitudes, personality, etc. require interviewing of those close to the victim and require triangulation from several sources to ensure accuracy. This may require the reinterviewing of distressed individuals, who may question the necessity of such considerations. Even through such attempts at corroboration, it is difficult to gain an accurate picture of the victim, as associates may hold a distorted view, through either genuine misunderstanding of the victim, deceit by the victim or more sinister personal reasons related to their previous relationships.
	Common errors
	Accepting statements at face value, e.g. 'She would never have gone home with a man she didn't know', being unable to recognize potential errors due to interpersonal factors, etc. The victim may have made an exception or she may have known the person without her friends knowing that she knew him. This may lead the investigation down the wrong path. Everything needs to be questioned and no information can be taken as correct until there is a good enough reason to do so.

(Left margin, first section: Analyse information)

(Left margin, second section: Analyse information)

	Strategies
	Seeking corroboration of every salient detail of victimology and being cognisant of such inaccuracies. Establishing what the victim would usually have done can be a vital step towards ascertaining where in her routine an outside influence might have changed the normal course of events. Trying to get the originating witness statement for each piece of information about the victim to prevent being distracted by hearsay within the investigation. Asking for CCTV etc. to be checked in order to confirm the victim's movements both at the time in question as well as on previous occasions to establish her usual behaviours and decisions. What would she usually wear, take with her, do or not do, etc.? Did she come into contact with potentially dangerous people as part of her job or where she lives? How does she come across, is she confident and socially competent or rather withdrawn? How would she interact with people in critical or confrontational situations? How might that have influenced the offender's behaviour?
Analyse information	**Difficult cognitive element –Highlight salient features of the offence and identify behavioural themes in offender's behaviour**
	Why difficult?
	Some offenders might display several different 'themes' within the same offence. Or there might not be any apparent theme distinguishable. Some behaviour may be so extreme it might draw too much attention to itself to consider the overall picture equally. Some behaviour may co-occur in the same offence but may appear contradictory on the surface. This is reliant on an understanding of offender behaviour, base rate frequencies, offender–victim interaction, environmental factors, co-occurrence of behaviours, thematic modelling of offence behaviour, anomalies and accuracy and completeness of information presented.
	Common errors
	Too narrow a focus on individual behaviours and lack of attention to more thematic interpretations. Single behaviours may differ somewhat but may still form part of the same overall theme. Offenders are more likely to remain consistent in their behavioural themes rather than in their single behaviours, which are more vulnerable to change and external influences. Not to look at the meaning of certain behaviours, and not questioning why certain actions were or were not performed by the offender.
	Strategies
	Recognizing the themes of behaviour exhibited by the offender. They may allude to the overall motive for the offence, whereas individual behaviours within a theme may vary. Trying to see the 'big picture' of behaviours rather than zooming in on single behaviours; they always need to be considered in context. Recognizing and clustering behaviours may help classify the offender to some extent and may allow for directed research. This could help identify the most likely background characteristics of the offender. Incorporating the salience of absent behaviour as well as that present.

	Difficult cognitive element –Assign the appropriate amount of meaning to an offender's behaviour
	Why difficult?
Analyse information	It may be hard to distinguish an offender's behaviours that were completely under the control of the offender, and behaviours influenced either by the victim or the environment/situation. Virtually every action or behaviour exhibited by the offender is open to interpretation and may infer many different explanations. For example, is tearing of clothing a functional act to gain access to the victim's genitals or a more expressive act to increase sexual arousal? Is the theft of a victim's handbag motivated by souvenir collection, for material gain, to identify her home address or to delay her seeking assistance through the removal of her mobile phone? Did the offender bind the victim to prevent escape or was this part of his sexual fantasy? Is a dismembered body reflective of psychopathology or a more functional act to facilitate disposal? Each and every behaviour has to be evaluated as to its role and meaning within the overall offence.
	Common errors
	To mistake something as fantasy driven and psychologically significant when it may be more reflective of functional activity. To try to find meaning and explanation through the dissection of every potentially 'bizarre' behaviour either out of context with the remaining behaviour, or where no such explanation is possible. To fail to take into account what the offender didn't do and the missed opportunities that were present for further behaviour.
	Strategies
	Distinguishing functional acts from expressive ones and providing a clear supporting rationale for inferences within the overall context of the offence. Accepting that not every detail is amenable to explanation. Making explicit to SIOs that such speculation should be avoided as often even the offenders might not be able to articulate why they did certain actions and even if they could, such explanations might have no investigative utility. Focusing on those aspects which are more reliable and investigatively useful. Being cognisant to what the offender did not do and incorporating this into behavioural interpretation.
	Difficult cognitive element – Use analysis of offender behaviour to direct interrogation of relevant databases, research literature and external expertise
	Why difficult?
Analyse information	In order to effectively identify relevant databases, research literature and external expertise, you need to have effectively analysed offender behaviour (in line with previously highlighted elements) and be fully cognisant with and have access to such resources. The research literature is somewhat disparate, with papers of relevance spread across many disciplines and subject areas. Communication with external expertise requires balancing the need for specific expertise against the disclosure of case-sensitive material that is outside the public domain.

	Common errors
	Requesting data be pulled off from databases that refer to quite common behaviours, relying on inappropriate behavioural analysis, relying on research papers without quality assuring the methodology, sample, caveats, etc., not being familiar with the associated research literature from related disciplines, not being aware of unpublished research, not sourcing the appropriate expertise, not asking the expert the pertinent questions.
	Strategies
	Develop and maintain close working relationships with those analysts routinely collating, coding and interrogating relevant behavioural databases. Maintenance of a historical and contemporary knowledge of, and access to, relevant research literature, both published and in press, through liaison and relationships with relevant academic institutions and individuals, as well as environmental scanning activity. Develop and maintain close working relationships with external experts and fully understand their specific expertise and limitations.
	Difficult cognitive element – Provide a behavioural Crime Scene Assessment (i.e. establish an enhanced understanding of the offence from a behavioural perspective)
	Why difficult?
Analyse information	a) This is reliant upon the accuracy, completeness and interpretation of information available for analysis. E.g. timings provided by witnesses may be incorrect; other witness sightings may have confused the victim with someone else; witnesses may mistake what actually happened on that specific night with what they remember what the victim would usually have done or what would usually have happened. Once you base your sequence of events on certain key points and they turn out to come from inaccurate information, this has an impact on the whole sequence and your inferences. Need to restrict interpretation to those aspects directly relevant to investigative activity and avoid unnecessary speculation.
	b) Try to establish if she was targeted or if she was a random victim, if the offender knew her, why they were both at the encounter site at the same time; if the offence was premeditated or if an encounter escalated into the offence.
	c) It is crucial to find out how well the offender knew the area and/or the victim, but this is often not very obvious from the available information.
	d) It is important to consider how much time the offender spent at the crime scene, which has to be inferred from the information available.

Common errors
a) Overreliance on accuracy of information without adequate quality control processes; not to caveat the fact that inferences are dependent on the accuracy of information; to make inferences too dependent on unreliable information.
b) Not researching enough what her routine activities were and not investigating why she would have strayed from them. Only questioning why she did certain things and not also why she did *not* do certain things when the opportunity was there.
c) Not to recognize the importance of establishing how familiar the offender was with the location – if he knew the area, this might offer a variety of investigative opportunities that should not be missed.
d) Not to realize how vital this piece of information can be and not to try and find out. Failure to acknowledge information gaps that may further support, refine or refute assessment. Unconscious influence of investigative interpretation of events affecting objectivity.
Strategies
a) Check and confirm the accuracy of all data you work with. Request any relevant incidences to be extracted from police systems about precursor offences, suspicious sightings or behaviours, indecent exposure etc. and other events that could have been committed by the offender. Find out if the victim had told anyone she had been accosted/harassed, etc.
b) Establish the link to the offender: he will either have a connection with the victim or with the crime site. If she just happened to be at that location when she was attacked and in the absence of any indications that she had been followed or lured there, one can hypothesize the offender had more of a link with the location and was there for a reason. If, however, the offence appears targeted and she had a routine of being there at that time, she may have been the intended victim and the offender has more of a link to her than to the location, as the location was down to her choosing and he was simply there because she was. Once it is established where the offender's link is (victim vs. location), investigative enquiries can focus on scrutinizing that link.
c) Visit the crime scene at the relevant time in order to establish how much knowledge of the locality was necessary to identify and access the scene, how good were the offender's choices, how much risk was he taking, how would he have known of the used locations or access routes, etc.?
d) Observe how long it would have taken to commit the offence to work out how long the offender remained at the crime scene. If he took his time this might indicate he knew there was a low risk of being discovered – but how did he know that? If the offence was indoors, does he live in the same building and know that the victim was living alone? If outdoors, does he know the location well enough to know that it is unlikely anyone will be walking past at that particular time and that he cannot be seen?

Analyse information

	Difficult cognitive element – Form hypotheses and inferences
Analyse information	
	Why difficult?
	List variants of your sequence of events, e.g. in the form of a hypothesis tree that displays all possible hypotheses and note which ones are the most likely and why. Provide support for or against each hypothesis with reference to psychological theory, relevant research findings and experiential knowledge. Ensure that the SIO will be able to understand the reasoning behind the different strengths of each hypothesis. Acknowledge the weaknesses of any opinions forwarded and emphasize the need to fill identified information gaps and seek consultation with relevant expertise to support, refine or refute assessment. Remain cognisant of the overriding aims of the assessment and link to investigative action. Adopt a 'scientific' approach in confirming or refuting a hypothesis that is capable of withstanding forensic scrutiny. Accept and manage expectation that a definitive assessment is often neither possible nor desirable, emphasizing the aim of prioritization and decision support.
	Common errors
	a) To be pressured into putting forward a definitive theory when you are unable to do so without being unscientific. Though more experienced SIOs may welcome an objective report, an SIO who is desperate and overwhelmed may want a firm conclusion from us rather than a scientific illustration of all the options and what is the most likely.
	b) Formulating a hypothesis early on and trying to prove it with the facts of the case. This can lead to biased thinking.
	Strategies
	a) Present all plausible theories and what does and does not support them. It would be unprofessional and unscientific to make a definitive statement as there is simply not enough certainty to do so until the offender has been caught and proven to have committed the offence. Science deals with probabilities. You can create a 'trinity' for offender behaviours by listing behaviours in three columns: facts, 'likelies' and unknowns. This will highlight the level of certainty for various inferences and what we know about specific facets of the offence. Draw up a hypothesis tree, listing each plausible hypothesis. Use a Toulmin system to back up or eliminate each hypothesis scientifically. Cross-reference bits from the trinity and create 'stories' or sequences of events of what might have happened, constantly checking them against the facts of the case to see if they can be disproven. This can help eliminate bias because you're looking at all the options and how they are or are not supported by the evidence. Use all the known facts to recreate the scene(s) as it was at the time, then let your stories play through and test them against available evidence. Try to exclude the most obvious scenarios first, i.e. that it was the partner or ex-partner. Only then is it usually advisable for a BIA to get involved.
	b) List each possible hypothesis and try to disprove them, which is easier than proving them. When you can reliably disprove a hypothesis, move on to the next one.

Difficult cognitive element – Provide a predictive 'profile' of the unknown offender
Why difficult?
Such features may be difficult to infer from a crime scene – developmental age may not correspond to actual age. Police hold records of previous convictions, but they are rarely if ever an accurate record of someone's entire criminal activities. Provision of likely background characteristics is dependent upon an accurate behavioural understanding of the offence and offender.Some criminals will learn very quickly from previous offences and may not have committed many 'build-up' offences previously, or they may have been so 'successful' that they have not been caught. This would create a discrepancy with the profile, if the assumption is that he has committed several similar offences but the police haven't caught him for them.The geography of the offender (where he lives) can often be established more reliably than other characteristics, however it may be difficult to check against suspects unless they actually live locally, as police often do not hold records on where offenders work or where their families or acquaintances live. Some characteristics inferred from the crime scene are not always usable for suspect prioritization unless they can be translated into likely previous convictions or unsolved precursor offences, e.g. sadistic behaviours and sexual fantasies. All inferences must be fully supported by sound rationale and presented in a manner easily understood by the SIO. The inferences must strike an appropriate balance between accuracy and utility. Inferences must be directly amenable to investigative action.
Common errors
Misjudging the balance between accuracy and utility. Failing to take into account the investigative implications of inferences and recommendations and/ or the investigative resources available. Basing inferences on inappropriate behavioural analysis and interpretation. Reliance on inappropriate datasets and research. Failing to ensure the SIO's understanding of how to utilize the 'profile' and highlighting the appropriate caveats to its use.
Strategies
Gain an accurate understanding of the investigative resources available. Provide sound supporting rationale for all inferences and recommendations made. Use database and research literature judiciously, and fully understand the data within the context of the current case. Communicate with the SIO both before report preparation and after delivery, to ensure their understanding of how to best utilize the advice provided and the caveats regarding its use.

Analyse information

Analyse information	**Difficult cognitive element – Produce or evaluate a suspect prioritization matrix**
	Why difficult?
	The elements of the matrix and their weightings will be used to decide which individuals the investigation is going to focus on first. Providing the appropriate weight to each inferred background characteristic such that certain individuals stand out from the more general backdrop of others within the pool of nominals is reliant upon the selection of the specific categories to be scored, the specific scores assigned to each category, and an in-depth understanding of methodological issues. The final result must be understandable and actionable by officers or analysts who are likely to be using such techniques for the first time and without the ongoing input from the BIA.
	Common errors
	Utilization of characteristics that whilst valid from a 'profiling' perspective, lack significant discriminatory power. Lack of clear operational definitions for the categories to be scored. Failure to consider mutual exclusivity and interdependence of categories. Failure to score the categories appropriately. Failure to recognize the investigative aims and/or resources supporting the prioritization matrix. Failure to ensure complete understanding by those tasked with nominal scoring and matrix implementation. Focusing too much on previous offences alone. The perpetrator may have committed offences the police are not aware of and may therefore fall through the net unless other characteristics are weighted adequately highly as well. Assuming that he has perpetrated a very similar offence before and not looking for less serious build-up offences.
	Strategies
	Test the proposed matrix against a series of real or simulated nominals to ensure avoidance of common methodological errors, and that it is prioritizing the type of individuals inferred in the manner intended. Ensure the SIO and associated analyst tasked with matrix actions are fully cognisant with its construction and use and oversee some initial trial testing ahead of full implementation.

demands table which details the processes, their various challenging cognitive elements, common errors made by novices and how to avoid them. The various psychological stages extracted from the BIAs' working process were grouped as follows by the researcher (first author):

- assessing the overall case;
- examining the SIO's reasoning process and personality style;
- analysing the information provided.

The first two of those stages may occur concurrently at the initial briefing stage, whereas step three produces the inferences and hypotheses that lead to the investigative advice provided. That stage is by far the most time consuming and indeed the main part of the BIA's work process. This will entail studying police reports, interview footage, examining other reports such as that of the pathologist, statements and crime scene photos, researching the area and various aspects of the offender's behaviour, putting together a potential sequence of events, drawing up different hypotheses and carrying out research using crime databases and academic literature. The analysis process often results in a *crime scene assessment* (see Chapters 2 and 3 for further details), which constitutes the main part of the report, and may also include creating a profile, or any of the other products and services deemed appropriate for the specific investigative needs (see Chapter 2 for a full review).

First, the BIA needs to make a judgement as to the overall nature of the case, what kind of advice or product they could provide to best support the investigation, and how their input is going to be received, interpreted and acted upon. Some cases do not necessitate a BIA's involvement, yet some SIOs may feel compelled to request them in order to appease the media's and the public's interest, or simply because they are stuck and are looking for new investigative leads, feeling they have already exhausted all avenues available to them. If the BIA decides that the case does contain enough behavioural information for them to work with, they observe how the SIO is running the investigation to decide how to best collaborate with the investigation team. The BIA needs to be judicious with their comments and suggestions lest the team should act on them prematurely before the BIA has a chance to receive, take in and analyse all the information in the case, after which they may refine their opinions and/or favour a different hypothesis. More experienced and confident SIOs are more likely to be cautious and to await the BIA's full report before making any crucial decisions. However, the BIA might not always encounter a receptive audience and there is an inherent risk of them being seen as an intruder or someone who was sent in to review and assess the investigation, rather than assist in it.

Once crucial assessments as to the type of involvement necessary and the personal dynamics involved have been made, the BIA will commence to analyse the wealth of materials available on the crime. This involves various reports, statements, photographs, videos, interviews, maps as well as research into the area, its social demographics and crime profile. The BIA always visits the crime site(s), if possible at the relevant time in order to ascertain the demographics of people who come across that location at that specific time. Through their analysis, they aim to identify and extract significant behaviours of the perpetrator, the meaning behind them, the sequence of events and what exactly happened during the commission of the crime, the decisions the offender took before, during and after the offence, his connection to the victim or the location and the possible motive for the crime. They will attempt to determine whether the offence was pre-planned or simply escalated out of an altercation, if the offender was impulsive or controlled, what his level of skill or experience is in terms of offending, how much time he spent at the crime scene and how much of a risk he was willing to take.

The BIA's analysis of the information will then lead to the creation of inferences and hypotheses, all of which will be noted and scrutinized in turn. The BIA has to check each inference against the facts and provide supporting evidence in the form of academic research and/or crime statistics to support or refute each inference made. The SIO will be informed of each hypothesis and their attached likelihood, in order that they are provided with the full range of possibilities, rather than a pre-selected subset, so that the SIO is able to make unbiased and well-informed decisions.

Lastly, the BIA provides investigative advice in their reports, which is based on the strongest and most likely inferences or hypotheses backed up by facts and research, as the main aim of their involvement is to provide advice that is useful to the investigation based on the psychology and behaviour of the offender. If necessary, they will also assist with prioritization of suspects by providing a profile depicting the most likely demographic parameters of the offender, based on major crime statistics.

Discussion – Study 1

The results of the cognitive task analysis for providing behavioural investigative advice identified a variety of intricate analytical processes and behavioural considerations aimed at dissecting psychological information in a criminal context, coupled with advanced interpersonal and communication skills at dealing with investigation teams and SIOs. Further, various features associated with expertise have been identified in the everyday workings of BIAs in the UK. Analysis of the data suggests that BIAs routinely engage in meticulous behavioural considerations in order to identify an offender's connection to a crime, either through the victim or the crime location. They utilize a large knowledge base of previous experience, academic research and major crime statistics to infer an offender's characteristics and generate hypotheses about the motive of the offence, and the offender's familiarity with the victim or the location. When called to assist in an investigation, a BIA makes an assessment as to whether their input is indeed warranted in the case at hand. In order to be able to support a case, there needs to be behavioural information regarding the offender to merit analysis. This is coupled with a sensitive assessment of the investigation at the time in order to ascertain which investigative steps have already been taken and what else should ideally be happening, which requires a highly developed set of interpersonal skills (see Chapter 1). The SIO may have requested the input of a BIA with a specific product in mind, yet the BIA may find that another kind of service may be more warranted, and they need to argue their case accordingly. Their most comprehensive product is the crime scene assessment, which is a meticulous analysis of the offence, its most likely aetiology, sequence of events, motive and most promising lines of enquiry. This assessment might lead to inferences about the offender, with weighted hypotheses and investigative suggestions.

Table 5.1 presents the results of the cognitive task analysis for the profession of being a Behavioural Investigative Adviser. They suggest a psychologically focused and meticulous cognitive procedure of assessment, research, interpretation and strategic as well as tactical decision making. The way that BIAs chunk information on various offender behaviours into themes rather than attempting to assign meaning to each individual behaviour, especially when it comes to assessing case linkage, is one of the hallmark aspects of expertise (Chase and Simon, 1973). The selective intake of specific bits of information rather than processing the entire data set equally, such as focusing on offender-led behaviour rather than reactionary behaviour, or assessing levels of threats and violence in the context of the surroundings and general risk of the situation, is another key feature attributed to expertise (Savelsbergh *et al.*, 2005). The BIAs' ability to notice abnormalities in the behaviour or to identify when opportunities presented themselves to the victim or offender which they did not take, are another facet of expertise (Militello *et al.*, 1997). Furthermore, the BIAs rely heavily on a strong and extensive empirical knowledge base of previous cases, which is also a feature commonly observed in experts (Militello *et al.*, 1997). The potential expertise of BIAs would appear to be of the perceptual kind, in that it aids the input and processing of information and behavioural models, rather than conceptual expertise, which is more commonly found in expert chess players and others who utilize superior skills in grasping concepts (Shanteau, 1985).

The findings of this study support the notion of expertise in professional BIAs in analysing and drawing meaning from crime scene behaviour that enables the provision of effective investigative advice from a complementary perspective to that of investigating officers.

Study 2: Cognitive processes in the Operative Fall Analytiker (OFA) in Germany

The term Operative Fall Analytiker translates to *operational case analyst(s)* and is equivalent to the Behavioural Investigative Adviser in the UK. The German infrastructure is such that each of the 16 states has its own team of OFAs covering that particular county. The role of the OFA team is to assist the investigation in the identification of information gaps in the case, enhance understanding of the crime, identify new lines of enquiry or prioritize existing ones, as well as prioritizing suspects. The official definition of providing *Operative Fall Analyse* translates to:

> a criminological process to enhance the understanding of the index crime in cases of murder and sexual violence as well as other suitable particularly meaningful offences, based on objective data and comprehensive information on the victim in order to identify advice to support the investigation and increase the level of understanding of the index offence.
>
> (Dern *et al.*, 2003).

Each OFA is a serving police officer, with the exception of one civilian clinical and forensic psychologist who joined the group of Bavarian OFAs in 2009. Since the team services a relatively small geographical area, there is no need for a nationally centralized point of contact and each local police unit phones the head of their respective OFA team directly as and when needed. The OFAs, whose numbers range from 2–5 per team in Germany, visit the police unit, are briefed on the case and visit the crime scene(s). If their support is deemed feasible, they provide the investigation with questionnaires which will guide and structure the information collation necessary for the analysis process. For instance, one questionnaire will request very detailed information on the victim to be collected. This can steer the investigating team in their initial or secondary questioning of witnesses and family of the victim. The completed questionnaires are then fed back to the OFA team. Since they have access to the police unit's IT system, they download the necessary reports and photographs. They speak to the coroner in a murder case to get their interpretation of injuries, which can shed light on the sequence of events and dynamics of the offence. Each OFA is provided with, and has access to, identical sets of information and initially, they work through the case information individually out of their office. If a case is highly complex, they may each be assigned different areas to concentrate on, e.g. victimology, location, etc. They spend a few days working through the information by themselves, making notes of their thoughts, identifying information gaps, making rudimentary initial inferences and identifying initial lines of enquiry, before commencing the analysis process that involves the whole team. For this group process, specific roles are assigned to the individual team members; one is the moderator, who takes the team through the various stages of discussion and points to cover, prompts each team member for their views and opinions, writes the protocol of the analysis process and structures inferences and hypotheses. Another OFA is the devil's advocate, whose task involves identifying counter-arguments to each hypothesis stated, who meticulously scrutinizes every inference and hypothesis until it can either be discarded or until it is solid and backed up by the facts, with as many weak points as possible eliminated. This process is aimed at ensuring that no bias can be introduced or maintained at the analysis stage, that each hypothesis is tested vigorously against the facts of the case, and that the team members do not acquiesce to anyone's opinion or personality or give in to peer pressure in the process. One of the other team members who is heading that particular case is required to clarify disagreements and make the decisions in cases where there are differing opinions as to the best course of action. At the analysis stage, the OFAs often create a list containing the facts, and note possibilities and assumptions on another sheet. They separate hard evidence (e.g. coroner's report, photographs, police reports) from uncorroborated information (e.g. witness statements, sightings, etc.) or speculation until assumptions can be verified to a high enough degree. This group process allows views to be challenged, alternatives to be considered and each hypothesis to be scrutinized. This also facilitates the examination of more hypotheses, as well as protecting against negative emotional side effects of intense cases. In complex investigations, tasks can be split up, e.g. one person has specific responsibilities and contacts and focuses only on victimology. The collegial team-setting allows for communicative exchange, which is thought to be beneficial for the mental health of each team member, as it functions as a buffer against the pressures inherent in any major investigation. Each possible hypothesis is listed and examined, and a hypothesis tree may be employed to visualize them (see Chapter 3 for an illustrative example from the UK). As a team, they go through all the facts of the case in segments: victim, injuries, crime scene, etc., to ensure that each member is in possession of the same facts and knowledge regarding the case. They identify problematic areas, i.e. facets that are unknown, e.g. they know where the victim was attacked and where the body was dumped but they don't know where the victim was murdered, or they don't know how the offender gained access to the building. They identify gaps in the information that prevent the OFAs to fill in a complete timeline of what happened, where, when and how. A part of the analysis process is also to identify behaviours that can potentially cause 'halo' effects, in that they are so bizarre or extreme they risk drawing too much attention to themselves, such as mutilation of the victim, for instance. People might be so preoccupied with trying to find the meaning behind such actions that they might get side-tracked away from the bigger picture and the offence itself. The OFAs are cognisant of the fact that, for some behaviours, there simply is no explanation; the offender may merely have been curious as to what he can do with a body and a knife, and there might not be an underlying necrophillic or otherwise pathological tendency in it. Again, the team approach can provide a buffer against such dangers of being side-tracked.

The OFAs have developed a systematically structured procedure setting out the steps of this analysis process:

1   **Overview**. This first step involves summarizing the case and what is known so far. Problematic areas are identified, e.g. unexplained actions taken by the victim or offender, lack of reliability of particular witnesses (e.g. due to intoxication at the time, dishonest character etc.) and information gaps are highlighted.
2   **Sequence of events.** During this stage, efforts are made to establish the *sequence* of events, i.e. how and where the offence started, how the offence developed and where and how it was concluded, up to the first report

to police. An assessment of the offence in terms of '*suitability and availability*' of the victim is made, i.e. was the victim attacked in an area where she was the only viable option, e.g. if no-one else was there at the time, or was she picked from a pool of many potential victims, such as an area busy with nightlife? Her suitability may have simply been dependent on criteria such as being female, alone and intoxicated. Further, the OFA team evaluates the *offending opportunity* that presented itself to the perpetrator, e.g. was he able to choose his victim from many potential victims, was he taking a high risk of being seen or was it a low-risk situation, was it a chance encounter in which he decided to offend spontaneously, did it escalate out of a different situation or was it *pre-meditated*?

3   **Behavioural assessment.** This stage is the most comprehensive part of the behavioural analysis the OFAs undertake. They examine the offender's *control* behaviours, i.e. how and why did he control the victim – was there a risk of her getting away or attracting attention or did he tie her up or gag her as part of his sexual gratification? Did he bring the items to control her with him or did he improvise with items from the scene or the victim? Did he threaten her verbally or physically to gain control or did he actually cause injury for that purpose? The next item the OFAs focus on is *violence*. They examine the level of violence used and its function, which can be either instrumental (violence is used in order to achieve a practical goal such as gaining the victim's compliance or causing her death), or expressive (the violence serves no practical purpose, and the only goal is emotive, to relieve the offender's emotional pressures, fulfil his curiosity or desires). Further, it needs to be ascertained whether violent actions were carried out in reaction to the victim's actions such as vigorous resistance, or whether violence was present from the start. The next point to be investigated is the *sexual* behaviour exhibited – which sex acts did the offender mean to carry out and which ones did he manage to carry out? Were they fantasy-led and ritualistic or fairly basic and functional? Did he do anything that could be classed as unusual? Was he trying to interact with the victim personally and attempting to establish some kind of intimacy or was he simply using her to fulfil his sexual needs? The offender's *verbal* behaviour is the next point of scrutiny; again it needs to be established what the purpose of his verbal interaction was: gaining compliance, gathering information on the victim, reassuring her, threatening her? If so, what did he say, did he reveal any information about himself, did he try to establish a conversation, did he remain silent, did he give any instructions, did he request any help from her, was his demeanour aggressive and intimidating or was he trying to calm the victim down, etc. Following this, the OFAs will examine the offender's use of *weapons*: were they actually used to inflict injuries or were they just used as a threat to gain compliance; did he bring them with him or find them at the scene; were there items available at the scene that he could have used but did not and if so, why didn't he use them? The next issue to be established is what the offender did to *conceal his identity/forensics* – did he attack the victim from

behind so she couldn't see him, did he blindfold her, did he wear a balaclava, did he wear gloves and a condom and remove or destroy forensic evidence, did he try to change his voice or accent? As part of the behavioural assessment, the OFAs also extract elements in the offender's behaviour that are not that typical for this type of offence and appear to *personalize* what he does, which might allow to draw conclusions about his motive for the offence and what he was trying to achieve. These would be things that would remove an element of anonymity from the offence for him and make it emotionally meaningful, such as calling the victim by a specific name, pretending she is someone specific, that he is someone specific, acting out a scenario through the offence, or doing something that is very personal to him but quite distinctive, which could also be referred to as a 'signature' behaviour. Further to these personalizing elements, OFAs attempt to identify any *salient* behaviours in the offence that stand out in some way which might warrant further consideration to see if they might hint at the personality of the offender, his motive, his connection to the victim, his psychopathology, his offending history, etc. These could be behaviours such as playing out a specific fantasy scenario through the offence, inflicting specific injuries, such as biting, a focus for injuries such as the breasts for instance, or anything else that may have been meaningful to the offender that goes beyond what is absolutely necessary in order to carry out the offence successfully. Finally, all the points extracted and examined as part of the behavioural assessment are pulled together in order to *characterize* the offender's behaviour, to create a big picture of what the offender wanted, what happened, what he did and how he did it. This process involves the assessment of the determination of the offender, how resistant he was to the stresses of the situation, ability to control the victim, etc. These details enable the OFAs to assess the offender's level of criminal competence and experience, which can lead to inferences about previous convictions and identification of any weaknesses.

4   **Assessment of motive.** Here, the OFAs differentiate between the *initial motive*, which in some cases may simply have been to achieve consensual intercourse, *escalation*, which may result out of the victim rejecting the offender's advances and him not being able to handle or tolerate that rejection, and in murder cases, the *motive to kill*. Not all murders are actually intended as such and they may well have started as either something less sinister, such as trying to pick up a woman on a night out, or on the other hand, as a robbery or a rape that escalated out of control. The preceding behavioural assessment should support this step, as it may inform the sequence of actions that occurred during the offence, if the victim was physically resistant, which may have heightened the offender's level of violence, and if it appeared that the offender lost control of his actions and entered a frenzy of violence or panic. The eventual killing motive must also be ascertained – it may either be expressive, such that the perpetrator actually wants to commit the act of killing his victim as he believes it will provide him pleasure, a thrill, a sensation of power, or satisfy his need for curiosity, for instance. Conversely, the

act of killing may be instrumental in that it serves the purpose of preventing the victim from being able to identify the offender, he needs a dead body to fulfil his necrophilic fantasies, or he wants to dismember the body in order to dispose of it more easily.

5   **Characterizing the offence.** This step involves creating a big-picture view of the offence, whereby the OFAs mentally 'zoom out' of the case, put aside the minor details and just look at the overall more distanced birds-eye view of what was going on. Sometimes, details can be distracting and individual behaviours can be too misleading in that they may be so extreme they can have a 'halo' effect that clouds everything else and absorbs the team's attention away from the actual big picture. Taking a more dissociated view of things allows for the overall offence to be evaluated more objectively.

6   **Offender profile.** At this stage, the level of premeditation, the offender's interaction with the victim, his level of control and risk-taking, his motives and whether he was familiar with the victim or the area are taken together and combined with research of appropriate statistics in order to identify the demographic parameters of offenders who, according to crime statistics, are usually responsible for offences such as the index offence. Statistically, the offender in question is most likely to have those same demographic parameters, which can then be used to prioritize suspects.

7   **Investigative advice.** The offender's knowledge of the victim or the crime scene, his level of premeditation, his interaction and motives are then used to identify lines of enquiry to the investigating team.

8   **Summary.** The facts of the case, what happened and how, what the offender's likely intentions were and how the investigation might want to proceed with this case is then summarized at the end of the presentation.

Results

The cognitive tasks and critical cues identified through the ACTA methodology by the researcher (first author) as being the integral elements of the cognitive OFA processes are listed in Table 5.2.

Table 5.2 Critical cue inventory[1] for making inferences and investigative suggestions in operational case analysis

Cue	Description	Potential inferences
Offence characteristics	Offence appears pre-mediated, planned out and prepared.	Offender more likely to live further away; offence less likely to have been spontaneous; offender likely to be older rather than younger[2]; if victim murdered it is more likely to have been part of the plan rather than accidental or due to escalation; offender may have visited encounter location previously and may have been seen by witnesses on those occasions.

(Continued)

Table 5.2 Cont'd

Cue	Description	Potential inferences
	Offence is of a violent and sexual nature.	There are likely to be precursor offences, anything that might have been a practice run (e.g. a male running into a woman and stealing her handbag, minor sexual assaults, indecent exposure, accosting, etc.), or minor incidences with a sexual connotation (stealing women's underwear from washing lines, 'peeping-Tom' offences, voyeurism, masturbating whilst watching females, etc.); such offences may have been committed by the same offender as the index offence, some incidents may not have been reported and the police should actively seek relevant information from the community around the encounter site as there may be forensic evidence to be gained or members of the public may have seen someone they either know or are able to describe;.
	Offender went to great lengths to make the body disappear and eliminate forensic evidence.	Offender more likely to be local: possibly has some connection to the victim, which he really does not want found out.
Crime scene observations	Victim is found undressed in an outdoor offence.	Offence is more likely to have taken place indoors, with the victim having been transported afterwards, meaning he may have used a car; complete undressing of victims occurs more frequently in indoor offences than outdoor offences; deposition/release site is less likely to have been the attack or main crime site.
	Offender broke into victim's home to attack.	Victim was targeted, either because offender knew her, had encountered her outside and followed her home, or because he knew he could gain access to her home when she is alone.
	Crime took place in victim's home but no sign of forced entry.	The victim may have known the offender well enough to let him in; he may have conned his way into the property on some kind of pretext; he may be skilled at picking locks; the victim may have returned home with him; she may have a routine of letting the cat or the dog in and out and unless she would have let him in voluntarily, he may have seen her do that when he was pursuing voyeuristic activities in the vicinity, and forced his way in as the door was opened.

Table 5.2 Cont'd

Cue	Description	Potential inferences
	Crime scene is victim's home, which appears pretty tidy.	Unless the victim is very tidy herself, the offender may have cleaned up after offence and may have disposed of broken glass or items, removed foot prints, blood, etc., which may be in the rubbish bins outside or near the property; items that are missing from scene might be of significance.
	Crime scene is victim's home, which appears very messy.	Unless the victim is very messy herself, there might have been a struggle – the neighbours might have heard it and there might be forensic evidence; items that are missing from scene might be of significance.
	A person is missing but their home appears to have been changed or staged.	The more effort an offender puts into staging a murder to look as if the person actually left voluntarily, the more he fears being connected to her, i.e. the more closely they may be associated.
	Encounter site is a rural location.	As there are no crime-attractors (e.g. night life, red-light district), the target backcloth is quite sparse, which means it is less likely the offender went there in order to hunt, but appears to have been there as part of his normal routine activities, and may therefore be local; he may have followed victim into this rural location from somewhere more lively in order to reduce the amount of potential witnesses; he may have been using a car rather than public transport; he may have been seen there by witnesses on previous, non-offending occasions.
	Murder appears to have resulted from an escalation, does not appear pre-meditated.	Offender may be acquaintance of victim, the situation might have escalated out of control and beyond his initial intentions; offender may be younger rather than older and less experienced in violent crime; offender may not be able to deal with pressure or unexpected events very well and may panic and overreact easily.
	Crime scene shows an overly violent struggle took place.	Offender may not be very adept at dealing with resistance in a controlled manner – might lose self-control when victim resists; might be inexperienced in exerting adequate amounts of control.

(Continued)

Table 5.2 Cont'd

Cue	Description	Potential inferences
Victimology	Victim pursued various scheduled activities at regular times.	If she was attacked at, or on her way to or from one of those activities, it is possible she was a specific target; offender knew when she was going to be at a specific place, may have targeted her; offender may have known her from one of those activities; may know her from seeing or encountering her travelling to or from those activities.
	Victim's work or social activities brought her into contact with high-risk individuals.	She may have been targeted by someone she knew from one of those activities or her job.
	Victim had spent time in a mental health institution.	She may have been targeted by someone she encountered in that context.
	Victim had mental health problems at the time of the offence.	Her mental state may have affected her decisions and whom she associated with; she may have been less risk-conscious or may have been taking risks deliberately; she may have been more vulnerable to exploitation and manipulation.
	Victim was promiscuous and very active sexually.	She may have come across offender in a location where she would usually meet men, she may have been chosen as a victim as she made herself sexually accessible more easily than other women; she may have fallen victim to a jealous ex-partner; may have been stalked by a previous partner; may have been attacked by one of her acquaintances; may have been attacked due to escalation when initial flirtatious exchange was terminated by her and offender did not accept her rejection; her sexual life may have had nothing to do with her attack at all.
	Victim had specific sexual preferences or pursued specific sexual practices.	Potential suspects and significant acquaintances or witnesses can also be sought out in circles that the victim may have frequented; the offence of murder may have been unintentional when victim was engaging in bondage or sadomasochism and things went wrong; her sexual life may have had nothing to do with her attack at all.

Table 5.2 Cont'd

Cue	Description	Potential inferences
	Victim is elderly.	Offender may have a sexual preference for older women; offender may have chosen older victim as she may be easier to control and subdue; offender focuses his criminal urges on older women for an internal reason; victim may look much younger than she is and offender may have assumed she was younger whilst he has no preference for older victims.
	Victim is very young.	Offender may have a sexual preference for younger females; offender may have chosen younger victim as she may be easier to control and subdue; victim may look much older than she is and offender may have assumed she was older whilst he has no preference for younger victims.
	Child victim was abducted and raped.	Offender most likely to be local.
Victim's injuries	Some injuries were carried out post mortem.	Offender might have felt quite secure in that location and felt no need to flee the scene straight away, indicating he knew no one would come and that he knew the location well, or if offence occurred in victim's home he may have known victim and knew no one would come; he may have been curious about the dead body; he may have necrophilic tendencies.
	Victim's body is found dismembered.	Offender may want to prevent identification of body; may want to make transportation easier; may want to make disposal of the body easier; may want keep parts of the body to mentally re-live offence.
	Superficial injuries.	Offender may have inflicted these injuries in order to gain compliance from the victim; may have been hesitant to cut more deeply; may be inexperienced in inflicting injuries.
	Reddening of the skin around the wrists and/or ankles.	Victim was tied up and potentially struggled; this may have been to prevent her from attacking offender or getting away; it may be part of offender's sexual script; victim may have engaged in bondage wilfully and may have initially consented to sexual activity when something changed in the offender's behaviour or the situation and the activity turned into a serious crime against her will; victim may have had intercourse with a partner during which she engaged in bondage but was attacked by someone else afterwards.

(Continued)

Table 5.2 Cont'd

Cue	Description	Potential inferences
	Injuries to lower arms.	Victim may have been defending herself from offender's attack, this may have prompted offender to tie her up or use more blunt violence to knock her unconscious or gain compliance and control; she probably wasn't tied up/compliant/unconscious straight away and offender unsuccessfully tried to control her without using ligatures, might be less experienced offender who probably hasn't tied up his previous victim(s) if there was one; if he is going to commit another offence of that nature he is more likely to tie her up sooner in order to avoid that level of physical resistance next time around.
	Victim sustained excessive injuries in tandem with defence injuries.	Offender may have panicked when victim resisted and over-compensated through excessive use of violence, is not very adept at exerting an appropriate amount of control to prevent resistance.
	Victim was knocked out and killed very quickly.	Offender's needs are focused on a unresponsive body rather than any interaction with the victim; pre-cursor offences might include cases of women being hit on the head and the offender making off rather than rape, anything involving immediate, focused violence.
	Murder appears very competent and goal-oriented.	Probably not the first murder offence, possibly not the last; probably did not happen out of an escalation but was pre-meditated.
Offender profile	Overall offence appears erratic, chaotic and unplanned.	Offender more likely to be younger (ca. between 15–25 years) rather than older (ca. 25–45 years, say).
	Offender broke into victim's residence in order to offend.	Offender likely to have committed burglaries previously and may have previous convictions for that, which means he may be on a police database.
	Offender took valuable items from victim.	Offender may have removed them for practical purposes such as delaying her ability to call for help or delaying identification of the victim; he may have stolen items for their value and he may have convictions for theft; he may have taken the opportunity for financial gain but has not stolen before.
	Victim was raped.	Offender likely to be generally criminal and criminally versatile, but does not necessarily have previous convictions for rape.

Table 5.2 Cont'd

Cue	Description	Potential inferences
	Offence is a sexual murder.	Offender likely to have previous convictions for rape and/or sexual assaults.
	Offender brought offence items (e.g. ligature, weapon, gloves, balaclava, etc.) with him.	Offence was premeditated and planned out; if the victim was not targeted specifically, the offender is likely to repeat this offence; offender left his home anticipating or even creating an opportunity to offend, he may therefore have travelled into a target-rich area specifically and may live further away than if he had offended spontaneously; offender more likely to have used transport than walked, as he had to conceal his offending 'kit'.
	Offender improvised 'tools' from crime scene, e.g. used telephone cord in victim's residence as ligature, used items of her clothing as ligatures or gags, used one of her kitchen knives as a weapon, etc.	Offence less likely to have been planned and offender may have spontaneously decided to offend or the offence escalated out of a less sinister situation; he may therefore have been in the area for a legitimate reason and is more likely to be local.
	Offender subjected victim to sadistic activities.	Offender may have previous convictions for arson and fire-setting, may have tortured and possibly killed animals, may have displayed a sadistic streak when he was growing up, may be sadistic perpetrator of domestic violence.
	Victim was buried in an outdoor location.	Offender was familiar with that location prior to body disposal, but he may be avoiding the area now, which may be noticed by others.
	One of the suspects changed his routine behaviour, is nervous, off sick, avoidant, overly indifferent or overly interested in media coverage of the case, avoids his usual social contacts, etc.	He might be trying to conceal his involvement in the offence, and topic areas he is trying to avoid might be worth exploring in greater detail during interview.

(Continued)

Table 5.2 Cont'd

Cue	Description	Potential inferences
	Offence occurred during day.	If offender resides with another adult, that person may be assuming he is out at work; he may not live with anyone else.
	Offence occurred during night.	If offender resides with another adult, that person may not be aware that offender was not at home during the offence, or they may have thought he was having a night out; offender may not live with anyone else.
	Offence occurred indoors but not at victim's address or encounter site.	Offence may have taken place at offender's address, which would mean he either lives alone or has access to a location which he could utilize to carry out the offence.
	Offender retained (some of the) victim's clothing.	Offender may cross-dress and further clues might be obtained from the cross-dressing community; if underwear was taken, precursor offences/incidences should be sought in which underwear was stolen from washing lines; he may simply have removed potential forensic evidence.

[1] Adapted from Klein, Calderwood, and MacGregor (1989).
[2] Age parameters refer to developmental age and maturity rather than physical age.

Table 5.2 lists various cues that the OFA team extract from an offence. No single cue can be used to make any one firm inference – it must always be viewed within the context of the overall offence and the other cues. Therefore, Table 5.2 cannot be used as a simple look-up table. Rather, one cue presents myriad possible inferences or explanations, each of which needs to be considered. The inferences in Table 5.2 are not listed in any particular meaningful order.

Offence characteristics

This is the first theme of critical cues as defined by the researcher (first author). This entails analysing the context and aetiology of the offence, in order to establish which event(s) led up to the victim and the offender coming together at the encounter site – did the offender cause the victim to be there, was he there in anticipation of potential victims, did she just happen to pass by and create a sudden opportunity, was it something that was prearranged and escalated or was it premeditated in its entirety? Further, the target backcloth is examined: how much effort did the offender have to make in order to find that victim? Was she a prostitute whom he would have easily gotten into his car and had intercourse with? Did he go into an area where there would be a large number of potential victims, such as prostitutes who put themselves in very high-risk situations, or women who join the nightlife, become intoxicated and make errors in judgement regarding their safety as a consequence? Conversely, was she the only available victim on a quiet road in a small village at night? If that was the case then it is less likely the offender sought out that area specifically to find a victim, and he may have been there as part of his own routine activities.

Crime scene observations

The facts gathered from the crime scene can reveal something about the practicalities of the crime and the most likely explanations or antecedents for those. For instance, if a naked body is found in a field, in bushes or in the woods, statistical analysis suggests that it is more likely the offence took place in an indoor location and the body was transported by car afterwards, according to previous offences in which a naked body was deposited outdoors. Unless there are visible drag marks or the victim's feet are dirty, it can be inferred that the offender was physically strong enough to carry the victim from the vehicle to the deposition site. The latter may also suggest where the closest suitable location is that can be accessed by car, which may hold geographic as well as forensic clues such as car interior fibres, tyre marks and foot prints, for instance. If the car appeared to have been parked on one specific side of the road or tyre marks show that it turned around, this may indicate the direction of where the offender came from or where he returned to, which may be indicative of the location of his residence (Büchler & Leineweber, 1991; Rossmo, 2000).

The offender's choice of victim and offence site can reveal if the victim was targeted specifically or if access to her could be ascertained through observation. If the offence took place in the victim's home, the offender may have felt safe in the knowledge that she would be alone for a certain amount of time, which may mean he either knew her or possibly has observed her previously and knew that she lived by herself. If there are no signs that entry was forced, he may have been to the residence previously for another reason and may have enjoyed a certain level of trust from the victim. Alternatively, he could have observed that the victim was not living with a male or family – for instance he may have been a contractor or delivery person who carried out some work at her or a neighbour's residence previously. The crime scene may also assist in determining the sequence of events and the levels of violence and control involved. If it appears that there was a struggle and items were broken or moved etc., this may indicate that the offender did not instantly gain and retain control over the victim. Neighbours can be canvassed for any audible or visible signs as well as the timing of that struggle. If the crime scene looks as if it was cleaned by the offender, dustbins in the immediate as well as surrounding location should be searched for traces of blood and fibres, which also applies to vacuum cleaners and washing machines in the building. The victim's friends or family might be able to advise on items that were moved or removed, which may hold further clues. The presence of a struggle can also imply that a murder was not necessarily part of the

offender's initial motive but may have escalated out of a verbal or physical altercation, or because the offender panicked and did not know how to silence the
victim or prevent her from alerting anyone. This may mean that he did not actually intend to kill the victim, that none or not all of the offence was premeditated,
that he may in fact be an acquaintance of the victim rather than a stranger who
was intent on killing someone, that he may not have been prepared for the entire
offence and that he may lack maturity and competence in controlling himself and
another person, be it verbally or physically. It is also vital to identify the offender's hunting style (targeted, premeditated, spontaneous, deliberate, etc.) in order
to form investigative advice from that.

Victimology

The most common route of investigation is through the victim, where the OFAs
seek to identify the motive for the crime and likely suspects. It is essential to
analyse who the victim is/was, how she presented herself, how she came across
to others, how she would have dealt with confrontation and upon encountering
strangers, whom she would usually associate or come into contact with, etc. A
victim who was rather reclusive and kept to herself most of the time will require
investigative focus on her work and the few activities she did pursue, such
as grocery shopping whereas a victim who was part of the drugs scene would
necessitate far more investigation around her associates and her usual habits.
However, if the victim does not appear to be the focal point of the crime, i.e. she
was a random victim, the investigation will need to focus on the crime scene
instead. This is because the offender either has a connection to the victim or the
encounter site. If that were not the case, he would simply not have been there. If
the victim had set routine activities, such as attending classes or meetings in the
evenings, and she was doing so very regularly, then any break in such routines
can become of interest when attempting to identify when and where in her routine
she may have been intercepted by the offender. Likewise, routine habits such as
locking or not locking front doors, wearing certain shoes or clothes for specific
purposes, setting your alarm every night just before you go to bed etc. can
become useful investigatively when one of these routines has been violated, e.g.
in cases where an offender attempts to disguise a no-body murder as a deliberate
disappearance by the victim, for which he attempts to simulate her routine habits
but gets it wrong.

Victim's injuries

This thematic area in the OFA team's analysis process is explored in order to
help ascertain the offender's motive(s), levels of competence in offending and
knowledge about the crime location. If it appears he felt comfortable taking his
time with the victim either when she was still alive or after he killed her, this
might imply that he had the knowledge that no one would arrive to interrupt
the offence, as he knew either the location or the victim well enough to make

that assumption. If the victim's body was dismembered one can safely assume the offender found a location secluded or secure enough in which he could perform this task without worrying about the blood, sounds, smells or items used alerting anybody. If the victim's body (whether alive or dead) shows a number of hesitation cuts, the offender may not be very experienced in stabbing people or he may have inflicted these superficial injuries in order to prevent the victim from struggling, implying she may not have taken potential previous threats of the offender's seriously enough. If the victim sustained defence injuries to her lower arms, this suggests that the offender did not gain control over the victim straightaway and she was putting up a fight. Again, this could hint at a lack of maturity and criminal experience on the offender's part. Whenever looking at offenders' behaviours, the OFA team is very cognisant of the fact that more attention needs to be paid to offender-led behaviour, i.e. those things he decides to do and carries out, rather than victim-led behaviours, which result from an interaction and are sometimes beyond the offender's control. For instance, an offender may have a knife on him with the intention of threatening the victim with it should she put up too much of a struggle. However, during the offence itself, if for instance her children are nearby, he might be able to gain compliance simply by threatening to do something to her children if she continues to fight him. Therefore, even if he did bring a knife, he may not need to use it, but the fact that the victim cannot report a knife present should not be read as the offender not having brought items with him, which would usually prompt the OFA into rating that offence as less premeditated and that the offender was less prepared to commit the crime on that particular night. Most non-spontaneous offenders plan out the first steps of the crime, but as soon as the victim becomes a part of the script, there are likely to be changes to his decisions due to possibly unexpected victim behaviour. These unexpected circumstances may provide vital bits of information about the perpetrator, as they can reveal how he deals with crisis situations, with resistance, external stress factors, interruptions, etc. Someone who remains calm and collected in acutely critical situations may be more likely to be mature, older and more experienced than someone who overreacts at the first sign of conflict, such as an offender who immediately becomes overly violent in response to the victim not being as compliant as he had anticipated.

Offender profile

The offender profile consists of demographic parameters most commonly found in other offenders who have previously committed similar offences. This means that they describe the most likely features of the offender, not a specific individual whom the police should be searching for. Profiles are generated in order to prioritize lists of suspects so that the investigation is able to start their process of elimination with the most likely suspects and then work their way down the list. Though the main features of a profile are the offender's geography, i.e. how local he was to the crime site(s), his previous convictions and mental maturity in terms of developmental age, other inferences can also be drawn, e.g. whether he knew the victim, if he has access to a car, comes into contact with various sites as part of his employment, has access to specific instruments or tools as part of his employment, whether he only offends at times at which he can legitimately be away from his home address and therefore lives with someone, etc. The offender's behaviours can help infer which crimes he has experience in, e.g. someone who broke into a house and rapes the person who lives there is very likely to have committed burglaries before then. Rapists are usually criminal across a range of activities and may not necessarily have a conviction for rape (Davies *et al.*, 1998; House, 1997; Wilson & Alison, 2005), whereas a sexual murderer is more likely to have committed rapes before (Soothill et al., 2002). If the offender also committed theft in the index offence, again it is likely he has done that to some extent previously and may well be on police databases for theft offences. Salient behaviours of the offence are utilized as search parameters on various crime databases, in order to extract attributes of offenders who generally display such features. The more salient those features are, the more fine-tuned the research can be, and the more precise the resulting profile parameters are.

Discussion – Study 2

The data collected from the OFAs contains various indicators of perceptual expertise in identifying behavioural links to offenders' psychology, knowledge and decision making. For instance, they call on their extensive knowledge base of previous cases, which constitutes a trait of expertise (Militello *et al.*, 1997); they draw on their in-depth understanding of major crime and investigative psychology, common offender behaviours during the commission of crimes, base lines of various behaviours, and the connection between mental health and criminal behaviour. The OFAs further selectively focus their information intake on those bits they know from research and experience to be the most indicative of the offender's knowledge of the victim or the location, his criminal experience, and his intentions and capacity, amongst other things (e.g. offender-led behaviours), which also suggests that they have accumulated expertise in evaluating behaviours in a major crime context (Savelsbergh *et al.*, 2005). Additionally, they group the entirety of available crime information into meaningful topic areas or chunks such as the offending opportunity, sequence of events, sexual behaviours, control behaviours, motives, escalation, etc., which can then be analysed in turn, providing mental processing aids commonly found in experts (Chase and Simon, 1973). Their extensive mental database of previous cases, common offending behaviours and baselines is also supportive in the OFAs' recognizing abnormalities in behaviour, missed opportunities and when something that should have happened did not happen, which is another trait of expertise (Militello *et al.*, 1997).

One of the main tools in their analysis is the systematic reconstruction of the offence, in which the facts of the case are used to detail each stage of the offence in order to produce a coherent scenario of what exactly happened and which bits of information are missing or where there were anomalies in behaviour, both the victim's or the offender's. This assists in making the dynamics of the offence as well as the decision-making process of the offender more transparent. Their team approach is preventative of a clash of personalities between any individual OFA and the SIO, and of the proliferation of any one team member's ego and ability to take full credit for the successful conclusion of a case. Their focus is not on identifying an offender or investigating the offence (that is the job of the investigating team), but on explicitly providing support to the investigation through the use of meticulous analysis and expert knowledge of behaviours and offender decision-making in major crime, which local police units may lack, as stranger rapes and murders are a less frequent occurrence than volume crime, which is usually the bread and butter of a police force. The OFA team gives credence discriminatorily to various sources of information – objective facts such as photos, videos, a coroner's report, socio-demographic information on the location and police reports as well as hard evidence are more influential on the analysis process than are witness statements and sightings, which can be less accurate and may mislead the analytical process.

The eventual report and a presentation by the OFA team to the investigating team is a summary of the group analysis process. It details each hypothesis considered and the information supporting or refuting it. It further lists all the gaps in the case, such as unexplained behaviours, time gaps, etc. Hypotheses and inferences are then turned into investigative advice and lines of enquiry, with an appreciation of the investigation's resources and capabilities. The OFAs then remain very involved in supporting the police unit in putting their advice into practice and fulfil a supporting role until the case is concluded. As experienced police officers, they also provide interview advice, sometimes carrying out the interviews themselves; they offer media advice, suggest questions to ask during house-to-house enquiries and other ad-hoc support as required, as well as being able to oversee how their advice has been put into practice. Furthermore, as more information comes in, be it through ongoing investigative efforts, the OFAs' advice having been applied or a member of the public providing more information, the analysis has to take that into account and the resulting investigative advice may need to be adjusted. The OFA team sees their primary role in providing dynamic investigative advice through the offender's connection with the victim or the crime scene, and to enhance the investigation's understanding of the offence. Due to their high level of involvement they may be called to testify in court.

Since the OFA team works with the investigation very closely and almost up until the conclusion of the case, they are able to review their contribution in light of the offender apprehended and convicted. This immediate feedback allows for a critical analysis of their performance and to further develop, improve and fine-tune their procedures. They can discuss things they may have missed and where their hypotheses were inaccurate, as well as solidifying reliable practices and considering them as a matter of routine. When an offender has been committed to prison and is allocated to a psychological treatment programme, the treating psychologist or psychiatrist may use the OFA team's analysis in order to better understand their patient's offending and to fine-tune their treatment accordingly.

General discussion

Cognitive aspects of expertise in processing of behavioural information and connecting behaviours to offenders' psychology and their decision making was apparent in both groups of participants – the German OFAs and the UK BIAs.

It appears the profession carried out by both groups of participants has evolved away from instinctive concrete statements and predictions of what an offender would be like – as was more common place up until the late 1990s – to a far more scientific approach with an extensive research background and probabilistic inferences, backed up meticulously by a scientific audit trail leading back to statistics on major crime and offenders. This fact-based approach is utilized by professionals who, as suggested by the current studies, have accumulated expertise in identifying and linking an offender's behaviours to his psychology, knowledge of the victim or the crime location as well as his decision making, and turning that information into investigative advice.

The profession of the BIAs/OFAs is one that has developed over time. Whilst they felt more confident to make concrete statements and inferences towards the beginning of their careers in the 1990s, investigative experience and a need for professional responsibility has caused them to err on the side of caution, to cover all possibilities and be accountable with regards to their inferences and statements. Their reports now contain clear 'audit trails' and rationales along with the scientific and factual backing for their inferences, and they are sure not to provide advice that may cause an SIO to falsely exclude a suspect simply because he does not match certain criteria. Their work is not to be utilized as evidence or to implicate anyone, yet is tailored to support investigations and SIOs' decision-making processes. With increased exposure to major crimes, the BIAs have also drifted further from the working practices and thought processes that novices are more likely to employ. The ACTA analysis suggests they are able to identify common pitfalls and natural tendencies to make false assumptions and to focus on what is the most obvious, and are prepared to counter these in order to be able to provide the best service possible. The ability to avoid such automaticity, i.e. being too guided by previous experience and becoming less meticulous with increasing confidence thought to be a by-product of expertise (Militello *et al.*, 1997), is a crucial skill of experts (Richler *et al.*, 2008).

The single activity of writing an offender profile is often mistakenly assumed to be the bread and butter of the BIA/OFA, when, in fact, it is only one of the tools they may choose from if appropriate for any one case. On the other hand, the crime scene assessment and the main analysis are very comprehensive and indeed the main products of the OFA's/BIA's; they are the processes that can lead to new lines of enquiry, identify forensic opportunities and the best way forward for the investigation. A profile is simply a prioritization tool that the media have sensationalized to such an extent that even some academics mistake it as representing and constituting the entire profession. Since the specification of the statistically most likely demographic parameters of the perpetrator (i.e. the profile) is only a by-product of the behavioural assessment that the OFAs/BIAs undertake and indeed a rather minor part of their report, basing an avenue of research upon it assuming that this would accurately assess the entire profession is a misguided undertaking. Conversely, if valid and appropriate pieces of research were to identify shortcomings in the methodology, it would be the BIA's/OFA's professional obligation to seek to improve on this particular aspect of their work, and their adjustments to laying a scientific audit trail show that they are more than willing to continue professionalizing their work and making it more transparent. The issue became problematic however, when the entire profession was questioned as to its validity simply because potential weaknesses were identified (justified though they were) in the processes of 'profiling'. In the UK and Germany, BIAs/OFAs are not just profilers – where necessary they will produce a profile for an investigation, however their remit is much wider than that; thus to discredit the entirety of their work based on flawed studies that focus on one single aspect of their work would be inappropriate and misleading.

The provision of behavioural investigative advice is a routine addition to complex major crime investigations throughout the UK as well as Germany and some other countries, mostly in cases of stranger murders and stranger rapes; however BIAs/OFAs may also be called in for serial rape offences, abductions or in missing person cases, amongst others. Despite its wide use, there is a clear lack of understanding about the remit, content and capacity of this specialized kind of advice, both amongst police who might hope for concrete and firm direction leading them to one specific suspect, yet also amongst academics and journalists. These groups of 'users' and 'observers' of the profession have, in many cases, failed to observe the evolution of the discipline, and may still be under the impression that what a BIA/OFA is supposed to do is attend a crime scene, close their eyes and replay what happened during the commission of the crime in their mind, to then declare the psychopathology, employment and appearance of the perpetrator, as well as whom he lives with. Since the actual processes that constitute the provision of behavioural investigative advice have hitherto not been scientifically explored and published to a great extent, it is understandable why many authors of news articles or academic papers have had to rely on their existing misconceptions. Most studies into 'profiling' have focused on the output generated by the profiler or BIA/OFA, i.e. only their reports and statements have been scrutinized. Such research has been both beneficial and misleading, in that some papers highlighted a lack of accountability and scientific 'audit trail' in reports as suggested in Alison *et al.* (2003), which prompted the NPIA's BIAs and Germany's OFAs into solidifying their working practices, backing up each of their statements with academic research and crime statistics, and therefore providing a positive shift in accountability and scientific method (Almond, Alison & Porter, 2007). The research into the accuracy of reports, statements and inferences however, has been problematic for the reasons mentioned above, i.e. that these studies (e.g. Kocsis, 2004; Kocsis *et al.*, 2002) in fact evaluated the accuracy of the general statistical basis of the statements, rather than the competence of the BIA/OFA or the benefit they offer to investigations. One might compare this false generalization to a doctor advising her patient to make major lifestyle changes in order to prevent another heart attack, for instance. Her advice may contain statements such as: exercise regularly, limit the amount of alcohol and cigarettes consumed, limit the amount of red meat, sweets and fatty foods eaten, reduce stress levels and listen to calming music in order to reduce the heart rate. If a researcher now was to measure how much of an effect any one of those pieces of advice in isolation had on the patient's future likelihood of having a heart attack, the flaw in the methodology becomes more obvious. First, if the heart patient only reduces his intake of sweets, yet still has choleric reactions to stressful situations, and did not heed any of the other pieces of advice given, his likelihood of having another heart attack may remain high. This, however, does not mean that the physician's advice was futile. It simply illustrates that a more holistic approach is needed in order to tackle the problem and that single statements extracted from a diagnosis or report cannot realistically be viewed in isolation. Second, it is now almost common knowledge that someone with a heart condition should take the above measures in order to reduce the risk of a recurrence of a cardiac episode. The patient's spouse and children may be telling him that quite regularly. However, that basic knowledge does not qualify them as doctors, and even though they may be aware of how to reduce the risk factors just as much as the physician is aware of them, this does not constitute the validity of designing a study in which physicians and lay people are compared as to their ability to provide advice to heart patients. Unfortunately, that is what some studies have done – relied on the common knowledge of some principles of offending in the population and used that as a measure of the BIAs'/OFAs' utility. Naturally, if these studies then state that lay people can perform just as well as BIAs/OFAs, the reputation of those professionals is tarnished, unless one looks deeper into the studies' design. In all research, it is vital to have picked the accurate variable to be measured, and to ensure that this variable is indeed representative of the issue to be researched.

The authors would argue that the above extraction of the BIAs'/OFAs' cognitive working practices highlights scientific thought processes and a reliance on facts and psychological research. This would suggest that providing behavioural investigative advice in the UK and Germany is a valid scientific addition to major crime investigations that cannot be likened nor reduced to subjective methods of the single activity of offender profiling, which do still appear in the media from time to time. It appears these professionals have developed a discipline that makes concerted efforts to back up claims, consider alternatives and to make the bases for their decisions clear and transparent. Therefore, it seems these are not the idle speculations of self-professed intuitive experts, but rather an experienced, considered view informed by many years of working on particularly complex cases of violent crime. Furthermore, hallmark features of perceptual expertise have been identified in the cognitive processes of BIAs/OFAs that would support the argument that qualified and experienced OFAs/BIAs have developed specific expertise in analysing behaviour for the purpose of providing investigative advice to police investigations.

Future directions

The inherent limitations of any study that works with the 'top people' in a particular field is the fact that the more specialized the profession becomes, the fewer potential experts there are to study. Consequently, the sample size of any expertise study will be much smaller than that of many other qualitative or quantitative studies, especially those that enjoy the luxury of being able to use a captive audience such as students as their participants. The current studies had only five and four participants in each group respectively, and even though that is a small sample size per se, it should be appreciated that the amount of data generated through the ACTA procedure is so comprehensive that it might well produce a data-overload if conducted with a much bigger sample size. Nevertheless, since the participants of the BIA study constituted 100 per cent of the NPIA BIAs working in the UK, and the OFA study's participants represented 100 per cent of acting senior OFAs in the German state of Bavaria, the researchers would argue that the representative strength of the samples might in fact be stronger than one which could be achieved by using 100 random people to represent a much larger population, as their values would always have to be averaged, as well as many outlier cases having to have to be excluded. Another potential limitation is that the ACTA process applied in this research might prompt the participant to voice more thoughts, alternatives and ideas in this study context than they would usually produce were they working in their normal environment. Such social desirability response bias (Arnold and Feldman, 1981) could not be eliminated by the researcher (first author) of this self-report study and its effect on the results is unknown.

It is suggested that future research attempts to replicate the promising findings of these studies with BIAs/OFAs of other countries in order to establish common ground and differences in working practices among the behavioural investigative advisers in different parts of the world. If a concerted effort could be made to standardise best practice across countries and to adopt the most successful techniques, these professionals as well as the populations they serve could benefit greatly from intelligent applications of psychology to police investigations. Furthermore, it would be interesting to investigate the extent of the expertise identified here. We have mentioned previously that expertise is domain-specific (Gilis *et al.*, 2008) and tied to a particular knowledge base (Militello *et al.*, 1997). Ascertaining which other uses such expertise in analysing behaviour could be applied to, as well as its boundaries, might have implications for further deployment of such professionals, or the development of training methods in other disciplines. In the meantime, the authors hope that the research presented here has made a valid starting point in revealing the cognitive science behind providing behavioural investigative advice, and strengthened the validity of the use of psychology in police work to support the effort to stop criminals from doing harm onto others.

References

Abernethy, B. (1987) 'Anticipation in sport: a review', *Physical Education Review*, 10: 5–16.

Abernethy, B., Gill, D.P., Parks, S.L. and Packer, S.T. (2001) 'Expertise and the perception of kinematic and situational probability information', *Perception*, 30: 233–52.

Alison, L. and Eyre, M. (2009) *Killer in the Shadows: the monstrous crimes of Robert Napper*, London: Pennant Books.

Alison, L., Smith, M.D., Eastman, C and Rainbow, L. (2003) 'Toulmin's philosophy of argument and its relevance to offender profiling', *Psychology, Crime and Law*, 9: 173–183.

Allard, F., Parker, S., Deakin, J. and Rodgers, W. (1993) 'Declarative knowledge in skilled motor performance: Byproduct or constituent?', in J.L. Starkes and F. Allard (eds), *Cognitive Issues in Motor Expertise*, Amsterdam: Elsevier.

Almond, L., Alison, L.J. and Porter, L.E. (2007) 'An evaluation and comparison of claims made in behavioural investigative advice reports compiled by the National Policing Improvement Agency in the United Kingdom', *Journal of Investigative Psychology and Offender Profiling*, 4: 71–83.

Arnold, H.J. and Feldman, D.C. (1981) 'Social desirability response bias in self-report choice situations', *Academy of Management Journal*, 24(2): 377–385.

Büchler, H. and Leineweber, H. (1991) 'The escape behaviour of bank robbers and circular blockade operations by the police', in E. Kube and H.U. Störzer (eds) *Police research in the Federal Republic of Germany: 15 years research within the "Bundeskriminalamt"*, Berlin: Springer-Verlag.

Canter, D.V. (2004) 'Offender profiling and investigative psychology', *Journal of Investigative Psychology and Offender Profiling*, 1: 1–15.

Chase, W.G. and Ericsson, K. A. (1982) 'Skill and working memory', in G.H. Bower (ed.) *The psychology of learning and motivation*, New York: Academic Press.

Chase, W.G. and Simon, H.A. (1973) 'The mind's eye in chess', in W.G. Chase (ed.) *Visual information processing*, New York: Academic Press.

Davies, A., Wittebrood, K. and Jackson, J.L. (1998) *Predicting the criminal record of a stranger rapist*, London: Home Office Policing and Reducing Crime Unit.

de Groot, A.D. (1946) *Het denken van den schaker. Een experimenteel psychologische studie* [The thinking of the chess player. An experimental psychology study], Amsterdam: Noord-Hollandsche Uitgeversmaatschappij.

Dern, H., Erpenbach, H., Hasse, G., Horn, A., Kroll, J, Schu, M. And Tröster, A. (2003) *Qualitätsstandards der Fallanalyse. Festlegung von Qualit ätsstandards für die Anwendung fallanalytischer Verfahren durch die Polizei des Bundes und der Länder*, Wiesbaden: Bundeskriminalamt.

Ericsson, K.A. (2005) 'Recent advances in expertise research: A commentary on the contributions to the special issue', *Applied Cognitive Psychology*, 19: 233–241.

Ericsson, K.A. and Kintsch, W. (1995) 'Long-term working memory', *Psychological Review*, 102: 211–245.

Ericsson, K.A., Charness, N., Feltovich, P. and Hoffman, R.R. (eds) (2006) *Cambridge handbook on expertise and expert performance,* Cambridge: Cambridge University Press.

Farrington, D.P. and Lambert, S. (1997) 'Predicting offender profiles from victim and witness descriptions', in J.L. Jackson and D.A. Bekerian (eds) *Offender profiling: Theory, research, and practice*, Chichester: Wiley.

Gilis, B., Helsen, W., Catteeuw, P. and Wagemans, J. (2008) 'Offside decisions by expert assistant referees in association football: Perception and recall of spatial positions in complex dynamic events', *Journal of Experimental Psychology*, 14(1): 21–35.

House, J.C. (1997) 'Towards a practical application of offender profiling: The RNC's criminal suspect prioritization system', in J.L. Jackson and D.A. Bekerian (eds) *Offender profiling, theory research and practice*, Chichester: Wiley.

Kalakoski, V. (2007) 'Effect of skill level on recall of visually presented patterns of musical notes', *Scandinavian Journal of Psychology*, 48: 87–96.

Keppel, R.D. and Weis, J.G. (1993) *Improving the investigation of violent crime: the homicide investigation and tracking system*, Washington, DC: National Institute of Justice.

Klein, G.A., Calderwood, R. and MacGregor, D. (1989) 'Critical Decision Method for Eliciting Knowledge', *IEEE Transactions on Systems, Man, and Cybernetics*, May/June: 462–472.

Kocsis, R.N. (2004) 'Psychological profiling of serial arson skills: an assessment of skills and accuracy', *Criminal Justice and Behavior*, 31: 341–361.

Kocsis, R.N., Hayes, A.F. and Irwin, H.J. (2002) 'Investigative experience and accuracy in psychological profiling of a violent crime', *Journal of Interpersonal Violence*, 17: 811–823.

Militello, L.G., Hutton, R.J.B., Pliske, R.M., Knight, B.J. and Klein, G. (1997) *Applied Cognitive Task Analysis (ACTA) Methodology*, San Diego, CA: Navy Personnel Research and Development Center.

Mislevy, R.J. (2010) 'Some implications of expertise research for educational assessment', *Research Papers in Education*, 25(3): 253–270.

Norman, G. (2005) 'From theory to application and back again: Implications of research on medical expertise for psychological theory', *Canadian Journal of Experimental Psychology*, 59: 35–40.

Prince, R. (2010) 'Fleshing out Expertise: the making of creative industries experts in the United Kingdom', *Geoforum*, 41: 875–884.

Richler, J.J., Gauthier, I., Wenger, M.J. and Palmeri, T.J. (2008) 'Holistic processing of faces: perceptual and decisional components', *Journal of Experimental Psychology, Learning, Memory, and Cognition*, 34(2): 328–342.

Rossmo, D.K. (2000) *Geographic Profiling*, Boca Raton, FL: CRC Press.

Salfati, C.G. (2000) 'The nature of expressiveness and instrumentality in homicide: implications for offender profiling', *Homicide Studies*, 4: 265–293.

Salthouse, T.A. (1991) 'Expertise as the circumvention of human processing limitations', in K.A. Ericcson and J. Smith (eds) *Toward a general theory of expertise*, Cambridge: Cambridge University Press.

Savelsbergh, G.J.P., Van der Kamp, J., Williams, A.M. and Ward, P. (2005) 'Anticipation and visual search behaviour in expert soccer goalkeepers', *Ergonomics*, 48: 1686–1697.

Shanteau, J. (1985) 'Psychological characteristics of expert decision makers', *Applied Experimental Psychology Series*, 85.

Snook, B., Eastwood, J., Gendreau, P., Goggin, C. and Cullen, R.M. (2007) 'Taking Stock of Criminal Profiling: a narrative review and meta-analysis', *Criminal Justice & Behaviour*, 34: 437.

Soothill, K., Francis, B., Ackerley, E. and Fligelstone, R. (2002) *Murder and serious sexual assault: What criminal histories can reveal about future serious offending*, London: Home Office.

Williams, A.M. and Burwitz, L. (1993) 'Advance cue utilization in soccer', in T. Reilly, J. Clarys and A. Stibbe (eds) *Science and Football II*, London: E & FN Spon.

Wilson, G. and Alison, L. (2005) 'Suspect prioritization in the investigation of sex offences: from clinical classification and profiling to pragmatism', in L. Alison (ed) *The forensic psychologist's casebook: psychological profiling and criminal investigation*, Cullompton: Willan Publishing.

APPENDIX 5.1

Extracting Expertise using Applied Cognitive Task Analysis

The desire of researchers to articulate and extract expertise has produced a variety of methods which attempt to identify crucial skills, strategies and processes in an expert that set them apart from everyone else. One large industry that benefits from such expertise extraction techniques is in IT, where programmers develop computer systems that aim to mimic and automate human decision-making processes in order to take over specific tasks and processes (Bonaceto & Burns, 2007). It is such cognitive processes that are also of interest in the field of behavioural analytical expertise. Methods used for extracting those processes attempt to model experts' cognition and knowledge. For this purpose, techniques of Cognitive Task Analysis have been developed that identify the crucial complex cognitive elements in a field of expertise, a job, a task or an action (Gordon & Gill, 1997; Schraagen, Chipman, & Shalin, 2000). Such methods focus on the cognitive elements that are central to decision-making, judgements and goal generation (Militello & Hutton, 1998). These techniques usually include high-level descriptions of the task in which the expertise is to be articulated, coupled with lengthy in-depth interviews with experts to extract cognitive strategies and other key mental processes. However, it has been found that Cognitive Task Analysis can be very draining on time factors (both the interviewer's but also the expert's), and on the whole is a rather lengthy process. Nevertheless, it was used as the core of a more economical technique, Applied Cognitive Task Analysis (ACTA, developed by Klein Associates Inc., Militello et al., 1997), which is a more efficient and less time-consuming approach (Militello & Hutton, 1998). The ACTA process requires the expert to articulate their work in a manner which will allow for crucial stages in the task to become apparent and their underlying cognitive processes to be examined. ACTA consists of three distinct parts: The Task Diagram, the Knowledge Audit, and the Simulation Interview.

In the *Task Diagram* phase, the expert is asked to break their task of expertise (i.e. their specific job or role) down into three to six consecutive subtasks. These subtasks are written down to provide a broad yet systematic overview of the job in question. The expert is then asked to identify which of those subtasks listed require the most cognitive skill in the form of making judgements, decisions, or requiring a great deal of cognitive processing. Those subtasks are again divided into three to six sub-subtasks by the expert. The resulting task diagram is then used as the framework for the in-depth interview that is to follow.

The *Knowledge Audit* explores the subtasks identified by the expert as requiring the most amount of cognitive skill during the task diagram interview. In the context of each of those subtasks, many skills associated with expertise are probed, including the ability to detect patterns, anomalies and opportunities, as well as being able to see the big picture and making inferences about the starting point and the likely outcome of a given scenario. Using this process, specific examples of aspects of expertise are elicited and it is established why novices might find some aspects difficult as well as identifying strategies and cues used by experts. This can provide vital insight into the differences between experts and novices in that particular task and can therefore elicit key issues that can be utilised in training novices. This phase of the ACTA process was developed to capture knowledge categories that are thought to best characterise expertise (Militello & Hutton, 1998).

During the *Simulation Interview*, the expert is guided through a specific scenario they might encounter during their work whilst the interviewer probes the cognitive processes the expert is going through. For each major event, decision or judgement during that simulation, the interviewer attempts to ascertain the expert's assessment of the situation at the time, what actions they would take, which cues led the expert to that assessment or action, and likely errors that might be made by a novice in that situation. One of the primary objectives of this phase of the ACTA process is to aid the understanding of decisions and judgements (Militello et al., 1997).

In order to feed back useful information to the experts or be able to develop training courses or experts systems, the information gathered during the ACTA interviews can be consolidated into a *cognitive demands table* (Militello & Hutton, 1998). This can provide a useful overview of the task at hand, and will also display its cognitive elements, demanding aspects, common errors and coping strategies. Further, a *critical cue inventory* can be constructed which was originally developed for use with the Critical Decision Method, another technique to elicit knowledge from experts (Klein, Calderwood, & MacGregor, 1989). This can display perceptual cues that experts identify by extracting patterns from seemingly random information that can then inform crucial inferences to be utilized by the investigation.

References

Bonaceto, C. & Burns, K. (2007) 'A survey of the methods and uses of cognitive engineering' In R.R. Hoffman (ed) *Expertise Out Of Context*, Lawrence Erlbaum Associates.

Gordon, S. E. & Gill, R.T. (1997) Cognitive Task Analysis. In C.E. Zsambok & G. Klein (eds.) *Naturalistic Decision-Making* (pp. 131–140). Mahwah, NJ. Lawrence Erlbaum Associates.

Klein, G.A., Calderwood, R., & MacGregor, D. (1989) '*Critical Decision Method for Eliciting Knowledge*', IEEE Transactions on Systems, Man, and Cybernetics, May/June, pp. 462–472.

Militello, L.G., Hutton, R.J.B., Pliske, R.M., Knight, B.J. & Klein, G. (1997) '*Applied Cognitive Task Analysis (ACTA) Methodology*' (Rep. No. NPRDCTN-98-4). San Diego, CA: Navy Personnel Research and Development Center.

Militello, L.G., Hutton, R.J.B. (1998) 'Applied cognitive task analysis (ACTA): a practitioner's toolkit for understanding cognitive task demands' *Ergonomics*, Vol. 41, No. 11, 1618–1641.

APPENDIX 5.2

Knowledge Audit

SUBTASK x from Task Diagram

	EXAMPLE	CUES & STRATEGIES	WHY DIFFICULT?
		What cues or strategies do you use in this situation?	*Why is this task hard for novices or why don't novices do that?*
Perceptual Skills Experts detect cues and patterns and make discriminations that novices can't see. Can you think of any examples here?			
Anomaly Experts can notice when something unusual happens. They can quickly detect deviations, or notice when something that should happen doesn't. Can you think of any examples here?			
Past and Future Experts can guess how the current situation arose and they can anticipate how the current situation will evolve. Can you think of any instance in which this happened, either where the experts were successful or novices fell short?			
Big Picture If you were watching novices, how would you know that they don't have the big picture?			

(Continued)

	EXAMPLE	CUES & STRATEGIES	WHY DIFFICULT?
		What cues or strategies do you use in this situation?	Why is this task hard for novices or why don't novices do that?
Tricks of the Trade Are there tricks of the trade that you use?			
Improvizing or Noticing Opportunities Can you recall a situation when you noticed that following the standard procedure wouldn't work? What did you do? Can you think of an example where the procedure would have worked but you saw that you could get more from the situation by taking a different action?			
Self-monitoring and Adjustment Experts notice when their performance is sub-par, and can often figure out WHY this is happening (e.g. high workload, fatigue, boredom, distraction) in order to make adjustments. Can you think of an example when you did this?			
Information Unless you're careful, misinformation can mislead you. Novices tend to believe whatever the information says. Can you think of examples where you had to rely on experience to avoid being fooled by misinformation?			
Scenario From Hell If you were going to give someone a scenario to teach someone humility – that this is a tough job – what would you put into that scenario? Did you ever have an experience that taught you humility in performing this job?			

APPENDIX 5.3

Simulation interview

Participant XX

Simulation Case

"Please review this case keeping in mind that I will be asking you about the decisions and judgements you are going to make in this investigation"

"Think back over this investigation. Please list the major events / decision-points / judgements that occurred during the incident."

Event / Decision Judgement /	Situational Assessment	Actions	Critical Cues	Alternative	Potential Errors
Major events / crucial points in the investigation	What do you think is going on here? What's your assessment of the situation at this point in time?	What actions, if any, would you take at this point in time?	What pieces of information led you to this situational assessment / action?	Are there any alternative ways you could interpret this situation? Are there any alternative courses of action that you would consider at this point?	What errors would a novice be likely to make? Are there cues they would miss?

APPENDIX 5.4

Task diagram

"Think about what you do when you provide Behavioural Investigative Advice (BIA) to a stranger murder/rape investigation. Can you break this task down into 3–6 steps? / Can you decompose this task into 3–6 subtasks?"

<u>Providing BIA to an investigation</u>

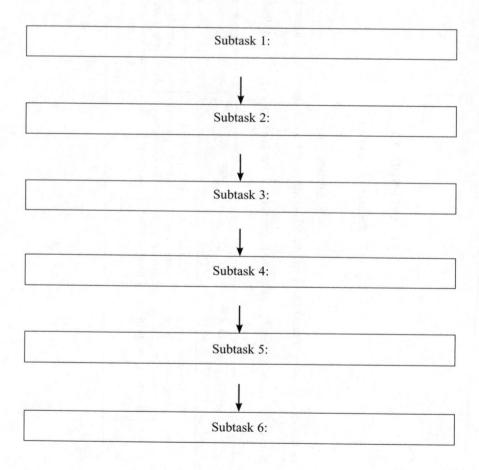

"Out of these subtasks you have just identified, which ones require the most cognitive skills? By that I mean judgements, assessments, problem-solving, decision-making and thinking skills"

"Can you decompose this subtask into 3–6 sub-subtasks?"

<u>Sub-Task Chosen</u>

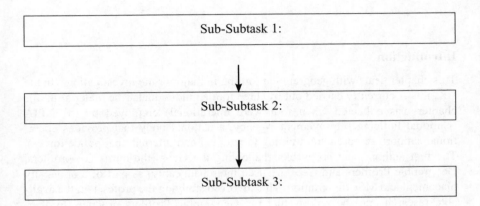

6 The cognitive expertise of Geographic Profilers

Susanne Knabe-Nicol and
Laurence Alison

Introduction

This chapter deals with geographic profiling in major crime investigations. In the UK, this is currently carried out by three trained individuals (the material in this chapter was collected when four were operational) employed by the NPIA (National Policing Improvement Agency, a national body that provides operational support, research and training to national and international police forces). The first author spent six weeks shadowing the Geos (the terms Geoprofilers, Geographic Profilers and Geos are used interchangeably) as part of a university placement and MSc dissertation. This involved studying the profession, the available research and the reports that the Geographic Profilers produce. Further, detailed one-to-one interviews were conducted by the first author as part of this qualitative study, to assess the cognitive processes involved in geographic profiling, along with a quantitative pilot study to examine the Geos' utility to investigations of single offences (as opposed to serial crimes).

Since geoprofiling is a highly specialized aspect of police work, the number of Geo experts available to study is extremely small. For this reason amongst others, this research relies principally on a qualitative consideration of the cognitive processes of Geos. Readers familiar with the field of geoprofiling will be aware that most research focuses on the accuracy and efficiency of prioritization of search areas or predictions of home locations when looking for the most likely base of an unknown serial offender. However, as far as the authors are aware, this is the first effort to examine geographic profiling from a more *holistic and process-driven approach*, rather than merely scrutinizing their output. To this end, Applied Cognitive Task Analysis (ACTA, *Militello et al.*, 1997) formed part of what we relied on in extracting and articulating the internal processes involved in geographic profiling. For a detailed description of the ACTA methodology, see Appendix 5.1 of this book.

As noted previously in this volume, there appears to be a widespread misconception of criminal profiling generally. With regards to geographic profiling specifically, this is often misrepresented as being 'just' a statistical tool for the identification of the most likely home base of a serial offender (Rossmo, 1997, 2000; Ratcliffe, 2004). However, the current research proposes that geoprofiling offers a range of outputs that may assist in major crime investigations beyond areas of prioritization. Further, we suggest that Geos might successfully be deployed in single offence cases rather than requiring three or more crimes in a series to generate useful material for the investigation. As we will outline, preliminary results suggest that the range of tasks Geos undertake and the techniques they apply are much more diverse and go well beyond using crime sites to produce a probability map of the most promising search areas (either manually or using specialized software). Furthermore, the quantitative study (Study 2) suggests that Geos may be able to successfully apply their expertise in analysing geographic behaviour to provide investigative advice in single offence cases, as opposed to only being able to assist when there is a serial offender under consideration.

Background

Academics and others have generally described geographic profiling along the lines of 'an investigative technique designed to aid police investigations into serial crimes' (Ratcliffe, 2004), or a 'strategic information management system designed to support serial violent crime investigations', (Rossmo, 2000), for instance. Even the operational community and the NPIA's website itself, stipulate that 'Geographic analysis...is based on the analysis of the locations of a connected series of offences' (NPIA, 2010). However, perhaps a more accurate and holistic definition might be as follows: 'a specialized subset of behavioural analysis directed at examining the geographic and temporal decision-making of an offender, in order to provide investigative advice'. This definition does not limit geographic profiling to serial crime.

There is a quantitative aspect to geoprofiling, which utilizes a number of crime site locations (e.g. encounter, attack, deposition and sighting sites) to infer the most likely base (usually home or work) of an offender. This aspect has also been 'automated' by computer systems that receive crime locations as input, and then output a map that indicates areas of varying degrees of probability that might contain the offender's home base. This pattern recognition process (whether carried out tacitly or with software) is possibly the single feature of geoprofiling that has received the most attention in academic literature, and has sparked some interesting academic debates (e.g. Snook, Canter & Bennell, 2002; Snook, Taylor & Bennell, 2004), including research comparing the accuracy of 'lay people' (students and police officers, i.e. not Geographic Profilers) using two heuristics, i.e. principles fundamental to geographic profiling (the circle hypothesis and the distance decay theory), with the accuracy of computer systems that were programmed based on the very same principles. The circle hypothesis suggests that a serial violent offender's residence is most likely to be found within a geographic circle that has as its diameter an imaginary line connecting the two offences in a series that are the furthest from each other (Canter & Larkin, 1993; Kocsis & Irwin, 1997; Tamura & Suzuki, 1997). The distance decay theory predicts a negative correlation between the distance from an offender's base and the amount of offences he commits in areas around that base (Brantingham & Brantingham, 1984). Snook *et al.*'s results indicated that lay persons could perform as well as, or better than the software at prioritizing search areas or indicating the most likely location of an offender's home base by arming them with these simple geographic 'rules of thumb'. Whilst instructive, these studies have sometimes drifted into misrepresentative generalizations about the profession and could, without clear reference to the restrictive caveats of the research, be utilized to throw the profession into question insofar as generating issues such as: 'if a layperson can do what the software or the experts can do, why do we need the software or the experts?' However, before we throw the baby out with the bathwater, we need to be very clear on what it is that Geo Profilers actually do. If it really is a simple matter of demarcating an 'x marks the spot' task, then Snook *et al.* may have a valid point. However, the current research shows that Geographic Profilers are not simply sitting in an office with a computer or a pen guessing where an offender might live. We need to examine what it actually is they do, rather than slip into simple straw-man arguments to decry the profession.

Snook *et al.* may indeed be correct in stipulating that software is not necessary to prioritize search areas in serial crime, and that it can be done manually/mentally by someone who understands the underlying statistical probabilities of geographic profiling. Certainly, accredited Geographic Profilers might be skilled and experienced enough to perform this task successfully. However, it should be clarified that it would be misleading to convey the impression that this one particular aspect of geographic analysis is representative of the entire discipline of geographic profiling, as in fact it is only one facet of it.

Expertise in geographic profiling

The aim of the placement was to focus on the qualitative side of geographic profiling, the expertise in geographic behaviour inherent within it, which has received little attention in operational or academic literature so far. This study examines the actual professionals who do the geographic profiling, rather than their reports and inferences. The sample size is small by definition, as it is a group of highly-specialized individuals under examination. The more specialized the demographic section of the population under investigation, the smaller the amount of potential participants in such research. NPIA Geo Profilers undergo a two-year internationally accredited training process. Further, they have many years of experience of operational police work and varied backgrounds in policing and academia. As such, and based on the perspective that domain-specific knowledge over a number of years can generate specialist skills, a core feature for discussion relates to the psychology of expertise in geographic profiling. Shanteau (1988) describes expertise as entailing superior perceptual and conceptual skills and as being domain-specific (Gilis *et al.*, 2008). Other skills include the ability to process large amounts of information more efficiently as chunks rather than single unrelated pieces of information (Chase & Simon, 1973), perceiving abnormalities or when something is amiss, and recognizing why one is thinking or doing what one is thinking or doing, i.e. possessing 'metacognitive' skills (Militello *et al.*, 1997). Further, experts are thought to have developed automaticity in their tasks of expertise, which greatly helps to reduce cognitive load (Militello *et al.*, 1997).

The aim of the placement was to identify, both through shadowing and observation as well as interviews, exactly what Geoprofilers actually do, and how they cognitively utilize their expertise. This exploratory process also led to the identification of various techniques and processes employed by the Geos, which are rarely if ever discussed in the research literature, yet may be vital to major crime investigations.

The Geos' ability to identify the most relevant information from what is sometimes an overwhelming number of documents, reports, interview videos, maps and statements, appears to be in line with expertise literature that refers to 'advance cues' (Abernethy, 1987; Williams and Burwitz, 1993; Abernethy et al., 2001) – i.e. an ability to identify and extract those particular bits of information that are most likely to have inferential or predictive value to the Geographic Profiler. Experts do not tend to take in more information per se; rather they take in information more selectively (Savelsbergh, Van der Kamp, Williams, & Ward, 2005), paying attention to those cues that are of value to making an accurate prediction or inference.

Within an ongoing investigation, many different individuals such as investigators, Behavioural Investigative Advisers, analysts and Geos might have access to identical sets of information. However, each individual involved in the investigation may use the available information differently, depending on their particular remit, skills, task, experience and expertise. A Geo will deal with information and data that can help generate inferences about an offender's movements and geographical and temporal decision-making processes. They attempt to reconstruct how the perpetrator came to choose the crime location(s), how he travelled, why he was at a particular place at a particular time, why he chose that particular victim, how he knew the location where the victim or target was attacked, how he knew a target or victim was going to be there, where he might have escaped to, and so forth. It is precisely this aspect of the Geographic Profilers' work, their expertise in providing investigative advice based on such crime information, which is going to be examined in Study 1.

Study 1 – Extracting the cognitive processes in geoprofiling

The participants for this study were the four Geoprofilers of the NPIA (data collected in 2008). Their ages ranged from 31 to 51, with the mean age being 45. There was one female and three males. Between them, they had 97 years' worth of operational experience, comprising roles such as Police Constable, Police Sergeant, Detective Constable, Detective Sergeant, Detective Inspector and Senior Crime Analyst, amongst others. Each of them held academic qualifications at either Bachelor's or Master's level. They were qualified Geographic Profilers accredited by the International Criminal Investigative Analysis Fellowship with an average of six years' experience as a Geographic Profiler.

The ACTA methodology is explained in detail in Appendix 5.1 and will therefore not be discussed in this chapter. It should be noted that this interviewing procedure was utilized in Study 1 because it was deemed fit for purpose. However, the researcher (first author) was not formally trained in ACTA, and drew her knowledge in conducting these interviews from the literature published by the developers of this process.

The output/result of the ACTA expertise extraction process was consolidated by the researcher into a cognitive demands table (Table 6.1) and a critical cue inventory (Table 6.2) for geographic profiling.

Table 6.1 Cognitive demands table for geographic profiling

Difficult cognitive element	*Why difficult?*	*Common errors*	*Cues and strategies*
Analyse information (schedule of offences, reports, statements, maps, demographic information, crimes plotted on maps) provided by investigation.	Information might be missing; information might be incomplete; information might be contradictory; information might be incorrect; information might be lacking in detail; there may be vast amounts of information to work through under time pressure; linkage difficult to establish if no forensics available and many errors can be made.	Novices often accept information given at face value; they might not question veracity of information given as they assume that investigators are right; lack confidence to question what was provided to them; are not aware that very often something will be missing or simply wrong; may not realise that different MO can be due to different opportunities or circumstances at the time rather than different offender; don't have the experience of seeing series of cases to know which range of variety/ differences is to be expected and which range is suspicious; might fail to link later crimes in different area as further away, which might actually be due to displacement; might make decisions about linkage too dependent upon behaviour and not considering time and geography enough.	Always question everything you're given; never accept anything at face value; always check everything for yourself; visit crime scenes; map information in your own tables; plot the crime sites on maps yourself; query if property deposition primary or secondary (i.e. deposited by offender or re-deposited by someone else who found item); analyse MO and behaviour to confirm linkage; always consider opportunities and target backcloth when trying to determine linkage rather than relying on behavioural information alone; be aware that police look for 'crimes', not necessarily 'incidents' that might have been caused by offender but not recorded, they could provide vital clues.

continued

Table 6.1 Cont'd

Difficult cognitive element	Why difficult?	Common errors	Cues and strategies
Identify patterns in spatial behaviour[1]	There might not be any apparent pattern; aspects common to offence sites might be personal to offender and therefore hidden to investigation; there might be offence 'outliers' that seem to defy an emerging pattern; linkage can be difficult to ascertain in the absence of forensic evidence – no guarantee that known offences are linked or that series is complete (i.e. there might be other related offences not included in this case); might not be clear if something is meaningful or might have happened by chance; need to attempt to extract offender's routine activity.	Novices might give up too soon; might fail to exclude outliers if necessary; might fail to see spatial behaviour in relation to temporal aspects of offences; might fail to visit crime sites to gain deeper understanding of locations and their potential significance; might not probe deeply enough into offender's decision-making process; might fail to investigate area surrounding crime sites e.g. access, demographics; might not analyse witness/ victim statements thoroughly enough to identify spatial information; novices often do not realise importance of post-offence movements and locations, such as property deposition sites that can reveal direction of escape, often towards residence; might not think to plot all information available to make sense of it; might not be aware of underlying psychological theories, of significance of extracting meaning from data; might not display/plot/ map information in meaningful way.	Always visit crime sites if at all possible; consider least effort principle and how it applies to each location – if it does not apply, what is the reason for it? Outliers might be due to unforeseen circumstances or due to displacement – consider setting aside from other offences in series; look for any spatial information in statements, request re-interviewing if necessary; always plot known post-offence information on map, identify routes between them; relate all data to routine activity, least effort principle and offender's choices; try to identify opportunities the offender did not take and identify why s/he did not take them; bear in mind police boundaries, ask for information from surrounding forces to ascertain all relevant crimes are included; look at where something happens and where nothing happens and ask: why? Be aware of the importance of routes, not only locations; try to infer offender's spatial awareness of area.

continued

Table 6.1 Cont'd

Difficult cognitive element	Why difficult?	Common errors	Cues and strategies
Identify patterns in temporal behaviour	Offences might occur at seemingly random times/ days; there might not be an obvious pattern or rationale for times chosen; linkage can be difficult to ascertain in the absence of forensic evidence – no guarantee that known offences are linked or that series is complete (i.e. there might be other related offences not included in this case); need to attempt to extract offender's routine activity.	Novices might give up too soon; might fail to exclude outliers if necessary; might fail to see temporal behaviour in relation to spatial aspects of offences; might fail to visit crime sites to gain deeper understanding of what goes on at locations and their potential significance; might not probe deeply enough into offender's decision-making process; might not analyse witness/victim statements thoroughly enough to identify temporal information; might mistakenly infer patterns when too little information available; may want to create and confirm hypotheses rather than test and question; don't look for information that would contradict their initial hypothesis; novices often misread an offence that is logged as having taken place during the early hours of a Saturday or Sunday as occurring on those days when in actual fact they should be taken as having occurred Friday or Saturday night as they are a continuation of that preceding day and activity.	Visit offence sites at the time the crime occurred if possible to learn about that location at that time of day/day of week; look for any temporal information in statements, request re-interviewing if necessary; question hypotheses once formulated, look at maths behind statistical findings; look for things that contradict hypotheses; avoid confirmation bias; question linkage; bear in mind offender's psyche: if offences seem to have seized after a media campaign some might assume offender stopped, but s/he may still linger around potential victims to enjoy the thrill of both reliving and imagining offending – CCTV might still capture him/her; create your own tables and maps to represent data meaningfully; compare locations to days of week.

continued

Table 6.1 Cont'd

Difficult cognitive element	Why difficult?	Common errors	Cues and strategies
Formulate hypotheses	Depends on accuracy, quality and completeness of information available; might be impossible if no patterns identifiable; suggestions made might be contrary to investigation's plan of action	Novices might lack confidence in proposing hypotheses that deviate from current line of enquiry; might not be able to justify hypotheses due to lack of thoroughness, research conducted and experience.	Make sure you can justify what you say; use experience of previous cases if similar; perform thorough research to back up inferences.

[1]Several issues mentioned within this table apply to both temporal as well as spatial analysis.

Table 6.1 displays the grouped elements of geographic profiling that were identified by the researcher as the most cognitively demanding, describing what their inherent difficulties are, which errors might commonly be made (e.g. by novices), and how those errors can be prevented. The data extracted for this study indicate that in terms of behavioural analysis for geographic profiling, there is no single discrete task that is adopted in isolation, but rather there appears to be a collection of diverse elements that are synthesized in a coherent, holistic manner to provide investigative leads. This section considers the ability to question and understand complex information, appreciate the influence of context over behaviour and the ability to recognize patterns in geomobile activity of offenders.

The first such element is the *analysis of information* provided by the investigation. This usually consists of a large file of documents, videos, photographs, statements, reports and maps. The first task of a Geoprofiler is thus to meticulously check the accuracy, quality and completeness of that data. According to the Geos' own experiences when starting out in the profession as well as observations made when training new recruits, common errors often made by less experienced individuals include accepting the information at face value and to assume that it has already been checked for accuracy and completeness by the officer providing it. It takes confidence to question something that is presented by a Senior Investigating Officer (SIO) and it may be that this is a quality which is usually developed with increasing experience and competence. Further, if looking at a series of offences supposedly perpetrated by the same offender, linkage analysis might be difficult to carry out for a novice as they have not yet accumulated enough experience to constitute a 'mental database' of baselines and the ranges of behaviours within serial offences, as reported by the Geos. If you don't know how much variety you can and should expect to see within different offences perpetrated by the same offender, you don't know how to differentiate between different perpetrators. When comparing such cases, it is vital to distinguish between offender-led behaviour and behaviour that was influenced by the victim or other, external circumstances, as those are less under the offender's control and therefore not always part of his 'plan' and not his preference, and may therefore not materialize again in another offence (Alison *et al.*, 2002). For instance, when analysing potential case linkage and the offender's choices made, in order to extract whether he was showing a preference for a certain type of victim, the Geoprofiler would first ascertain what the target backcloth was like in the area at the relevant time. If the offender appears to have chosen female victims of a certain age and attire in his offences, it might be false to assume that those criteria were in fact necessary parameters for his choice of victim, when in fact most of the females in that area at the time were dressed that way. If, however, the victim was the only one who had a certain notable appearance or characteristic and appears to have been targeted by the offender when there seem to have been a number of alternative victims available, the Geo would be more willing to consider that there was something specific about that particular female that he was looking for. The level of risk involved would also be considered, e.g. did he accept a higher risk to attack that particular female when it would have been easier to attack one of the others? The offender's particular choice of a target would fall into the category of offender-led decisions, whilst general target backcloth and victim availability would be included under the external circumstances. Offender-led decisions are more personal to the offender and could investigatively be more informative. The same applies to choice of weapons or other offence items, such as ligatures, gags, etc. If the offender specifically carries items with him, rather than simply choosing spontaneously from what is available at the crime scene (tree branches or rocks as weapons, victim's clothing as gags or ligatures, etc.), then the items he deliberately chose in advance are again more informative of his planning, his means and how he wanted the offence to be committed, than are the items used spontaneously and opportunistically. Therefore, one cannot use the fact that for instance, in most offences, a bra was used to tie the victim's hands and in another case, a belt was used, to state that the cases are not linked. In fact, the victim who was tied up with her belt may not have worn a bra, or the belt may have been easier to get to. The offender-led behaviour in this instance would be the fact that he did not bring the actual ligature item with him, such as a cable or a rope, but that he was willing to use something of the victim's. The specific type of item used, however, is down in part to victim's choice in terms of which items of clothing she has on, and external circumstances, i.e. what is available. A Geo would use only offender-led behaviours when determining case linkage, rather than external or victim-led determinants.

Strategies employed by the Geos in order to analyse information in the best way possible, include:

1   Questioning and checking everything for themselves by corroborating and cross-referencing information from statements with other sources,

double-checking crucial bits of information with the investigating team, visiting the crime scene themselves rather than just accepting descriptions and creating their own maps and offence matrices rather than relying on ones prepared by others. If the police say they have an offender on CCTV at a certain time, the Geo double-checks to see if the footage really shows the offender or if the whole team just acquiesced to someone declaring that person to be the offender; if Geos are given a proposed series of offences they check carefully if the crimes really do appear to be related rather than accepting that they are and possibly falsely including an unrelated offence in the analysis.

2   Keeping an open mind about alternatives, for instance considering that the victim's associates might be deliberately misleading the investigation with their statement in order to conceal their involvement in the offence; having a constant awareness of all possible circumstances and aetiologies of the crime and what might have happened rather than working with only one hypothesis.

3   Potentially tasking police with identifying other incidents that would not have been recorded or crimed, but might be related. For instance, in a rape enquiry, an offender who appears to have a fetish for female lingerie might have stolen his victim's underwear in the index offence (the offence in question), but upon further investigation and house-to-house enquiries in the relevant area, the police might discover that several women had underwear stolen from their washing lines on previous occasions, and might even have seen someone in the area (although there was no rape). Such information may not have been registered as a crime by the police, yet it might provide further investigative and forensic opportunities. When an investigation is faced with an extreme and violent index offence, it would be quite rare for the offender not to have left a trail of previous 'build-up' offences or behavioural 'try-outs' where the offender practised approaching an unwilling victim, which did not amount to a full assault, as such incidents may have culminated in the index offence (Townsley, Smith & Pease, 2005), and an offender's fantasy-led sexual behaviours can evolve throughout his offence series (Woodhams, Hollin & Bull, 2007). The Geos reported that this contextualization of the index offence was a learned behaviour and also based on experience that was not naturally considered by novices.

Recognizing *patterns in the offender's spatial behaviour* is another challenge that Geographic Profilers come across. The Geo aims to identify how familiar the offender was with the various known locations, why he was there and what his spatial decision-making process was. For instance, is that location an element of his every-day cognitive map, which is a mental representation of the area(s) he is familiar with and frequents on a regular basis (Rossmo, 2000), and was he there due to his legitimate routine activities such as work, commute, leisure, etc. (Brantingham & Brantingham, 1981) when he encountered the victim by chance? Or did he identify the location as suitable when he came across it through his routine activity and then deliberately came back to it in order to use it as an offence site? Within the broader remit of experts identifying patterns of activity and behaviour (Militello *et al.*, 1997) is the issue of post-offence movements. Offenders frequently return to their base (e.g. home or work) after an offence (Büchler & Leineweber, 1991; Rossmo, 2000) and this information can be extracted from victim or witness statements, following the directionality of property deposition, CCTV (closed-circuit television), use of stolen cards, or timed witness sightings etc. After taking risks by committing a serious offence, home might seem safe and attract the offender back. The identification of such patterns might be hindered by the fact that some offence locations will not bear an obvious or logical justification, and might be based on entirely personal and internal choices. Further, when examining several crime scenes with regards to their having been used by the same offender, one scene might look like an 'outlier', a location that is geographically quite distant or behaviourally (when looking at MO) different from the cluster of other offences. This might either not form part of the series or might simply differ from the other offences under consideration because of other circumstances, chance, displacement, etc. If that outlier appears to skew the overall pattern, the Geo has to make a decision on whether they should include it in their examination or leave it out and thereby exclude it from analysis. For instance, if in a proposed series there are five offences in which the victim appears to have been a random choice and it is likely that she simply posed the least risk and was available from a larger pool of potential victims, whereas in another offence it seems she was picked out and followed for some time, these differences in offender-led targeting might suggest that the offences may not be linked, as target choices are largely up to the offender (Bennell and Canter, 2002; Bennell and Jones, 2005; Grubin *et al.*, 2001). The Geo will use themes of an offender's decisions as a holistic big-picture view of the offence to distinguish between crimes committed by different offenders, in order to put together those which are more likely to be linked. Another example might be a number of cases in which the offender appears to have transported his victims in his car as part of the offence. When another case comes in, in which some of the offence behaviours overlap, but no transport was used and far shorter distances were travelled, in addition to the offence being rather far away from the proposed series, this specific offence might initially be excluded from analysis until an overall picture of the proposed series has been established.

Furthermore, locations need to be examined in relation to temporal information. A specific street or a footpath in a field can be used by a very different demographic of people during the night, especially weekend nights, than during the day. A park or path through a green may be frequented by dog walkers, joggers, parents with prams and the elderly during daylight hours, whereas it might be deserted at night or attract members of the alcoholic community, prostitutes, the gay community or may be used by groups of young people to congregate and socialize away from adult supervision. Each crime location should be visited at the time the crime was committed in order to ascertain who can be encountered there at the relevant time. The Geoprofiler aims to identify the opportunities that presented themselves to the perpetrator and why he did or did not take them. In particular, not taking an opportunity (i.e. absence of a specific behaviour or action) may be especially revealing, for example if the offender apparently rejects the 'least effort principle' (Godwin, 1996; Reber, 1985). This principle suggests that in any given situation in which a person is presented with a number of alternative courses of action, paths to choose from or decisions to make, they will, all other factors being equal, choose the one which requires the least effort. This might relate to a location which can be reached by either walking up the hill or taking a more even path, when they would both require the same amount of time, in which case the principle would predict that the person will choose the even path which would be easier to walk. Alternatively, if an employee is free to choose from a number of tasks, each of which carries the same amount of professional recognition and new skills to be acquired, they are more likely to choose the one that is somewhat easier to master. Each of the offender's decisions and actions needs to be scrutinized in relation to this principle, as humans are thought to always choose the easiest option out of a selection of those with other comparable pros and cons.

The next cognitively demanding element of geographic profiling is the extraction of a *temporal pattern* from the offender's actions. Many similar principles apply here as in the spatial pattern: least effort principle (Godwin, 1996; Reber, 1985), routine activity theory (Brantingham and Brantingham, 1981) and targeted vs. random victim. Experts often routinely adopt counter-intuitive routes to question their own inferences and thereby make deliberate efforts to search the evidence for information that not only supports their hypotheses, but also that which contradicts them. This assists them in avoiding confirmation bias (Almond et al., 2008) and asymmetric scepticism (Ask and Granhag, 2005, see also Chapter 3). A Geo infers from the offence or sighting times whether the area in question is linked to his home base, work base or social activity. For instance, the location of an offence that occurred late at night but that offers no late-night entertainment, shops or other reasons why someone would be there, indicates that the offender may reside around that area. On the other hand, crime timings in the centre of town that are around rush-hour and commuter times (e.g. 7am–9am or 4pm–6pm) are more indicative of being tied into an offender's route to and from work. A phenomenon that Geographic Profilers routinely consider is displacement. In another case where there had been a series of attacks on lone females after a night out, media appeals had warned women about walking by themselves and the offences appeared to have stopped. However, the Geo advised the police to put surveillance in place at times and in locations the offences had previously taken place, being aware that rapists can enjoy the thrill of anticipation and re-living offences, even if they are not offending at the time, and indeed the perpetrator was caught observing females walking home on the first night of surveillance. Such displacement may be temporary and offending might resume once the offender feels things have calmed down. Alternatively, he might move his offending to another location, which the Geo needs to be vigilant of when considering case linkage. Different locations do not necessarily mean different offenders. In a serial offences investigation, the Geo reported they mapped the offences out and made notes of their timings, which revealed that the offence that occurred at the earliest time of the day, and that which occurred at the latest time of the day, were the two most South-Eastern located offences in the series. The Geo was able to infer from this that those offence sites may have involved the least travel and were therefore closer to the offender's home base, which, after a focusing of investigative tactics on that area, turned out to be true.

The last demanding cognitive element identified for geographic profiling is the *formulation of hypotheses*. This step is dependent upon the Geo's ability to infer patterns in the offender's choice(s) of crime sites; these can include an observation point (a location that shields the offender from view yet allows him to observe potential targets), encounter site (where victim and offender meet for the first time), attack site (where the offender attacks the victim), the actual location where the crime was carried out, body disposal (where the offender disposes of the victim's body) and property deposition site (where the offender might leave items used during the offence, such as weapons, or items belonging to the victim, such as her phone, wallet, etc.), sightings of the offender after the crime, and offender's use of stolen bank cards after the offence, etc. It also depends on the times he offended, and on the accuracy and completeness of information held by the police. The nature and use of those locations by the offender is highly signif-icant. One Geo reported to have learned from experience that attack sites are much closer to the offender's home than victim release or body deposition sites, which can be rather far away. Especially the locations that occur later at night tend to be closer to the offender's home base, thereby further guiding the inves-tigation's geographical focus. Furthermore, it is possible that the investigating team already have their own theories about the crime in question and that they might have imparted those to the Geo. In that case it is vital for the Geoprofiler not to be influenced by the SIO's opinion and to remain objective at all times. Again, it requires confidence to make inferences and suggest courses of action that are contrary to what the investigating team have been assuming and working towards so far. Therefore, it is vital that the Geo's inferences are backed up by research, statistics and evidence. An expert has to be able to justify their opinions in order to show to others why they have or have not come to any particular conclusion. For instance, the investigation may have been focusing on the murdered victim's partner – if however the Geographic Profiler believes she was murdered by someone else, they need to illustrate to the police how they came to that conclusion. This might be in the form of showing routine behaviours by the victim and her partner, none of which include any of the crime sites except the encounter site, suggesting she may have encountered the offender in an area where she was for some reason, but he then took her to a place he was familiar with that neither she nor her partner ever frequent or even know about. In order for the SIO to agree to a shift from one line of enquiry to another, they will want to be convinced that they are doing the right thing, therefore the Geo has to be very clear and plausible in their argumentation and refer back to literature which also suggests that murderers tend to take their victims into areas they are already familiar with, be it because they know it provides a relatively safe opportunity to offend, or because they can access and leave it without risking being seen as it is quite desolate, or they may be able to return home more easily. In cases where there is an absence of such academic backing for specific conclusions, Geos reported making reference to previous cases they worked on to which the index offence bears some similarities. This anecdotal comparison may actually be more relatable to the SIO, as it is just in their line of work. Experts are known to have this ability to draw from a large, relevant experiential knowledgebase in order to inform their decision making (Militello *et al.*, 1997). Another aspect of crime that Geos routinely scrutinize in order to try and understand the offender's decision-making process is the victimology. It is important to determine why the victim was where she was when the encounter or attack took place; if she was there regularly, it is possible she may have been targeted and the offender either followed her or encountered her there before. If she was there for the first time and became a victim by chance, it is more likely that the location is tied into the perpetrator's routines which makes the location the focus of investigative attention.

Table 6.2 displays a critical cue inventory that consolidates some of the data acquired through the ACTA process. It should be noted that this cannot be treated as a 'look-up' table for what any specific cue means and which particular infer-ence it leads to; rather it lists cues which might hint at several (sometimes incom-patible or contradicting) inferences as well as inferences which might follow a combination of several specific cues. One cue can therefore reveal little in isola-tion and must be combined with others in order to allow for an accurate conclu-sion to be drawn. If any conclusion can be refuted by a fact of the case, it might have to be excluded from the decreasing pool of possible inferences. If there is both strong supportive yet also contradictive information regarding any one conclusion, the accuracy and specificity of the inference needs to be reviewed. Ultimately, the most plausible inference is that which cannot be disproved by accurate facts, but is supported by them. This table therefore simply illustrates some of the options that need to be considered as possibly accounting for each of the facts; however these possible considerations are by no means complete.

A Geo performs a detailed temporal analysis, identifying (especially in serial cases) which days of the week and which times of the day the offender chooses to offend. One might surmise that an offender can only offend when certain conditions are met: he must be unsupervised so he can commit his crime; he must have access to a suitable victim, crime site, and accessories/tools if required; he must know where to find a victim who is unguarded (or find a victim by chance), where to take her and where to release her or dispose of the body; he must be able to be away from home or work to find his victim or commit the crime (unless he lures her into his residence or place of employment) without arousing suspicion of anyone in his household (e.g. a spouse or other family member) or place of work.

The above set of conditions assumes that the offender's criminal activity is separate from his work routine activity and he offends in his 'free' time. However, another scenario is possible, in which the pattern of offending is tied into his work routine, e.g. he offends on his way to or from work, or he attacks victims whilst he is working. Some forms of employment might actually bring the offender into contact with potential victims, if he is a contractor, delivery person, or of another profession that facilitates his visiting the homes of other people. Conversely, potential victims might be coming to him, e.g. if he works in some premises that are visited by customers, patients, clients, students, etc. If his attacks seem to take place in the morning, late afternoon and possibly at lunch times, that suggests that offending is concentrated around his work routine, when he is travelling to or from work, for instance. In that case, a Geo would attempt to identify commuting routes and timings of travel in order to suggest opportunities for forensics, surveillance or apprehension at the right place at the right time.

In serial cases, the lengths of time between offences may be of significance as well. The occasions on which he offends might be dictated by external factors such as opportunity, or they might be under the influence of more personal,

Table 6.2 Critical cue inventory[1] for making inferences and investigative suggestions in geographic profiling

Cue	Description	Inference
Temporal analysis	Offender only active on specific days of the week.	On those days offender might engage in activities (work, social) that bring him in contact with potential victims; might not have access to victims or opportunities to offend on other days; might depend on his job in some way to bring him into contact with victims or access to opportunities to offend; offences occurring late at night on a Friday/Saturday evening might be due to offender being in area for social activity rather than living nearby.
	Offender not active on specific days of the week.	Might have constraining commitments on those days, e.g. work, family, social activities that hinder offending; might not have opportunities to offend on those days; victims/targets might be less accessible or available on those days.
	Crimes committed within specific times of day.	Might be due to target availability at specific times; might be due to offender being only free to commit around those times; might be due to offender having opportunity to come into contact with potential targets around those times; might be times of day where risk of being identified/disturbed is the lowest; if offences occur in morning and late afternoon and/or lunch time they might be related to work base rather than residence; offences/activities that occur late at night tend to be closer to offender's home.

(continued)

Table 6.2 Cont'd

Cue	Description	Inference
	Intervals between offences are regular.	Offending opportunities might be dependent upon regular legitimate activities of offender, either geographically or temporally.
	Intervals between offences are shortening.	Offender's need to offend might be heightening, risk of escalation of violence/ number of targets etc. in order to 'outdo' previous offences.
	Intervals between offences are lengthening.	Displacement might be at play; heightened media and police attention might be causing offender to 'lie low' for a while before he resumes offending or might displace offending to another area; potential victims might be more alert – target backcloth changes.
Spatial analysis	Offences occur in close proximity to each other within a definable area.	Offender might be of the 'hunter' type and hence local, living within a few kilometres of the crime sites, therefore offending and living area overlap; might be 'commuter' type who has defined area as hunting ground and travels out of his own area to this hunting ground in order to offend – those two areas do not overlap. Hunter type: focus of offender's spatial awareness likely to be within that definable crime area; probably goes about daily legitimate activities in that space; might live, work or frequent that area; might have detailed local knowledge; Investigation should focus on the locality. Commuter type: investigative focus should lie on reasons to visit that area and the means to do so. How would he travel there, who travels there and from where etc.
	Offences occur at seemingly random locations and with great distances between each other.	Offender might be of the 'commuter' type and travel into area specifically to offend; might live further away but likely to have some knowledge of area surrounding crime sites.
	Offences tend to be near main roads.	Might be due to higher target availability; might be due to presence of easy access and escape routes; might be due to unfamiliarity with side streets; might be due to better access to (own) transport on main roads; targets might be spotted from road, might be hunting while driving; might be of 'commuter' type.

(continued)

Table 6.2 Cont'd

Cue	Description	Inference
	Offences tend to take place in quieter areas.	Might have followed victim until out of sight; might have detailed knowledge of access and escape routes to and from area; might know area well and be local; might be aware of CCTV and higher risk of witnesses on main roads; might be after targets in quieter locations (e.g. in burglary).
	Offences tend to take place in central business or non-residential areas.	Might be of commuter type; less likely to be living in area; might have been in area in order to offend rather than following his routine activity.
	Offender seems to use vehicle yet is cautious about not being seen.	Probably due to using own vehicle that might identify him rather than using stolen car.
	Travel pattern of crime series seems to be directional.	Might be of commuter type; less likely to be local.
	Offender known to have been travelling in specific direction when victim was encountered by chance.	Might have been travelling home, likely to be local, with possible base in direction of original travel path.
Victimology	Many victims travelled similar paths before being attacked.	Might have been spotted and followed by offender at a certain location they all passed through.
		Might have been lying in wait until a suitable victim comes along.
	Offender seems to attack victims of specific demographics (e.g. age, gender).	Might spend time observing potential targets where they can be encountered; might use those 'observation points' to choose victim; if potential victim availability limited to particular area offender might have to travel in to offend (possibly of commuter type).
	Victims/targets are of a specific and rare type/ limited target availability	Might have to travel into area(s) to locate targets, might be of commuter type.

(continued)

Table 6.2 Cont'd

Cue	Description	Inference
	A house burgled is in concealed location.	Offender might have known of potential target, might have chosen that house deliberately rather than randomly; likely previous reconnaissance activity to identify access and escape routes.
	Burglaries of commercial premises seem to be work of professional burglar.	Less likely to be local; might be of commuter type.
Post-offence movement	Offender seems to escape in specific direction after committing offence.	Might be heading towards home; might be heading towards transportation; might be heading towards some other base of relative safety.
	Offender defies least effort principle by not choosing most easily available escape routes.	There must be a rationale for his/her choice of escape route, likely escaping towards an area of significance.
	A house burgled is on a sloping road.	Offender most likely escaped in down-hill direction (according to least effort principle).
Miscellaneous	Specific source material used in arson attack.	If origin of source material can be identified that might add another 'location' on crime map which offender is likely to have visited, this is therefore on his mental map and possibly part of routine activity.
	Offences tend to be on linear route.	Perpetrator might attack whilst en route between locations rather than venturing out from home base.
	Offences seem to carry a high risk with them from the start.	It is likely they occurred well into the series – identify earlier offences he might have started with that were less risky as they might be the beginning of the series.

[1]Adapted from Klein, G.A., Calderwood, R., & MacGregor, D. (1989).

internal pressures and desires. If these intervals between offences become longer, this might be due to displacement, media and police activity, or increased vigilance of potential victims, etc. (Rossmo, 2000). On the other hand, if they appear to be shortening, and that happens in tandem with increasing levels of violence exhibited during his crimes, it may be that there is an escalation in the perpetrator's offending behaviour, with his need for violent/sexual gratification increasing and his level of dangerousness rising accordingly. It could be that offenders experience a decrease in excitation generated from the repetition of a crime that initially provided them with a 'thrill', which might lead to offence escalation in order to experience that same stimulation.

Spatial analysis might indicate whether the offender is of the 'hunter' or 'commuter' type. The former are those who maintain a connection to their home base, from which they venture out in order to commit an offence and then return to it (Canter and Larkin, 1993). Their 'offending space' therefore overlaps with their routine activity space as the offender is more likely to know the area he offends in from his legitimate routine activities (e.g. travelling to and from work, going shopping, socializing, etc.). The crime sites he chooses are likely not to be very distant from his home base and indeed, according to the circle hypothesis, his base is likely to be close to the centre of a circle that encompasses all offences in a series (Canter and Larkin, 1993; Kocsis and Irwin, 1997; Tamura and Suzuki, 1997). The commuter-type offender, on the other hand, uses an offending space which does not overlap with his normal routine activity space (Rossmo, 2005). He might commute to those areas due to the target availability there, and the crime sites are likely to be further away from his home location than in the case of a 'hunter'. Offences that appear to have been committed by a 'hunter' are more likely to provide investigative leads, as the offender has a strong connection to the crime sites that will be the focus of investigation. With a 'commuter' type offender on the other hand, this connection is much weaker or indeed lacking, and investigative leads may be harder to come by as the offender specifically travelled to those places to offend, rather than having a natural connection to them.

The Geographic Profiler will also examine the streets in which offences took place, or in which the offender was lying in wait until he spotted potential targets. Use of main roads might hint at a lack of local knowledge or the use of a car or public transport, whereas use of back roads suggests familiarity with the area if the offender chose those locations, or that he followed victims into those areas, in which case familiarity is more difficult to infer. Identifying where the offender was prior to an attack, even if that location is not an actual crime site, might produce valuable information about possible forensic as well as investigative opportunities. If he spent some time there on the lookout for a suitable target, he might have dropped a cigarette butt or left a fingerprint, footprint or other forensic clues behind. The fact that he was aware of such an appropriate observation point might further suggest something about his knowledge of the area and his means of transportation. Any geographical information can be of great use to the Geo in order to form a holistic picture of the offender's geography, not just the crime sites. Therefore, it is vital that interviewing officers extract any such information from victims and witnesses, as they may be able to give an account of where the offender approached them from, i.e. where he was when she walked by perhaps, or in which direction he escaped. This pre- and post-offence movement potentially holds a lot of valuable information to inform the Geoprofiler's analysis. If, for instance the victim just got off a bus and was attacked a few hundred meters away from the bus stop with the offender approaching her from behind, is it possible he was on the same bus but she did not notice him? In this case there might be CCTV footage of him held by the bus company. Though it might be easy not to realize the importance of information such as where the victim was coming from and what she had been doing prior to the attack, this can hold vital clues as to how she was spotted and selected by the offender. If it appears that several victims were walking along the same road in the centre of town prior to being attacked in a much quieter area, then the actual attack locations might have nothing in common with each other or even with the offender, whereas the location where they were spotted and then followed from might be where the offender was lying in wait for someone suitable to come past. Therefore, that 'observation spot' is the one location that was consciously chosen by the offender, and it might be the one that provides the most robust and reliable investigative leads. This area may hold more clues than the actual attack site, and it is up to the interviewers to extract such information. Another example might be that witnesses or the victim report the offender as not wearing warm clothing such as gloves, a scarf or a coat, when the temperatures were very low. This might imply that he either had a car or his residence was nearby, and he did not have to be outside very long. Proper questioning should also be able to identify where the offender escaped to. For instance, he may have seemed to disappear into a residential street, which might again suggest familiarity, his home or that he had a car parked there; alternatively, if he went to a main road, that might hint at the possibility that he does not live in that particular area, but again might now be seeking means of transportation. Most offenders tend to return home after having committed an offence (Büchler & Leineweber, 1991; Rossmo, 2000). In a case in which the victim was walking along a footpath and was attacked outdoors, the Geo was able to determine that the target backcloth was not particularly rich at the time, in that there were not many other potential victims using that path, which led to the inference the victim was either targeted specifically or that the attack was opportunistic. The Geo further observed that where the victim was walking and attacked could have been spotted from a road nearby, therefore a driver might have seen the victim and spontaneously decided to commit the offence. The victim reported where the offender escaped to after the offence and it turned out that a car was seen parked there, probably the offender's car. As this location was some distance away from the offence site and it was not the closest location available to leave the car (defying the least effort principle), the Geoprofiler inferred that the deliberate caution exercised by the offender not to be seen in his car might mean he was using his own car (rather than a stolen, borrowed or a company car) and that he was probably recognizable in some way, both of these inferences hinting at someone who was local to, and familiar with the area.

Rather than crime locations being a deliberately sought-out destination, they might also be of an opportunistic nature, in which an individual commits an offence because an opportunity presented itself, whilst he was actually en route somewhere else for a legitimate purpose. In that case, it should be noted in which direction the offender appeared to have been travelling and where he came from. This will provide starting points for the identification of witness sightings, which CCTV cameras to collect information from, etc. In such rather spontaneous offences, it might also be beneficial to identify other opportunistic facets, such as items used that might have been obtained whilst the offender was on his way somewhere. For instance, in an arson series, where it appeared that fast food boxes were used to start fires in people's houses, a Geo would seek to identify where those items came from in order to extract where the offender had been. Those fast food outlets might be able to provide police with more information on the perpetrator, as well as CCTV footage.

Discussion – Study 1

The aim of Study 1 was to articulate the processes utilized by Geographic Profilers, as well as to ascertain the breadth of their role. Results of the expertise extraction process indicate that they perform, amongst other things, a variety of meticulous analyses in order to provide specific kinds of targeted support to criminal investigations. These processes are the detailed and careful examination of case materials for temporal analysis, spatial analysis, victimology, extraction and interpretation of post-offence movement, amongst others. They combine these facets of the offence for the formulation and scrutiny of hypotheses and holistic inferences in order to provide investigative advice to the SIO.

Historically, geographic profiling has only been discussed in the context of providing operational support when trying to apprehend a serial offender by determining an area most likely to contain the offender's base. However, approximately 39 per cent of all cases the NPIA's Geoprofilers worked on until 2008 were single offences (statistics collated by the NPIA's Geographic Profilers between 2002–2007) The bulk of their case load were rape series (27 per cent), single murder cases (20 per cent), missing person cases or no-body murders (10 per cent), robbery series (8 per cent) and single rapes (7 per cent), with other case types such as serial cases of burglary, indecent exposure, arson, murder and abduction making up between 1–6 per cent each.

The Geo will attempt to ascertain both the routes taken by the offender to locate a victim and to evade capture after the offence. These aspects can be crucial when attempting to determine where the offender came from and in which direction they escaped, especially the latter being indicative of a possible anchor point (Büchler & Leineweber, 1991; Rossmo, 2000), which is often their place of residence. Further, they infer from the available materials what the offender's movements were, how he might have selected the victim(s), if he was positioned in a certain location to spot and observe potential targets, and how he has come across those. In a case mentioned previously, a Geo reported that females were being attacked when walking home once they had reached small residential side streets in an area away from the town centre, which did not seem to be connected to each other. The Geo overlaid the paths taken by the victims from the town centre where they had been on a night out, and even though there was no connection between the various attack sites, they were found to have used the same road leading into the residential area. The Geo used that information on a potential observation point of the offender's to inform proactive investigative techniques (e.g. cameras, surveillance, etc.) and the offender was indeed caught through those measures. The Geoprofiler will also map the offences temporally and spatially. This provides an overview of when the offences took place. In both single and serial cases a late hour can be indicative of close proximity to the offender's base; in serial cases a Geo can observe on which day of the week, time of day, specific weather conditions, etc. (crimes occurred in order to extract a pattern), where they took place, and a combination thereof (to infer who would be at a specific location at a specific time). Such an analysis can be of great assistance in building up a picture of who the offender was targeting, where and how he was targeting victims, how he knew potential victims would be there, how and where he attacked and how he got away from the scene afterwards, amongst other things. Even words used by the offender can contain geographic information or hints at the offender's familiarity with the area, for instance if he knows names of local places that are only known to residents, or refers to specific bus routes, etc. Analyses of this nature can then inform investigative suggestions about where and at what times to implement surveillance measures, dispatch undercover officers, where and when to make appeals for information from the public, and also, how to prioritize search areas and suspect lists. Performing such analyses and preparing a report can take a Geo up to two weeks, which they use to work through materials, putting together tables and diagrams, conducting research, constructing and scrutinizing hypotheses and drawing inferences that can then aid investigative decision making. For each decision taken or not taken by the offender, the Geo tries to determine the 'why' or 'why not' in order to extract the reason for the offender's actions.

Interestingly, when geographic profiling was first conceptualized and applied to crime investigations, it was indeed used primarily to identify the area most likely to contain the base of a serial offender. Canter (2003), for instance, stated that if an offender's base is not located within a circle encompassing his crimes, then it is 'not of any value exploring any further the use of geography for detection' (p. 129). Similarly, Bennell, Snook and Taylor (2005) note that they see little value in examining factors such as crime sites, target backcloth, land use, arterial routes and barriers or temporal patterns, to name a few (p. 34). However, a professional modern-day UK Geoprofiler would dismiss such statements very quickly, as detailed analyses of the choice of locations, movements, access and escape routes, timings and choice of victims can provide a wealth of information that can lead to identifying investigative strategies and successful lines of enquiry. It appears then, that the original definition of geographic profiling as a technique that provides a geographic focus for search efforts to determine the most likely area of residence of a serial offender is incomplete. Nowadays, Geographic Profilers utilize expertise in geographic behaviour in a variety of ways. For instance, one Geo reported a case in which the area determined likely to contain the home base of the offender was quite large, over 30km. Although in theory, a DNA screen in that area would have had a fair chance of identifying the offender, the Geo suggested a media appeal that focused on asking callers very particular questions to identify males with specific connections to the area. Once such a person was identified through the appeal, the investigation had the offender's name and had saved a considerable amount of money on not completing a DNA-screen of the entire area.

So why does expertise matter?

Tables 6.1 and 6.2 display the Geographic Profilers' expertise applied to numerous single spatial and temporal cues, aspects and facets of an analysis. Expertise research findings indicate that experts are generally highly sensitive to the cues that are the most likely to be of relevance to their specific task at hand (Savelsbergh *et al.*, 2005). It transpired that expert Geoprofilers routinely examine many different issues including possible hunter/commuter typology, access and escape routes, timings and demographics at particular times, amongst other things. Nevertheless, being an investigative expert also entails questioning the most likely hypothesis that results from statistical probabilities, rather than applying it faithfully. In an operational setting in which the future of possible victims might be at stake, it is crucial to be resistant to the blind application of acquired knowledge. Decisional components are likely to become deeply embedded in an expert's working mind and might become resistant to the influences of the individual case (Richler *et al.*, 2008). However, the 'common errors' column in Table 6.1 lists a variety of cautions considered by the Geoprofilers. This indicates they are well aware of common pitfalls and the dangers of taking things for what they seem. Indeed it appears that this caution and routine questioning of the information provided, and of their own conclusions, are part of their training and also based on experience. Therefore, being a *true* expert might include as one of its requirements the ability to counteract one's expertise, which might bring with it cognitive-load reducing qualities such as automaticity (Shanteau, 1987). This might be unique to specific tasks of expertise, such as geographic profiling. This is because in this particular profession, many details of offences and offenders are unknown and are deliberately covert or misleading. In other tasks of expertise, such as the sight-reading of sheet music, for instance, there is generally less risk involved in applying automaticity and rapid pattern-recognition (Waters, Townsend & Underwood, 1998), apart from the music to be read being more complex than the instrumentalist initially assumed. Such processes reduce the amount of detail that needs to be processed. However, a Geographic Profiler must be alert to each single aspect of a case in order to make accurate inferences and suggestions, lest they should jeopardize the investigation. This seems to be a quality that is acquired through thorough training in this specific field, thereby quite possibly necessitating specialized experts for specific tasks rather than individuals with an all-round function, which is likely to result in analyses that are less profound and detailed. It takes close to two years to become a qualified Geographic Profiler accredited by the International Criminal Investigative Analysis Fellowship, which the NPIA's Geos are recognized by. The training structure includes one and a half months spent studying statistics and probabilities, two months studying violent and serious crime and two months of offender profiling. The studies conducted in this paper seem to imply that this training of experts is a necessity well worth its investment as the first step to developing the Geos' expertise. This expertise appears to equip Geographic Profilers to be able to achieve a well-balanced synthesis of attention to detail with a holistic analysis of the case: the crime location, for instance, will be analysed as to its access and escape routes, where someone might have parked or where they might have been watching potential targets from, and the detailed knowledge someone must have had about it in order to weigh up its opportunistic value against any risk. Besides this meticulous dissection of detail, the Geo also considers the overall nature of the location, whether it is a crime attractor or generator (e.g. a night club, a red-light district, etc.) and who would be frequenting that area at the time the offence occurred. The Geos noted the importance of getting to know the area at the relevant time, in order to understand its demographics and target back cloth.

Study 2: What can geoprofiling contribute to single-offence cases?

Geographic Profilers were provided with case materials of two types of real-life single offences that were unfamiliar to them: one type were single offences with only one known crime location; the other type had several crime sites for each offence. They were instructed to work through those materials and produce inferences and investigative suggestions that were then evaluated as to their utility to the investigation. Operationally, Geos have been providing support for single case investigations for a number of years; however, as far as the authors are aware, no research has been conducted as yet to test their utility in such cases. This study will therefore examine investigative suggestions and inferences produced by the Geoprofilers and compare them to the actual investigations' outcomes, i.e. the steps that in real life actually did lead to the identification of the offender, in order to ascertain what the utility of their input to those particular investigations would have been. Due to space limitations, this pilot cannot be reported in full in this chapter; therefore, full statistics are not presented here but were included in the original study (Knabe, 2008).

Since the task of geoprofiling is dependent upon the availability of spatial and temporal information, it is hypothesized that Geoprofilers will be able to provide useful suggestions and accurate inferences in single cases with multiple locations, yet will fail to be of investigative utility in offences involving one site only.

Participants

Due to operational commitments and time limitations, only two of the four Geographic Profilers (the youngest and the oldest one, one male, a retired police officer; one female, a former senior crime analyst) were able to take part in this study. This particular piece of research should therefore be viewed as a pilot only, which requires replication with the full set of Geos.

Materials

Case information was provided by the NPIA's Serious Crime Analysis Section (SCAS). The participants were not familiar with the cases. They were provided with materials of 13 single-offence cases in total, of which there were two murder cases with multiple locations (e.g. different encounter, attack, property disposal, body deposition sites, etc.), three murder cases with only a single location (i.e. encounter, attack and deposition site are identical), two rape cases with multiple locations and six rape cases with a single location. These cases were randomly chosen and provided in an anonymized format by the NPIA's Serious Crime Analysis Section, based on their suitability with regards to type (murder or rape) and crime location (single or multiple). Participants were given the case information and maps depicting the relevant location(s); however, crime data and locations cannot be published for confidentiality reasons. The Geos were also given details about these cases such as scene/locations addresses, victim information (demographic information only, no names), offender description (if available), a brief summary of the offence and circumstances and, if available, details of the forensics recovered from the scene(s). Again, these details cannot be reproduced here, due to confidentiality requirements. Participants noted their investigative suggestions, rationales and inferences on a response sheet.

Procedure

The Geoprofilers were provided with materials to work through in their own time. They were allowed to use all resources available for this exercise (e.g. libraries, the internet, academic research, maps, etc.). They then filled in their response sheets that were fed back to the researcher. This non-laboratory-based approach is a relatively realistic replication of how Geographic Profilers usually operate: in real life, they are provided with relevant case information they take away to work on. They use a variety of resources available that might be of use and return the finished 'product', i.e. a report, by an agreed deadline. However, in order not to encroach on their full-time operational capacity, case information for this study was kept to a minimum, as they were given a number of cases to work on and full reports by the Geos were not required.

Results

Coding

Participants' responses were transferred from their response sheets onto a spreadsheet. Their investigative suggestions, location inferences (i.e. where they thought the offender might live) and other inferences (e.g. 'The offender has detailed knowledge of the location') were coded by the researcher so that each statement that could be identified as a suggestion or inference was assigned a score between zero and three based on its usefulness/accuracy and specificity in relation to each case's actual outcome. Inter-rater reliability was not ascertained at the time and results should therefore be treated with caution. Furthermore, it should be noted that test-re-test reliability has not been established and future studies may want to address this issue in order to solidify the methodology of this pilot.

'*Suggestion*' scores were obtained by using the following coding system:
0 = ineffectual
1 = general and useful
2 = somewhat defined and useful
3 = specific and useful

Utility and specificity were ascertained by taking into account the actual real-life investigation's outcome and how the offender was caught. It is essential to consider the specificity of suggestions as it is vital for an investigation team to allocate resources reasonably. A suggestion like *"Do a DNA screen'* is very vague and is potentially much more costly and time-consuming than 'Do a DNA screen of all males over the age of 15 living within 2km of the offence location'. If a DNA screen in that particular case did not help progress the investigation, both those suggestions would have been coded as 0 (ineffectual). However, if a DNA screen did lead to the identification of the perpetrator, the first example statement above would have received a 1 (general and useful) whereas the second statement would have received a score of 3 (specific and useful). A specific suggestion is therefore seen as being of higher value than a vague or general one. In a police investigation, it is of utmost importance that advice be precise and of operational utility as well as based on thorough research and rationales.

Many suggestions were noted down on the response sheet that were perfectly reasonable and might well have aided an investigation (e.g. setting up CCTV cameras, initiating covert operations, doing media appeals etc). However, if they did not lead to the apprehension of the offender in the specific cases utilized for this study, they were also coded as ineffectual. This is because particular cases were used here rather than hypothetical scenarios and in each investigation there might be various leads that are followed, yet only one might resolve the case. The utility of Geoprofilers' input in 13 specific cases was examined for this study, hence it had to be taken into consideration whether a suggestion would actually have helped *in this particular case* or not, rather than determining if it is generally good practice to implement a specific suggestion, which in most cases, would indeed have been the case.

'*Location*' inferences were coded similarly using the following system:
0 = inaccurate
1 = general and accurate
2 = somewhat defined and accurate
3 = specific and accurate

Therefore a location inference stating 'The offender is likely to be local' would have received a 0 if inaccurate and only a 1 if accurate, whereas 'The offender is likely to live within 1.5km of x location' would have received a location score of 3 if accurate, yet also a 0 if inaccurate.

> *'Other inferences'* were coded similarly, using the following system:
> *0 = inaccurate / missing*
> *1 = general and accurate*
> *2 = somewhat defined and accurate*
> *3 = specific and accurate*

Such inferences might include statements like '…seems to indicate he has familiarity with the area' which again would have received a lower specificity ranking if accurate than a statement such as '…seems to indicate he has been to building x before'.

'Spot-on suggestions' were also determined by the researcher and were those that would have led directly to the identification of the perpetrator, if acted on by the investigation. For instance, if the offender in the actual case was in fact caught through CCTV at a particular location and the Geo included the suggestion to use CCTV at that spot on their response sheet, then that statement would have been counted as a spot-on suggestion. Each participant's suggestions were counted and the number of spot-on suggestions in relation to the total number of suggestions was determined as their spot-on percentage score.

The suggestive utility (*Sugg_Utility*), location accuracy (*Location*) and inference accuracy (*Inference*) scores are a combination of the specificity of the Geoprofiler's input and its accuracy. On each of those three measures, a maximum score of 3 could be obtained according to the coding system above. If the suggestion was ineffective or the inference was inaccurate (or no inference was made), a 0 was given; if the suggestion was general and useful or the inference was general and accurate it was given a score of 1; if the suggestion was somewhat defined and useful or the inference was somewhat defined and accurate it obtained a score of 2; and if the suggestion was specific and useful or the inference was specific and accurate it was given a score of 3. The spot-on score depicts the percentage of how many of the suggestions made would have identified the perpetrator.

To test the hypothesis that the Geoprofilers would be able to provide useful input on single cases with multiple locations, yet fail to do so for cases with only one location, the participants' scores for rape and murder cases were combined (single sites for both crime types vs. multiple sites for both types) to allow for a direct comparison between the two crime site classes (single vs. multiple locations). As the numbers of cases were not equal (there were four multiple location cases and nine single location cases), percentages of the maximum score that could have been achieved were calculated and compared, rather than total raw scores. For example, in the four cases containing multiple locations, the maximum amount of scores for suggestive utility, location and inference was 12 respectively, as each input could achieve a maximum of 3, which is multiplied by the number of cases.

Correlational analysis revealed a high correlation for location inferences and other inferences ($r = 0.654$, p [two-tailed] <0.05). In other words, if a participant achieved high scores on one of those measures, they were also likely to achieve high scores on the other.

As Table 6.3 suggests, the most utility was gained from Geoprofilers' inferences about where the offender might be living (mean location score $= 1.53$ with the minimum possible score $= 0$ and the maximum possible score $= 3$). The least accuracy was achieved with other inferences (mean inference score $= 0.78$) which included statements such as 'is likely to have familiarity with the area'.

Figure 6.1 shows that the utility of Geoprofilers' investigative suggestions is roughly equal for single cases with either multiple locations (41 per cent of maximum utility scores achieved) or a single location (47 per cent achieved). However, on the other three measures the Geos performed markedly better in the cases containing multiple locations. In those instances, 30 per cent of their suggestions were spot-on compared to only 15 per cent in single location cases. Similarly, they achieved 75 per cent of the maximum location inference score when working on cases with multiple locations compared to 52 per cent in single location cases. For multiple locations, 52 per cent of the maximum inference scores were achieved whereas only 15 per cent of the maximum inference score was achieved in the single location cases.

Discussion – Study 2

The aim of this pilot was to measure what, if anything, Geographic Profilers can contribute to single cases, i.e. those that are investigated without a connection to any other offence thought to have been committed by the same perpetrator. It was predicted that Geos would make some useful suggestions and accurate predictions for cases involving multiple locations, yet will fail to be of utility in cases involving a single location only. Contrary to this hypothesis, results indicate that the Geographic Profilers were of investigative utility even in cases

Table 6.3 Descriptive statistics for suggestions' utility, accuracy of inferences and locations and percentages of spot-on suggestions

	N	Range	Minimum	Maximum	Mean	Std. Deviation	Variance
Sugg_Utility	13	2.67	.33	3.00	**1.3538**	.81204	.659
Spot_On (%)	13	80.00	.00	80.00	**20.0769**	25.75028	663.077
Location	13	3.00	.00	3.00	**1.5385**	1.26592	1.603
Inference	13	2.00	.00	2.00	**.7885**	.82819	.686

involving only a single offence, albeit considerably less so than in cases for which multiple locations were known. Even though this was only a pilot study and replication on a larger scale involving all Geographic Profilers and an equal amount of cases for each case type is recommended, these initial findings suggest that Geoprofilers make accurate location inferences about where the offender is likely to be living or operating from, in 52 per cent (single location offences) to 75 per cent (multiple location cases) of cases (see Figure 6.1). This indicates that their input might indeed be of utility to single case investigations. The results from this pilot study were so promising that they effected a policy change within the NPIA's Serious Crime Analysis Section to include the Geographic Profilers automatically when a new case comes in for analysis, be it single or serial. Hitherto, the Geos got involved only when either recommended by designated personnel within the NPIA, or if an investigation specifically requested their involvement. Nevertheless, it should be borne in mind that this pilot would necessitate replication with the whole geographic profiling team and would also need to include ascertaining inter-rater reliability, as at present, the researcher was the only person carrying out the encoding of participants' responses, which might make the results more subjective than would have been the case with two researchers coding the data independently.

The distinction between single offences with a single site and single offences with multiple sites is of great significance. The former refers to crimes in which the encounter, attack, victim release / body dump and property deposition sites are identical. In other words, the offender encounters a victim, carries out the attack in that same location and then leaves without moving the victim or disposing of

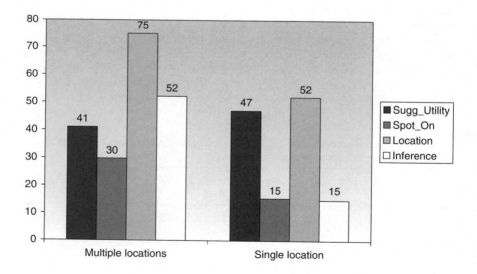

Figure 6.1 Comparison of Geoprofiling Utility Percentage for single Cases with either multiple Locations or a single Location.

property anywhere else. In this case, there is only one known location that can be included in the analysis. The alternative with multiple sites is one where the offender might encounter a victim in one location, take her somewhere else to carry out the rape/murder, possibly take her further to release her or dump the body, and perhaps deposit property taken or objects used in the attack in yet another locality, which is often on the way back to his base (Büchler & Leineweber, 1991; Rossmo, 2000). In such circumstances, there are several crime locations to work with, and there is far more potential for drawing inferences about the offender's movements (before, during and after the offence), familiarity with the area and decision-making process. Knowledge of further locations may also be gained from other information such as sightings, CCTV or mobile phone data, for instance.

Forty-one per cent of multiple and 47 per cent of single case *investigative suggestions* were seen as helpful. In terms of o*ther inferences,* 52 per cent of inferences for multiple locations and 15 per cent of inferences for single location cases were rated as accurate. It is currently not known to the authors which ratios (i.e. a suggestion-to-helpful-suggestion ratio and an inference-to-accurate-inference ratio) is classifiable as ineffective, moderately effective or very effective. In order to be able to put these numbers into perspective, one would need to examine the utility of other people's suggestions (for instance those of police investigators, for the same cases as those used in this study) or the Geos' own suggestions in serial cases, in order to ascertain whether these figures are operationally valuable or not. Such comparisons have not been carried out; however, in a related study which has not been published (Knabe, 2008), police investigators were given maps with serial crime site locations and details (time and location) of those mapped offences, and their output was scored on the same measures that were used on the Geographic Profilers in this study. The investigators' suggestive utility was between 5 per cent and 10 per cent. They were working on serial cases rather than single cases, therefore having more crime sites available, which, according to Rossmo (2000) should increase the likelihood of being able to correctly infer an offender's home base; on the other hand, they were given less information than the Geos. Therefore, a direct comparison would not be appropriate. Nevertheless, this great discrepancy in utility of investigative suggestions between the police investigators and the Geographic Profilers in those two studies seems to indicate that the Geos' scores achieved in this study are markedly higher than those of non-geographic experts, even when the police officers were provided with more crime sites (eleven sites in one study and nine in the other, both being serial offences).

The matter is somewhat different though with the *spot-on* scores for both case classes (single and multiple locations). This pilot study suggests that for cases with multiple locations, 30 per cent of the Geographic Profilers' suggestions (and 15 per cent in single location offences) would have directly led to the identification of the offender. Even though these numbers might appear relatively low when viewed in isolation, it should be noted that the fact that almost one in three of the Geos' suggestions (in multiple location cases) would have led the investigation straight to the apprehension of the perpetrator might be of high investigative utility indeed.

Interestingly, *location inferences* and other *inferences* were highly correlated ($r = 0.654$). Although further analyses would need to be conducted on this relationship, it is possible that both types of inferences are dependent upon similar factors, for instance the amount and detail of information provided, or the skills of the person making the inferences, etc. Although scores on one of these measures seem to increase as scores on the other increase, *location inference* scores did appear to be markedly higher than other *inference* scores across all four case types (see Figure 6.1). It is not known at this stage if that difference in accuracy is due to the expertise of Geoprofilers in geographic matters, or whether it is simply easier to make accurate location inferences than other investigative inferences. It might be beneficial to design a study in which Geographic Profilers would make both types of inferences as one group, to then be compared to Behavioural Investigative Advisers (BIAs) as the other group. One might argue that, traditionally, location inferences might be the domain of the Geos and many other inferences might be the realm of the BIAs, hence it would be interesting to ascertain if one of those two aspects was really somewhat 'easier' to make than the other, or if they are indeed expertise/domain specific.

It is possible that the relative reliability of participants' location inferences as compared to other inferences might be partly due to the fact that violent crimes were used as case materials in the present studies. Research suggests that violent offenders commit their crimes closer to a base than those who commit property offences, for instance (LeBeau, 1987; White, 1932). Therefore, it is not clear if property crimes had been used as case materials, whether the strength of location inferences would have remained this strong.

Conclusion

Geographic profiling is an investigative technique that spans well beyond its most commonly known remit of prioritizing search areas for serial offences. The findings of this paper, yet also the researcher's time spent studying the Geographic Profilers, suggest that they utilize fine-tuned techniques and skills to be able to provide investigative support in a variety of formats to a variety of cases. Their expertise in analysing temporal and spatial patterns, examining movements and routes as well as many other aspects that might add information to the data matrix allows them to provide advice on both single as well as serial cases. It seems that this expertise is developed through a thorough prescribed training process as well as firsthand operational experience. The Geoprofilers get involved when a known suspect needs to be located, when a body needs to be found in order to start a case against a suspect, when covert operations need to be set up, when areas need to be prioritized, when a single violent crime has been committed and when people have gone missing in suspicious circumstances.

Although Study 2 suggested that the presence of multiple known locations in a crime significantly increases the Geos' investigative utility (as opposed to having a single location only), the Geographic Profilers seemed to have been able to provide a high level of useful advice and make correct inferences in single cases. This pilot study might have been the first one to investigate the utility of geographic profiling in single cases, and these preliminary results look promising. Though geographic profiling has been thought to be used mainly to support serial crime investigations, the UK's Geos have been working successfully on a large number of single case investigations for years, and the pilot study points towards the validity of that work. Clearly, more research is needed into geographic profiling of single cases, however it seems that current definitions of the technique as a tool primarily or even solely for the apprehension of serial offenders is evidently inaccurate.

The purpose of this chapter was to scrutinize the profession of Geographic Profilers and to examine their utility in an operational setting. The Geographic Profilers were found to have the ability to infer geographical knowledge and familiarity with an area as well as an offender's routines, from the temporal and spatial distribution of known locations, the offender's degree of preparation, his access and escape routes, speech and target selection. Their profession entails the analysis of a large amount of sometimes ambiguous information with the aim of extraction of the above patterns and cues. Geos attempt to determine why an offender chose a particular location or victim, and how that rationale can be used by police to advance the investigation.

As far as the authors are aware, most if not all previous published work has discussed geographic profiling from an academic, quantitative and theoretical perspective; however this paper attempted to apply academic rigour to the actual operational setting of geographic profiling in order to gain the most accurate and detailed insight possible. Therefore, only professionals who would in reality be working on serious investigations were selected as participants, specifically, Geographic Profilers. The cases they were given to work on were real-life investigations. Furthermore, the case materials they were provided with were similar to those that were available to the investigating officer at the time, without any guarantee of offender typology or target backcloth.

The research presented in this chapter suggests the presence of an inherent expertise in analysing and drawing meaning from geographic behaviour that has developed in Geographic Profilers, which enables them to create a holistic picture of an offender's use of space and time, and to use that understanding to produce investigative advice.

References

Abernethy, B. (1987) 'Anticipation in sport: a review', *Physical Education Review*, 10: 5–16.

Abernethy, B., Gill, D.P., Parks, S.L. and Packer, S.T. (2001) 'Expertise and the perception of kinematic and situational probability information', *Perception*, 30: 233–252.

Alison, L., Bennell, C., Mokros, A. and Ormerod, D. (2002) 'The personality paradox in offender profiling: a theoretical review of the processes involved in deriving background characteristics from crime scene actions', *Psychology, Public Policy & Law*, 8: 115–135.

Almond, L., Alison, L., Eyre, M., Crego, J. and Goodwill, A. (2008) 'Heuristics and biases in decision making', in L. Alison and J. Crego (eds) *Policing Critical Incidents: Leadership and Critical Incident Management*, Cullompton: Willan.

Ask, K. and Granhag, P. (2005) 'Motivational Sources of Confirmation Bias in Criminal Investigations', *Journal of Investigative Psychology and Offender Profiling*, 2: 43–63.

Bennell, C. and Canter, D.V. (2002) 'Linking commercial burglaries by modus operandi: tests using regression and ROC analysis', *Science and Justice*, 42: 153–164.

Bennell, C. and Jones, N.J. (2005) 'Between a ROC and a hard place: a method for linking serial burglaries by modus operandi', *Journal of Investigative Psychology and Offender Profiling*, 2: 23–41.

Bennell, C. Snook, B. and Taylor, P. (2005) 'Geographic Profiling – The debate continues: ten problems with the Rossmo and Filer defence of computer profiling', *Blue Line Magazine*, October 2005.

Brantingham, P.J. and Brantingham, P.L. (1981) *Environmental criminology*, Thousand Oaks, CA: Sage Publications, Inc.

Brantingham, P.J. and Brantingham, P.L. (1984) 'Patterns In Crime', New York: Macmillan.

Büchler, H. and Leineweber, H. (1991) 'The escape behaviour of bank robbers and circular blockade operations by the police', in E. Kube and H.U. Störzer (eds) *Police research in the Federal Republic of Germany: 15 years research within the "Bundeskriminalamt")*, Berlin: Springer- Verlag.

Canter, D. (2003) *Mapping Murder: Walking in the killer's footsteps*, London: Virgin Books.

Canter, D. and Larkin, P. (1993) 'The environmental range of serial rapists', *Journal of Environmental Psychology*, 13: 63–69.

Chase, W.G. and Simon, H.A. (1973) 'The mind's eye in chess', in W.G. Chase (ed.) *Visual information processing*, New York: Academic Press.

Gilis, B., Helsen, W., Catteeuw, P. and Wagemans, J. (2008) 'Offside decisions by expert assistant referees in association football: perception and recall of spatial positions in complex dynamic events', *Journal of Experimental Psychology*, 14(1): 21–35.

Godwin, M. (1996) *Mapping Human Predators: the geographical behaviour of fifty-four American serial killers*. Online. Available HTTP: < www.geocomputation.org/1996/abs040.htm> (accessed 4 October 2010).

Grubin, D., Kelly, P. and Brunsdon, C. (2001) *Linking serious sexual assault through behaviour*, London: Home Office, Research Development and Statistics Directorate.

Klein, G.A., Calderwood, R. and MacGregor, D. (1989) 'Critical Decision Method for Eliciting Knowledge', *IEEE Transactions on Systems*, Man, and Cybernetics, May/June: 462–472.

Knabe, S. (2008) 'Geographic Profiling Under The Microscope: a critical examination of the utility of geographic profiling and expert geographic profilers', unpublished Master's thesis, University of Liverpool.

Kocsis, R.N. and Irwin, H.J. (1997) 'An analysis of spatial patterns in serial rape, arson, and burglary: the utility of the circle theory of environmental range for psychological profiling', *Psychiatry, Psychology and Law*, 4: 195–206.

LeBeau, J.L. (1987) 'The journey to rape: geographic distance and the rapist's method of approaching the victim', *Journal of Police Science and Administration*, 15: 129–136.

Militello, L.G., Hutton, R.J.B., Pliske, R.M., Knight, B.J. and Klein, G. (1997) *Applied Cognitive Task Analysis (ACTA) Methodology (Rep. No. NPRDCTN-98-4)*, San Diego, CA: Navy Personnel Research and Development Center.

NPIA (2010) *Geographical Profiler*. Online. Available at HTTP: <http://npia.police.uk/en/6857.htm> (accessed September 2008).

Ratcliffe, J.H. (2004) 'Crime Mapping and the training needs of law enforcement', *European Journal on Criminal Policy and Research*, 10: 65–83.

Reber, A.S. (1985) *The Penguin Dictionary of Psychology*, Harmondsworth: Penguin.

Richler, J.J., Gauthier, I., Wenger, M.J. and Palmeri, T.J. (2008) 'Holistic processing of faces: perceptual and decisional components', *Journal of Experimental Psychology*, Learning, Memory, and Cognition, 34(2): 328–342.

Rossmo, D.K. (1997) 'Geographic profiling', in Jackson, D.A. Jackson, J.L. and Bekerian, D.A. (eds) *Offender profiling: Theory, research and practice*, Chichester: Wiley.

Rossmo, D.K. (2000) *Geographic Profiling*, Boca Raton, FL: CRC Press.

Rossmo, D.K. (2005) 'Commentary: geographic heuristics or shortcuts to failure? response to Snook et al.' *Applied Cognitive Psychology*, 19: 651–654.

Savelsbergh, G.J.P., Van der Kamp, J., Williams, A.M. and Ward, P. (2005) 'Anticipation and visual search behaviour in expert soccer goalkeepers', *Ergonomics*, 48: 1686–1697.

Shanteau, J. (1988) 'Psychological characteristics of expert decision makers', *Acta Psychologica*, 68: 203–215.

Snook, B., Canter, D.V. and Bennell, C. (2002) 'Predicting the home location of serial offenders: a preliminary comparison of the accuracy of human judges with a geographic profiling system', *Behavioral Sciences and the Law*, 20: 1–10.

Snook, B., Taylor, P.J. and Bennell, C. (2004) 'Geographic Profiling: The Fast, Frugal, and Accurate Way', *Applied Cognitive Psychology*, 18: 105–121.

Tamura, M. and Suzuki, M. (1997) 'Criminal profiling research on serial arson: examinations of circle hypothesis estimating offender's residential area', *Research on Prevention of Crime and Delinquency*, 38: 13–25.

Townsley, M., Smith, C. and Pease, K. (2005) 'Using DNA to catch offenders quicker: serious detections arising from criminal justice samples', *Jill Dando Institute of Crime Science*.

Waters, A.J., Townsend, E. and Underwood, G. (1998) 'Expertise in musical sight reading: a study of pianists', *British Journal of Psychology*, 89: 123–149.

Williams, A.M. and Burwitz, L. (1993) 'Advance cue utilization in soccer', in T. Reilly, J. Clarys and A. Stibbe (eds) *Science and Football II*, London: E & FN Spon.

White, C.R. (1932) 'The relation of felonies to environmental factors in Indianapolis', *Social Forces*, 10: 498–509.

Woodhams, J., Hollin, C.R., and Bull, R. (2007) 'The psychology of linking crimes: a review of the evidence', *Legal and Criminological Psychology*, 12: 233–249.

7   Familial DNA prioritization

Adam Gregory and Lee Rainbow

Introduction

Having already discussed *what* Behavioural Investigative Advisers (BIAs) do (see Chapters 2 and 3), the aim of this chapter is to explore in greater detail exactly *how* BIAs synthesize their expertise within the investigative arena. We have already been quite vocal in our criticism of naive academic commentaries of behavioural investigative advice within this volume, highlighting the rather simplistic straw man argument concerning lack of scientific reliability and validity as somewhat disingenuous. The aim of this chapter is to demonstrate contemporary BIAs' continued development of robust scientific methodologies in an attempt to further educate the misinformed spectator and to support the notion of continuing professionalism within the discipline of Behavioural Investigative Advice.

In this chapter we focus on the relatively new investigative tool of familial DNA analysis to demonstrate such evolving contributions from BIAs. We begin with a brief introduction of the underlying forensic science, before making explicit the methodological and analytical advancements developed by the authors to significantly enhance success in offender identification.

It is highlighted that such service provision is only available from the National Policing Improvement Agency's Crime Operational Support Section (NPIA COS) due to the multidisciplinary expertise and access to sensitive and confidential data required. As such, the services and products described in this chapter should not be taken as representative of standard BIA provision within the UK.

Background

The UK's National DNA Database (NDNAD) has become one of the most potent tools in the resolution of major crime investigations. References to a 'DNA hit' have become common parlance within media reporting and investigative arenas. Indeed, 'crime scene' DNA profiles (i.e. DNA recovered from the scene of a crime that is believed to belong to the unknown offender) are matched to the profiles of known individuals on the NDNAD at a rate of over 100 a day across all offence types, with an average 48 rape and 23 murder offences matched every month (NPIA, 2010). However, what is perhaps less well known and certainly less well understood is that an increasing number of major crime investigations are being detected through a less direct application of the NDNAD – that of 'familial DNA searching'.

If a DNA profile can be retrieved from the scene of an undetected homicide, rape or other serious crime then the primary hope for the police is that it will match against a known individual whose DNA profile has already been loaded onto the NDNAD. Since the inception of the NDNAD in 1995, it is estimated that over five million individuals (NPIA, 2010) have been sampled and their DNA retained within this central UK database. However, with a population of 60 million, and a continuous increase in individuals reaching the age of legal responsibility, even a database of five million people does not guarantee detection through this simple matching process.

Familial DNA searching is a secondary process whereby a DNA profile (typically assumed to be that of an unknown offender) is searched across the NDNAD to identify potential close relatives of an offender when the offender's DNA profile is not present.

Since 2003, the process has been undertaken in more than 180 major crime investigations, leading to the apprehension of a significant number of offenders. Analysis of available data reveals a total of 33 offenders have been directly identified through familial DNA searching, responsible for 13 murders, 40 serious sexual offences, seven armed robberies, one kidnap and three offences relating to child abandonment. The first conviction to be obtained through the use of familial DNA searching of the NDNAD was in 2004.

The science

As outlined above, familial DNA searching is a search of the NDNAD to identify potential close relatives of an offender when the offender's DNA profile is not present on the NDNAD. It works on the general principle that people who are related are likely to have more DNA in common than those who are not, and thereby seeks to identify individuals on the NDNAD who have a greater genetic similarity to the unknown offender and hence a greater potential to be related.

DNA is inherited and all members of a family will share certain amounts of DNA. Children will share half their DNA with their father and half with their mother. The extent to which siblings will share their DNA is variable, but they will tend to share a larger proportion of DNA than unrelated persons.

Adapted from proven, validated methodologies utilized in paternity testing, familial DNA searching expresses a 'likelihood ratio' (LR) for each person on the NDNAD, calculated by considering which DNA components (or alleles) are shared by individuals on the familial search list and the perceived offender, and how frequently these occur within the general population. The strength of the evidence for a familial relationship is formalized as an LR, through comparison of the probability of observing the degree of genetic similarity if the person is *related* to the offender, with the probability of observing the degree of genetic similarity if the person is *unrelated* to the offender. A genetic LR can thus be expressed in its simplest terms as:

Probability of observing this degree of genetic similarity if the person is related to the offender

---

Probability of observing this degree of genetic similarity if the person is unrelated to the offender

Due to the differing patterns of genetic inheritance between parents/children and siblings, two different search algorithms result in two separate results lists being produced from the NDNAD; one for potential parent/child (P/C) relationships and one for potential sibling (Sib) relationships.

In simple mathematical terms, anyone with a LR greater than 1 would be seen as more likely to be related to the unknown offender whilst those with an LR of less than 1 would be more likely to be unrelated.

However, due to the laws of probability and the large number of individuals on the NDNAD, in practice the number of individuals with an LR greater than one is typically many thousands. This presents a significant problem to investigators who do not have the resources to research such large numbers of individuals and families for a potential link to the offender. Whilst the potential relatives of the unknown offender are ranked by the magnitude of the LR, finite resources typically result in only the very top of these lists being actionable in terms of further investigative research.

Prioritization

In recognition of these issues, some attempts have been made to further prioritize these lists, utilizing criteria such as age and geographic location. Relying on assumptions regarding offender geography (i.e. offenders tend to commit crime close to home), lack of familial dispersion (i.e. relatives of the offender are likely to live close to the offender and hence close to the offence location) and familial age distribution (i.e. parents of the offender are more likely to be 25 years older than the offender than 15 years older), the original familial DNA search results are reprioritized in an attempt to raise the level of potential relatives above purely genetic similarity. However, as is often the case with the application of forensic science techniques to what is in fact an investigative arena, the structure and parameters of the search and the interpretation of the results it creates are critical factors in its overall success. Given that the estimations of age and geographic association are often those proposed by the Senior Investigating Officer (SIO), their validity and utility in cases not previously supported by a BIA or a Geographic Profiler is likely to be rather variable. Furthermore, as is often the case with police investigation more generally, the implementation of these factors is by way of 'filters', ruling individuals in or out, rather than attempting to integrate the factors to support a more holistic prioritization.

Such considerations can be made explicit with reference to the following example. Consider a rape offence in which predictions were made that the offender would be between 20 and 40 years of age, would reside within five miles of the crime scene and have previous convictions for violent offending. Whilst filters could easily be set on the basis of these predictions – looking only for violent offenders between 20 and 40 residing within five miles – we could easily miss someone. A known sex offender, 30 years of age, living within one mile of the crime scene but with no violent pre-cons would be effectively eliminated. Furthermore, since the parameters are quite broad, even the number of individuals matching all factors may be too large for the investigation to effectively manage, with no discrimination evident between them. Of those individuals who 'pass' these filters, should we be more interested in a 20 year old living within 100 yards of the scene, or a 32 year old who lives four miles away?

Whilst employing the right filters can, and indeed has, resulted in the swift identification of offenders' relatives within familial DNA searches, the process is unnecessarily risky, necessitates additional assumptions having to be made and lacks both the methodological rigour and critically the resultant prioritization one might expect from such a system.

BIA Methodology

The authors have been strong advocates of the principle that searching for relatives of an unknown offender through the use of familial DNA should not be a purely genetic exercise. However, we have been equally vocal that the degree of methodological and empirical rigour inherent in the genetic aspect of the process should be replicated in other more behavioural facets of equal relevance to the offence(s) under consideration.

Common BIA practice in the above scenario would be to utilize a 'matrix' approach in which individuals are scored against each of the relevant categories in terms of whether they match or not, but also, where applicable, how well they match. In this way, the system identifies the best matches overall but also allows for the situation in which someone matches well on only two out of the three categories. They are not 'filtered out', but simply deprioritized relative to those who match the predictions even more closely.

An offender commits an offence at a fixed point in time, in a location of his choosing. These crucial facets of the crime should not be overlooked when one undertakes a familial DNA search. Behavioural science, and the discipline of behavioural investigative advice in particular, provides us with a greater understanding of where offenders may choose to offend, and why, and also the extent to which estimations of their most likely age can be deduced from a careful examination of 'crime scene' data. Harnessing the relevant research and empirical data as well as the expertise of practitioners in the field should allow for prioritization to be achieved in these two areas. Indeed this is no more than BIAs currently offer to major crime investigations as routine advice (see Chapter 2).

If, as is proposed here, accurate age assessments can be made for the offender and reliable predictions made as to his probable association to the crime scene, we have the starting point for effective 'behavioural' prioritization of his potential relatives.

Knowledge of an offender's likely age allows for prediction of the most likely age of his parents as well as any siblings and children he may have. Similarly, identifying that an offender has knowledge of, and therefore an association to, a particular geographic area may well relate closely to similar knowledge held by his family members, or at least a prediction that their own geographic associations may not be too far away.

In terms of familial DNA searching, it is therefore proposed that a prioritization system should take account of all relevant factors, as well as have the ability to discriminate between those matching to differing degrees. The factors should be objectively weighted according to relevant, reliable data and the resultant values combined into a meaningful 'composite' value (i.e. a value that takes account of the relative and appropriate contribution of genetics, age and geographical association). This is achieved through the development of LRs for both age and geographic association.

Age

In order to calculate an LR with respect to age, we first need to derive an accurate age estimation for the offender. As it is beyond the scope of this chapter to detail the complexities, methodology, data and caveats concerning such a process, for the purposes of the present discussion, an accurate (or at least a BIA inferred) estimation will be assumed.

In order to prioritize individuals in relation to age, we are essentially comparing the age of individuals returned from the familial DNA searches against that which we would expect for any of the offender's potential relatives. For example, if the estimated age of the offender were to be determined as being between 37 and 47 years, a 34-year-old male from the parent–child familial list is probably too old to be a son of the offender and certainly too young to be his father. Conversely, a 75-year-old female from this list has a *relatively* high probability of being the mother of the offender.

As with the calculation for 'genetic LR', once the offender age prediction has been made, we need to consider the difference between the estimated offender age and the age of an individual returned in the familial DNA search list under two hypotheses:

A   the probability of observing the age of an individual returned from the familial DNA search if the individual is *related* to the offender;
B   the probability of observing the age of an individual returned from the familial DNA search if the individual is *unrelated* to the offender.

An LR for age can then be calculated by dividing the first probability by the second. These calculations will differ according to which familial search is being considered – the parent–child (P/C) search, or the sibling (Sib) search.

Parent–child search

With respect to hypothesis 'A', UK statistics for the ages at which mothers and fathers have children were analysed in order to compute the probabilities of parents having children at different ages. These figures were retrieved from the Home Office for National Statistics in England and Wales, the General Register Office for Scotland and the Northern Ireland Statistics and Research Agency (births recorded between 1964 and 2005; total number of births considered for mothers: 30,477,118; total number of births considered for fathers: 30,444,905). Probabilities were calculated separately for mothers and fathers and utilized in the following way:

- predicting the age of the offender's mother – mother age data;
- predicting the age of the offender's father – father age data;
- predicting the age of the offender's potential son – father age data;
- predicting the age of the offender's potential daughter – father age data.

By way of example, the probabilities associated with a mothers' age at childbirth are given in Figure 7.1 and Table 7.1.

Reference to Figure 7.1 and Table 7.1 illustrate some interesting findings. For example, it can be seen that women are approximately twice as likely to have a child at the age of 28 as they are at 33. The probability of a female having a child at the age of 19 is very similar to the probability aged 31, and so on. It is also noteworthy that at the extremes it becomes very unlikely ($p < 0.01$) that a female will give birth to a child prior to the age of 16, or after the age of 38. This is important since whilst there will of course be exceptions to these national trends, from a probability perspective, in familial DNA terms and relative to other birthing ages, these ages can be objectively deprioritized.

In order to compute the probabilities of observing the age of individuals returned from familial DNA search lists if unrelated to the offender – Hypothesis 'B' – statistical data representing the age profile of the UK (by year of birth) have been used (data taken from mid-year population estimates for 2008, obtained from the Office for National Statistics [ONS], 2010).

As a concrete example, if an offender is believed to be 25 years old and a female returned from the familial DNA (P/C) search list is 52 years old (i.e. born in 1959), the age at which she could have given birth to the offender would be 27. As such reference to Table 1 reveals that the probability of observing a 52-year-old female if she is the mother of the offender is 0.064125. The probability of observing a 52-year-old female if the individual is unrelated to the offender is simply the probability of observing an individual born in 1959. Reference to the ONS data reveals this to be 0.013404127.

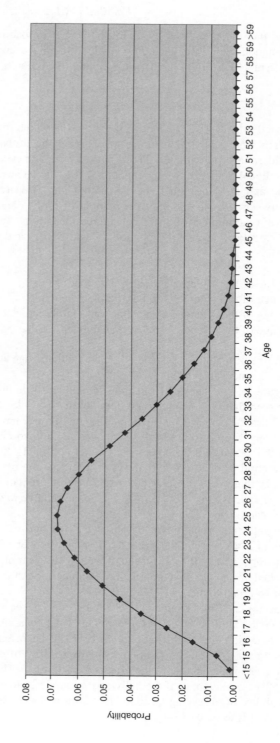

Figure 7.1 The probabilities of mothers' age at childbirth.

Table 7.1 The probabilities of mothers' age at childbirth

Age	Probability	Age	Probability	Age	Probability	Age	Probability
<15	0.001596	23	0.065171	32	0.035593	41	0.002841
15	0.006409	24	0.067930	33	0.030082	42	0.001713
16	0.015950	25	0.068302	34	0.024931	43	0.000948
17	0.025977	26	0.066886	35	0.020069	44	0.001017
18	0.035563	27	0.064125	36	0.015714	45	0.000007
19	0.043515	28	0.059908	37	0.012147	46	0.000002
20	0.050687	29	0.054935	38	0.009055	47	0.000001
21	0.056480	30	0.048043	39	0.006446	>47	<0.000001
22	0.061265	31	0.042068	40	0.004294		

The LR with respect to age can then be calculated by dividing the first probability (under hypothesis A – related) by the second (under hypothesis B – unrelated), such that:

LR(age) = p (hyp. A) / p (hyp. B)
LR(age) = 0.064125 / 0.013404
LR(age) = 4.784020

However, given that in an operational scenario we are considering the offender to be within a specified *age range*, this methodology has been adapted to account for such ranges rather than discrete, individual values. As such, relevant probabilities are averaged to provide an overall probability of each person on the familial DNA search list actually being a parent or child of the offender. For example: if an offender is believed to be between 22 and 32 years, and a female returned from the familial DNA (P/C) search list is 48 years old (born in 1962), the age at which she could have given birth to the offender ranges from 16 to 26 years.

Under the above circumstances, the probabilities for each age between 16 and 26 years (from Table 7.1) would be averaged to yield the overall probability of a 48-year-old woman being the correct age to be the offender's mother (see Table 7.2).

Therefore, in this example the overall probability of observing a 48-year-old female from the P/C familial DNA search list if the female is the offender's mother is 0.050702.

The probability of observing a 48-year-old female if unrelated to the offender would simply be that of a UK female happening to have been born in 1962 by chance. Again from the ONS data this probability can be stated as 0.014580.

As such, the LR with respect to age can be calculated as:

LR(age) = p (hyp. A) / p (hyp. B)
LR(age) = 0.050702 / 0.014580
LR(age) = 3.477503

Table 7.2 Probability of observing a 48-year-old female if related as a mother to the offender (if the offender's estimated age is 22–32 years old)

Age of mother (at birth of child)	Probability (if related)
16	0.015950
17	0.025977
18	0.035563
19	0.043515
20	0.050687
21	0.056480
22	0.061265
23	0.065171
24	0.067930
25	0.068302
26	0.066886
Mean	**0.050702**

To put this statistical result into context, it can be seen that a 48-year-old female returned from the familial DNA search analysis is almost three and a half times more likely to be the mother of the offender (with an estimated age of 22 to 32 years) than chance.

By way of contrast, if we consider the age LR for a 70-year-old individual from the parent–child list, the corresponding calculations produce a value of only 0.2659, almost the exact inverse of the LR for the 48-year-old (i.e. this time it is the unrelated probability which is approximately three and a half times greater than the related).

Sibling search

With respect to potential siblings, in order to deduce the probabilities required under hypothesis 'A' (i.e. related to the offender) we are interested in how many years tend to separate full (same mother and father) siblings. Unlike parental data however, no relevant national statistics exist. Therefore a survey was undertaken to identify the frequencies with which specific age differences between sibling pairs occur. The age differences for 248 sibling pairs from 108 families (opportunistically sampled) were computed. In doing this, the ages of a total of 277 individuals were considered (*mean age* = 29.2, *SD* = 12.8). The mean number of siblings in each family was 2.56 (*SD* = 0.77). Fifty-eight per cent of the families had two siblings, 30 per cent had three siblings, 9 per cent had four siblings, and 3 per cent had five siblings. None of the families surveyed had more than five siblings.

As we are concerned with the direction of the age difference (for computational purposes) and not just the age difference per se, the frequencies of each age difference were halved to generate directional values for one sibling being a

Table 7.3 The probabilities of different age differences between siblings

Age Diff.	Probability	Age Diff.	Probability
+10	0.014113	−1	0.036291
+9	0.014113	−2	0.118952
+8	0.024194	−3	0.104839
+7	0.020162	−4	0.064516
+6	0.026210	−5	0.044355
+5	0.044355	−6	0.026210
+4	0.064516	−7	0.020162
+3	0.104839	−8	0.024194
+2	0.118952	−9	0.014113
+1	0.036291	−10	0.014113
0	0.024194		

particular number of years 'older' or 'younger' than another. The probability values for age differences from +10 to −10 are illustrated in Table 7.3.

As with the parent–child search, because we are working with an estimated age range for the offender, the probabilities for the relevant range of potential age differences must be identified and averaged to give the overall probability value.

For example, if an offender was estimated as being 20 to 30 years of age, and we are interested in the probability of a 27-year-old male being related to him as a sibling, the probabilities for each age difference between −3 and +7 would be averaged to yield the overall probability of a 27-year-old being the correct age to be the offender's sibling (see Table 7.4).

Once again, in common with the calculations for the parent–child search, the probability of an individual being 27 'by chance' (i.e. under hypothesis 'B') is simply the probability of being born in 1983, this is found to be 0.013424.

As such, the LR with respect to age can be calculated as:

LR(age) = p (hyp. A) / p (hyp. B)
LR(age) = 0.063600 / 0.013424
LR(age) = 4.737783

This implies that the chance of observing a 27-year-old individual from a familial DNA search if they are in fact a sibling of the offender is almost five times higher than observing this aged individual if they are unrelated (i.e. by chance).

By way of contrast, if we consider the age LR for a 40-year-old individual from the sibling search, the corresponding calculations produce a value of only 0.213160, almost the exact inverse of the LR for the 27-year-old (i.e. this time it is the unrelated probability which is approximately five times greater than the related).

Table 7.4 Probability of observing a 27-year-old male if related as a sibling to the offender (if the offender's estimated age is 20–30 years old)

Relative ages	Age Diff.	Probability (if related)
20 & 27	+7	0.020162
21 & 27	+6	0.026210
22 & 27	+5	0.044355
23 & 27	+4	0.064516
24 & 27	+3	0.104839
25 & 27	+2	0.118952
26 & 27	+1	0.036291
27 & 27	0	0.024194
28 & 27	−1	0.036291
29 & 27	−2	0.118952
30 & 27	−3	0.104839
Mean		**0.063600**

Geographic association

The general premise that underpins our familial DNA methodology with respect to geographic association is that family dispersion tends to happen over relatively small distances, rather than very large ones. In other words when moving from a family home, individuals tend to move elsewhere in the same locality, or to areas in close proximity, rather than relocate to towns and cities more geographically distant. Whilst one may expect regional differences to exist across the UK in terms of migration patterns, the above relationship can generally be expected to follow a 'distance decay' function, with the probability of identifying a family member decreasing as distance from the crime scene increases. Such expectation is supported from analysis of census data (Champion, 2005), which, notwithstanding the fact that there will always be exceptions, supports the notion that from a prioritization perspective we are *most likely* to find relatives of serious crime offenders in the same broad geographic areas as the offenders themselves.

One of the most consistent and compelling criminological/criminal psychological research findings is that offenders tend to commit their offences in areas they know and in which they feel comfortable (e.g. Brantingham and Brantingham, 1981). Quite routinely these areas are found to be those around their own homes – their geographic movements being as relevant to their day to day lives as their criminal activities. Patterns identified in the analysis of serious crime offenders appear to adhere equally well to these general rules (e.g. Davies and Dale, 1995; Rossmo et al, 2004), meaning that the sorts of offences for which familial DNA searches may be commissioned are likely to have been committed by offenders with strong links (typically through residence) to the areas in which they offend. As such, in most cases we can expect the offender to live close to the location of his crime(s) and the offender's relatives to live relatively close to the offender.

A further enhancement of this principle, utilized in our familial DNA prioritization methodology, is to acknowledge other geographic sites of relevance to the offender and his potential relatives in addition to the current offence location and possible residence. By working closely with both the Serious Crime Analysis Section (SCAS) and the Police National Computer (PNC), we are able to match individuals returned in a familial DNA search with their corresponding records on the PNC, resulting in other geographic associations becoming visible to us. These would potentially include previous addresses, places frequented, offence locations, relevant custody locations and so on. These additional details allow for a more complete picture of an individual's geographic associations to be developed, upon which more effective prioritization can be based.

It is worth considering the potential benefits of this richness of data for investigations. As highlighted above, more simplistic approaches to the prioritization of familial DNA search results have been attempted with respect to geographical association. However, the geographic information available from the NDNAD relates only to the police station at which that person's DNA sample was taken at the time they were loaded to the database. This location may or may not be a good indicator of where the individual actually resides, where they offend, where they work, etc. Such an association may, for example, be the result of criminal activity whilst at university or whilst attending a party at a location of no relevance to the offender. By extension, it could have little relevance in terms of where the individual's family members are most likely to be found. Furthermore, this geographic reference point is static in the sense that it will not change even if the offender goes on to offend or live in a completely different area of the country.

Also available to us through the PNC, and of significant potential relevance given the familial nature of what we are seeking to prioritize, is the place of birth of the individual. One can imagine a scenario in which a family member has moved from an area in which he or she used to co-reside with the offender to elsewhere in the country, particularly if the offence under investigation happens to be from 20 or 30 years ago (a fairly common scenario given the revisiting of historical cases such advancements in forensic science often promote). If the offence location is geographically close to the family birthplace, a relative now residing and offending hundreds of miles away could still be linked back to the area of interest through their place of birth. Such success would even result in cases where the offender had also distanced himself from the scene of the crime in subsequent years.

In order to prioritize individuals in relation to geographic association then, we are essentially comparing the geographic associations of individuals returned from the familial DNA search lists with what would be expected for any of the offender's potential relatives.

If, for example, we believed an offender has a geographical association with Rochdale, we might propose that an individual who could be geographically linked to Rochdale via any information recorded on the NDNAD or the PNC (birthplace, residence, offending, etc.) should be of high priority. Next we would need to recognize that those with links to nearby Manchester may be more likely to represent potential relatives than individuals with geographic associations solely within Plymouth or Aberdeen, and so on.

In practice, prior to calculating an LR with respect to geographic association, we need to first evaluate the strength of association between the offender and the location or locations in which he has chosen to offend. It would make little sense to provide an investigation with prioritization criteria for potential family members if we were not confident that there was even an association between the offence location(s) and the offender.

Provided we are confident that the choice of crime site(s) reflects the offender's underlying knowledge of the area (as is typically the case) we need to deduce the following for each person returned in a familial DNA search:

A   the probability of observing the distance between the relevant crime location(s) and the closest geographic association of the individual if they are *related* to the offender;
B   the probability of observing the distance between the relevant crime location(s) the closest geographic association of the individual if they are *unrelated* to the offender.

With respect to hypothesis 'A', calculations are performed utilizing census data relating to individuals' migration patterns. Probabilities of various distances existing between family members were deduced as a way of most closely modelling likely familial dispersion. An excerpt of the data used is provided in Table 7.5.

Table 7.5 Probability of moving particular distances (UK) *Adapted from UK Census, 2001*

Distance moved (to closest km)	Probability of moving this distance
0	0.158
1	0.123
2	0.096
3	0.073
4	0.056
5	0.042
6	0.031
7	0.023
8	0.018
9	0.013
10	0.010
11	0.008
12	0.007
13	0.006
14	0.005
15	0.005

Whilst the above data could be used to calculate discrete probabilities for the distances from the crime site of each individual returned from the familial DNA search lists (i.e. 3.42 kms, 13.86 kms, etc.), this level of discrimination exceeds the overall aims of *prioritization*. It is deemed sufficient for operational purposes to assign geographic zones. The size (i.e. radius) of these zones is determined by a number of factors including the likely strength of association between the offender and the crime scene, the nature of the area itself (urban/rural), the proximity of the offence location to major towns or city centres, the location of force or postcode boundaries (used in the calculation of population figures) and additional factors relating to the police processes in the area, such as the location of relevant police stations, local DNA sampling procedures and so on.

The probability value with respect to hypothesis 'B' will simply be the probability of randomly selecting an individual living within any specified area by chance. This is calculated by dividing the population of the areas of interest (i.e. the 'zones') by the population of the UK as a whole. UK statistics for the population of areas by postcode (from the 2001 Census) are utilized in order to calculate these probabilities.

As an illustrative example, if an offence took place at location 'X' within Greater Manchester (and we are confident that the choice of crime site reflects the offender's underlying knowledge of the area), a series of zones can be constructed as illustrated in Figure 7.2.

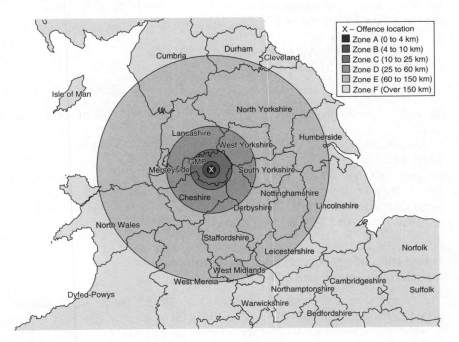

Figure 7.2 Geographic zones radiating from the crime site (i.e. area of offender geographic association).

Table 7.6 Geographic Likelihood Ratios (LRs) for each of the six prescribed zones

Zone	Range (km)	Likelihood Ratio (LR)
A	0–4	78.45
B	4–10	9.73
C	10–25	2.75
D	25–60	0.93
E	60–150	0.33
F	150–2000	0.17

Reference to Table 7.5 reveals that the probability of observing an individual from the familial DNA search list having a geographic association within 4 km of the area (Zone A) of offender geographic association (i.e. crime site) if related to the offender is 0.506 (i.e. 0.158 + 0.123 + 0.096 + 0.073 + 0.056).

The probability of observing an individual from the familial DNA search list living within 4km of the crime site if the individual is unrelated (hypothesis 'B') is the population of the prescribed zone divided by the population of the UK as a whole. In this example, such a probability would equate to 0.00645 (368,154/ 57,103,927).

The LR with respect to geographic association for Zone A (0–4 km) can then be calculated by dividing the first probability (under hypothesis A – related) by the second (under hypothesis B – unrelated), such that:

LR(geo) = p (hyp. A) / p (hyp. B)
LR(geo) = 0.506 / 0.00645
LR(geo) = 78.45

Table 7.6 illustrates the 'distance decay' nature of the zones' LRs from the above example.

As such, an individual returned from the familial DNA search list who has a geographic association within 14 km of the crime site, for example, would be assigned an LR(geo) of 2.75 and is therefore almost three times more likely to be a relative of the offender than chance, compared with an individual with a geographic association 120 km from the crime site who is three times more likely to be unrelated to the offender than related.

Integration of genetics, age and geographical association – composite of LR

The central argument presented in this chapter is that the key to successful prioritization of a familial DNA search list is the implementation of a system in which the potential relatives of the offender are prioritized according to how well they match across all three available prioritization facets, derived from a combination of behavioural and forensic analysis. It is asserted here that this prioritization process must be objective and empirically sound, recognizing the relative contribution of each category within it.

Given the starting point of 'genetic' LRs produced by the forensic service providers, the repeated use of such LRs for both age and geographic association ensures internal consistency and the ability to compare 'like with like'. The probability calculations for both age and geographical association are derived from either almost complete population datasets or sufficiently representative samples, and thus can arguably be viewed as at least as valid and robust as the LRs calculated by the forensic service providers (i.e. those producing the familial DNA search results based upon genetic similarity). Similarly, the use of LRs avoids the common fallacies and errors of statistical reasoning which result from a misunderstanding of conditional probabilities and multiple testing.

Given the assumption that genotype, age and geographic association are all independent of one another (whilst it cannot be definitively stated that genotype and geographic association are independent, given that no known link has been reported between particular DNA components and specific geographical areas such independence has been assumed) the overall or 'composite' LR for individuals returned from fDNA search lists can be calculated by multiplying the respective LRs for genetic similarity, age and geographic association for each individual, such that:

$$LR(comp) = LR(gen) \times LR(age) \times LR(geo)$$

By adjusting the genetic LR in this way, to take into account an individual's age and geographic association, those individuals who are more likely to be relatives of the offender will become more readily identifiable from the more general backdrop of the list, whilst still preserving the appropriate weight assigned to them through their genetic similarity.

As an illustrative example, if we take a number of hypothetical individuals returned from a familial DNA search process, each with an identical (genetic similarity) LR, we can more readily appreciate the effect of introducing age and geographic association LRs to the prioritization process (see Table 7.7).

For the purposes of the example, the specified age range of the offender is 22 to 32 years (in line with 'P/C' age example outlined above), with a geographic association defined within zones (in line with 'geographic association' example outlined above).

Perhaps the best example of the strength of this methodology is illustrated by comparison of similarly aged individuals living within similar proximity to one another, which from a prioritization perspective was previously impossible to any degree of sophistication or robust accountability. Reference to Table 7.7 reveals that it is now possible to support the prioritization of a 40-year-old female living 6 km from the crime site, over a 48-year-old female living 12 km from the crime site, for example. When one further factors in the relative weight of the genetic similarity revealed through the familial DNA search results, the application of this methodology provides a significantly enhanced product for operational policing.

Table 7.7 Composite LR scores based on genetic similarity, age and geographic association

Individual returned from Familial DNA search list		Genetic similarity	Age	Geographic Association	Composite	Prioritised Rank
Age	Geographic Zone	(LR)	(LR)	(LR)	(LR)	
40	A	5,000	1.1399	78.45	447,125.8	2
40	B	5,000	1.1399	9.73	55,456.14	5
40	C	5,000	1.1399	2.75	15,673.63	7
48	A	5,000	3.4775	78.45	1,364,049	1
48	B	5,000	3.4775	9.73	169,180.4	3
48	C	5,000	3.4775	2.75	47,815.63	6
70	A	5,000	0.2659	78.45	104,299.3	4
70	B	5,000	0.2659	9.73	12,936.04	8
70	C	5,000	0.2659	2.75	3,656.125	9

Conclusions

As highlighted in Chapter 2, the role of the Behavioural Investigative Adviser has evolved significantly in recent years, and contemporary BIAs are now utilizing their knowledge and experience of both serious crime and scientific methodology to develop new ways of supporting major crime enquires. The development of an enhanced prioritization system for familial DNA search results represents one of the many examples of such evolution.

Reflection on such contributions from BIAs promotes a number of salient conclusions. First, they provide further support for the notion that BIAs are now fully integrated within the investigative process and are able to provide significant contributions across a range of investigative domains. Second, they demonstrate that BIAs are now fully cognisant with state of the art forensic techniques and can proactively synthesize their skills to enhance such products in line with pragmatic investigative objectives. Finally, and perhaps of greatest significance, they serve to remind that whilst 'forensic science' products are typically accepted at face value by the police service and the wider public as 'truly scientific', the work of BIAs is continually questioned within an agenda of 'bad science'. This chapter serves to demonstrate that many of the contemporary contributions from BIAs share the same scientific credentials of their 'physical science' counterparts, and that BIAs are perhaps uniquely placed to enhance the fruits of such scientific advancements through the application of robust scientific methods of their own.

References

Brantingham, P.J. and Brantingham, P.L. (eds) (1981) *Environmental Criminology*, Beverly Hills: Sage.

Champion, T. (2005) 'Population movement within the UK', in R. Chappell (ed.) *Focus on People and Migration*, Basingstoke: Palgrave Macmillan.

Davies, A. and Dale, A. (1995) *Locating the Stranger Rapist*, London: Police Research Group.

NPIA (2010) *National DNA Database Statistics*. Online. Available HTTP: <www.npia. police.uk/en/13338.htm> (accessed 19 November 2010).

Office for National Statistics (ONS) (2010) *Mid Year Population Estimates 2008*. Online. Available HTTP: <http://www.statistics.gov.uk/downloads/theme_population/mid2008-improved-migration-revised-13-05 10.zip> (accessed 1 November 2010).

Rossmo, K., Davies, A. and Patrick, M. (2004) *Exploring the geo demographic and distance relations between stranger rapists and their offences* (Special Interest Series No. 16), London: Home Office.

8   Child pornography offenders

Towards an evidenced-based approach to prioritizing the investigation of indecent image offences

Michelle McManus, Matthew L. Long and Laurence Alison

Offences relating to indecent images of children (IIOC) have seen a dramatic increase and are now acknowledged as a global problem (Wolak, Finkelhor and Mitchell, 2009) presenting fresh challenges for law enforcement in terms of managing the sexual exploitation of children (Calder, 2004). Perhaps the simplest question the police face is whether an indecent image offender is committing, or is likely to commit contact sexual abuse against a child (Eke, Seto and Williams, 2010)? Recent studies have begun to explore the specific relationship between possession of the actual IIOC and the likelihood of being a contact offender (Long *et al.*, under review; McCarthy, 2010). These studies have been based on a corpus of knowledge that has effectively examined three questions: (1) What are the key features of IIOC offending? (2) How do offenders use IIOC within their offending? (3) How prevalent are contact sexual abusers within indecent image offender samples? This chapter will therefore present an overview of the three questions and then describe the current issues within contemporary studies around the ability to prioritize IIOC offenders.

Defining child pornography: indecent images of children

In terms of defining 'child pornography', several researchers (e.g. Calder, 2004; Beech, Elliott, Birgden & Findlater, 2008) have adopted the definition proposed by Edwards (2000): 'child pornography is a record of the systematic rape, abuse and torture of children on film, photograph and other electronic means' (p. 1). However, according to Beech *et al.* (2008), abusive imagery of children can also include what they refer to as ' "everyday" or "accidental" naked images of children' (p. 219). Some individuals with a sexual interest in children possess images and videos that are legal (e.g. magazine photographs of children). Thus, it may be more productive to consider child imagery on a continuum, ranging from legal imagery to those at the extreme end depicting sexual assault (Taylor, Holland and Quayle, 2001; Quayle, 2004). Indeed, solely concentrating on the illegal content of an individual's collection limits understanding of the meaning applied by the offender to specific material, which may be indicative of a sexual interest in children. For instance, individuals may gain pleasure from obtaining legal images to complete a series or 'story' (Quayle & Taylor, 2002). It should be noted that

Table 8.1 SAP image levels indicating levels of indecent images of children (IIOC)

Level	Description
1	Images depicting erotic posing with no sexual activity
2	Non-penetrative sexual activity between children, or solo masturbation by a child
3	Non-penetrative sexual activity between adults and children
4	Penetrative sexual activity involving a child or children, or both children and adults
5	Sadism or penetration of, or by, an animal

throughout this chapter the preferred term indecent images of children (IIOC) is used as the authors believe this term best reflects the illegal and indecent nature of this crime.

In the United Kingdom the Sexual Offences Act (2003) extended the Protection of Children Act (1978), introducing new offences to deal specifically with the exploitation of children through indecent images of children (Sentencing Guidelines Council, 2007). Formalized in a Court of Appeal case, the Sentencing Advisory Panel (SAP) introduced guidance on the levels of IIOC, which in ascending order depict the seriousness of the offence. Table 8.1 represents the five 'types' or 'levels' of IIOC (in ascending order) cited by the Sexual Offences Act 2003: Definitive Guideline (Sentencing Guidelines Council, 2007, p. 109).

Unlike other typologies (e.g. the COPINE scale; see Taylor *et al.*, 2001), the levels set out by the Sentencing Guidelines Council do *not* include legal images of children or material that does not depict erotic posing (but nevertheless portrays children either fully clothed or in their underwear). This is because, under UK law, such content is not illegal and would not be used for sentencing offenders (Beech *et al.*, 2008).

In addition, the Sentencing Guidelines Council (2007) stipulates the importance of the victim age when assessing seriousness of the offence. It states that images which portray children under the age of 13 should incur a higher starting point for sentencing than those images featuring 13–15 year olds. Similarly, images possessed of victims aged 16/17 years carry a lesser starting point for sentencing than IIOC depicting children aged 13–15 years. The Internet Watch Foundation (2008) identified zero to ten year olds featuring in 69 per cent of IIOCs, with 24 per cent of IIOC featuring a child less than six years old. In their observations they state a clear trend is emerging where IIOC are depicting children younger and younger. A similar age trend has also been reported by Gallagher *et al.* (2006) and Webb, Craissati and Keen (2007) who found that the majority of their internet offenders possessed images of children ten years old or below (86 per cent). There is no doubt the younger the victim the greater power and control an offender holds (Taylor and Quayle, 2003) due to their restricted ability to know and communicate what is happening is wrong. Taylor *et al.* (2001) suggest that the age of the child, the amount of IIOC, the way it is organized and whether it contains private material should also be considered when defining IIOC. Indeed, these considerations are reflected within the sentencing guidelines as aggravating factors (Sentencing Guidelines Council, 2007).

Within the academic literature three key questions have been addressed in an attempt to explain the relationship and whether IIOC offenders constitute a new type of offence or new way of offending (Bourke and Hernandez, 2009).

What are the key features of IIOC offending?

Internet World Stats (2008) state there are currently over 1.5 billion internet users across the world. Since there is no single, regulatory body governing its use, the ability to control its content is limited (Beech *et al.*, 2008). Individuals who have a sexual interest in children are free to form social networks, referred to as virtual communities (Renold *et al.*, 2003) with other like-minded people. Quayle and Taylor (2002) state this can potentially empower and justify sexual interest in children. This has subsequently impacted upon the availability of 'Indecent Images of Children' (IIOC) causing an 'explosive growth in child pornography' (Schell *et al.*, 2007, p. 47).

The internet also functions in such a way that it allows individuals to engage with others who share the same pro-offending attitudes (Beech *et al.*, 2008). The quantities and ease of access to indecent images and other like-minded individuals enables an offender to normalize child sexuality, subsequently they begin to objectify the child and the actual harm that takes place (Beech *et al.*, 2008). The immediacy of the internet may act as reinforcement with the behavioural response likely to develop. If this is combined with masturbation the behaviour can become highly reinforcing (Gifford, 2002) and can encourage an individual to further disengage in social interaction with the real world, potentially increasing any social problems that originally existed (Morahan-Martin and Schumacher, 2000; Quayle, Vaughan and Taylor, 2006).

How do offenders use IIOC within their offending?

The role of IIOC within an individuals' offending behaviour (i.e. in terms of its function and relationship to contact offending) has been the subject of much debate, with no conclusive answers being drawn (Taylor and Quayle, 2003). One argument postulates that IIOC are part of the development of offending potentially leading to contact sexual behaviour with a child (Buschman *et al.*, 2010, Sullivan, 2002), while others state the IIOC act as a diversion from escalating their behaviour (Riegel, 2004). Another perspective considers that some offenders are already contact abusing children and use IIOC as another part of their paedophilic lifestyle, when for example, access to children is restricted (Bourke and Hernandez, 2009).

IIOC as part of development of offending

Quayle and Taylor (2002) suggest IIOC may provide a blue print educating an offender how to abuse a child. It has been argued that those who view pornography can become desensitized to the material with repeated viewing conditioning arousal, resulting in the individual seeking out more violent, explicit images (Zillman and Bryant, 1986). Sullivan and Sheehan (2002) refer to this within IIOC as fantasy escalation effect. It has been suggested that IIOC are an aid to fantasy enabling internet offenders to search and select material they find most arousing (Quayle and Taylor, 2002). One aspect of the fantasy is the creation of an unrealistic expectation of child sexual encounters. The images often portray children smiling and somewhat complicit in the activity, enabling offenders to cognitively distort children as sexual beings (Howitt and Sheldon, 2007). This can increase cognitive distortions reducing inhibitions to contact abuse against a child (Print and Morrison, 2000), or as Sullivan (2002) posits, spiral their offending behaviour by fantasizing with images. The images may serve as a motivational factor 'triggering subsequent grooming behaviours' (Buschman *et al.*, 2010, p. 208).

IIOC as diversion from contact offending

Riegel (2004) conducted an anonymous survey and found that 84.5 per cent of participants stated viewing erotica did not increase any desires to contact abuse, with 83 per cent believing it acted as a substitute for contact abuse. More generally, research agrees that not all offenders who use IIOC to facilitate arousal will inevitably develop into contact offenders (Seto, Hanson and Babchishin, 2011; Sullivan and Beech, 2004; Osborn *et al.*, 2010).

The increased ability of IIOC offenders to relate to fictional characters may somewhat hinder them from progressing onto contact abusing a child regardless of their failure to desist collecting (Elliott *et al.*, 2009). A recent meta-analysis by Babchishin, Hanson and Hermann (2011) examining characteristics of IIOC offenders stated increased self-control and other psychological barriers may be the difference between offender groups that inhibits these offenders from acting out their paedophilic fantasies. Research on cognitive distortions within IIOC (non-contact) and contact offender samples has further highlighted the apparent barriers for IIOC offenders (Elliott *et al.*, 2009). Contact sexual offenders have been reported to have lower cognitive distortions regarding children as sexual beings in that they have first-hand experience of their sexualization (Howitt and Sheldon, 2007). Elliott *et al.* (2009) reported that contact child sexual offenders (with no IIOC offence) had more cognitive distortions specifically in their ability to accept the harmful consequences of their behaviour, believing the child enjoyed the abuse. Conversely, internet offenders seem to be more aware of the damage caused to child victims, however they manage to continue their internet sexual offending by minimizing their actions as a 'passive viewer' (Elliott *et al.*, 2009, p. 88).

IIOC used as part of an already established paraphilic lifestyle

Bourke and Hernandez (2009) suggested a new type of offending where the child sexual offender uses IIOC as an extension of their already paraphilic lifestyle.

Their self-disclosure data suggested most offenders were already contact abusing before becoming involved in IIOC. Similarly, Sheehan and Sullivan's (2010) recent study on producers of IIOC also concluded that the internet may provide 'post-hoc justification rather than a primary precipitating factor' (p.164) for contact abuse. Nevertheless, the 2,369 per cent increase in the overall number of contact sexual offences disclosed within Bourke and Hernandez's (2009) study may suggest that sexual fantasies using IIOC to stimulate and reach masturbatory fantasy are rarely limited to fantasy.

How prevalent are contact sexual abusers within indecent image samples?

Contact sexual abusers do exist within IIOC offenders. The ongoing debate is in what proportion and what stages. A recent meta-analysis found approximately 12 per cent of IIOC offenders have historically contact offended against a child, increasing to 55 per cent when using self-report data (Seto *et al.*, 2011). Interestingly, they found the Bourke and Hernandez (2009) self-reporting data, that 84.5 per cent of IIOC offenders had contact offended against a child, was a statistical outlier. As can be seen from Table 8.2, there is significant variance in findings regarding prevalence of contact offending within IIOC samples.

However Table 8.2 is interpreted, there appears to be a subgroup of IIOC offenders who pose a high risk of contact offending. The task for the police is therefore to try and determine who poses significant risk and prioritize the protection of those children.

Table 8.2 Prevalence rates of contact sexual offenders among IIOC samples

% Contact offence	N	Source	Reference
84.5% ($n = 131$)	155	Self-report	Bourke and Hernandez (2009)
57.4% ($n = 62$)	108	Self-report	Neutze, Seto, Schaefer, Mundt, and Beier (2009)
55.3% ($n = 21$)	38	Self-report	Buschman and Bogaerts (2009)
47.8% ($n = 11$)	23	Self-report	Quayle and Taylor (2003)
43% ($n = 43$)	100	Previous charges	Seto, Cantor, and Blanchard (2006)
32.8% ($n = 42$)	128	Self-report	Coward, Gabriel, Schuler and Prentky (2009)
20.9% ($n = 99$)	473	Arrests	Wolak, Finkelhor and Mitchell (2009)
13.0% ($n = 28$)	215	Convictions	Sullivan (2007)
10.9% ($n = 54$)	494	Previous convictions	Elliot, Beech, Mandeville-Norden, and Hayes (2009)
6.7% ($n = 2$)	30	Previous convictions	Laulik, Allam, and Sheridan (2007)
5% ($n = 15$)	301	Previous charges/ convictions	Seto and Eke (2008)
4.8% ($n = 11$)	231	Previous conviction	Endrass, Urbaniok, Hammermesiter, Benz, Elbert, Lauchbacher and Rossegger (2009)

Can offenders be differentiated according to their use of IIOC?

There is a lack of research that has examined the differences between contact and non-contact offenders in terms of their IIOC possession. Research that does exist has tended to concentrate on IIOC offenders without contact offences rather than comparing them to contact offenders. In a recidivism study with a follow-up period of one and a half to four years, Osborn *et al.* (2010) used the risk matrix 2000 revised and found none of their internet sex offenders went on to sexually reoffend regardless of their risk categorization. None of the high-risk offenders were found to possess images at the SAP level five. They concluded that the level of image possessed had no impact on their potential risk of reoffending. This finding may not be surprising as Gallagher *et al.* (2006) found the 'most serious images were the least numerous', (p. 63). Furthermore, they found when examining video IIOC, level four IIOC as the highest percentage with level five the lowest, indicating the format of the image may have an impact on possession. Conversely, Laulik, Allam and Sheridan (2007) reported the majority of internet offenders possessed images at level four or five. These two studies illustrate the variety of findings in emerging research in relation to IIOC type and level. Larger studies concentrating on the level of IIOC available for offenders have reported a continuing trend with a significant proportion of websites (58 per cent) showing images at levels four and five (Internet Watch Foundation, 2008). Although it is unclear whether these trends are related to risk, research has acknowledged the importance of understanding how the possession of images at any SAP level relates to risk of harm to children (Carr and Hilton, 2009).

A recent American study that has examined how IIOC possession relates to risk is McCarthy (2010). She sampled 107 offenders (56 non-contact offenders; 51 contact offenders) convicted of IIOC offences, in the aim of identifying potential risk factors associated with contact sexual abuse. She found that contact offenders were significantly more likely to possess larger child pornography collections than non-contact offenders. She also concluded that contact offenders were more likely to engage in grooming behaviours than non-contact offenders (such as sending adult pornography to potential victims; however this would constitute a different offence within the UK). Usefully, McCarthy (2010) has attempted to establish that differences between the offender groups and their IIOC offending behaviour exist however, as with Long et al. (under review), caution should be exercised with small effect sizes.

From a UK perspective, Long *et al.* (under review) examined the differences between contact and non-contact offenders within their IIOC offending behaviour and possession. This study examined 60 offenders, 30 contact and 30 non-contact offenders who had been convicted of possessing, making or downloading IIOC in both still and movie format. The aim of the study was twofold. First, was to examine whether there were differences between contact and non-contact offenders in terms of their IIOC possession. Second, was to examine whether images possessed by contact offenders related to their contact offence. Contact offenders were found to have significantly fewer IIOC (still and movie IIOC). This pattern was also found when analysing still images and movies separately. Contact offenders possessed a significantly lower proportion of Level 1 movies (i.e. IIOC depicting erotic posing with no sexual activity). On the other hand, contact offenders were significantly more likely to own a greater proportion of Level 3 still IIOC (i.e. images depicting non-penetrative sexual activity between adults and children) and Level 4 IIOC (penetrative sexual activity between adults and children). In summary, contact offenders possessed more severe imagery proportionally. Long *et al.* (under review) hypothesize that the behaviour depicted in the IIOC could relate to the offences *known* to have been committed. This may suggest contact offenders preferred IIOC at similar levels of abuse to those offences they are committing, a notion hypothesized by Quayle and Taylor (2002). In terms of whether images possessed by contact offenders related to their contact offence, the more severe the contact offence committed, the higher the level of IIOC in the offender's possession. The gender and age of the children in the IIOC was associated with the gender and age of the contact offence victims. Furthermore, contact offenders were more likely to display polymorphic behaviour (those who possessed IIOC depicting children of both genders also contact offended against both genders) and a smaller age range within their IIOC possession. Finally, when examining criminal histories, contact offenders were significantly more likely to have a conviction for non-sexual offences (i.e. theft) when compared with non-contact offenders. Similar results have been found with stranger rapists (Davies, Wittebrood and Jackson, 1998). In summary, contact offenders appeared more specific in their IIOC possession and it related to their contact offending.

Conclusions

This chapter has described the three questions relating to IIOC: (1) What are the key features of IIOC offending? (2) How do offenders use IIOC within their offending? (3) How prevalent are contact sexual offenders within IIOC samples? It has also detailed recent exploratory studies that indicate that there are differences between contact and non-contact offenders within their indecent image possession. Before defining what gaps remain and what this means for policing is it worth reflecting on what is already known. First, IIOC are widely available, affordable and have social networks associated with it. IIOC are likely to be here to stay. Second, there are debates as to how the IIOC are used but essentially they are used as part of the contact offending, to complement it or to divert from it. Finally, in terms of prevalence of contact offenders in IIOC offender groups, while there is little agreement in how many IIOC offenders are contact offenders, it is agreed that a sub-group exists that presents a real risk to children. In terms of policing, the real question is how do the police identify those that present a high risk? Any empirical research that can assist with this will allow the police to deliver the requirement to 'focus the available resources in a way which best protects the public from serious harm' (MAPPA, 2009, p. 32).

In many respects the fact that the high-risk sub-groups do exist may encourage further research and police activity, in order to ascertain and understand where the risk lies. As Glasgow (2010) emphasizes, police and researchers have a rich source of data available with a golden opportunity to develop risk assessments. Without risk assessments, as Carson and Bain (2008) note, risk factors may be based upon practitioners' experience, however it should be remembered that any risk factors should be based upon quality empirical research, wherever that has been undertaken (Carson and Bain, 2008). Although the current research on IIOC is far from achieving this, the problem has been identified. The exploratory studies outlined in this chapter have taken tentative steps towards identifying factors that suggest the likelihood of contact offending. By examining the detail of IIOC cases and identifying factors that suggest likelihood of contact offending, there is the possibility of preventing and ceasing contact sexual abuse. It is acknowledged that there are difficulties in using such data with issues of undetected contact offences (Buschman *et al.*, 2010; Bourke and Hernandez, 2009), differences in recording information (Alison and Canter, 2005). Furthermore, researchers must remain cognisant that a risk assessment tool should be validated against a relevant offender group and be empirically grounded in the risk factors, with a proven track record in the research literature (Kemshall, 2003), before they can be effective.

This need to manage risk may be one of the most significant changes in policing and law enforcement generally in recent years (Ericson & Haggerty, 1997). Policing now has a tighter focus on risky offenders (Kemshall & Wood, 2008). In order to make a decision of risk the police should take the risk assessment and likelihood of reoffending, any relevant intelligence and previous convictions to inform their decision of risk (MAPPA, 2009). For IIOC offences there is still some way to go to achieve this; however research has begun to assess likelihood factors, and with increased research and understanding it will hopefully progress to the development of risk assessments. In the meantime, such studies provide policing with an empirical basis to assist and inform decisions with the aim of safeguarding children.

References

Alison, L.A. and Canter, D. (2005) 'Rhetorical shaping in an undercover operation: the investigation of Colin Stagg in the Rachel Nickell murder enquiry', in L.A. Alison (ed.) *The forensic psychologist's casebook: psychological profiling and criminal investigation*, Cullompton: Willan Publishing.

Babchishin, K.M., Hanson, K.R. and Hermann, C.A. (2011) 'The characteristics of online sex offenders: a meta-analysis', *Sexual Abuse: A Journal of Research and Treatment*, *23(1)*: 92–123.

Beech, A.R., Elliott, I.A., Birgden, A. and Findlater, D. (2008) 'The internet and child sexual offending: a criminological review', *Aggression and Violent Behavior*, 13: 216–228.

Bourke, M.L. and Hernandez, A.E. (2009) 'The "Butner Study" redux: A report of the incidence of hands-on child victimization by child pornography offenders', *Journal of Family Violence*, 24: 183–191.

Buschman, J. and Bogaerts, S. (2009) 'Polygraph testing internet offenders', in D. Wilcox (ed.) *The use of polygraph in assessing, treating, and supervising sex offenders: a practitioner's guide*, Chichester: Wiley-Blackwell.

Buschman, J., Wilcox, D.K., Oelricj, M. and Hackett, S. (2010) 'Cybersex offender risk assessment: an explorative study', *Journal of Sexual Aggression*, 16(2): 197–209.

Calder, M.C. (ed.) (2004) *Child sexual abuse and the internet: tackling the new frontier*. Lyme Regis: Russell House.

Carr, J. and Hilton, Z. (2009) 'Child Protection and self-regulation in the Internet industry: the UK experience', *Children and Society*, 23: 303–308.

Carson, D. and Bain, A. (2008) *Professional risk and working with people*, London: Jessica Kingsley.

Coward, A.I., Gabriel, A.M., Schuler, A. and Prentky, R.A. (2009) 'Child internet victimization: project development and preliminary results', poster presented at the American Psychology and Law Society Conference, San Antonia, TX, March.

Davies, A., Wittebrood, K. and Jackson, J.L. (1998) *Predicting the criminal record of a stranger rapist*, London: Home Office.

Edwards, S.S.M. (2000) 'Prosecuting "child pornography": Possession and taking of indecent photographs of children', *Journal of Social Welfare and Family Law*, 22: 1–21.

Eke, A.W., Seto, M.C. and Williams, J. (2010) 'Examining the criminal history and future offending of child pornography offenders: an extended prospective follow-up study', *Law and Human Behavior*, *17*: 201–210.

Elliot, I.A., Beech, A.R., Mandeville-Norden, R. and Hayes, E. (2009) 'Psychological profiles of Internet sexual offenders: Comparisons with contact sexual offenders', *Sexual Abuse: A Journal of Research and Treatment*, 21(1): 76–92.

Endrass, J., Urbaniok, F., Hammermeister, L.C., Benz, C., Elbert, T., Laubacher, A. and Rossegger, A. (2009) 'The consumption of Internet child pornography and violent and sex offending', *BMC Psychiatry*, 9: 43.

Ericson, R.V. and Haggerty, K.D. (1997) *Policing the risk society*, Oxford: Clarendon Press.

Gallagher, B., Fraser, C., Christmann, K. and Hodgson, B. (2006) *International and Internet child sexual abuse and exploitation: research report*, University of Huddersfield: Centre for Applied Childhood Studies.

Gifford, J.H. (2002) 'Emotion and self-control', *Journal of Economic Behavior and Organisation*, 49: 113–130.

Glasgow, D. (2010) 'The potential of digital evidence to contribute to risk assessment of internet offenders', *Journal of Sexual Aggression*, 16(1): 87–106.

Howitt, D. and Sheldon, K. (2007) 'The role of cognitive distortions in paedophilic offending: Internet and contact offenders compared', *Psychology, Crime and Law*, 13(5): 469–486.

Internet Watch Foundation. (2008) *2008 Annual and Charity Report*, Cambridge: Internet Watch Foundation.

Internet world stats. (2008) *Internet world stats*. Online. Available HTTP: <http://www.internetworldstats.com/> (accessed 13 August 2010).

Kemshall, H. (2003) *Understanding risk in criminal justice*, Maidenhead: Open University Press.

Kemshall, H. and Wood. J. (2008) 'Partnership for public protection: key issues in the multi-agency public protection arrangement (MAPPA)', in C. Clark and J. McGhee (eds) *Private and confidential? Handling personal information in social and health services*, Bristol: Policy Press.

Laulik, S., Allam, J. and Sheridan, L. (2007) 'An investigation into maladaptive personality functioning in Internet sex offenders', *Psychology, Crime and Law*, 13(5): 523–535.

Long, M.L., Alison, L.A., McManus, M.A. and McCallum, C. (under review) 'Child pornography offenders: A comparison between contact and non-contact offenders possession of indecent images of children'. *Sexual Abuse: A Journal of Research and Treatment*.

McCarthy, J. (2010) 'Internet sexual activity: A comparison between contact and non-contact child pornography offenders', *Journal of Sexual Aggression*, 16(2): 181–195.

MAPPA Guidance (2009) *MAPPA Guidance version 3.0*, London: National MAPPA team.

Morahan-Martin, J. and Schumacher, P. (2000) 'Incidents and correlates of pathological internet use among college students', *Computers in Human Behavior*, 16: 13–29.

Neutze, J., Seto, M.C., Schaefer, G.A., Mundt, I.A. and Beier, K.M. (2009) 'Predictors of child pornography offenses and child sexual abuse in a community sample of pedophiles and hebephiles', unpublished manuscript.

Osborn, J., Elliott, I.A., Middleton, D. and Beech, A.R. (2010) 'The use of actuarial risk assessment measures with UK internet child pornography offenders', *Journal of Aggression, Conflict and Peace Research*, 2(3): 16–24.

Print, B. and Morrison, T. (2000) 'Treating adolescents who sexually abuse others', in C. Itzin (ed.) *Home truths about child sexual abuse: influencing policy and practice*, London: Routledge.

Protection of Children Act (1978) c. 37 O.P.S.I.

Quayle, E. (2004) 'The impact of viewing on offending behaviour', in M.C. Calder (ed.), *Child sexual abuse and the internet: Tackling the new frontier*, Lyme Regis: Russell House.

Quayle, E., and Taylor, M. (2002) 'Child pornography and the internet: Perpetuating a cycle of abuse', *Deviant Behavior: An Interdisciplinary Journal*, 23: 331–361.

Quayle, E. and Taylor, M. (2003) 'Model of problematic internet use in people with sexual interest in children', *CyberPsychology & Behavior*, 6: 93–106.

Quayle, E. Vaughan, M. and Taylor, M. (2006) 'Sex offenders, Internet child abuse images and emotional avoidance: the importance of values', *Aggression and Violent Behavior*, 11: 1–11.

Riegel, D.L. (2004) 'Effects on boy-attracted pedosexual males of viewing boy erotica (letter to the editor)', *Archives of Sexual Behaviour*, 33: 321–323.

Renold, E., Creighton, S.J., Atkinson, C. and Carr, J. (2003) *Images of abuse: a review of the evidence on child pornography*, London: NSPCC.

Schell, B.H., Martin, M.V., Hung, P.C.K. and Rueda, L. (2007) 'Cyber child pornography: a review paper of the social and legal issues and remedies – and a proposed technological solution', *Aggression and Violent Behavior*, 12: 45–63.

Sentencing Guidelines Council (2007) *Sexual Offences Act 2003: Definitive Guideline*. Online. HTTP Available <http://www.sentencingcouncil.org.uk/docs/web_Sexual OffencesAct_2003.pdf> (accessed 19 January 2011).

Seto, M.C. and Eke, A.W. (2008) 'Predicting new offenses committed by child pornography offenders', paper presented at the 27th Annual Conference of the Association for the Treatment of Sexual Abusers, Atlanta, GA, October.

Seto, M.C., Cantor, J.M. and Blanchard, R. (2006) 'Child pornography offenses are a valid diagnostic indicator of pedophilia', *Journal of Abnormal psychology*, 115: 610–615.

Seto, M.C., Hanson, K.R. and Babchishin, K.M. (2011) 'Contact sexual offending by men with online sexual offenses', *Sexual Abuse: A Journal of Research and Treatment*, 23(1): 124–145.

Sexual Offences Act (2003) c. 42 O.P.S.I.

Sheehan, V. and Sullivan, J. (2010) 'A qualitative analysis of child sex offenders involved in the manufacture of indecent images of children', *Journal of Sexual Aggression*, 16(2): 143–167.

Sullivan, C. (2007) *Internet trades of child pornography: profiling research—update*, Wellington, New Zealand: Department of Internal Affairs. Online. Available HTTP: <http://www.dia.govt.nz/pubforms.nsf/URL/Profilingupdate2.pdf/$file/Profilingupdate2.pdf> (accessed 28 October 2010).

Sullivan, J. (2002) 'The spiral of sexual abuse: a conceptual framework for understanding and illustrating the evolution of sexually abusive behaviour', *NOTANews*, 41: 17–21.

Sullivan, J. and Beech, A.R (2004) 'Assessing Internet Sex Offenders', in M. Calder (ed.) *Child Sexual Abuse and the Internet: tackling the new frontier*, Dorset: Russell House Publishing Limited.

Sullivan, J and Sheehan, V. (2002) 'The internet sex offender. Understanding the behaviour and engaging the assessment and treatment issues', Paper presented to the 21st Annual Conference of ATSA (The Association for the Treatment of Sexual Abusers) Montreal, Canada.

Taylor, M. and Quayle, E. (2003) *Child pornography: An internet crime*, Hove: Brunner-Routledge.

Taylor, M., Holland, G. and Quayle, E. (2001) 'Typology of paedophile picture collections', *Police Journal*, 74; 97–107.

Webb, L., Craissati, J. and Keen, S. (2007) 'Characteristics of Internet child pornography offenders: a comparison with child molesters', *Sex Abuse*, 19: 449–465.

Wolak, J., Finkelhor, D. and Mitchell, K.J. (2009) *Trends in arrests of "online predators"*, Crime Against Children Research Center. Online. Available HTTP: < http://www.unh.edu/ccrc/internet crimes/papers.html> (accessed 8 November 2010).

Zillman, D. and Bryant, J. (1986) 'Shifting preferences in pornography consumption', *Communication Research*, 12: 560–178.

Part II

Professionalizing the product

Lee Rainbow

In Part 1, the focus of discussion was directed at the *process* of behavioural investigative advice provision. As with any consumable however, success or failure is dependant upon not only the processes underpinning eventual delivery, but on the actual product itself. It is no good having the best production line in the world, employing the best available technology and operational best practice if the final product is unwanted or not fit for purpose.

Somewhat surprisingly, this aspect of behavioural investigative advice has received remarkably little attention in the research literature, as reflected in the relative contribution of this section to the volume as a whole. Whether this is due to the previously highlighted focus on a negative research agenda determined to debunk the underlying theoretical tenets of the discipline rather than seek to enhance its potentially beneficial contribution remains unclear. What is clear however is that the role of the final product is at least as critical in the ongoing professionalization of behavioural investigative advice as the processes behind it, and require just as much attention and evidence-based best practice as its more theoretical and methodological bedfellows.

Curiously, given the status of behavioural investigative advice as a consumable service, little attention had previously been paid to what the customer actually wanted in relation to such delivery. The usual market mechanisms have been somewhat ignored, with the service providers themselves assuming and determining customer needs. In Chapter 10, Cole and Brown provide the first systematic analysis of customer need through proactive customer consultation. The results provide much food for thought for contemporary practitioners in terms of current divergence between supply and demand, although aspirations towards ultimate convergence must be recognized as over simplistic and potentially both achievable and undesirable.

The remaining chapters expand on the findings from customer-focused preferences to consider the presentation of advice, inferences and recommendations from a more psychologically informed perspective. Chapters 11, 12 and 13 all cover the interpretation and utilization of advice, summarizing the pitfalls and methods to avoid misinterpretation of advice and risk. They illustrate the subtleties and important influences of the way in which advice is communicated. In the early 1990s little if any thought was given to the extent to which communication errors and misunderstandings could derail enquiries with both parties (BIA and police officer) mutually misunderstanding one another. These chapters illustrate those effects and provide some clarity on how such claims can be most effectively conveyed to reduce uncertainties.

Chapter 12 also reinforces the notion of how communication and the details of the profile itself can either steer the officer in the wrong direction or, on the other hand, provide a benefit by encouraging him or her to rethink their hypothesized framework and remain open-minded and receptive to new information. Much of this work borrows its approach from the traditional decision-making approaches enshrined in Kahneman and Tversky's seminal work on heuristics and biases, and there can be little doubt that this approach provides considerable benefit in considering the impact of such advice on the enquiry – specifically in terms of availability and confirmation bias.

In addition to recognizing the possibilities and limitations, we need to be mindful of how these various contributions are articulated. Given the many unknowns and the variation in the success of, for example, linking as opposed to deriving characteristics, it is important to communicate the rationales upon which claims are made and the certainty (or uncertainty) of any specific given claim. Much has been researched and written about the extent to which miscommunication has led to inappropriate judgements and decisions about risk, and yet relatively little attention has been paid to this within this particular forensic domain. Almond, Alison and Porter address this in Chapter 13 with what we believe is the only study of its kind to explore the importance of ensuring that advice could be written clearly, unambiguously and with reference to clear backing as to its origin. Such scarcity of attention is pertinent given Rainbow's practitioner view (this volume) that such issues 'represent the most significant advancement in the professionalization of BIA in the UK'. This final chapter also serves to end the volume on a positive note, highlighting significant improvements in contemporary practice over more historical activity.

9 What do Senior Investigating Police Officers want from Behavioural Investigative Advisers?

Terri Cole and Jennifer Brown

Introduction

BIA: *How can a BIA be of assistance in this case?*
SIO: *I would like the name, address and Criminal Record Office number of the offender please.*

This quote outlines an apocryphal conversation between a Behavioural Investigative Adviser (BIA) and Senior Investigating Officer (SIO). Typically the BIA is invited to an investigation and attempts to ascertain 'what the SIO wants' in relation to support and advice. Sometimes the BIA can provide the advice specified by the SIO, but on other occasions the BIA will state why this may not be possible and provide alternative suggestions as to the type of advice that may be more appropriately provided and investigatively effective. Whilst such one on one consultation and agreement over terms of reference is necessary for the provision of appropriate advice in an individual case, there is a significant gap in the research literature in identifying what SIOs want from BIAs, when they want advice, and in what format. It is argued here that if BIAs are to be of optimal use to investigations, identification of SIO needs and wants is a necessary prerequisite for the provision of useful and relevant behavioural advice. This chapter takes a proactive customer focused approach, innovatively asking SIOs themselves what they actually want in relation to behavioural investigative advice. Through tasking the investigators to describe a difficult to detect murder investigation in which they were SIO, the role and potential role of a BIA, from the viewpoint of the SIO, has been explored and explicitly articulated for the first time within a UK context.

Previous research – satisfaction surveys

Previous attempts that have indirectly considered the requirements of the investigation have focused upon satisfaction surveys, in order to elicit how happy investigators were with the services they had previously received from BIAs. The largest published study of its kind in the UK to date remains the research undertaken by Copson (1995), who surveyed detectives regarding the usefulness of 184 'offender profiles'. Whilst the majority of survey participants found the profiles operationally useful (82.6 per cent) and nearly all stated they would probably or definitely use a profiler again (92.4 per cent), this view was not dependent on the profile assisting in solving the case (14.1 per cent), as they rarely led directly to the identification of the offender (2.7 per cent). However the profiles were said to further the investigator's understanding of the case or offender (60.9 per cent) and/or reassure their own judgements regarding the case (51.6 per cent).

Whilst the findings of this survey are of interest, the results should be interpreted with caution. The data are now somewhat dated – Copson (1995) questioned investigators who had used profiling during the period 1981–1994. As such the results relate to the more historic practice of 'offender profiling' and do not relate to the contemporary provision of behavioural investigative advice that reflects a quite distinct operating landscape (see for example Rainbow, 2008; Rainbow and Gregory, 2009). Furthermore, as almost half of the profiles studied (47.8 per cent) represented the contribution of just two individuals, such biased sampling may have unduly skewed findings. Perceptions regarding accuracy of profiles may also be related to the identity of the BIA, the personal belief the officer has in profiling (Kocsis and Hayes, 2004) or influenced by whether the advice supports or challenges their own beliefs (Marshall and Alison, 2007; see Chapter 12). Moreover, satisfaction was only sought retrospectively, *after* the investigations had ceased and hence opinions could have been influenced by the outcome of the case. Details such as at what stage of the investigation (e.g. how much was known, or was the investigation at a dead end) or what happened to the advice (was it followed, was it accurate) may also unduly influence satisfaction, yet in the Copson study, only 16.3 per cent of advice was directly acted upon. Whilst the retrospective study therefore provided broad indications of investigators satisfaction with historic profiling advice in the UK, it did not explicitly elicit the ways in which behavioural investigative advice could best help (or hinder) current and future investigations.

Overall findings from satisfaction surveys indicate historic profilers' reports were of assistance in focussing the investigation, prioritizing suspects, saving time, generating new ideas, furthering their understanding of the offender and ensuring a complete investigation has been conducted (Copson, 1995; Douglas unpublished, cited in Pinizzotto, 1984; Haines, 2006; Jackson, Eshof and Kleuver, 1997; Wilson and Soothill, 1996). Some initial inferences in relation to what investigators want can be therefore be extrapolated from such findings – for example investigators did not appear to expect the adviser to solve the case; however they did appreciate information that furthered their understanding of the offence, reassured their own thoughts or focused the investigation. Nevertheless satisfaction surveys are largely descriptive with little or no conceptual levels of analysis, and actually tell us little about what SIOs want or when they want particular information.

Current research – SIO interviews

Research objectives

In recognition of this identified gap in the research literature, the current study set out to address the following research objectives:

- to identify what information SIOs want from BIAs in relation to:
  - ○ the products and services they ideally would like to receive; and
  - ○ the type of offender background characteristics they felt would assist their enquiries;
- to identify at what point in an investigation – i.e. the timing of when SIOs want assistance from BIAs; and
- the format in which the SIOs want the advice presented.

This is done in a systematic way using qualitative analysis of semi-structured interviews that were theoretically informed by the Pragmatic Psychology approach (Fishman, 1999).

Participants

SIOs are the main clients of BIAs. Such individuals are the lead decision makers throughout the course of the investigation, and it is they who decide whether or not to engage and utilize behavioural investigative advice. As such, research participants were identified from a purposive sample of serving or recently retired SIOs having specific experience in relation to difficult to detect murder investigations. Through consultation with the National Crime Faculty (NCF, a precursor to the current National Policing Improvement Agency, NPIA) a total of 12 SIOs were identified by means of the following criteria:

- having specific experience in difficult to detect murder investigations;
- the cases for discussion were detected;
- their current availability for interview; and
- to ensure a regional representation of forces from England and Wales including both metropolitan and provincial areas.

All participants had served at least 20 years as a police officer at the time of interview and all were very experienced in working on hard to solve enquiries within the Criminal Investigations Department (CID). All had used behavioural investigative advice in their investigations. In the event, one SIO having initially agreed to be interviewed withdrew due to operational contingencies. Of the remaining participants, one was a Detective Chief Inspector, seven were Detective Superintendents and three were Detective Chief Superintendents. One was from the London Metropolitan Police Force, one from Greater Manchester Police and the others were from different Provincial Police Forces (i.e. outside of the major cities) throughout England and Wales.

The 'boundary problem' of how many cases to look at (or interviews to conduct) alongside how much detail to go into, was considered. Given the exploratory nature of this qualitative research, the unusual and specific nature of the topic and design using in-depth semi-structured interviews, the initial use of 11 participants was considered adequate (see Morse, 2000). The practicalities of conducting more interviews were tempered by reaching saturation point in data collection, in other words when there was a repetition rather than discovery of new information. Once all the SIO contacts were interviewed and their interview data analysed, the number of interviewees and information gleaned was reviewed and the decision taken that increasing the number of interviews was unlikely to yield any additional insights.

Interview procedure

Having identified and selected participants fulfilling the research requirements, they were initially telephoned, and then follow up confirmation letters and agreements outlining ethical considerations were sent. All of the interviews took place between 5 August 2002 and 7 January 2003, at times and locations requested by the interviewees.

The semi-structured interviews were designed to elicit the individual's experiences, thoughts and perspectives in relation to a specific difficult to detect murder case the investigator (interviewee) had been in charge of. There were a set of introductory contextual questions asking about the general role of an SIO. These were progressively refined to discuss behavioural investigative advice. The main questions asked are outlined below:

1   What is your role as an SIO?
2   Can you talk me through a difficult to detect murder investigation in which you were SIO?
3   Did you use a BIA?
    •   At what stage were they brought into the investigation? Why then?
    •   From your perspective what type of behavioural advice was of assistance?
    •   What else do you think may have benefited the investigation to have known regarding the likely suspect?
4   From your perspective, how would such advice link into potential lines of enquiry?
5   In your view, when would this type of information be useful?
6   In what format would you find the information useful?

Within questions 2–4, a 'timeline' was composed highlighting at which stages information came into the investigation, the resultant actions and investigative decisions, and the actual/potential role of a BIA within this. Interviewees were encouraged to refer to their own notes and files as necessary. This method enabled the results to be more reliable and not solely reliant on recall. This also provided insight into the investigators' actual *behaviour* rather than purely their *account* of intended or ideal action.

Results

What products and services are required?

Table 9.1 summarizes the products from the BIA deemed to be of greatest assistance to the interviewees when conducting their enquiries in relation to the suspect. These are generally related either to the generation of suspects, or the handling of them once identified.

Table 9.2 outlines the products the interviewees wanted from the BIA when considering the incident itself. These were categorized as relating either to the crime scene or the SIOs' role in managing the case.

What information is required in relation to background characteristics?

The following information relating to the potential offender was highlighted by the SIOs as being of use to them:

- relationship to the victim;
- age;
- ethnicity or ethnic appearance;
- previous criminal history;
- living arrangements;
- education;
- employment;
- access to potential weapons;
- specialist knowledge – for example tying knots or martial arts;
- general lifestyle – what we expect the offender to do day to day;
- hobbies;
- sociability;
- way they conduct themselves/demeanour;
- medical conditions;
- family background;
- do they abuse their wife, children or pets? and;
- aspirations.

Interviewees articulated that *any* background information would be of use to them in trying to trace the offender, and that these should not merely be limited

Table 9.1 Products SIOs wish to receive from BIAs – related to potential suspects

Related to suspect:	Product
Generation	Background characteristics.
	Questionnaires and schedules for the purpose of conducting house to house enquiries – to glean as much relevant information (e.g. from potential witnesses) as possible.
	Interview strategies for witnesses – e.g. to glean relevant information for subsequent behavioural investigative advice (in conjunction with relevant police personnel).
Handling	Prioritization of suspects or persons of interest to the investigation for example for intelligence led DNA screens.
	Focus for house searches – to detail what information one may expect to find in a suspect's house, which for example may appear inadvertent to the untrained eye, but may provide useful intelligence information.
	Interview strategies for suspects – e.g. to initiate communication (in conjunction with relevant police personnel).

Table 9.2 Products SIOs wish to receive from BIAs – related to the incident

Related to:	Product
Crime Scene	Crime scene interpretation – possible sequence of events, interactions between offender, victim and witnesses, things that 'don't fit' or appear disparate.
	Consideration of motivation or the reasons why the offence occurred in that way at that particular place and time.
	Generation, testing and revision of hypotheses – acting as an objective scientist, viewing things from a different perspective and considering alternatives (in line with the investigative thinking specified in the ACPO Murder Manual, 2006).
	Offence linkage on the basis of similarities and differences in offence behaviour where no forensic links exist.
Incident management	Prioritization of actions and messages coming into the incident room.
	Aid with management of team welfare and assistance in boosting morale in protracted investigations or when things go wrong.
	What and how to release details to the media to use this resource in the best way – e.g. utilization of witness testimony research to prompt relevant memory from appropriate witnesses.
	Risk assessment of future offending – to assist resource prioritization and deployment.
	Prioritization of lines of enquiry that appear more likely to lead to relevant persons of interest.
	Search – attempting to locate persons of interest, suspects, offenders, crime scenes, body or weapon recovery sites; potential routes and methods of travel to and from scenes (in conjunction with geographic profilers and police personnel as appropriate).

to those features searchable in police systems. The added value is to prime investigating officers to the potential value and interpretation of evidence, exemplified by the following observation:

> What I need is for when my detectives go to the door, that they use their intuition, something clicks about this individual and if that individual fits the kind of profile you have come up with, and there is something about him that they are not happy with, I would expect those individual officers to pursue that to their satisfaction and ultimately to my satisfaction…it's not just about previous convictions.
>
> (Officer I: 889–945)

When information is required

The investigators were also asked about the appropriate timing of assistance – i.e. when they would like to receive behavioural investigative advice. There was some disagreement about when BIAs could assist. Some SIOs stated they would not consider a BIA within the first 24 hours as they are too busy and two suggested waiting 72 hours. However others suggested it was crucial to get BIA assistance as soon as possible and most of the interviewees acknowledged that although the SIO may be busy with other endeavours during the initial hours of an enquiry, early contact and assistance from a BIA would be beneficial for an early indication of motive or analytical comparison to historical cases.The following were provided as reasons for this early request for advice:

> When you start at that early stage there are things that you [the BIA] would be looking at that would ring bells, whereas I'm [the SIO] talking about how am I going to exploit forensic on her [the victim], I've got a hell of a lot going on in my mind.
>
> (Officer C: 400–411)

> At the outset with cases like this I think that an SIO needs whatever help he can get to rationalise what we are dealing with.
>
> (D: 110–115)

A repeated suggestion was for advice to be supplied throughout the course of the enquiry, with the BIAs recurrently 'touching base' with the investigation so as initial findings could be continually refined as necessary as more information becomes available, as exemplified below:

> If we had a murder today and you came tomorrow, we sat down, these are my initial thoughts, I would find that useful, and they may be refined as more information comes in.
>
> (Officer E : 863–867)

The format in which they want the advice presented

SIOs wanted succinct reports, with a summary of suggestions, submitted in writing, via secure means and within agreed timescales. They also wanted reports which were evidence based – i.e. supported with statistical data, research or experience regarding specific similar cases. This would provide them with greater justification on which to base their investigative decisions.For example one SIO said:

> I want someone to say to me, look this is likely to be a kid between 14 and 18 with this sort of background and it's based on the fact that we've dealt with 500 murders in the last 10 years in the database, 100 of which fit this MO and on 86 occasions it was someone who fitted this profile.
>
> (Officer K: 923–929)

Six of the interviewees highlighted the benefit of a verbal presentation of findings, e.g.:

> They were spellbound because it's not a case of, we're here with the answers, but we're here with some thoughts, and it was a really electric meeting I thought and they suddenly got the respect of the team.
>
> (Officer D: 875–880)

Written advice *in combination with* initial verbal briefing would be the ideal, provided the verbal advice was consistent with what was reflected later in writing:

> On the spot, verbal…but always documented afterwards.
>
> (A: 415–426)

> I'd go up the scene…we'd walk and just have a chat…and in the office we had the boards up…and it helped me to start to get my head around about the hypothesis…the report, is the disclosable document…so to complete the audit trail…you're going to get ½ hour of my time, what we've got to make sure is what you say is reflected in this report.
>
> (Officer C: 605; 000–096)

This was a persistent theme throughout the interviews: that dialogue with and presentation to the management or investigation teams was advocated as beneficial, but a written report is vital to complete an investigator's audit trail.

Expectations

Current convergence with contemporary practice

Much of the advice requested by SIOs is consistent with what previous authors have stated is currently being provided i.e. crime scene assessment; hypothesis generation; offence linkage analysis; background characteristics; prioritization of persons of interest; interview and media advice (e.g. Rainbow and Gregory, 2009, see Chapter 2; West, 2001).

Background characteristics requested as being of use to the SIOs are those which are often incorporated into current BIA reports. BIAs have access to databases, such as the one held by the Serious Crime Analysis Section (SCAS) at NPIA, which holds data on serious sexual offences and murder regarding both detected and undetected offenders. This information can provide a BIA with empirical backing for many such background offender features, and undergoes strict quality control procedures to ensure the reliability of the dataset as far as possible.

The SIOs wish for submission of reports within agreed timescales is commensurate with ACPO guidelines for adherence by UK BIAs (Rainbow, 2008; see Chapter 1) and is an accepted part of professional practice. The length of the timescale is dependent upon the nature and needs of the enquiry, the needs of the BIA (who may need time to read and analyse paperwork, collate data and research, write a report and have it peer reviewed) and the availability of all relevant and requested case related information. Nevertheless once timescales have been negotiated, there are rarely reasons why these should not be adhered to (e.g. illness or deployment to another more serious offence).

The SIOs wanting the submission of written reports is reflective of earlier considerations by Gudjonsson and Copson (1997) who highlighted the danger of verbal reporting as the advice can be easily misunderstood and misinterpreted. It is also in accordance with ACPO guidelines for adherence by UK BIAs (Rainbow, 2008; see Chapter 1).

In relation to the format of advice provision, the SIOs wanted reports disseminated in a secure manner. The NPIA BIAs have access to an internal police email network and their reports are usually submitted via this secure means. SIOs wanted succinctly written reports with an executive summary. This is also advocated by Alison, McLean, and Almond (2007), and there are guidelines as to how BIAs can best articulate findings to investigators (e.g. Alison, Goodwill, and Alison, 2005; Rainbow, 2008; see Chapter 1), which can be used by practitioners. For example Alison *et al.* (2005) highlight the crucial need to set out the background details – including contact numbers and background competence of authors; instructions and origin of report (terms of reference); caveats, limitations and sources of any inferences made; and a summary of the case. This introduction can then be followed by the actual behavioural analysis, and finally the investigative recommendations arising from the analysis should be articulated. An exemplar report is included by Alison *et al.* (2005) to illustrate their recommendations.

Current divergence with contemporary practice

It is important to understand the viewpoint of the SIO to ensure subsequent behavioural investigative advice will be tailored to an investigation's specific needs.

However, the information sought needs to have some level of predictive validity, and needs to be feasibly and reliably recoverable from datasets, experience or research available to the BIA. Ultimately it also needs to pragmatically assist the enquiry.

Some services the SIOs requested such as assistance with house to house questionnaires, prioritization of messages coming into the incident room, and assistance with the management of team welfare and boosting morale, are areas in which BIAs do not currently routinely provide advice. In addition there is a potential conflict for the BIA in promoting innovative practice and providing 'what SIOs want', and the ethical dilemma of stepping beyond their recognized professional boundaries of expertise. Other persons (e.g. occupational psychologists) may be better placed to assist in providing some of the advice (e.g. boosting morale). At the present time, further exploration of these additional areas of request from SIOs would be worthwhile to ascertain precisely what it is they want (e.g. specific counselling services; organizational support, etc.), which would then enable further consideration of who may be best placed to provide it.

When asked what they wanted to know in relation to an offender's likely background characteristics some of the SIOs alluded to what they did not want. For example they stated some behavioural investigative advice they had previously received was not definitive. Yet clearly behavioural science is probabilistic, and rather than a criticism of content, this appears more a case of miscommunication between the SIO and BIA. It should be articulated by the BIA from the beginning of the investigation that behavioural advice is based upon levels of probability that are rather lower than say DNA evidence (with which the police are familiar). Such comments therefore reveal the need for further communication and understanding of the role of BIAs in investigations. Similarly, comments that 'nothing could be done with it', or 'it was merely a re-hash of what was already known', should have now in part been rectified with the continued evolution of contemporary behavioural investigative advice and its focus on investigative utility. Such criticisms reinforce the recognition that BIAs need not only to report behavioural understanding and inferences to the SIO, but also to incorporate their advice into practical suggestions regarding how the investigation could proceed and practically use this advice. Such comments are also supportive of earlier discussion regarding proficient terms of reference being set and adequate, continuous communication.

Also in relation to what SIOs may not want, it was commented upon that reports sometimes 'stated the obvious'. This was a somewhat more negative connotation than the wording of the questionnaire used by Copson (1995), where the majority of investigators stated the profile 'reassured their own judgement'. It is true that merely reinforcing one's own beliefs (which may be 'obvious' to that individual) may not add anything new however, and using a BIA merely as an 'insurance policy' may be a waste of this resource. As such SIOs need to be better informed that where possible BIAs should be used interactively to advance the enquiry rather than merely verify their own judgements. However, providing validation of investigators' thoughts from a different (behavioural) perspective could be worthwhile triangulation for the enquiry, providing them with an additional and perhaps more scientific basis to reinforce their investigative decision making and enhance investigative audit trails.

Some of the information requested on the SIO 'wish lists' is just not available. For example whilst investigators want information regarding the offender's probable lifestyle, hobbies and aspirations, there is simply no such data available within the policing environment to empirically support such speculation. Investigations may collect such information regarding known offenders on an ad hoc basis, but the extent of research conducted on any individual offender is usually based upon what other offences it is believed they may have committed, or for information which may be required at trial. Such data is almost exclusively stored within individual force recording systems, and therefore not easily retrievable nationally. Some preliminary work and pilot analysis of what is contained in data systems by different investigations for detected murder enquiries was undertaken by Cole (2010). There were huge individual differences regarding how much data were collected on offenders, even though all had been convicted of difficult to detect murders. In future it may be that greater data collection and collaboration is required between police forces and other agencies nationally (e.g. prisons, probation, schools, etc.) to utilize the information they may hold regarding offenders, which may assist BIAs and investigations in this vein. A similar lack of relevant published research findings further compromises BIAs' ability to provide SIOs with inferences relating to more 'lifestyle' aspects of the unknown offender, rendering any such speculation completely absent of any sound supporting rationale.

Also in relation to the background characteristics of offenders, some of the investigators commented they wanted to be provided with features that were neither too broad, nor too narrow in terms of the characteristics provided. For example, predictions of global traits are unlikely to be of great use to them (Alison *et al.*, 2002). Labelled the 'bandwidth-fidelity trade off' Alison *et al.* (2002, p. 126) explains how predicting very generic behavioural themes allows only general information to be inferred about an offender's background, but would not be able to lead to more specific background characteristic predictions. So predicting that the offender is likely to be a male, aged between ten and ninety years, may be accurate, but practically is of limited value to the investigation in the narrowing of their potential suspect pool. Predicting the offender is likely to be aged between 20 and 25 years would be far more useful, yet is less likely to be accurate as the potential margin of error is greater. However to be of practical assistance a balance must be sought, and prediction of the somewhat more specific traits are required if the advice is to be of assistance to investigations, yet this cannot be at the expense of the reliability of the claims. This is a problem BIAs have to consider and weigh up in every case. Whilst the SIO may want specifics, the BIA has to be cognisant to the reliability (and potential unreliability) of providing such advice.

Concerning the format of advice, although all parties recommend the provision of written reports, sometimes in a live operational environment this may not be possible – when giving real time advice during an interview with a suspect for example. In such instances, based on the combined wishes of practitioners, it is suggested that notes are made either by the BIA, the investigation team, or a minute taker, and subsequently agreed by all, which can provide a reliable summary of the advice provided.

Furthermore the SIOs wanted findings presented back to investigation teams for discussion and comment. Whilst this has occurred in some cases, currently this appears to be the exception rather than the norm due to the workloads of all involved. However, although time consuming, such presentation not only ensures the investigation team has a clear understanding of the report, but also means its content and implications can be discussed and evaluated in view of investigative priorities. In addition it proactively imposes another meeting between the BIA and SIO, enhancing the BIA's continued engagement and communication with the enquiry, providing another opportunity for each profession to learn more about the other's respective roles. It also enables the BIA to gain valuable feedback on if, why and how their findings can be used. It is suggested that in future this should be considered as best practice when feasible. In Germany for example the operational case analysts (OFA teams who do a similar role to the BIAs in the UK) routinely present their findings back to the investigation teams, and work far more closely with the investigation until the conclusion of the case (see Chapter 5).

The SIOs' statements – that they wanted reports with statistical, research or experientially evidenced recommendations to give them a better foundation on which to base their decisions – echoes academic discussions by Alison and colleagues (Alison *et al.*, 2003; Alison *et al.*, 2005; Almond, Alison, and Porter, 2007) who have outlined the need for BIAs to provide explicit rationale and backing for the advice they provide. A series of studies have tested the strength of an argument's component parts by examining the claim or opinion proffered by the BIA (see Chapter 13). The Copson (1995) study also highlighted this as an area that lacked consistency with huge individual differences between BIAs (then profilers), with the frequency of supporting explanation for inferences made ranging from 7 per cent to 48 per cent between individual practitioners. Certainly studies have demonstrated that the substantiveness of arguments made in BIA reports is improving (Alison *et al.*, 2003; Almond *et al.*, 2007), with a contemporary BIA sample demonstrating 'very large positive difference' (Almond *et al.*, 2007, p. 1), clearer boundaries and a more evidence-based presentational format when compared to previous non-NPIA advice (Alison *et al.*, 2003). However out of 805 claims made in 47 of the contemporary reports, still only 34 per cent had formal evidence or a rational that is not yet ideal nor readily commensurate with 'what the SIO wants'.

Currently contemporary BIAs utilize relevant police data regarding previous cases where possible, use experience and incorporate related research in order to attempt to back up and rationalize claims made. Where appropriate, these contributions are supported by explicit caveats relating to factors such as sample size and relevancy to the current case, and presented in a format easily accessible by SIOs.

The difficulty for BIAs however is that appropriate research, based upon large, relevant samples is lacking, which links what is known about the offence to known socio-demographic information or characteristics of the offender. In an attempt to address some of the knowledge gap, a further study by Cole (2010) has statistically analysed police data, identifying any patterns between what is known from the crime scene, and the background characteristics of the offender (in detected cases) in difficult to detect murder offences. Research of this kind is one step towards providing BIAs statistical backing for inferences made when working on cases and enables them to incorporate appropriate findings into their reports. However further research of this nature is required.

Conclusion

This chapter has outlined novel exploratory research, which has for the first time focused upon the needs of the BIA's customer – the SIO. It has identified what experienced SIOs have stated are their needs, and as such is an important first step in order to appropriately tailor future research and practice.

These initial results demonstrate that whilst much of what SIOs want BIAs currently deliver, there remains some residual divergence. BIAs are sometimes unable to provide what is required as they simply do not have the expertise required. SIOs may want additional products and services, and future research and practice needs to explore precisely what is required and who may be best placed to deliver it. Similarly some of what the SIOs want is unavailable due to a paucity of relevant research or relevant empirical datasets, and as such any benign temptation to deliver such customer requirements must be appropriately and judiciously balanced against the potential of serious professional, scientific and ethical compromise.

Moreover the BIA may be *able* to provide what was requested by the SIO, but on the basis of their own experience in serious crime investigation think that they can offer an alternative which would be of more use to the enquiry. Some of the advice may not be directly in line with what the SIO initially expected but whilst BIAs have a duty to deliver what is asked when appropriate, they also need to make investigators aware that 'what they want' is not always feasible or best for their enquiry. It should be recognized that the BIA and SIO working together in a professional and ethical way can only enhance the quality and success of investigations.

It is hoped that preliminary results will light the way for future research into this area and promote the expansion of relevant research activity to address the current areas of divergence. It is for practitioners and researchers alike to take cognisance of these illuminating customer views and continue to develop the discipline of behavioural investigative advice in the most effective manner possible.

References

Alison, L., Goodwill, A. and Alison, E. (2005) 'Guidelines for profilers', in L. Alison (ed.), *The Forensic Psychologist's Casebook*, Cullompton: Willan Publishing.

Alison, L., McLean, C. and Almond, L. (2007) 'Profiling suspects', in T. Newburn, T. Williamson and A. Wright (eds), *Handbook of Criminal Investigations*, Cullompton: Willan Publishing.

Alison, L., Bennell, C., Mokros, A. and Ormerod, D. (2002) 'The Personality Paradox in Offender Profiling: a theoretical review of the processes involved in deriving background characteristics from crime scene actions', *Psychology, Public Policy & Law*, 8(1): 115–135.

Alison, L., Smith, M.D., Eastman, O. and Rainbow, L. (2003) 'Toulmin's Philosophy of Argument and its Relevance to Offender Profiling', *Psychology, Crime & Law*, 9(2): 173–183.

Almond, L., Alison, L. and Porter, L. (2007) 'An Evaluation and Comparison of Claims Made in Behavioural Investigative Advice Reports Compiled by the National Policing Improvements Agency in the United Kingdom', *Journal of Investigative Psychology and Offender Profiling*, 4(2): 71–83.

Cole, T. (2010) 'Behavioural investigative advice in difficult to detect murders: a pragmatic psychological approach', unpublished PhD dissertation, University of Surrey.

Copson, G. (1995) *Coals to Newcastle? Part 1: a study of offender profiling*, London: Police Research Group Special Interest Series, Home Office.

Fishman, D.B. (1999) *The case for pragmatic psychology*, New York: New York University Press.

Gudjonsson, G.H. and Copson, G. (1997) 'The Role of the Expert in Criminal Investigation', in J.L. Jackson and D.A. Bekerian (eds), *Offender Profiling, theory, research and practice*, Chichester: Wiley.

Haines, M. (2006) 'Criminal Profiling use and belief: A survey of Canadian police officer opinion', unpublished honour's thesis, Memorial University of Newfoundland St. Johns.

Jackson, J.L., van den Eshof, P. and de Kleuver, E.E. (1997) 'A research approach to offender profiling', in J.L. Jackson and D.A. Bekerian (eds), *Offender Profiling: Theory, Research and Practice*, Chichester: Wiley.

Kocsis, R.N. and Hayes, A.F. (2004) 'Believing is seeing? Investigating the perceived accuracy of criminal psychological profiles', *International Journal of Offender Therapy and Comparative Criminology*, 48: 149–160.

Marshall, B.C. and Alison, L.J. (2007) 'Stereotyping, congruence and presentation order: Interpretative biases in utilizing offender profiles', *Psychology, Crime & Law*, 13(3): 285–303.

Morse, J.M. (2000) 'Determining sample size', *Qualitative Health Research*, 10: 3–5.

Pinizzotto, A.J. (1984) Forensic psychology: Criminal personality profiling, *Journal of Police Science and Administration*, 12: 32–40.

Rainbow, L. (2008) 'Taming the Beast: the UK approach to the management of behavioural investigative advice', *Journal of Police and Criminal Psychology*, 23(2): 90–97.

Rainbow, L. and Gregory, A. (2009) 'Behavioural Investigative Advice: a contemporary view', *The Journal of Homicide and Major Incident Investigation*, 5(1): 71–82.

West, A.G. (2001) 'From Offender Profiler to Behavioural Investigative Advisor: the effective application of behavioural science to the investigation of major crime', *Police Research and Management,* 5(1): 95–108.

Wilson, P. and Soothill, K. (1996) 'Psychological Profiling: Red, Green or Amber?', *The Police Journal,* 1: 12–20.

10 Interpreting claims in offender profiles

The role of probability phrases, base-rates and rerceived dangerousness

Gaëlle Villejoubert, Louise Almond
and Laurence Alison

Traditionally, profiling has been defined as the process of predicting the likely socio-demographic characteristics of an offender based on the information available at the crime scene (Alison, Mclean, & Almond, 2007). In the last ten years, however, a change of emphasis from the exclusive focus on the offender and his likely 'psychological profile' to myriad broader issues involved in investigating crime – such as interview strategies, DNA intelligence led screens, risk assessments and geographical profiling – has emerged. As a result, offender profilers are now more broadly referred to as 'Behavioural Investigative Advisers' (BIA). Despite this, BIA reports still typically contain claims about the likely characteristics of offenders expressed with varying uncertainty qualifiers to indicate the extent to which the enquiry team can expect each claim to be true. Uncertainty qualifiers may encompass vague, verbal probability qualifiers such as *probably, possibly, unlikely*. For example, 'the offender is *probably* a male'. They can also include precise numerical expressions such as, 'There is a 60 per cent chance that the offender will be white'. If a claim is not qualified by a verbal or a numerical uncertainty phrase, then the profiler is indicating to the enquiry team that the claim is certain. For example in the absence of any uncertainty qualifier, the statement, 'the offender will have previous convictions' might be understood as a statement of complete certainty.

To verify that profilers duly reported the uncertainty surrounding their claims, Collins and Alison (2002) content analysed 26 offender profiles constructed by a range of profilers, the majority of which were produced during the years 1996–2000. They identified 107 different verbal probability qualifiers, which they argued could be divided into two broad categories: a 'possible' low-probability category (i.e. characterising claims as having a low probability of being true) and a high-probability category (i.e. characterising claims as having a high probability of being true). However, 46 per cent of the claims examined were not characterised by any uncertainty qualifier at all, suggesting that they may be perceived as statements of certainty (a situation which is extremely unlikely in any field of expert advice).

However in a contemporary study, Almond, Alison, and Porter (2007) examined 47 behavioural investigative advice reports produced by the National

Policing Improvement Agency in the year 2005 and discovered that 18 per cent of all the claims were unqualified. This more recent figure is comparatively lower than that observed by Collins and Alison (2002). Almond et al. (2007) coded the remaining claims as either verbal or numerical qualifying expressions, with the verbal probability expressions divided into the same two high/low categories previously identified by Collins and Alison (2002). Results revealed that 59 per cent of these qualifiers could be coded as 'probable' and only 5 per cent as 'possible'. The statistical terms were also categorised as either high or low probability qualifiers. Similar results emerged from this analysis: 16 per cent of these qualifiers represented a probability higher than 50 per cent, whilst only 2 per cent represented a probability of less than 50 per cent. So, overall, this line of research has shown that most claims presented within contemporary BIA reports were qualified by verbal probability expressions and were presented as highly probable statements of certainty.

The fact that probability expressions are now used in most profiling claims is reassuring, since investigators can more readily assess the significance of the inferences drawn from claims when they are qualified by varying levels of certainty. However, exactly how qualifiers affect the interpretation of the claims is currently unknown. There are some well-documented examples of disastrous errors caused by differential understanding and usage of verbal probabilities. For example, Karelitz and Budescu (2004) discussed the costly consequences of the different interpretation of the term 'fair chance' by the U.S Joint Chief of Staff and the Central Intelligence Agency which led to the Bay of Pigs invasion in 1961. In a similar vein, if a Senior Investigating Officer (SIO) were to misinterpret the strength of an offender profiling claim, this could have serious consequences for the investigation. A misunderstanding about the likelihood of an offender having pre-convictions (and thus appearing in a Police National Computer record) could, if unchecked, direct an enquiry down an unproductive route. For that reason, it is important that research considers how verbal and numerical probabilities affect uncertainty interpretations. This will give profilers and BIAs a better awareness of pertinent issues when constructing their reports and will help to minimise any misinterpretations between themselves and the SIO.

There is a large body of decision-making literature that examines the interpretation of probability words and expressions. Several studies have revealed that, paradoxically, although people prefer to communicate uncertainties with verbal probability expressions they prefer to receive it with numerical probability expressions (Brun & Teigen, 1988; Erev & Cohen, 1990). Speakers' preference for verbal expressions is generally said to occur because words, as opposed to numbers, are thought to be better understood by those who receive the information. In contrast, decision-makers who receive uncertain information tend to think they will make more accurate inferences based on numerical information, although this belief is not necessarily correct (Erev & Cohen, 1990).

In the remainder of this introduction, the paper considers the research on verbal probabilities and uses this as a basis for predicting how verbal probabilities may affect the interpretation of profiling claims.

Inter-individual variability in numerical interpretations of probability words

When communicating uncertainty, the vocabulary people use to express states of uncertainty is rich and varied. In an effort to investigate the numerical meaning of verbal probabilities, Reagan, Mosteller and Youtz (1989) found that over 282 different verbal probability expressions had been used in 37 studies of verbal uncertainty. As well as being numerous, verbal probabilities are also very vague (Brun & Teigen, 1988; Reagan *et al.*, 1989; Teigen & Brun, 1995). Unsurprisingly, the most robust finding in studies of verbal uncertainty communication is the extremely high variability in individuals' interpretation of numerical probabilities conveyed within a verbal probability expression. Although people perceive the meaning of verbal probabilities consistently (individuals derive the same interpretation across multiple situations), there is a wide variation across different individuals in the interpretation of verbal probability expressions (Teigen & Brun, 1995).

Wallsten, Budescu, Rapoport, Zwick, and Forsyth (1986) argued that individuals' interpretations of verbal probability expressions are best understood in terms of membership functions. Memberships range from 0 for a numerical value that cannot be conveyed by the verbal probability to 1 for a numerical value that is typically conveyed by the verbal probability. Membership functions assign a degree of membership to all the values of the probability scale for any given probability expression. Membership functions thus describe how verbal probability expressions map on the different values of the numerical probability scale for different individuals. They specify the meaning of a particular verbal probability expression by defining (i) its range of possible numerical interpretations, (ii) the symmetry of the mapping and (iii) the probability value which has the highest membership value. For example, non-null membership values for the word *likely* spread from $p = .08$ to $p = 1$, indicating that *likely* could be interpreted to refer to almost any numerical probability value. On average, the maximum membership value (the membership function's *peak value*) for *likely* is assigned at a probability of .85 (Budescu, Karelitz, & Wallsten, 2003). This suggests that *likely* will be interpreted by most people as conveying an 85 per cent probability. Whereas membership functions are generally quite stable for a given individual, they can vary greatly from an individual to another (Budescu & Wallsten, 1995). This line of research suggests that considerable variation in individuals' numerical interpretations might also be observed within the context of profiling claims. Therefore, we hypothesised that individuals' membership functions of verbal probability expressions qualifying profiling claims would be heterogeneous (Hypothesis 1).

Perceived behavioural characteristic base-rates will affect numerical interpretations

In addition to high variability across different individuals' interpretations, several external factors, such as the outcome's base-rate as well as its seriousness have also been shown to have substantial effects on the numerical interpretation of verbal probabilities. Thus, the peak, spread and shape of probability words' membership functions also depends on the context within which any given claim arises (Budescu & Wallsten, 1995). Thus, a *likely* outcome can be thought to have different numerical probabilities of occurrence depending on its perceived base-rate probability. For example, compare the following two statements:

(1) It is *likely* that it will snow in Liverpool, England, next December.
(2) It is *likely* that it will snow in the Aspen ski resort, U.S., next December.

The word *likely* will receive different numerical interpretations depending on context. In interpreting the level of uncertainty communicated, individuals tend to combine the range of values which they feel are expressed by the word *likely* with contextual information about the base-rate of the outcome being predicted (in this case, the probability of snow in December in the two locations specified). Thus, when asked to give numerical interpretations for such outcomes, individuals typically assign higher numerical values to 'likely' when it qualifies a high base-rate outcome rather than a low base-rate outcome (Wallsten, Fillenbaum, & Cox, 1986; Weber & Hilton, 1990). In the example above, individuals would assign a higher numerical value to Statement 2. Consequently, one might expect that a high base-rate offender characteristic would be assigned a higher numerical probability than a low base-rate characteristic, despite them being qualified by the same probability word (Hypothesis 2).

More dangerous behavioural characteristics will be perceived as more likely

As discussed previously the perceived severity of the outcome qualified is an additional contextual feature. Individuals tend to interpret a given probability word as more probable when it qualifies a severe outcome in a medical scenario (Bonnefon & Villejoubert, 2006; Weber & Hilton, 1990). Assuming the physician is polite and will try to 'sugar-coat' severe – hence threatening – news, individuals infer that the true numerical probability of the severe outcome is much higher than that usually communicated by the physician's probability qualifier (Bonnefon & Villejoubert, 2006). This 'severity effect' may also play a role in interpreting profiling claims because a severe outcome has potentially harmful consequences, the perceived dangerousness of an offender characteristic may, for example, also influence the numeric interpretation. This study consequently hypothesised that a dangerous offender characteristic statement would be assigned a higher numeric probability function than a harmless characteristic, even where qualified by the same probability word (Hypothesis 3).

Perceived likelihood will depend on characteristic framing

Probability words used to qualify an outcome can be assigned a variety of different numerical interpretations, depending on (i) individuals' personal membership functions for these words, (ii) on the outcome's base-rate or its severity. Furthermore, recent research suggests that the way an outcome is framed will also affect how likely it will be perceived.

Verbal probability qualifiers generate different perspectives on the perceived probability of an occurrence or non-occurrence (Moxey & Sanford, 2000; Teigen & Brun, 1995). Some probability words and expressions such as *probable* or *a small chance* are said to have a 'positive directionality'. This means that they focus our attention on a possible occurrence of the outcome characterised. Alternatively, when an outcome is qualified by a negative probability term such as *doubtful* or *not quite certain*, they focus our attention on non-occurrence.

A direct consequence of 'perspective effect' is that when an outcome is framed positively, individuals prefer using positive probability words to qualify uncertainty. For example, when a medical examination reveals positive reactions to *some* of the tests, individuals prefer to say, that it is *possible* the patient has the disease, thus representing a 'positive verbal probability'. Conversely, they will prefer to use a negative word and say, for example, that it is *uncertain* whether or not the patient has the disease when told that *not all* the tests showed positive reactions. A mirror pattern occurs when individuals are told of the quantities of tests showing negative results (Teigen & Brun, 2003).

Generally, systematic relationships between the directionality of a given probability expression and the shape and location of its membership function are observed. Thus, positive phrases are typically interpreted as conveying probabilities above .5, whereas negative phrases are typically interpreted as denoting probabilities below .5. The membership functions of positive probability expressions are, therefore, positively skewed with peak values above .50. In contrast membership functions of negative probability expressions are negatively skewed with peak values below .50 (Budescu et al., 2003).

Typically, profiling claims most often refer to behavioural characteristics that may or may not be true of the suspected offender. Thus, the perceived level of uncertainty associated with a given behavioural characteristic may depend on whether the characteristic is presented in a positive frame (i.e. *presence* of an offender characteristic) or in a negative frame (i.e. *absence* of an offender characteristic). The current paper hypothesises that the perceived level of uncertainty associated with a given probability word such as likely would be higher when this word qualifies a positively framed characteristic ('the offender *has* a history of sexually inappropriate behaviour') compared to when it qualified negatively ('the offender *does not have* a history of sexually inappropriate behaviour') (Hypothesis 4a). Similarly, probability words chosen to express a given numerical probability such as *80 per cent probability* may convey a higher level of uncertainty when qualifying a positively framed characteristic rather than a negatively framed characteristic (Hypothesis 4b).

Perceived likelihood will depend on profiling claim framing

A given profiling claim may focus on the chances that a target attribute is true or will occur vs. the chances that the alternative target attribute is not true or will not occur. For example, a profiler could say that, 'it is *likely* that the offender *has* a short temper' (positive frame) or, 'it is *unlikely* that the offender *does not have* a short temper' (negative frame). Thus profiling claim framing entails both the framing of the behavioural characteristic and its associated probability. Research on the role of description framing has shown that when an alternative is described as offering a 90 per cent chance of success, it will be more often endorsed than when it is described as offering a 10 per cent chance of failure, even though the two descriptions are formally equivalent (Levin & Gaeth, 1988; Russo & Schomaker, 1989). Thus the numerical interpretation of a verbal uncertainty qualifier should be higher when inferred from a positively framed claim such as 'It is likely that X' rather than from a negatively framed claim such as 'It is unlikely that X' (Hypothesis 5a). Conversely, we expected that the probability word chosen to express the numerical probability of a claim would convey higher levels of uncertainty when it was inferred from a positively framed claim (e.g. there is a 70 per cent probability that X is true) rather than from a negatively framed one (e.g. there is a 30 per cent probability that X is not true) (Hypothesis 5b).

Low-probability characteristics will be understood as confirmations

Although high numerical probabilities are typically expressed with positive probability words such as *very probable* and low probabilities, this is not always the case with negative words such as *very improbable*. An event with an 80 per cent probability may be described as *not completely certain*, whilst an event with a 20 per cent probability may be described as *possible*. In fact, low probabilities outcomes (10 per cent-probability, 25 per cent probability outcomes) are more often interpreted as asserting an outcome rather than denying it (Teigen & Brun, 1995). Moreover, Evans (1998) demonstrated the existence of a 'matching bias', defined as the tendency to only consider information whose lexical content matches that of the information presented in the propositional rule to be tested. We consequently hypothesised that where a behavioural characteristic is mentioned in a profiling claim, this would still be judged as more likely to represent the characteristic of the offender even when the claim that qualifies the characteristic is assigned a low numerical probability (Hypothesis 6).

Experiment

Profilers use probability phrases to indicate the level of uncertainty of any given claim. Previous research has shown that profilers use various verbal and numerical probabilities expressions to convey such uncertainties (Collins & Alison, 2002). However, there is currently no research examining how these terms can affect the interpretation of offender profiling claims. Based on existing literature on the interpretation of verbal probabilities, we formulated a number of hypotheses concerning the factors that will affect the interpretation of the uncertainty qualifying profiling claims. These hypotheses were tested using an online questionnaire.

Method

Participants

Seventy participants (20 men, 45 women, 5 did not specify their gender, mean age = 28.5 years, SD = 11.3 years) were recruited through postings on the University of Liverpool website and through forensic e-mail groups. The majority (75 per cent) of participants were White British. Half were employed and 44 per cent were still studying. Forty-one per cent had achieved a post-graduate degree, 27 per cent a degree and 21 per cent had achieved A-levels.

Design

All participants completed the same online questionnaire containing 48 questions presented in two sections. The first section presented a series of questions aimed at testing the effect of the different contextual factors we had identified on the numerical interpretations that could be assigned to probability words or on the choice of verbal probability words. The second section was aimed at assessing the variability in individuals' numerical interpretations of verbal probabilities using membership functions for a series of expressions qualifying different offender characteristics.

Materials and procedure

The first page of the questionnaire introduced the study as part of a larger project examining the content of offender profiles and behavioural investigative advice and the ways in which such advice is interpreted and used. Participants were reminded that their answers would remain confidential and anonymous. Before beginning the questionnaire, participants were asked to indicate that they consented to participate in the study and that they were aware that they could withdraw from the study at any time.

The hypotheses were tested by displaying a series of statements presented as originating from a number of offender profiles that had been compiled to assist the police in their apprehension of an unknown suspect. Participants were asked to read each statement carefully and answer the associated question.

In order to examine the variation that exists across individuals' interpretation of verbal probability words (Hypothesis 1), we elicited membership functions for ten different words using the Multiple Stimuli Method (Budescu et al., 2003). So, after having read an offender profiling claim such as 'It is *very probable* that the offender will be male', participants were presented with 11 10-point Likert scales, corresponding to 11 levels of numerical probability (0 per cent, 10 per cent, up to 100 per cent probability). For each of the probabilities presented (0 per cent, 10 per cent, etc.), participants were asked to indicate the extent to which the profiler could have had this probability in mind when making his claim.

Table 10.1 Offender profiling claims used to test for Hypothesis 1

Claim
1. It *suggests that* the offender will have previous sexual convictions
2. It is *very likely* that the offender will have a manual unskilled occupation
3. It is *uncertain* whether the offender will be employed
4. It is *likely* that the offender will be aged 50 years or older
5. It is *somewhat doubtful* that the offender will live in the local area
6. It is *possible* that the offender will not live in the local area
7. It is *very unlikely* that the offender will be married
8. It is *probable* that the offender will be single
9. It is *quite unlikely* that the offender will be aged less than 25 years old
10. It is *improbable* that the offender will have previous convictions

They reported their answer by selecting a number between 1 (absolutely not) and 10 (absolutely). Table 10.1 summarises the 10 probability phrases examined alongside the offender characteristic they qualified. The selection of these terms was based on the most regularly used terms in the contemporary sample identified by Almond et al. (2007).

The effect of base-rates on the interpretation of the uncertainty associated with offender profiling claims (Hypothesis 2) was examined using three pairs of claims. The same probability phrase qualified either a high base-rate offender characteristic or a low base-rate characteristic. A similar manipulation was used to assess the effect of perceived dangerousness on the interpretation of the uncertainty associated with offender profiling claims (Hypothesis 3). Table 10.2 summarises the claims used for this section. For each of these claims participants were asked, 'What do you think the chances are that the offender [characteristic]? ____ %'.

Table 10.2 Claims presented to participants as a function of base-rate and dangerousness

Dimension manipulated	Probability phrase		
	...*will probably be*...	...*is possibly*...	...*is likely to*...
Base-rate			
High	...of White British origin	...of Christian faith	...have previous convictions
Low	...of Chinese origin	...of Pagan faith	...have previous convictions for fraud
Dangerousness			
High	...a sexual predator	...a psychopath	...kill again
Low	...a homosexual	...a postman	...return to the crime scene

To evaluate the effect of characteristic framing on the level of probability assigned to a given probability word (Hypothesis 4a), we presented the following two pairs of claims where the same probability phrase qualified either a positively framed behavioural characteristic or a negatively framed characteristic (the words in brackets were presented in the claim using a negative frame):

(a) It is likely that the offender will (will not) have a history of sexually inappropriate behaviour.
(b) It is probable that the offender will (will not) be a loner.

In order to collect comparable judgements, participants were asked to evaluate the chances that the offender *did* present the target characteristic when it was positively framed, but they were asked to evaluate the chances that the offender *did not* present this characteristic when it was negatively framed.

We used a similar procedure to evaluate the effect of characteristic framing on the probability word used to convey a given level of numerical probability (Hypothesis 4b). However, we used the same numerical probability to qualify either a positively or a negatively framed characteristic and we asked participants to complete a sentence using their own preferred probability word. The two claims used were:

(c) There is an 80 per cent probability that the offender will (will not) have a pre-conviction for violence.
(d) There is a 60 per cent probability that the offender will (will not) live within one mile of the crime scene.

As for the previous set of claims, to collect comparable judgements, participants were asked to choose a word to convey the probability that the offender *did* present the target characteristic for positively framed characteristics and a word to convey the probability that the offender *did not* present it for negatively framed ones.

The effect of claim framing on the numerical interpretation of verbal probabilities (Hypothesis 5a) was tested by presenting the following two claims qualified by opposite probability words *and* opposite characteristic framings:

(e) It is probable (rather improbable) that the offender will (will not) collect pornography.
(f) It is likely (rather unlikely) that the offender will (will not) be insecure with women.

In both cases, participants were asked to evaluate the chances that the offender presented the characteristic mentioned in the claim (e.g. the chances that the offender *would be* insecure with women). In a similar vein, the role of claim framing on the choice of verbal words to qualify a given numerical probability (Hypothesis 5b) was examined by presenting two identical claims qualified by complementary probability values and characteristics. The claims used were:

(g) There is a 70 per cent probability (a 30 per cent probability) that the offender will (will not) have a short temper and be quite aggressive.
(h) There is an 80 per cent probability (a 20 per cent probability) that the offender will (will not) have children.

Once again, in both cases, participants were asked to verbally express the chances that the offender would present the characteristic mentioned using their own preferred choice of words.

Finally, we wanted to examine whether suspects who presented a behavioural characteristic mentioned in a profiling claim would be judged more likely to be the offender even when the claim that qualified the characteristic yielded a low numerical probability (Hypothesis 6). To this end, we presented the following three different claims, which were either qualified with a low or a high probability:

(i) There is a 10 per cent probability (a 75 per cent probability) that the offender is a construction worker.
(j) There is a 25 per cent probability (a 70 per cent probability) that the offender is aged between 18 and 25 years.
(k) There is a 20 per cent probability (a 80 per cent probability) that the offender will be single.

Each claim was presented with the same summary information about the age, the marital status and the occupation of four suspects (see Table 10.3). In each case, participants were asked to rank order the suspects from the most likely to the least likely to have committed the offence.

Results

Inter-individual variability

We expected to observe considerable variability between individuals in their interpretation of verbal qualifying profiling claims (Hypothesis 1). Figure 10.1 presents the membership functions for each probability phrase used. The error bars

Table 10.3 Summary suspect information presented to test for Hypothesis 6

Suspect no	Age	Marital status	Occupation
1	28	Single	Unemployed
2	21	Co-habiting	Soldier
3	41	Divorced	Construction worker
4	44	Married	Lorry driver

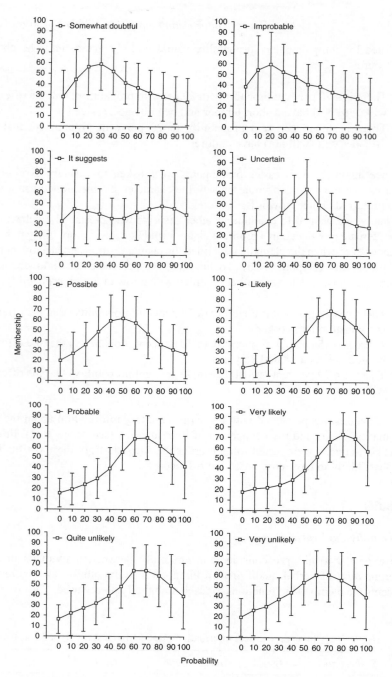

Figure 10.1 Membership functions for each of the ten probability words qualifying behavioural characteristics in offender profiling claims based on the judgements of all 69 subjects tested. Points represent the mean membership for a given probability. Vertical lines depict standard deviations from the means.

Table 10.4 Membership functions statistics for the probability words used to test for Hypothesis 1

Probability word	N	Peak			Min		Max		Skew	
		M	SD	Cv (%)	M	SD	M	SD	M	SD
Improbable (10)	62	33.1	31.5	95	10.5	16.5	78.5	22.5	0.26	0.52
Somewhat doubtful (5)	62	37.3	29.9	80	9.7	15.5	76.8	22.8	0.15	0.46
Uncertain (3)	64	41.9	26.4	63	14.8	15.6	83.8	20.5	0.03	0.35
Possible (6)	62	49.5	25.6	52	12.3	13.6	85.3	18.2	0.01	0.41
Suggests (1)	63	50.0	37.2	74	14.8	18.6	78.1	26.3	0.03	0.63
Very unlikely (7)	62	60.8	28.2	46	20.3	20.4	92.3	12.5	−0.12	0.46
Quite unlikely (9)	62	63.9	24.5	38	23.5	20.3	91.5	14.5	−0.16	0.42
Probable (8)	62	68.4	22.2	32	21.8	18.3	94.4	10.2	−0.22	0.41
Likely (4)	58	68.8	19.6	28	25.5	19.9	95.3	9.0	−0.20	0.40
Very likely (2)	64	73.3	26.5	36	29.1	22.3	95.3	13.8	−0.29	0.49

Notes: The words are sorted by their mean peak value. The numbers in brackets refer to the associated claim used as reported in Table 10.1.

(denoting the means' standard deviations) further indicate the extent of the variability in interpretations dependent on the verbal probability term used. Table 10.4 presents the membership functions, mean peak, minimum and maximum values, together with standard deviations and coefficients of variation. There was little agreement amongst individuals concerning the numerical probability typically conveyed within a verbal probability phrase. This latter point is further illustrated by Figure 10.2, which represents histograms representing the distributions of the peak values assigned to any given word. These graphs reveal that phrases such as *it suggests* are especially ambiguous. The phrase is interpreted by some individuals as signifying a probability lower than 20 per cent, whilst others interpret this as conveying a probability greater than 60 per cent similar variations exist for *probable, unlikely* or *quite unlikely*, which are assigned peak values that encompass the whole scale of probabilities. Greater consensus was found for the phrases *somewhat doubtful* or *improbable*, which were interpreted as denoting probabilities lower than 20 per cent by the majority of individuals. Similarly, *uncertain* or *possible* were generally understood as typically conveying a 50 per cent or less probability. The phrases *likely* and *very likely* were generally understood to convey higher numerical values, ranging from 40 per cent to 100 per cent for *likely* and 60 per cent to 100 per cent for *very likely*.

The role of perceived base-rate and dangerousness of offender characteristics

Beyond inter-individual variability in the interpretation of verbal probability phrases, we also expected to demonstrate how contextual features, such as the perceived base-rate of a given offender profiling claim (Hypothesis 2) and the

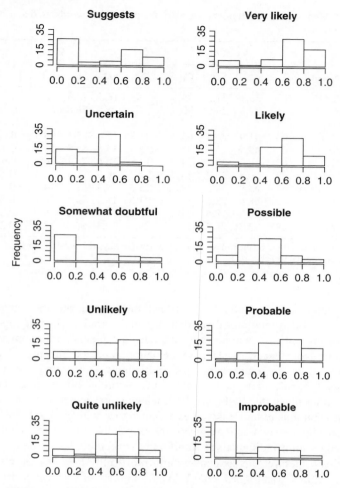

Figure 10.2 Histograms of the membership functions peak values for each of the ten probability words qualifying behavioural characteristics in offender profiling claims.

perceived dangerousness of the claim (Hypothesis 3) influence interpretation. Both hypotheses were tested using a 3 (probability word) × 2 (high vs. low base-rates/Dangerousness) within-subject Analysis of Variance (ANOVA). Figure 10.3 presents the mean probability judgements observed for each probability word (*probably, possibly* and *likely*) associated with (i) high and low base-rate levels, and (ii) high and low levels of dangerousness. The probability word used to qualify the claim had a significant effect on the numerical probability assigned to the claim; $M^{probably} = 57.96$, SE $= 2.12$; $M^{possibly} = 39.26$, SE $= 2.03$ and $M^{likely} = 61.86$, SE $= 1.79$; $F(2, 136) = 80.81$, MSE $= 249.18$, $p < .001$ for claims with differing base-rates; $M^{probably} = 60.54$, SE $= 1.98$; $M^{possibly} = 37.99$,

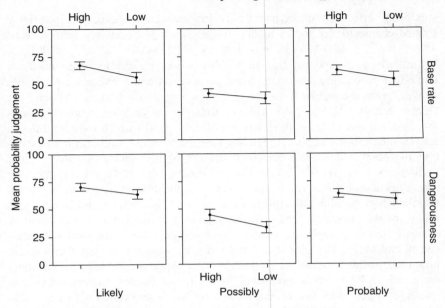

Figure 10.3 Mean probability judgements as a function of probability word, base-rate and dangerousness levels. Error bars depict confidence intervals around the means.

SE = 2.11 and M^{likely} = 66.59, SE = 1.70; $F(2, 138)$ = 118.03, MSE = 269.55, $p < .001$ for claims with differing dangerousness.

As anticipated in Hypothesis 2, numerical probability judgements were also influenced by the claims' perceived base-rates. High base-rate claims systematically led to higher mean probability judgements; M^{high} = 57.08, SE = 1.56; M^{low} = 48.98, SE = 2.18; $F(1, 68)$ = 19.25, MSE = 352.83, $p < .001$. Similarly, and in line with Hypothesis 3, claims related to more dangerous behaviour characteristics were perceived as more likely than those related to more benign characteristics; $M^{\text{dangerous}}$ = 59.06, M^{benign} = 51.01, $F(1, 69)$ = 19.25, MSE = 245.24, $p < .001$. The interactions effects were not significant in either analyses; $ps > .15$.

The role of characteristic framing

We hypothesised that the perceived level of certainty associated with *likely* or *probable* would differ depending on whether these words qualified a positively framed characteristic (e.g. the offender *will* have a history of sexually inappropriate behaviour) compared to when it qualified a negatively framed one (e.g. the offender *will not* have...). The words *likely* and *probable* elicited similar numerical probability judgements; $F(1, 68)$ = 0.45, MSE = 230.24, $p = .51$. In line with Hypothesis 4a, however, the valence of the behavioural characteristic had a significant effect on mean probability judgements. As expected, positively framed characteristics led to higher judgements than negatively framed ones; $M^{positive} = 62.34$, $M^{negative} = 54.36$, $F(1, 68) = 17.21$, MSE $= 255.63$, $p < .001$.

Similarly, we expected that probability words chosen to communicate a numerical probability associated with positively framed characteristic would convey greater certainty than those with a negatively framed characteristic (Hypothesis 4b). A total of 98 different probability expressions were elicited by the questions associated with claims (c), (d) and (g), (h) which were used to test for Hypotheses 4b and 5b, respectively (see the 'Method' section for a description of these claims). We presented the probability phrases elicited by our participants to a new set of 20 independent coders and asked them to provide the most typical probability value representative of the phrases listed. We then used the median probability value given for each word by the independent coders as proxy for the degree of certainty communicated by participants. The resulting scores were not normally distributed so we analysed these data with Wilcoxon-signed ranks tests. The tests results and summary statistics for Hypothesis 4b are presented in the first half of Table 10.5. As expected, the level of certainty communicated by words associated to positively framed characteristics was generally higher than that communicated by words associated with negatively framed characteristics. This trend, however, was only statistically significant for claim (c) 'There is an 80 per cent probability that the offender will (will not) have a pre-conviction for violence'.

The role of profiling claim framing

Previous results revealed that the same probability word or probability value will convey different levels of certainty depending on whether it is associated with a positively framed characteristic or a negatively framed one. We also hypothesised that logically equivalent claims would be seen to convey different levels of certainty, depending on the valence of the frame used. In order to test

Table 10.5 Wilcoxon-signed ranks test results for Hypotheses 4b and 5b

	Ranks							
Claims	*Positive*			*Negative*			*Ties*	
	N	*M*	Σ	*N*	*M*	Σ	*N*	*z*
Behavioural characteristic framing (Hypothesis 4b)								
(c)	32	18.97	59.00	40	14.75	607.00	23	− 4.33*
(d)	15	19.03	285.50	16	13.16	210.50	28	− 0.74
Claim framing (Hypothesis 5b)								
(g)	44	25.41	1118.00	3	3.33	10.00	11	− 5.87*
(h)	49	28.70	1406.50	4	6.13	24.50	8	− 6.13*

[‡]$p < .001$.

Hypothesis 5a, we compared the perceived level of certainty based on positive claims (e.g. It is *probable* that the offender *will…*) to that associated with negative claims (e.g. It is *rather improbable* that the offender *will not…*). A printing error in the questionnaire prevented the use of statements (f) as the characteristic was framed positively in both claims. Hypothesis 5a was, however, confirmed by comparing judgements based on the positive framing of claim (e) to those based on its negative frame equivalent. Thus, the average probability that the offender collected pornography was judged higher by participants informed that it was *probable* that the offender *would* collect pornography (positively framed claim) compared to participants informed that it was *rather improbable* that the offender *would not* collect pornography (negatively framed claim); $M^{positive} = 62.77$, SD = 19.53, $M^{negative} = 47.99$, SD = 29.40, $t(68) = 4.15$, $d = 0.60$, $p < .001$.

Similarly, we hypothesised that probability words chosen to communicate a numerical probability associated with positively framed claim would convey more certainty than those chosen to communicate the same probability associated with a negatively framed claim (Hypothesis 5b). We used the same procedure used to test for Hypothesis 4b to analyse the degree of certainty communicated by probabilities phrases elicited. The tests results and summary statistics for Hypothesis 5b are presented in the second half of Table 10.5. As anticipated, probability words qualifying the same statement generally conveyed a higher level of certainty when based on positive rather than negative claims.

The impact of low-probability statistics on suspect identification

Our last hypothesis concerned the impact of matching behavioural characteristics on perceived likelihood of guilt. We expected that suspects who presented a behavioural characteristic mentioned in a profiling claim would be judged more likely to be the offender *even* when the claim qualified the characteristic with a low numerical probability (Hypothesis 6). To test this hypothesis we computed the proportion of positive identifications (i.e. identifications of a suspect as either most likely or second most likely to have committed the offence) depending on whether or not a suspect description contained a characteristic matching the offender's characteristic as well as the stated probability that the offender would present this characteristic. A total of 1,649 identifications were available (four suspects × three offender characteristics × two levels of probability for the offender characteristic × 70 subjects – missing data).

Overall, suspects who presented a matching characteristic were positively identified 77.3 per cent ($N = 415$) of the time, whereas suspects who did not were positively identified 42.7 per cent ($N = 1234$) of the time. The rate of positive identifications was thus significantly higher when suspects' descriptions matched a characteristic of the offender; $\chi^2(1, N = 1649) = 165.56$; $p < .001$. As expected, the stated probability of the offender presenting the named characteristic did not have an effect on positive identifications. Suspects were equally likely to be positively identified when the offender's characteristic was associated with a low probability or with a high probability; $\chi^2(1, N = 1649) = 0.005$; $p = .94$.

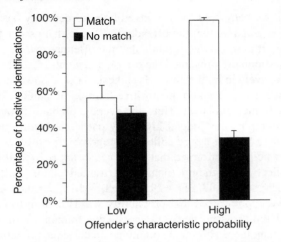

Figure 10.4 Percentage of positive identifications as a function of suspect–offender matching and offender's characteristic probability. Error bars depict confidence intervals around the percentages.

There was, however, an interaction between the probability of the offender presenting a characteristic and whether or not a suspect's description matched this characteristic, as shown in Figure 10.4. Suspects were always more likely to be positively identified when they presented a matching characteristic with the offender but the effect of suspect–offender description matching was significantly more pronounced when the offender was said to be highly likely to present the matching characteristic. This result demonstrates that the matching bias is even stronger for high probability matching statements.

Discussion

The aim of this research was to examine how probability expressions affect the interpretation of the information provided in offender profiles. Based on an online questionnaire we were able to demonstrate that uncertain claims about offenders are interpreted differently by different people. Our results showed that several uncertainty expressions led to considerable variation. Although participants generally agreed that phrases such as *improbable* or *somewhat doubtful* communicated very low probabilities, phrases such as *uncertain* or *possible* consistently were interpreted to communication probabilities at around chance level. Expressions such as *likely* and *very likely* clearly communicated higher probabilities above 50 per cent chance, whereas other expressions, such as *it suggests* were found very ambiguous and were interpreted as denoting very low probabilities *or* very high probabilities. This interpretative diversity may induce an illusion of valid communication, which could result in misunderstandings between a behavioural investigative adviser's intended meaning and the

Senior Investigating Officer's (SIOs) interpretation (Budescu & Wallsten, 1985). Such opportunities for miscommunication have been shown to be higher for verbal opposed to numerical risk communication both experimentally (Budescu, Weinberg, & Wallsten, 1988) and in field (medical) settings (Bryant & Norman, 1980). However, relying on numerical probability estimates may not always be possible, especially in an arena, where there is a relative paucity of hard, scientific facts. Therefore, when uncertainty can only be characterised verbally, BIAs may wish to focus on the least ambiguous terms.

Our results also demonstrated how base-rates and perceived dangerousness influenced the way in which uncertain claims are interpreted. Thus, verbal probability expressions associated with a high base-rate claim led to higher subjective judgements of the probability of the claim being true compared to low base-rate claims. Similarly, extending upon the well-documented severity effect in medical contexts (Bonnefon & Villejoubert, 2006; Weber & Hilton, 1990), our research showed that more dangerous offender characteristics were perceived as more likely to occur. One strategy to counteract such effects might be to put greater emphasis on the uncertainty of a claim when it relates to a high base-rate or highly dangerous characteristic. For example, if a BIA concludes that it is *probable* that an offender may be a sexual predator (a dangerous characteristic), they could report that it is *possible* in order to prevent SIOs to overestimate the probability of such a claim being true. Conversely, one could temper the uncertainty associated with low base-rate claims or claims relating to a benign characteristic.

The results also confirmed that the framing of behavioural characteristics presented in profile claims also affected the perceived probability of occurrence. The same probability word was interpreted as denoting a lower level of uncertainty (i.e. a higher probability of occurring) when referring to the presence of a characteristic in an offender rather than its absence. This was also true for numerical probabilities: a given numerical level of uncertainty was communicated with probability expressions denoting less uncertainty when the numerical probability referred to the presence rather than the absence of a behavioural characteristic. Another framing effect was observed between logically equivalent claims either presented in a positive frame or in a negative frame. Thus, a claim presented in a positive frame (e.g. 'it is probable that the offender would collect pornography') led to higher subjective probabilities for the claim being true than when the same claim was presented in a negative frame (e.g. 'it is rather improbable that the offender would not collect pornography'). Once again, the same effect of claim framing was found when the original claim was qualified by a numerical probability: probability words qualifying a claim conveyed a higher level of certainty when they were based on positive claims than when they were based on negative ones. From a general standpoint, these results both confirm and expand upon previous results by Teigen and Brun (2003), in which the interpretation of verbal probabilities depended on claim framing in general contexts and had not systematically distinguished the role of characteristic vs. claim framing on the uncertainty conveyed by a statement qualified by a probability phrase.

With regards to issues directly relevant to offender profiling, these results suggest that BIAs may need to consider what is the most appropriate way to frame behavioural characteristics (as either present or absent) or claims (as either true or not true) when reporting uncertain claims. Research has shown that where individuals are encouraged to engage in deeper processing of such information, they are less likely to draw biased interpretations of risk information in general (Kahneman, 2003; Natter & Berry, 2005). In particular, framing effects are reduced when recipients are encouraged to think about the claim in both a positive frame and its negative equivalent (Maule, 1989; Maule & Villejoubert, 2007). These results suggest that an SIO's interpretations of a BIA's profile claims will be less influenced by framing effects if such claims are presented both with positive and negative frames, thereby reducing interpretive error. Likewise, SIOs may consider reframing claims they read in the opposite frame in order to avoid being erroneously influenced by the way in which the claim is presented.

Finally, our results have shown that when prioritising suspects based on profile claims, suspects are more often classified as being either the most likely or the second most likely to have committed an offence if they present a characteristic that matches the offender characteristic in the profile claim. Such positive identifications were systematic when the claim was qualified by a high probability, although were still highly prevalent when the claim was qualified by a low probability. Individuals tend to rely on a similarity heuristic to make probability judgements (Kahneman & Frederick, 2002). It is therefore possible that individuals rely on such heuristics when they judge that the suspect who most resembles the offender was the most likely to have committed an offence. This is not necessarily an issue where the probability that the offender presents the characteristic is also high. However, where the characteristic in the behavioural claim is reported as having a low probability of occurrence, this could lead to erroneous prioritisation, where suspects presenting a matching characteristic are given too much priority.

Needless to say, a weakness of the study was the reliance on a non-police sample. However, previous studies in both lay samples and experts have revealed similar issues (Maule & Villejoubert, 2007). Thus, whilst important to test the transferability of such findings operationally, our results are probably indicative of general findings. Moreover, although advice concerning probable offender characteristics is rarely used in court, especially in the UK (Alison, Bennell, Mokros, & Ormerod, 2002), similar fact evidence in behavioural analysis has been used in the courts and is, therefore, actively listened to and read by members of the jury (Alison, West, & Goodwill, 2004). As such, our results yield interesting prospects for a greater appreciation of how such advice is interpreted beyond the remit of investigative experts. Indeed, other areas of advice also bear examination, including the interpretation of covert surveillance and other forms of law enforcement and military/security intelligence. Alison and Crego (2008), amongst many others, have indicated how high stake decisions might be made based on uncertain information and how, in many cases, such uncertain information may come from external sources (e.g. from other agencies, expert adviser reports, source management and handlers etc.). An increased awareness of interpretative frameworks that may occur across this range of contexts, as well as research-informed advice on how such reports could be best constructed could prove invaluable.

Conclusion

The present research offered a comprehensive overview of ways in which uncertain profiling claims may be misinterpreted. As we mentioned in the introduction, research that is directly relevant to improve the quality of behavioural investigative advice is scarce. A major contribution of the present research was to extend results from previous research examining risk communication in medical and business settings to the domain of investigative advice. Raising awareness of these issues should assist in improving the quality of the provision of such advice and the interpretation and utilisation in operational contexts. Decision-makers who receive uncertain information tend to think they will make more accurate inferences based on numerical information, although this intuition is not necessarily correct (Erev & Cohen, 1990). Therefore, SIO's preferences for numerical information as well as the accuracy of their inference made on the basis of verbal and numerical information could be tested in future experiments.

Acknowledgements

This research is part of a larger project funded by the Leverhulme Trust with support by the National Policing Improvement Agency. The authors are grateful to Lee Rainbow and the Behavioural Investigative Advisers at the National Policing Improvement Agency for comments on this study.

References

Alison, L., & Crego, J. (2008). *Policing critical incidents: Leadership and critical incident management.* Devon: Willan Publishers.

Alison, L., Mclean, C., & Almond, L. (2007). Profiling suspects. In T. Newburn, T. Williamson, & A. Wright (Eds.), *Handbook of criminal investigation.* Cullumpton: Willan Publishers.

Alison, L., West, A., & Goodwill, A. (2004). The academic and the practitioner: Pragmatists' views of offender profiling. *Psychology, Public Policy and Law, 10,* 71–101.

Alison, L., Bennell, C., Mokros, A., & Ormerod, D. (2002). The personality paradox in offender profiling: A theoretical review of the processes involved in deriving background characteristics from crime scene actions. *Psychology, Public Policy and Law, 8,* 115–135.

Almond, L., Alison, L., & Porter, L. (2007). An evaluation and comparison of claims made in behavioural investigative advice reports compiled by the national policing improvements agency in the United Kingdom. *Journal of Investigative Psychology and Offender Profiling, 4,* 71–83.

Bonnefon, J. F., & Villejoubert, G. (2006). Tactful, or doubtful? Expectations of politeness explain the severity bias in the interpretation of probability phrases. *Psychological Science, 17,* 747–751.

Brun, W., & Teigen, K. (1988). Verbal probabilities: Ambiguous, context-dependent, or both? *Organizational Behavior and Human Decision Processes, 41,* 390–404.

Bryant, G., & Norman, G. (1980). Expressions of probability: Words and numbers. *New England Journal of Medicine, 302,* 411–427.

Budescu, D., & Wallsten, T. (1985). Consistency in interpretation of probabilistic phrases. *Organizational Behavior and Human Decision Processes, 36,* 391–485.

Budescu, D. V., & Wallsten, T. S. (1995). Processing linguistic probabilities: General principles and empirical evidence. In J. Busemeyer, R. Hastie, & D. L. Medin (Eds.), *Decision making from a cognitive perspective.* New York: Academic Press.

Budescu, D., Karelitz, T., & Wallsten, T. (2003). Predicting the directionality of probability words from their membership functions. *Journal of Behavioral Decision Making, 16,* 159–180.

Budescu, D., Weinberg, S., & Wallsten, T. (1988). Decisions based on numerically and verbally expressed uncertainties. *Journal of Experimental Psychology: Human Perception and Performance, 14,* 281–294.

Collins, S., & Alison, L. (2002). How certain are offender profilers about the claims they make? Internal report for the National Crime and Operations Faculty, Hook, Bramshill.

Erev, I., & Cohen, B. L. (1990). Verbal versus numerical probabilities: Efficiency, biases, and the preference paradox. *Organizational Behavior and Human Decision Processes, 45,* 1–18.

Evans, J. St. B. T. (1998). Matching bias in conditional reasoning: Do we understand it after 25 years? *Thinking and Reasoning, 4,* 45–82.

Kahneman, D. (2003). A perspective on judgment and choice: Mapping bounded rationality. *American Psychologist, 58,* 697–720.

Kahneman, D., & Frederick, S. (2002). Representativeness revisited: Attribute substitution in intuitive judgment. In T. Gilovich, D. Griffin, & D. Kahneman (Eds.), *Heuristics and biases: The psychology of intuitive judgment.* Cambridge: Cambridge University Press.

Karelitz, T., & Budescu, D. (2004). You say "probable" and I say "likely": Improving interpersonal communication with verbal probability phrases. *Journal of Experimental Psychology: Applied, 10,* 25–41.

Levin, I. P., & Gaeth, G. J. (1988). How consumers are affected by the framing of attribute information before and after consuming the product. *Journal of Consumer Research, 15,* 374–378.

Maule, A. J. (1989). Positive and negative decision frames: A verbal protocol analysis of the Asian Disease problem of Tversky and Kahneman. In H. Montgomery, & O. Svenson (Eds.), *Process and structure in human decision making.* Chichester: Wiley.

Maule, A. J., & Villejoubert, G. (2007). What lies beneath: Reframing framing effects. *Thinking and Reasoning, 13,* 25–44.

Moxey, L. M., & Sanford, A. J. (2000). Communicating quantities: A review of psycholinguistic evidence of how expressions determine perspectives. *Applied Cognitive Psychology, 14,* 237–255.

Natter, H. N., & Berry, D. C. (2005). Effects of active information processing on the understanding of risk information. *Applied Cognitive Psychology, 19,* 123–135.

Reagan, R., Mosteller, F., & Youtz, C. (1989). Quantitative meanings of verbal probability expressions. *Journal of Applied Psychology, 74*, 433–442.

Russo, J., & Schomaker, P. (1989). *Decision traps*. New York: Schuster & Simon.

Teigen, K., & Brun, W. (1995). Yes, but it is uncertain: Direction and communicative intention of verbal probabilistic terms. *Acta Psychologica, 88*, 233–258.

Teigen, K., & Brun, W. (2003). Verbal probabilities: A question of frame? *Journal of Behavioural Decision Making, 16*, 53–72.

Wallsten, T., Budescu, D., Rapoport, A., Zwick, R., & Forsyth, B. (1986). Measuring the vague meanings of probability terms. *Journal of Experimental Psychology: General, 115*, 348–365.

Wallsten, T., Fillenbaum, S., & Cox, J. (1986). Base rate effects on the interpretation of probability and frequency expressions. *Journal of Memory and Language, 25*, 571–587.

Weber, E., & Hilton, D. (1990). Contextual effects in the interpretation of probability words: Perceived base rate and severity of events. *Journal of Experimental Psychology: Human Perception and Performance, 16*, 781–789.

11 Stereotyping, congruence and presentation order

Interpretative biases in utilizing offender profiles

Benjamin C. Marshall and Laurence Alison

This chapter was previously published in the journal, *Psychology, Crime, and Law*. Reproduced with kind permission.

Introduction

Investigative decision making is a domain where experience is a highly regarded commodity (Oldfield, 1997; Smith & Flanagan, 2000). However, arguing against the clinical, *experiential* approach to profiling, Alison and Canter (1999) emphasize that, whilst the value of previous casework should not be dismissed, inferences based solely on opinion are potentially subject to all the "distortions, biases and shortcomings associated with the frailties of human decision making" (p. 29). Such shortcomings include a tendency to use a limited number of simplifying cognitive heuristics when making complex judgements (Bar-Hillel, 1980; Ginosar & Trope, 1980; for a review see Kahneman, Slovic, & Tversky, 1982). Although no doubt highly adaptive from an evolutionary perspective (Arkes, 1991), too heavy a reliance on heuristics can be potentially damaging to criminal investigations through inappropriate misallocation of resources, discrimination against "favoured" suspects, promoting false confessions and so on. Similarly, ignoring such advice when pertinent, well documented and thoroughly researched because that advice is inconsistent with the investigator's particular beliefs can prove equally dangerous. It has been shown that investigating officers' subjective opinions can influence the lines of questioning used during interview so that the interview is used to *prove* the subjective suspicions, rather than to objectively search for the truth (Baldwin, 1993).

Empirically derived offender profiles potentially provide scientific justification to complement experiential judgements, and to identify and avoid potential biases. However, thus far, very little research has investigated the effect profiles have on investigators' judgements. Instead, research has typically considered either the accuracy of the predictions that a profile contains (e.g. Kocsis, 2003, 2004; Kocsis, Hayes, & Irwin, 2002), the *perceived* accuracy of the predictions (e.g. Alison, Smith, & Morgan, 2003; Kocsis & Hayes, 2004; Kocsis & Heller, 2004; Kocsis, Irwin, Hayes, & Nunn, 2000; Kocsis & Middledorp, 2004) or the *perceived* usefulness of offender profiles in genuine investigative scenarios (e.g. Copson, 1995; Jackson, Van Koppen, & Herbrink, 1993). Other studies (e.g. Alison, Smith, Eastman, & Rainbow, 2003; Alison, Smith, & Morgan, 2003) draw attention to the lack of robustness or clearly articulated processes in profiling suggesting that some profiles contain redundant, unsubstantiated and ambiguous statements that are potentially harmful to investigations, either by way of leading it in the wrong direction or adding spurious support to investigative biases that may already be influencing proceedings.

This study explores the possibility that even well prepared, empirically derived and robust offender profiles may be susceptible to being interpreted in a way that serves to reinforce previously existing investigative biases. Further, it is proposed that the point at which a profile is introduced into the investigation may be critical to the perception, influence and utilization of psychological investigative advice. Needless to say, this may not prove problematic where the investigative "steer" is correct and where the profile is empirically sound (indeed, it should lead to a more speedy resolution of the case). However, where the initial bias is inaccurate and the investigator is either reinforced by a profile that is consistent with that bias or chooses to ignore a profile that challenges it, problems can emerge. It is therefore important to understand how such information is interpreted and to identify whether particular biases emerge in using profiling reports.

The representativeness heuristic and stereotypic bias

One of the most prominent heuristics in decision-making literature is the representativeness heuristic (Tversky & Kahneman, 1971). This states that individuals often judge the probability that event A originates from process B, or that process B will generate event A, by the degree to which A is similar to, or representative of B (Tversky & Kahneman, 1974). The representativeness heuristic is particularly relevant to stereotypic bias since stereotypes concern judgements made about individuals due to their representativeness to a particular group or class of individuals. To illustrate this, Kahneman and Tversky (1973) set a task where participants were given a description of an individual and asked to estimate the likelihood that the individual described was either an engineer or a lawyer. They found that participants based their decision more on whether the description given conformed to a stereotype of an engineer, rather than whether the individual described was selected from a sample either comprising 70 per cent engineers or just 30 per cent.

Despite stereotypic bias in the legal system being of concern to sociologists for some time (White, 1975) and bias within the police force receiving particular attention in recent years (Macpherson, 1999), some authors maintain that the problem is endemic (Ford, 2003). Moreover, Devine (2001, p. 757) has suggested that, "even those who consciously renounce prejudice have been shown to have implicit or automatic biases that conflict with their nonprejudiced values". Therefore, investigating officers may be biased towards preconceived stereotypes when making judgements and decisions, even if this bias is not consciously acknowledged.

Belief persistence

The phenomenon known as belief persistence implies that, once formed, beliefs are remarkably resistant to change (Ross & Anderson, 1982). Even if an initial belief is based on an arbitrary value, it can still influence subsequent judgements. Tversky and Kahneman (1974) termed this effect "anchoring", observing that individuals tend to "anchor" themselves to a given value and make subsequent judgements by adjusting from this starting point. Anchoring occurs because the adjustments are typically insufficient, which subsequently results in a bias toward the starting value.

As well as being influenced by arbitrary values, belief persistence effects have been found to occur even when the information the belief is founded on is discredited, situations which should logically result in the complete eradication of the belief (Ross, Lepper, & Hubbard, 1975). Davies (1997) suggested that such effects may be caused by individuals cognitively generating causal explanations, which lend support to this mis-information. Consequently, when the information is discredited the cognitively generated explanation, connecting antecedent to consequence, remains. In a series of experiments, Davies (1997) found that individuals who generated explanations for event outcomes produced significantly more persistence in their beliefs than when simply provided with explanations by the experimenter.

Davies' notion that cognitively generated explanations are more persistent than "ready-made" explanations is supported by the literature on persuasion and attitude change. For example, Janis and King (1954) found that active participation in giving a speech resulted in more attitude change than the passive act of listening to one. More recently, the elaboration likelihood model of persuasion (Petty & Cacioppo, 1986) proposes that individuals who think about the issues and evaluate arguments in a persuasive message (cognitive elaboration) engage in *central processing*. Petty and Cacioppo suggest that central processing leads to attitudes that are stronger, more persistent, and more resistant to counter-persuasion than attitudes formed by *peripheral processing*, in which individuals devote little cognitive effort to the issues and arguments they are presented with. It is possible that police investigators may be particularly susceptible to belief persistence effects since some authors argue that officers generate story-like narratives in order to make sense of the information they are presented with during the course of an investigation (Innes, 2002).

Confirmation bias

An individual's persistence in sticking with a particular belief potentially limits the influence an offender profile can have on the direction of an enquiry. In particular, a profile may have greater influence when supporting beliefs than when contradicting them. Therefore, far from reducing the impact of investigative biases, they may actually serve to reinforce them because of a tendency for individuals to rate evidence that supports their beliefs as "more convincing" and "better conducted" than evidence, of no less probative value, that opposes their views (Lord, Ross, & Lepper, 1979). Ross and Anderson (1982) termed this confirmation bias, suggesting that individuals selectively search, recollect, or assimilate information in a way that lends spurious support to a hypothesis under consideration. Certainly, Copson's (1995) "Coals to Newcastle" report stated that over 50 per cent of offender profiles were considered "operationally useful" because they *reinforced* the officer's own belief. The survey does not make clear how "useful" the advice was perceived to be when it was incongruent with the officer's beliefs.

Timing effects

It is interesting to note that Copson's (1995) survey also reports that 54 per cent of profiles were requested *after* the direction of the inquiry had already been established. Since belief persistence and confirmation bias are both dependent on a belief being instilled *before* presentation of further evidence, it follows that the timing of psychological advice in situations such as criminal investigations may prove a significant factor in how the advice is interpreted and used.

The importance of timing has been established in other criminal justice scenarios. For example, Brekke and Borgida (1988) found that expert testimony was more effective when presented early in a courtroom trial than when it was presented toward the end. Brekke and Borgida proposed that, "once jurors had the opportunity to interpret the case facts in light of their own preconceptions, their resulting beliefs and intuitive theories were less influenced by expert testimony... [but] when presented early in the trial, [the expert testimony] may serve as a powerful organizing theme or basis for a juror's initial impression of the case." (pp. 381–383). Similarly, Bodenhausen (1988) reported that a stereotype's prejudicial effect only held in conditions where it was activated before the presentation of the evidence. The suggestion was that it was not the stereotype per se that influenced judgement, but rather that the stereotype prompted selective processing of the subsequent information; stereotype-primed participants tended to remember more incriminating evidence than exonerating evidence.

The present study

The aims of this study are threefold: (a) to identify the range of different decision-making strategies used in interpreting investigative information and profiles; (b) to establish the extent to which profiles influence this process of interpretation – in particular whether certain decision-making strategies are more or less resistant to change; and (c) to identify whether it makes a difference if the profile is introduced before examination of the investigative material or after the individual has made a clear judgement.

Specifically, this study aims to test the following five hypotheses:

1   That individuals will be biased toward a suspect who is representative of a stereotype when judging the likelihood of guilt in an investigative context.
2   That in the face of disconfirming evidence, individuals will be more *persistent* to beliefs of guilt when the suspect is representative of a stereotype than when the suspect is not representative.

3   That belief persistence will be greater when individuals engage *central* cognitive processes, such as cognitive elaboration of the evidence, than when individuals rely on more *peripheral* cognitive processes.
4   That individuals will demonstrate a confirmation bias when interpreting a profile and that this confirmation bias will be particularly pronounced with individuals who engage in central cognitive processes.
5   That in all cases, the influence of a profile will be greater when presented before the presentation of the evidence than after.

Method

Participants and design

Two hundred and twenty-two individuals, recruited by opportunity and snowball sampling participated in an internet-based questionnaire, the completion of which was voluntary. On entering the questionnaire, participants were randomly assigned to one of eight conditions (described below). When each condition reached its quota it was deactivated, this was repeated until quotas for each condition were met. Not all participants fully completed the questionnaire and some questionnaires were submitted more than once. Duplicated entries and those that failed to answer a minimum of the first three questions were removed from the analyses. In total, 18 questionnaires were removed from the sample, leaving 222 (from 240).

In order to test the hypotheses a $2 \times 2 \times 2$ design was employed. To manipulate representativeness of the suspect to a stereotype, the first factor was whether the suspect presented to the participant described a "stereotypical" or "atypical" suspect, i.e. whether the description was congruent or incongruent with the stereotype for this type of offender (a child sexual abuser). The second factor concerned whether the profile presented to the participant was congruent or incongruent with the suspect they were presented with (i.e. a stereotypical or atypical suspect). Finally, the third factor concerned the order of presentation with either the profile being presented before the suspect or the suspect presented before the profile. Table 11.1 gives a description of the conditions and a demographic breakdown of the participants in each.

Materials

The materials were adapted from an example given by Blau (1994) of circumstances surrounding a series of sex offences. The scenario was modified to represent a series of offences against children (aged between 10 and 12 years old) since it was felt that this type of offence would provide a better opportunity to test representativeness in line with unfounded stereotypes highlighted in the literature (e.g. Groth, Hobson, & Gary, 1985/2002; Kirby, 1993). Three pieces of information were presented to the participants: the series background, details of a suspect, and an offender profile.

Table 11.1 Conditions and participants' age and gender

Order of condition	Suspect	Mean profile	Presentation	Participants		Age (SD)
A	stereotypical	stereotypical	suspect first	$n = 28$	12 female, 16 male	33.1 (12.1)
B	stereotypical	atypical	suspect first	$n = 24$	8 female, 16 male	29.8 (8.1)
C	atypical	stereotypical	suspect first	$n = 26$	13 female, 13 male	30.4 (7.0)
D	atypical	atypical	suspect first	$n = 28$	19 female, 9 male	38.0 (12.9)
E	stereotypical	stereotypical	profile first	$n = 28$	13 female, 15 male	31.7 (10.8)
F	stereotypical	atypical	profile first	$n = 30$	19 female, 11 male	29.4 (10.0)
G	atypical	stereotypical	profile first	$n = 30$	12 female, 18 male	34.0 (10.4)
H	atypical	atypical	profile first	$n = 28$	12 female, 16 male	28.8 (5.7)
Total ($n = 222$)	–	–	–	108 female 114 male		32.0 (10.2)

Background information

Each questionnaire begins with a description of the series of offences followed by a brief physical description of the assailant as described by the victims. The offender's *modus operandi* was then described outlining the offender's behaviour during the assaults, the level of violence involved, and the nature of the sexual acts (the background information is given in more detail in the appendix).

Suspect information

Participants were presented with one of two suspect descriptions. The stereotypical suspect was designed to be congruent with the stereotypical child molester as described in the literature (Groth *et al.*, 1985/2002; Kirby, 1993): Around 40 years of age, unemployed, unskilled and unkempt, has problems forming and maintaining relationships and is morally deviant. In contrast, the atypical suspect was constructed to be at odds with this stereotype yet still plausible in view of statistics for this kind of offender (see Kirby, 1993): young, employed, educated, socially confident and married with children. In short, the atypical suspect appears to be a normal, well-adjusted member of society. Care was taken to maintain evidential equality between the suspects. They were both consistent with the physical description of the assailant described in the series history in terms of height, hair colour, accent, and the presence of a tattoo. Both were said to have been identified by witnesses following the broadcast of an E-FIT. Finally, both suspects were said to live locally and to own pornography. The stereotypical and atypical suspects are compared in Table 11.2.

Offender profile

Participants were shown one of two bogus offender profiles: stereotypical or atypical. Although these profiles were constructed by the first author, to establish realism the statements were based on a genuine profile presented in outline by

Table 11.2 Stereotypical vs atypical suspect comparison

Stereotypical suspect	Atypical suspect
44-year-old white male	26-year-old white male
6 ft 2 inches tall	6 ft 2 inches tall
Dark blond hair	Dark blond hair
Described by local people as a loner with few close friends	Described by local people as a regular guy with traditional family values
Unmarried and currently single; lives alone in an apartment complex half a mile from where the crimes took place	Lives with his wife and two young children in a semi-detached house half a mile from where the crimes took place
Unemployed	Works in the postal sorting office in town
Described by local people as being insecure with women	Described as a dedicated family man
One previous girlfriend (lasted 6 months)	Before marriage the suspect was sexually adventurous and had many sexual partners
Fairly heavy user of alcohol	Physically fit, does not take drugs, and avoids excessive alcohol consumption
Described as having a short temper and can be quite aggressive	Described by local people as an assertive man who likes to get what he wants
Collects pornography	Collects pornography
He is from a poor, working class family	He is from a fairly wealthy, middle-class family
Dropped out of school at 15 before taking his O levels	He graduated from university with a degree in management
Grew up in the area and his accent reflects this	He grew up in the area and his accent reflects this
Tattoo on left arm	He has a tattoo on his left arm

Alison, Smith, and Morgan (2003) (for full details of the profile see Douglas, Ressler, Burgess, & Hartman, 1986). The profiles derived for this study are in line with what Alison (2005) refers to as "traditional trait based profiles", that is, they provide a pen portrait of the offender as a kind of list of attributes. Such profiles are similar to the vast majority of popular accounts of what profilers do, and, in fact, represent the vast majority of such profiles provided in the USA. The stereotypical profile was designed to be consistent with the stereotypical suspect in this study while the atypical profile was constructed to be consistent with the atypical suspect. Both profiles predicted the offender to live locally and to own a pornography collection. The stereotypical and atypical profiles are compared in Table 11.3.

In the suspect-first conditions (conditions A through D), the suspect was presented before presentation of the offender profile, whereas in the profile-first conditions (conditions E through H), the offender profile was presented first.

Procedure and dependent measures

The experiment was introduced as a study to improve investigative decision making. Participants were told that the study involved a series of sexual assaults

Table 11.3 Stereotypical vs atypical profile comparison

Stereotypical profile	Atypical profile
In most crimes of this nature the offender is unemployed.	In most crimes of this nature the offender is employed in some form of skilled or office job.
The offender will usually be single and live alone.	The offender will usually be married, often with children of his own.
The offender will probably be sexually inexperienced or sexually inadequate; if any, he will have had one or two very short consensual sexual relationships.	The offender will be sexually exploratory, and will probably have had several sexual partners.
The offender will own a pornography collection.	The offender will own a pornography collection.
Most offenders live within 2 miles of the scene of the crime.	Most offenders live within 2 miles of the scene of the crime.
Many will have some form of alcohol or drug dependency.	Many offences of this type do not involve the use of alcohol or drugs.
Offenders of this sort are often aggressive individuals with low levels of frustration tolerance.	Offenders of this sort are often perceived by others as being quiet, self-assured individuals.
Sex offenders of this nature will usually have at least one previous criminal conviction.	Sex offenders of this nature try to avoid police attention and usually have no previous criminal convictions.
Offenders typically have misplaced moral beliefs.	Offenders typically appear to have normal moral and belief structures.
Offences like this are characteristically committed by individuals of approximately 40 years of age (average).	Offences like this are characteristically committed by individuals of approximately 25 years of age (average).
Most are aged over 30.	Most are aged under 30.
This type of sex offender often has difficulty in maintaining relationships and will probably have few friends.	This type of sex offender often has superficial charm, and will probably be fairly popular.
The offender will probably not have been educated beyond the minimum age of 16. It is unlikely he will have gone to university.	The offender will probably have been educated beyond the age of 16 and is likely to have gone to university.

against young girls and were advised that, should such material cause discomfort or distress, they were not obliged to take part in the study and could leave the questionnaire at any time. It was also explained that the results would be anonymous and strictly confidential. Participants were then told to imagine they were acting as the Senior Investigating Officer in charge of investigating the series and to read over the subsequent materials in the order presented.

After the presentation of the suspect, participants were asked to estimate the likelihood that the suspect was guilty of the series of offences. Judgements were made by marking a point on a 21-point scale ranging from 0 (not at all likely to be guilty) to 100 (extremely likely to be guilty) in five-point increments. After presentation of the profile, participants were given the chance to revise their estimate of guilt and asked to indicate how significant the offender profile was in making their decisions. Again, this was measured by participants marking a point on a 21-point scale ranging from 0 (not at all significant) to 100 (extremely significant) in five-point increments. In conditions where the profile was presented before the suspect only one estimate of suspect guilt was recorded.

Content analysis

In order to explore what cognitive strategies were being employed, participants were asked to give a brief account of the reasoning behind each of their responses. Participants' justifications for their judgements were content-analysed into four categories, described in the results section. Inter-coder reliability was established by calculating Cohen's (1960) kappa statistic across a random sample of 16 cases, divided equally between the four conditions, coded by two untrained coders. This resulted in a kappa coefficient of 0.83, indicating almost perfect agreement (Landis & Koch, 1977).

Results

Please note that non-parametric tests of significance are used throughout this section since almost all distributions do not meet the assumptions for parametric analyses.

Initial beliefs and cognitive strategies employed

Participants in conditions where a suspect was presented prior to a profile (conditions A through D) provide an opportunity to assess pre-profile beliefs held by participants and what strategies were used to generate these beliefs.

The representativeness heuristic would predict that, given no further information, participants presented with a "stereotypical" suspect, would judge more highly the probability of guilt than participants presented with an atypical suspect. However this was found not to be the case (stereotypical suspect: $M = 49.8$, SD $= 19.7$, median $= 50$; atypical suspect: $M = 50.5$, SD $= 17.2$, median $= 50$, $U = 1394$, $z = -0.6$, $p = $ NS). What is notable, however, is the degree of variance *within* the conditions. Judgements for the stereotypical suspect ranged from 10 to 95, whereas judgements for the atypical suspect ranged from 15 to 90. This degree of variance implies that participants were interpreting the same information in very different ways, irrespective of whether they had the "stereotype" or not. This challenged the assertion (at least within this set of participants) that the stereotypical suspect created for this study really did represent a commonly agreed view of a sex offender. Similarly, the atypical suspect was not widely viewed as atypical, with a similarly wide range of perceptions about the likelihood of his guilt.

In order to explore the strategies being used, a content analysis dictionary was generated to code participants' justifications for their decisions. These were coded into four broad cognitive strategies:

1   *Physical evidence*. This refers to judgements based on the physical evidence, i.e. "he was identified by four witnesses", "he has a tattoo", etc. It also incorporates other "evidence" that is taken at face value, for example "he lives nearby" without elaborating further on the importance of the evidence. This apparent low-level cognitive effort reflects Petty and Cacioppo's (1986) concept of "peripheral processing".

2   *Representativeness*. This category refers to judgements made on the basis of the suspect's resemblance, or non-resemblance, to a preconceived stereotype. This includes statements such as "he seems like the type" or "he's a family man, therefore it's unlikely".

3   *Cognitive elaboration*. This category includes participants who have considered the evidence beyond that given to them in the questionnaire. In Petty and Cacioppo's (1986)'s terms, this category encompasses participants who have engaged in "central" processing of the evidence. This includes elaborating on the relevance of certain factors and/or generating causal explanations to justify the suspect's guilt or innocence. This might include statements such as, "his job allows him to be at the scene without drawing attention to himself" or, "this suspect would have smelt of alcohol and would have acted more violently".

4   *None reported*. The final category captures those participants who fail to provide enough (or any) details to classify their response.

Table 11.4 depicts the strategies employed by participants when estimating guilt for both the stereotypical and atypical suspects before the presentation of a profile. It should be noted that these categories are not mutually exclusive; more than one strategy could be coded for any one participant.

Table 11.4 shows that, in the absence of a profile, most participants (66 per cent) rely on physical evidence to make a judgement. In addition, many (40 per cent) cognitively elaborate on the significance of the evidence and/or generate causal explanations to justify reasons that make the suspect more or less likely. Just over 20 per cent of participants mentioned that the suspect was, or was not,

Table 11.4 Strategy employed before presentation of profile

Strategy evident	Total (n = 106)	Stereotypical suspect (n = 52)	Atypical suspect (n = 54)	χ^2
Physical evidence	66% (70)	63.5 % (33)	68.5% (37)	0.30[†]
Cognitive elaboration	40% (42)	48.1% (25)	31.5% (17)	3.05[†]
Representativeness	22% (23)	17.3% (9)	25.9% (14)	1.16[†]
None reported	18% (19)	13.5% (7)	22.2% (12)	1.38[†]

[†] p = NS.

the "type" of person they would usually associate with this sort of offending. In most of these cases (14 out of 23), this strategy was employed to indicate how unlikely the atypical suspect was, rather than how likely the stereotypical suspect was. However, no significant differences were found in which strategies were used when comparing participants presented with stereotypical and atypical suspects.

Since participants were found to use a combination of strategies in making their judgements, in order to determine which strategies were being used to formulate which judgements, it was necessary to determine which was the *dominant* strategy and whether they thought the suspect was likely to be guilty or not guilty (the direction of judgement). When one strategy was employed, this was simply considered the dominant strategy. However, where two or more strategies were evident, the dominant strategy was determined in one of two ways. Where the strategies used conflicted with each other, i.e. "He doesn't sound like the typical paedophile, but then the physical evidence is quite persuasive." the dominant strategy was deemed to be the strategy that was congruent with the direction of judgement. In instances where the strategies used were in agreement with each other, i.e. "he fits the stereotype, has been identified by witnesses, is sexually frustrated and has the time to be there", classification of the dominant strategy was determined as the strategy that required the most cognitive effort, with physical evidence reflecting low effort, representativeness reflecting medium effort and cognitive elaboration reflecting high effort. This is based on the Petty and Cacioppo (1986) proposition that attitudes are stronger when individuals think more about the issues involved.

The majority (86 per cent) of participants used a score of between 45 and 55 to indicate no initial belief. However, it was clear from the justifications given by a few participants that they interpreted the scale differently. For example, some considered a score of 50 out of a 100 as a 50 per cent chance of guilt and therefore a high likelihood, so reported a score of 20 or 25 to indicate no initial belief. Similarly, a few (5 per cent) participants believing the suspect likely to be more guilty/not guilty than not, gave a score of 50. Consequently, where possible, the justifications participants gave of their responses were used to determine the direction of judgement rather than the score. Where this was not clear, a score of 50 was taken as the "no initial belief" mid-point, with scores above or below taken as likely to be guilty, and not likely to be guilty, respectively.

Table 11.5 depicts the dominant strategies used by participants and the direction of judgement in each case. The table suggests that most participants (40 per cent) based their decisions on the physical evidence alone, mostly in favour of the suspect's guilt. Almost one-third of participants (31 per cent) engage in cognitive elaboration to determine a judgement. Interestingly, cognitive elaboration was used mostly in determining a stereotypical suspect as unlikely to be guilty, whereas the strategy was used more often in judging an atypical suspect to be the likely offender, χ^2 (2, $n = 33$) = 6.11, $p < 0.05$. Perhaps surprisingly, just one in ten participants (10 per cent) claimed to have based their judgement on the suspect's representativeness to a preconceived "type". As expected, for the

Table 11.5 Dominant strategy and direction of judgement before presentation of profile

	Stereotypical suspect (n = 52)			Atypical suspect (n = 54)		
Dominant strategy	*Total (n = 106)*	*Guilty*	*Not guilty*	*No judgement*	*Guilty*	*Not guilty*	*No judgement*
Physical evidence	39.6% (42)	15% (8)	6% (3)	13% (7)	24% (13)	2% (1)	19% (10)
Cognitive elaboration	31.1% (33)	12% (6)	21% (11)	6% (3)	9% (5)	4% (2)	11% (6)
None reported	18.9% (20)	4% (2)	2% (1)	10% (5)	4% (2)	4% (2)	15% (8)
Representativeness	10.4% (11)	6% (3)	2% (1)	4% (2)	0% (0)	7% (4)	2% (1)
Total		37% (19)	31% (16)	33% (17)	37% (20)	17% (9)	46% (25)

stereotypical suspect, this strategy was used more in favour of guilt, whereas for the atypical suspect it was used in opposition of guilt, χ^2 (2, $n = 33$) = 5.08, $p < 0.05$, one-tailed.

Belief persistence and the influence of the profile

Profile influence was calculated by subtracting participants' pre-profile judgements from judgements made following the presentation of the profile. For example, a participant who made a pre-profile judgement of 40, but then increased it to 60 following the profile, scored 20 (60–40) on profile influence. Table 11.6 depicts the mean guilt likelihood for conditions E through H before and after the introduction of a profile and the degree of influence the profile effected.

Table 11.6 reveals that there is a general trend for judgements to move in the direction of the profile. That is, where a profile is congruent with the suspect description, participants increase their estimates for the likelihood of guilt, and conversely, where a profile conflicts with a suspect description participants decrease their estimates. In order to accept the second hypothesis, that in the face

Table 11.6 The influence of the profile

Condition	Suspect/Profile		Pre-profile judgement	Post-profile judgement	Profile influence
A	Stereotypical/ Stereotypical	mean (SD)	48.6 (17.5)	55 (19.3)	6.4 (10.1)
		median	55	55	0
B	Stereotypical/ Atypical	mean (SD)	51.3 (22.3)	38.8 (19.6)	−12.5 (13.4)
		median	50	40	−12.5
C	Atypical/ Stereotypical	mean (SD)	51.5 (14.9)	39.6 (21.0)	−11.9 (17.5)
		median	50	37.5	−2.5
D	Atypical/Atypical	mean (SD)	49.5 (19.3)	65 (20.3)	15.5 (17)
		median	50	70	12.5

of disconfirming evidence, individuals will be more persistent in their belief of the guilt of the offender (when he is representative of a stereotype), the magnitude of profile influence in condition C needs to be significantly less than the magnitude of profile influence in condition B. However, this difference is not significant, $U = 307.5$, $z = -0.9$, $p = $ NS.

An examination of the variance suggests that participants' responses are still far from unanimous. This suggests that some participants are strongly influenced by the profile, while others are not. In order to measure the degree to which the initial cognitive strategy affects the subsequent influence of the profile, the sample was divided into three groups that describe the effect the profile has on the participants' initial beliefs: *challenges belief*, where a profile conflicts with the participant's estimate of guilt, *reinforces belief*, where a profile is congruent with the participant's estimate of guilt and *no initial belief*, where the participant made no initial judgement either way. Since it was found that participants, given the same material, differed in their estimations of a suspect's likelihood of guilt, some believing they were likely, others believing they were unlikely, these categories are independent of the conditions described in the Method section.

Table 11.7 depicts the belief change (the magnitude of profile influence) when a profile is introduced into the scenario. The table suggests that when faced with disconfirming evidence, belief persistence is stronger in conditions where participants make their initial judgement by cognitively elaborating on the evidence than for participants basing their judgements on physical evidence or representativeness. In fact seven out of the 12 (53.8 per cent) participants basing their initial judgement on cognitively elaborated evidence did not change their judgement at all, resulting in a median score of 0. In contrast, all six (100 per cent) participants employing representativeness as their dominant strategy changed their judgement

Table 11.7 Profile influence by dominant strategy

| Dominant strategy (n) | | Magnitude of belief change | | | |
		Total	Profile reinforces	Profile challenges	No initial judgement
Physical evidence (42)	Mean (SD)	9.4 (12.5)	7.7 (12.1)	12.9 (15.9)	8.2 (10.1)
	Median	0	0	7.5	0
Representativeness (11)	Mean (SD)	20.0 (21.9)	2.5 (3.5)	35.0 (19.0)	1.7 (2.9)
	Median	15	2.5	32.5	0
Cognitive elaboration (33)	Mean (SD)	12.3 (14.9)	11.7 (13.0)	11.3 (17.5)	14.4 (15.1)
	Median	10	10	0	15
None reported (20)	Mean (SD)	12.3 (13.2)	9.0 (8.9)	2.5 (3.5)	15.0 (14.9)
	Median	7.5	10	2.5	15
Total	Mean (SD)	11.9 (14.7)	9.1 (11.6)	15.8 (18.7)	11.2 (12.9)
	Median	5	5	10	5

following the profile. A Mann–Whitney U-test found this difference to be significant, $U = 11.5$, $z = -2.34$, $p < 0.05$. These results support Hypothesis 3, that belief persistence will be greater for judgements based on central cognitive processes than when judgements are based on peripheral processes such as representativeness. The fact that those basing their judgements on physical evidence are the least influenced by a profile strongly suggests that this group includes many individuals who do not believe in the value of traditional, trait-based forms of offender profiling.

Confirmation bias

Table 11.7 also depicts the measure of profile influence when an initial belief is supported by the subsequent profile. It appears that participants who based their pre-profile judgement on cognitive elaboration use the profile to reinforce their previous judgement to a greater extent than participants basing their judgements on other strategies. Conversely, participants basing judgements on the representativeness heuristic were the least reinforced by the profile. However, this difference fails to reach statistical levels of significance, $U = 143.0$, $z = -1.08$, $p = NS$.

Confirmation bias exists when individuals place more weight on confirming evidence than they do on disconfirming evidence of no less probative value. Figure 11.1 shows the differential between the confirming and disconfirming effects of the profile for all cognitive strategies. This was calculated by subtracting the magnitude of belief change for instances where a profile challenges a belief from the

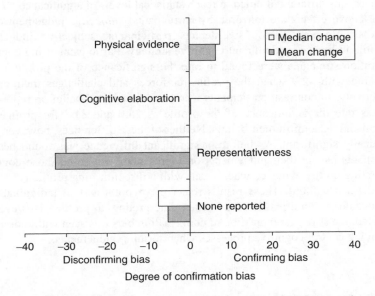

Figure 11.1 Differential between confirming and disconfirming influence of profile by cognitive strategy.

Table 11.8 Subjective profile influence by dominant strategy

Dominant strategy (n)		Subjective profile influence			
		Total	Profile reinforces	Profile challenges	No initial judgement
Physical evidence (42)	mean (SD)	42.0 (29.3)	45.4 (31.6)	32.5 (17.7)	31.5 (23.6)
	median	50	50	32.5	25
Representativeness (11)	mean (SD)	57.7 (34.8)	25.0 (35.4)	81.7 (22.9)	31.7 (17.6)
	median	50	25	92.5	30
Cognitive elaboration (33)	mean (SD)	53.5 (33.5)	57.5 (37.3)	42.9 (31.7)	62.2 (30.1)
	median	60	67.5	40	70
None reported (20)	mean (SD)	54.5 (24.3)	62.0 (13.5)	32.5 (17.7)	55.0 (27.2)
	median	65	65	32.5	65
Total	mean (SD)	49.6 (30.6)	51.3 (32.2)	53.4 (32.0)	45.4 (28.5)
	median	50	55	52.5	50

magnitude of belief change for instances where a profile reinforces a belief. The long bar seen extending into the disconfirming region of the graph indicates a strong disconfirming bias for participants basing their judgements on representativeness. These participants were found to be significantly more influenced by a profile that disconfirms their beliefs than one that supports it ($U = 0$, $z = -2.012$, $p < 0.05$). In contrast, participants using cognitive elaboration appear to show the highest degree of confirmation bias, that is, they appear to be more influenced by a profile that reinforces their judgement than they are to one that challenges it. However, this differential failed to reach statistical levels of significance.

The above effects are mirrored by participants' *subjective* judgement of the profile's influence. Table 11.8 depicts participants' subjective judgements of profile influence by dominant cognitive strategy. Participants using cognitive elaboration strategies were found to rate the significance of the profile as 57.5 compared with 42.9 when the profile reinforces and challenges their beliefs, respectively. In contrast, participants who base their initial belief on representativeness rate the significance of the profile as 25.0 and 81.7 for profiles that confirm and disconfirm their beliefs. Neither of these differences, however, were statistically significant. As before, a significant difference was found between participants basing their judgements on representativeness and those cognitive elaborating on the evidence when faced with a disconfirming profile ($U = 13.8$, $z = -2.12$, $p < 0.05$). These results reject the hypothesis that individuals will demonstrate a confirmation bias when interpreting a profile. However, as predicted, the strongest indication of confirmation bias was seen with individuals employing central cognitive processes when forming judgements.

Timing effects

Table 11.9 compares the subjective degree of profile influence made by participants in the profile-first conditions (conditions E to H) with participants in the

Table 11.9 Subjective profile influence by order of presentation

		Profile influence		
Stimulus		*Suspect first*	*Profile first*	*U (z)*
Stereotypical suspect/	mean (SD)	43.0 (31.5)	68.8 (24.4)	203 (–3.1),
stereotypical profile (conditions A/E)	median	47.5	72.5	*p* < 0.001
Stereotypical suspect/	mean (SD)	42.5 (24.3)	64.0 (21.7)	188 (–3.0),
atypical profile (conditions B/F)	median	45	65	*p* < 0.001
Atypical suspect/	mean (SD)	54.2 (29.2)	61.8 (23.9)	333 (–0.9),
stereotypical profile (conditions C/G)	median	57.5	67.5	*p* = NS
Atypical suspect/	mean (SD)	57.9 (34.4)	57.3 (28.2)	380 (–0.2),
atypical profile (conditions D/G)	median	65	65	*p* = NS
Total	mean (SD)	49.6 (30.6)	63.0 (24.6)	4593 (–3.3),
	median	50	65	*p* < 0.001

suspect-first conditions (conditions A to D). The table demonstrates that when all conditions are considered, the profile appears to have more influence when presented *before* a suspect rather than after. This effect is particularly pronounced for conditions where a stereotypical suspect and a stereotypical profile are presented (conditions A and E). These results lend strong support to the hypothesis that a profile has greater influence when presented before the presentation of a suspect than after.

Discussion

This study explored whether and to what extent individual cognitive strategies influenced the interpretation of investigative information in making judgements of a suspect's guilt. Specifically, it examined how an offender profile might enhance or inhibit these perceptions. Contrary to expectations, participants did not generally view the "stereotypical suspect" constructed for the study as any more likely to be guilty than the "atypical suspect". Indeed, there was a very wide range of responses to both suspects, with some individuals in each group drawing on the representativeness heuristic or cognitive elaboration to either include or exclude the suspects as likely candidates for having committed the offence. This finding challenges previous arguments that the representativeness heuristic accounts for a number of decision-making errors (Tversky & Kahneman, 1974). In the absence of further information, participants were reluctant to resort to the suspect's representativeness to a stereotype in making judgements, with many participants engaging in more sophisticated cognitive processes instead – elaborating on the importance of, and generating causal hypotheses from, the evidence.

A second apparent contradiction was the finding that individuals drawing on the representativeness heuristic were *not* resistant to changing their view in light of disconfirming profile information. Indeed, those relying on representativeness appeared to use the profile as a device to challenge their view and to reconsider their prior belief regarding perceived guilt or innocence. In contrast those who relied on cognitive elaboration, a strategy in which the information is processed more deeply, did appear to persist with their beliefs. This suggests a possible explanation for greater resistance to being influenced by the profile lies in the principle of belief persistence as a function of cognitive effort.

The absence of belief persistence effects for participants using representativeness as the dominant cognitive strategy can be explained through the literature on persuasion and attitude change by considering that a profile represents the opinion of an "expert". The credibility of the source has long been considered a significant factor in persuasive communication (Hovland & Weiss, 1952), and its mediating influence on stereotypic judgements has also already been recognized (Macrae, Shepherd, & Milne, 1992). Consequently, the influence of a disconfirming profile on stereotype-based judgements may not be a function of the *facts* presented within the profile so much as *who* these facts are presented by.

The fact that those participants basing their beliefs on more central cognitive processes appeared more resistant to the influence of the profile also finds support in literature concerning the influence of an expert. For example, Petty and Cacioppo's (1986) elaboration likelihood model suggests that the credibility of the source is more important when the issue being discussed engages peripheral cognitive processes (i.e. cognitive heuristics such as representativeness) than when it engages central cognitive processes, such as cognitive elaboration.

An obvious limitation of this study lies in the fact that a non-police sample was used in an artificial environment (online questionnaire). Thus, the extent to which these findings transfer is of course questionable. For example, it is likely that many police officers consider themselves "experts" in these matters. However, evidence suggests that police perceive greater accuracy in a profile written by an "expert" than one by an unspecified author (Kocsis & Hayes, 2004) and that police are not actually better than science students at predicting offender characteristics (Kocsis, 2003; Kocsis et al., 2000, 2002). Further discussion of the limitations of using a non-police sample are discussed below.

In instances where participants' stereotypic beliefs were supported by the profile, far from showing confirmation bias, almost no change in belief was observed at all. This could be explained through the profile merely reaffirming what their preconceptions already told them. Some participants even commented that the profile was "obvious" or "added nothing new". At first glance, this absence of confirmation bias is encouraging. However, there is a danger that the profile might instead be serving to reinforce a stereotype. Some participants commented that profiles are dangerous and should not be used for this very reason, i.e. that profiles "fuel stereotypes" and create "witch-hunts". This could have significance to profiling in investigative settings where a profile perpetuates a stereotype in one investigation, with the stereotype then inappropriately biasing subsequent ones.

Although not statistically significant, there appeared to be a tendency for confirmation bias to be more likely amongst participants engaging in cognitive elaboration. In these cases, participants demonstrated belief persistence when the profile was incongruous with their views, yet reinforced their beliefs when the profile supported them. This parallels Lord *et al.*'s (1979) study on confirmation bias, which suggests that evidence in support of a participant's viewpoint is judged as more convincing than evidence opposing it.

The finding that offender profiles were judged more influential when presented before rather than after the presentation of a suspect is consistent with Brekke and Borgida's (1988) suggestion that expert evidence presented early in a trial acts as an organizing theme, from which subsequent judgements are made. This suggests that the risk of potentially undesirable effects, such as belief persistence and confirmation bias might be minimized by presenting an offender profile early into an investigation, rather than after the enquiry team has invested considerable effort in the case, only to then call in a profiler as an "insurance policy". Historically, at least in the UK, psychological advice has rarely been requested early in investigations. Copson (1995) reports that in 54 per cent of cases where psychological advice is given, it had been requested *after* the direction of the case had been established. It is acknowledged that bringing external advice into investigations at an early stage is not likely to be considered cost efficient since the complexity of a case is still likely to be largely unknown at such a point. However, there may be cases where early indications suggest that the resolution of the crime may not be straightforward, particularly in crimes such as sexual homicide and stranger rape.

Limitations and future research

Caution must be exercised when applying findings and conclusions from this study to a genuine investigative context, not least because of the nature of the sample employed. A police sample would be more familiar with the case materials, have more investigative experience and, as discussed, may consider themselves as having more expertise than the sample employed in this study. Needless to say, before one can claim any major significance for these effects within a policing environment, one would have to replicate the study with a police sample, preferably under higher fidelity circumstances.

Despite the large sample, another limitation concerns the relatively small cell sizes across the eight conditions which may have comprised the likelihood of demonstrating clear findings, with several results approaching but failing to reach significance. This problem was confounded by the proportion of participants relying on physical evidence alone to base their judgements and the large proportion of participants gravitating to the mid-point of the scale indicating they believed the suspect to be neither likely nor unlikely to be guilty. While in many cases the use of physical evidence as a dominant strategy may reflect the participants reluctance to determine, or admit to determining guilt on anything other than solid evidence, it is likely that if the physical evidence had not been so compelling, many might have been forced into using alternative cognitive strategies. However, it is also possible that without such compelling physical evidence, even more participants may have gravitated to the mid-point of the scale. To counter this, replication of this study may consider revising the scale so that there is no "mid-point" to gravitate towards.

Implications

While acknowledging the limitations to the study described above, the argument that understanding the ways in which cognitive strategies are used in interpreting investigation still stands. The fact that such a wide range of responses and justifications was given by participants given identical stimuli is itself of significant interest. Although this was a non-police sample, if similar variations in judgements exist within a law enforcement environment, this alone highlights the need for a systematic procedure for evaluating how officers make sense of complex information and how they interpret behavioural and psychological advice. Readers are referred to Alison, Smith, Eastman and Rainbow (2003) for an example of such a procedure. Such issues may also be pertinent in juror studies, specifically in the way in which individuals interpret profiling or behavioural advice in court.

The finding by Copson (1995) that over 50 per cent of profiles were considered "useful" because they "reinforced" officers' views provides compelling support for the possible significance of confirmation bias and other heuristics. Further, one might expect greater cognitive effort in real enquiries and less use of representativeness. Indeed, Innes (2002) suggests that police attempt to understand a crime by generating cognitive narratives and causal explanations to link a suspect's personality and circumstances with the events of the crime in question. In this study, these were the selfsame cognitive processes that appear to be most at risk of belief persistence and confirmation bias. Greater physical resources will also be relevant in real enquiries and so prior investment will be high. A potential danger then may lie in a situation where the enquiry team have invested heavily in a given suspect or type of suspect and are unwilling to challenge their own views in light of well constructed profiling advice. Thus, it may prove extremely difficult for an adviser to construct a report that will seriously encourage critical re-evaluation if that report is inconsistent with prior beliefs.

Appendix 1: Series history and modus operandi

Series history

The following considers a series of reports of sexual assaults between April and July 2002. All evidence and information relating to this series has been reviewed. Psychological interviews were carried out with the three victims. The first, assaulted on 10 April was 11 years old. The second, a 12-year-old victim, was assaulted 22 May. The third was a 10 year old girl who was assaulted on 5 July.

From this information, the man responsible for these attacks is estimated to be tall, between 6 ft and 6 ft 3 inches in height. He speaks with a local accent, with a calm voice. He wears no aftershave and has no other noticeable scent.

His hair is either brown or dark blond. He is pale-skinned. He has a tattoo on his left arm.

Modus operandi

The style of attacks in these offences is fairly consistent. All the victims were local girls, aged between 10 and 12 years. The offender appears to have knowledge of the area in which he operates. During the attacks, he follows the same sequence:

1 Grabs the victim securely and shields her vision with a blindfold.
2 Wears a hood, a towel, or shirt around his face or dark glasses to hide his identity.
3 In both cases, the victim was walking home from school. He walks her away from her route to a secluded spot nearby. He tells the victim not to make any noise, cry or resist his efforts.
4 In each case he first demands a kiss by asking the victim to stick out her tongue. He then fondles the victim and, finally, attempts intercourse. He does not require the victim to remove all of her clothes nor does he remove his clothes entirely. From the fondling stage he keeps his victim blindfolded with a piece of his own clothing (a scarf, a hat, gloves).
5 After the assault, he gets the victim to put back on any removed clothing and guides her away from the secluded spot, leaving the blindfold on. In each case, he warns her not to look. He then leaves very quietly and calmly.

References

Alison, L. J. (2005). *The Forensic Psychologist's Casebook: Psychological Profiling and Criminal Investigation*. Devon: Willan.

Alison, L. J., & Canter, D. V. (1999). Professional, legal and ethical issues in offender profiling. In D. V. Canter, & L. J. Alison (Eds.), *Profiling in policy and practice* (pp. 21–54). Aldershot: Ashgate.

Alison, L. J., Smith, M. D., & Morgan, K. (2003). Interpreting the accuracy of offender profiles. *Psychology, Crime & Law, 9*, 185–195.

Alison, L. J., Smith, M. D., Eastman, O., & Rainbow, L. (2003). Toulmin's philosophy of argument and its relevance to offender profiling. *Psychology, Crime & Law, 9*, 173–183.

Arkes, H. R. (1991). Costs and benefits of judgment errors: Implications for debiasing. *Psychological Bulletin, 110*, 486–498.

Baldwin, J. (1993). Police interviewing techniques: Establishing truth or proof? *British Journal of Criminology, 33*, 325–252.

Bar-Hillel, M. (1980). The base-rate fallacy in probability judgments. *Acta Psychologica, 44*, 211–233.

Blau, T. H. (1994). *Psychological services for law enforcement*. Chichester: John Wiley and Sons.

Bodenhausen, G. V. (1988). Stereotypic biases in social decision making and memory: Testing process models of stereotype use. *Journal of Personality and Social Psychology, 55*, 726–737.

Brekke, N., & Borgida, E. (1988). Expert psychological testimony in rape trials: A social–cognitive analysis. *Journal of Personality and Social Psychology, 55*, 372–386.

Cohen, J. (1960). A coefficient of agreement for nominal scales. *Educational and Psychological Measurement, 20*, 37–46.

Copson, G. (1995). *Coals to Newcastle? Part 1: A study of offender profiling*. London: Home Office Police Research Group: Special Interest Series.

Davies, M. F. (1997). Belief persistence after evidential discrediting: The impact of generated versus provided explanations on the likelihood of discredited outcomes. *Journal of Experimental Social Psychology, 33*, 561–578.

Devine, P. G. (2001). Implicit prejudice and stereotyping: How automatic are they? Introduction to special section. *Journal of Personality and Social Psychology, 81*, 757–759.

Douglas, J., Ressler, R., Burgess, A., & Hartman, C. (1986). Criminal profiling from crime scene analysis. *Behavioral Sciences and the Law, 4*, 401–421.

Ford, S. (Executive Producer) (2003). *The secret policeman* [Television broadcast], 21 October 2003. London: British Broadcasting Corporation.

Ginosar, Z., & Trope, Y. (1980). The effects of base rates and individuating information on judgments about another person. *Journal of Experimental Social Psychology, 16*, 228–242.

Groth, A. N., Hobson, W. F., & Gary, T. S. (1985/2002). *The child molesters: Clinical observations*. Available online at: http://mhawestchester.org/mhaeducation/incestmono7.asp

Hovland, C. I., & Weiss, W. (1952). The influence of source credibility on communication effectiveness. *Public Opinion Quarterly, 15*, 635–650.

Innes, M. (2002). The 'process structures' of police homicide investigations. *British Journal of Criminology, 42*, 669–688.

Jackson, J. L., Van Koppen, P. J., & Herbrink, J. C. M. (1993). *Does the service meet the needs? An evaluation of consumer satisfaction with specific profile analysis and investigative advice as offered by the Scientific Research Advisory Unit of the National Criminal Intelligence Division (CRI), The Netherlands*. Leiden: NSCR.

Janis, I. L., & King, B. T. (1954). The influence of role playing on opinion change. *Journal of Abnormal and Social Psychology, 49*, 211–218.

Kahneman, D., Slovic, P., & Tversky, A. (Eds). (1982). *Judgment under uncertainty: Heuristics and biases*. Cambridge: Cambridge University Press.

Kahneman, D., & Tversky, A. (1973). On the psychology of prediction. *Psychological Review, 80*, 237–251.

Kirby, S. (1993). The child molester: Separating myth from reality. PhD thesis, University of Surrey.

Kocsis, R. N. (2003). Criminal psychological profiling: Validities and abilities. *International Journal of Offender Therapy and Comparative Criminology, 47*, 126–144.

Kocsis, R. N. (2004). Psychological profiling of serial arson offenses: An assessment of skills and accuracy. *Criminal Justice and Behavior, 31*, 241–361.

Kocsis, R. N., & Hayes, A. F. (2004). Believing is seeing? Investigating the perceived accuracy of criminal psychological profiles. *International Journal of Offender Therapy and Comparative Criminology, 48*, 149–160.

Kocsis, R. N., & Heller, G. Z. (2004). Believing is seeing II: Beliefs and perceptions of criminal psychological profiles. *International Journal of Offender Therapy and Comparative Criminology, 48*, 313–329.

Kocsis, R. N., & Middledorp, J. (2004). Believing is seeing III: Perceptions of content in criminal psychological profiles. *International Journal of Offender Therapy and Comparative Criminology, 48*, 477–494.

Kocsis, R. N., Hayes, A. F., & Irwin, H. J. (2002). Investigative experience and accuracy in psychological profiling of a violent crime. *Journal of Interpersonal Violence, 17*, 811–823.

Kocsis, R. N., Irwin, H. J., Hayes, A. F., & Nunn, R. (2000). Expertise in psychological profiling. *Journal of Interpersonal Violence, 15*, 311–331.

Landis, J. R., & Koch, G. G. (1977). The measurement of observer agreement for categorical data. *Biometrics, 33*, 159–174.

Lord, C. G., Ross, L., & Lepper, M. R. (1979). Biased assimilation and attitude polarization: The effects of prior theories on subsequently considered evidence. *Journal of Personality and Social Psychology, 37*, 2098–2109.

Macpherson, M. (1999). *The Stephen Lawrence inquiry*. Cm. 4262-I. London: The Stationary Office.

Macrae, C. N., Shepherd, J. W., & Milne, A. B. (1992). The effects of source credibility on the dilution of stereotype-based judgments. *Personality and Social Psychology Bulletin, 18*, 765–775.

Oldfield, D. (1997). What help do the police need with their enquiries? In J. L. Jackson, & D. A. Bekerian (Eds.), *Offender profiling: Theory, research, and practice* (pp. 107–133). Chichester: John Wiley & Sons.

Petty, R. E., & Cacioppo, J. T. (1986). The elaboration likelihood model of persuasion. *Advances in Experimental Social Psychology, 19*, 123–205.

Ross, L., Lepper, M. R., & Hubbard, M. (1975). Perseverance in self perception and social perception: Biased attributional processes in the debriefing paradigm. *Journal of Personality and Social Psychology, 32*, 880–892.

Ross, R., & Anderson, C. A. (1982). Shortcomings in the attribution process: On the origins and maintenance of erroneous social assessments. In D. Kahneman, P. Slovic, & A. Tversky (Eds.), *Judgement under uncertainty: Heuristics and biases* (pp. 129–152). Cambridge: Cambridge University Press.

Smith, N., & Flanagan, C. (2000). *The effective detective: Identifying the skills of an effective SIO*. Police Research Series, Paper 122. London: Home Office.

Tversky, A., & Kahneman, D. (1971). Belief in the law of small numbers. *Psychological Bulletin, 2*, 105–110.

Tversky, A., & Kahneman, D. (1974). Judgment under uncertainty: Heuristics and biases. *Science, 185*, 1124–1131.

White, G. F. (1975). Public responses to hypothetical crimes: Effect of offender and victim status and seriousness of the offense on punitive reactions. *Social Forces, 53*, 411–419.

12 An evaluation and comparison of claims made in behavioural investigative advice reports compiled by the National Policing Improvement Agency in the United Kingdom

Louise Almond, Laurence Alison and Louise Porter

This chapter was previously published in *The Journal of Investigative Psychology and Offender Profiling.* Reproduced with kind permission.

Traditionally, offender profiling has involved the process of predicting the likely socio-demographic characteristics of an offender based on information available at the crime scene. In the last ten years, however, a broader definition of offender profiling has emerged that recognizes the range of fruitful, reliable, tested and transparent evidence-based methods by which psychologists might provide advice to the police during investigations (Alison, McLean, & Almond, 2007). This has, more recently, involved practitioners adopting the term 'Behavioural Investigative Adviser', which reflects a change of tack from the exclusive focus on the offender and his likely 'psychological profile' to the myriad issues that are involved in investigating crime. Extending well beyond attempts to set suspect parameters or explain the behaviour of offenders in one-off critical incidents, advisers can now assist on issues such as DNA intelligence-led screening, risk assessments, geographical analysis, veracity of victim statements and the linkage analysis (Alison, McLean, & Almond, 2007). This paper will use the terms offender profiling and behavioural investigative advice interchangeably, as some researchers and practitioners refer to the process as offender profiling whilst others refer to the process as behavioural investigative advice.

Academic work on the evaluation of offender profiling to date has sought to examine the contributions of such advice to police investigations, e.g. in terms of their accuracy (Copson, 1995; Pinizzotto & Finkel, 1990). This has led to recognition that judgements of profile accuracy are often subjective and particularly problematic where the advice offered is ambiguous or unverifiable (Alison, Smith, & Morgan, 2003; Kocsis & Hayes, 2004).

The Association of Chief Police Officers (ACPO) working group has also expressed concerns in relation to the type of advice given by a range of offender profiling 'experts' (ACPO, 2000). In particular, ACPO policy has led to each profiler signing up to a new set of working conditions with the evaluation of any advice offered central to the new system. ACPO currently audits every accredited Behavioural Investigative Adviser (BIA) once a year, this evaluation includes a checklist of particular variables, i.e. 'Does the report state the agreed terms of reference?', 'Does it include the BIA qualifications and/or background?', 'Does it contain caveats?', etc. However, there is currently no agreement as to how the reasoning process behind the inferences made might be evaluated and how such profiling reports can be deconstructed.

Alison, Smith, Eastman, and Rainbow (2003) reviewed how Toulmin's (1958) philosophy of argument could be applied as an evaluation process as it provides both a possible framework for evaluating profiles and a model to assist individuals in constructing such reports. Alison *et al.* (2003) argued that the strength of a 'Toulminian' approach lies in its ability to deconstruct arguments into their constituent parts, thus allowing for close scrutiny of the strengths and weaknesses of various aspects of the argument.

Toulmin suggested that arguments contain six interrelated components (see Figure 12.1): (1) the claim; (2) the strength; (3) the grounds; (4) the warrant; (5) the backing and (6) the rebuttal. In terms of profiling advice, a claim is a statement made by the profiler about the case (e.g. 'the murderer is under 30 years old'). In order to substantiate this claim, certain components must be present:

1   Strength: this indicates the extent to which the enquiry team should rely on the claim being true; strength may be described in semantic terms such as, 'probably', 'possibly', 'certainly', or as a statistical probability (i.e. 'an 87 per cent chance that…').

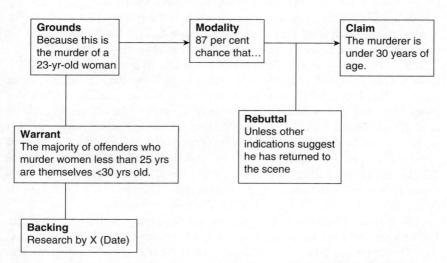

Figure 12.1 Toulmin's structure of argument using a hypothetical 'profiling' example (Alison *et al.*, 2003).

2   Grounds: the grounds are the support for the claim; i.e. the specific aspect of the case that has led the profiler to make the claim (i.e., 'because this is the murder of a 23-year-old woman').
3   Warrant: this authorises the grounds; that is, it describes why a specific aspect of a case has led the profiler to make a particular claim (i.e., 'the majority of offenders who murder women less than 25 years old are, themselves, <30 years old').
4   Backing: this is the formal support for the warrant and comes in the form of a citation to a specific example(s) of research (i.e. 'research by X (date)') or reference to established databases (i.e. CATCHEM).[1]
5   Rebuttal: this sets out the conditions under which the claim ceases to be likely, or must be adjusted (i.e., unless other indications suggest he has returned to the scene'). Thus, if further evidence comes to light, the claim can be adjusted accordingly.

Alison *et al.* (2003) argued that there were several reasons why Toulmin's philosophy of argument could serve as a useful way of exploring the construction of profiling advice. First, there are few clear bases upon which such advice is given. Thus, a framework in which we can deconstruct the constituents of any given claim allows us more readily to penetrate weak arguments. If any of the components are missing, we can more readily appreciate in which ways the claim is weak or problematic. ACPO recognizes the importance of the report clearly outlining the differences between speculative statements and facts. In this way the investigator can measure the weight and significance that can be attached to any inference or conclusion. Second, Toulmin asserts that his approach links closely with that of legal argument. Increasingly, there is pressure on investigating officers to consider carefully the potential legal ramifications of employing profiling advice in their inquiries because it may jeopardize the enquiry (Ormerod, 1999). Toulmin's approach allows for a rationale and justification for the procedures set in motion over and beyond, 'we did this because the profiler suggested it'.

Toulmin's framework was first applied to the area of profiling by Alison *et al.* (2003). They analysed a sample of 21 offender profiles, the majority of which were produced from 1997–2001 (*n* = 16). The 21 profiles contained 880 statements that were claims made about the characteristics of the offender(s). Alison *et al.* (2003) reported that 82 per cent of these claims were unsubstantiated. That is, in terms of Toulmin's system, they involved simply a claim with no form of justification at all. Just under 15.5 per cent included some grounds for the claim, 1.2 per cent involved illogical grounds for the claim, and 1.4 per cent also incorporated a warrant with backing as well as grounds. Therefore only 12 statements out of 880 included the full gamut of the Toulminian framework.

Alison *et al.* (2003) also analysed the confirmability of the claims given. Over 50 per cent were unverifiable and only 30 per cent of the claims were capable of being proved false. Nearly 25 per cent of the claims were ambiguous and 6 per cent had multiple outs by referring to a given characteristic *and* its opposite or alternative.

Although Alison *et al*'s study was based on a very small and somewhat limited sample of profiles, their results did reveal some weaknesses in offender profiles that have been used in the last ten years, particularly the lack of backing contained within the claims. Alison and Canter (1999) have previously pointed out that there are many problems inherent in not including the bases for opinions presented in profiles. These include the inability to evaluate the material, the potential for misunderstanding the report, the inability to acquire a cumulative basis for providing profiles, and the inability of profiles to stand up to legal scrutiny if raised in court. Alison *et al.* (2003), therefore, argue that Toulmin's framework can provide a basis upon which to encourage professionalism, to ensure the highest standards to professional integrity, and to help prevent the worst excesses of speculation and lack of accountability.

Given the criticisms and recommendations highlighted by Alison *et al.*'s (2003) research, the present study will apply Toulmin's philosophy of argument to examine a contemporary sample of profiling reports produced by the UK's National Policing Improvement Agency (NPIA), in order to assess whether the process of constructing reports has improved. The NPIA employs five full-time BIAs who carry out 80–90 per cent of the profiling reports carried out in the UK. The study will also compare the results of this contemporary sample with the results of previous samples in order to investigate whether they contain a greater proportion of substantive arguments.

Method

Materials

Reports

Forty-seven profiles written by the NPIA BIAs in the year 2005 were collated for analysis. All of the reports had been used in major inquires; 24 involved a murder, 12 a rape, 8 sexual assault, 1 artifice, 1 sabotage and 1 suicide. Forty reports involved a single incident, seven involved a series of incidents. The reports were representative of previous years' NPIA BIA reports in terms of type of offence and single/series incident, this was confirmed by the NPIA lead adviser. All of the profiles involved UK inquiries.

Content analysis dictionary

The authors constructed a content analysis dictionary. The dictionary was divided into four sections:

Section A referred to the report as a whole and included variables contained within the ACPO evaluation checklist. The following variables were coded as present if the report contained, Variable 1, the 'date' on which it was written; Variable 2, details of the 'BIA's qualifications and/or background'; Variable 3, 'caveats' relating to the methodological and/or legal limitations and implications of the report; Variable 4, clear description of the BIA's understanding of the brief, written as explicit 'terms of reference'; and Variable 5, details of what 'materials' were used, i.e. crime scene visits, witness statements, photographs. Variable 6 referred to the "report type," i.e. briefing, veracity, linking.

Section B referred to each separate claim made by the BIA. A claim was defined as any opinion given by the BIA. The following variables were coded as present or absent for each individual claim: Variable 7, 'grounds', would be coded if the claim contained information from the incident that provided support for the claim; Variable 8, 'warrant', coded whether the reasons why the grounds are a basis for the claim were given; Variable 9, 'backing', is the formal support of the warrant (often empirical); Variable 10, 'rebuttal', is any conditions under which the claim ceases to be probable and, therefore, needs to be adjusted accordingly; and Variable 11, 'modality', is the strength of the claim, which can be in semantic or statistical terms.

Section C refers to the confimability of each separate claim made by the BIA. The following variables were coded as present or absent for each individual claim: Variable 12, 'verifiable', claims could be verified post-conviction and could be easily measured (e.g. 'the offender had previous history of violent behaviour' can be verified by checking police records); Variable 13, 'falsifiable', was only coded if the claim could be proved false (e.g. 'the offender will be male' can be falsified by observing the offender's gender); Variable 14, 'ambiguous', indicates claims that were vague or open to interpretation and, therefore, difficult to confirm or measure (e.g. 'the offender will have poor social skills'). Variable 15, 'multiple outs', refers to claims in which the BIA refers to a given characteristic and its alternative or opposite (e.g. 'the offender could be married or divorced').

Section D refers to any investigative recommendations made by the BIA that were specifically linked to a particular claim. Therefore, for each claim that was made, the investigative recommendations that were linked to that claim were coded.

Procedure

The reports were coded by the first author using the content analysis dictionary described previously. This dictionary was based on Alison *et al.*'s (2003) original content analysis dictionary which only included variables that had an inter-rater reliability of more than 0.65. The coder was instructed to code each report with a presence or absence for each variable in section A. Having done this, the coder was then instructed to identify each claim contained within the report, a claim constituted any opinion given by the BIA. The coder was then instructed to code each claim with a presence or absence for each of the variables in sections B, C, and D.

Results

Section A

Of the 47 reports, 81 per cent (38) gave the date of the report, 83 per cent (39) described the BIA's background and/or qualifications, and 77 per cent (36) included caveats relating to the legal and/or methodological limitations of the report. Ninety-eight per cent (46) indicated explicit terms of reference and 87 per cent (41) indicated in detail what materials were used. Although these figures are high, this information is required by the ACPO checklist and, therefore, should have been present in all of the reports.

Section B

The 47 reports yielded 805 claims. The average number of claims per report was 17 ($SD = 7.58$); the minimum number of claims made was four and the maximum was 39.

There were several different types of claims made: behavioural (i.e. 'The offender will probably have returned to the crime scene'), geographical (i.e. 'It is highly likely that the offender will live within two miles of the crime scene'), linking (i.e. 'Due to the similarity in the offending behaviour it is very likely that these two crimes are linked'), offender characteristics (i.e. 'The offender is likely to be a white male'), temporal (i.e. 'The offence was likely to have been committed between 10 a.m. and 2 p.m.'), and veracity (i.e. 'The presence of these particular behaviours indicates that this is unlikely to be a false allegation'). Table 12.1 shows that the majority of the claims related to the behaviour or characteristics of the offender.

Of those 805 claims, 96 per cent (776) had grounds for the claims and 63 per cent (506) had a warrant, which provided a link between the grounds and the claim. Table 12.2 illustrates what formal support, if any, was given for the warrant. This formal support could take the form of specific research studies, existing databases (such as CATCHEM), the BIA's personal experience of working on similar cases, forensic analysis or existing theories. Only 34 per cent (274) of the claims contained any formal backing; of those, the majority were studies or databases. Therefore, while the proportion of claims that contained grounds was very high, the number containing a warrant and backing was much lower. Only 10 per cent (86) of claims included rebuttal, i.e. indication as to the conditions in which the claim ceases to be probable.

Table 12.1. Type of claim

Type of claim	Frequency	Percentage of total claims (per cent)
Offender characteristics	305	38
Behavioural	281	35
Geographical	108	13
Veracity	46	6
Linking	42	5
Temporal	23	3

Table 12.2. Type of backing

Type of backing	Frequency	Percentage of total claims (per cent)
No backing	531	66
Database	126	16
Study	107	13
Experience	30	4
Forensics	10	1
Theory	1	0.1

The modality, or indication of the strength of the claim, was coded on a scale. Table 12.3 illustrates the type of modality that was present in the claims. In 18 per cent (144) of claims no modality was present, indicating that the claim was made with great certainty. This figure is reasonably low, however, which is encouraging, as it is very unlikely that a profiler could be certain that a claim they were making was definitely accurate. The majority of the claims were indicated as 'probable'.

Section C

In terms of confirmability, 70 per cent (567) of the claims were verifiable and 43 per cent (347) were falsifiable. Therefore, over half of the claims cannot be proved correct (or incorrect) post-conviction. However, we recognize that this is largely due to the nature of some of the characteristics, where, despite an offender displaying a particular characteristic, evidence may not be available to the investigation (e.g. previous violent behaviour, previous sexually inappropriate behaviour). A small number of the claims were ambiguous, 8 per cent (65), and a small number contained an alternative or opposite claim, 7 per cent (57).

Section D

As Table 12.4 shows, investigative recommendations were made in 85 per cent (40) of the reports. In total, 246 recommendations linked to a claim were made.

Table 12.3. Type of modality

Type of modality	Frequency	Percentage of total claims (per cent)
Semantics-probable	474	59
Definite	141	18
Statistics > 50%	128	16
Semantics-possible	43	5
Statistics < 50%	15	2

Table 12.4. Investigative recommendations

Investigative recommendation	Frequency	Percentage of total claims (per cent)
Lines of enquiry	126	15.7
Prioritisation of suspects	95	11.8
Forensic analysis	12	1.5
Risk of future offending	6	0.7
Interview	3	0.4
Surveillance	2	0.2
Media	1	0.1
Other experts to contact	1	0.1

The average number of recommendations per report was five ($SD = 3.9$); the minimum recommendations made were zero and the maximum was 14. The majority of these were prioritisation of suspects (11.8 per cent) and new lines of enquiry (15.7 per cent).

Variations in argument structure

Although all the reports produced by the NPIA BIAs could be classified as an offender profile or behavioural investigative advice, they do produce several different types of reports. These are:

- *Behavioural assessment* – a crime scene assessment, where a greater understanding of the offence, from a behavioural perspective, is forwarded in the absence of offender considerations.
- *Briefing* – initial thoughts ahead of a fuller, more detailed product, the identification of potential BIA contribution or an operationally focussed brief review of relevant literature.
- *Full report* – the expected product of behavioural support, with terms of reference met with accompanying rationale, explicit inferences, investigative suggestions, etc. (as distinct from a briefing report).
- *Full report with linking* – all linkage reports should represent 'full' reports in that they should include all the criteria (i.e. rationale, evidence, etc.) outlined earlier for a 'full' report. This may, however, relate to linkage being part of a 'full' profile report where background characteristics are also inferred and prioritised.
- *Linking report* – an opinion being forwarded regarding the likelihood of two or more offences being committed by the same person.
- *No body murder* – the provision of behavioural advice (often relating to assisting the prioritisation of search strategies) in cases of (suspected) murder where no body has been recovered to date.
- *Review* – a review of previous profiling advice.

- *Supplementary* – additional reports that are produced after a 'full report' and that address additional aspects not known at the time of the original report preparation, recognising the dynamic nature of investigations, or to clarify aspects of the original 'full' report.
- *Veracity* – provision of an opinion regarding whether an allegation of sexual assault is based upon a true incident or has been fabricated.

Table 12.5 illustrates whether warrants and backing were absent for each report type. As the table shows, the level of warrant and backing differed in terms of the report type. For example, in the review report, a very high number of the claims had no warrant (83 per cent) and none of the claims had any backing. Approximately 50 per cent of the claims made in the briefing and 'no-body' murder reports did not contain a warrant, and a large number of these claims did not have any backing. In the briefing reports, 92 per cent (99) of the claims had no formal support or backing. However, the veracity and linking reports contained a higher percentage of warrants and backing. Only 18 per cent (8) of the veracity claims did not have a warrant, and these veracity claims on the whole contained some form of backing (73 per cent). Although only one-third of claims in the full report did not have a warrant, a large number (64 per cent) did not have any backing. Due to the nature of the reports, it is unsurprising that the review and briefing reports contained less warrant and backing for their claims. However, the proportion of claims containing a warrant and backing in both the 'no body' murder reports and the full reports was quite low.

Table 12.6 illustrates whether warrants and backing were absent for each claim type. As the table reveals, the level of warrant and backing differed in terms of the type of claim being made. For example, over 50 per cent of behavioural claims did not contain a warrant and 89 per cent had no backing. Similar levels were shown in the temporal claims. The veracity, linking and geographical claims had much higher levels of warrant and backing. However, one in three of the

Table 12.5. Report type and whether warrant and backing was used

Type of report	Number of claims	per cent of claims with no warrant	per cent of claims with no backing
Review	18	83 (15)	100 (18)
Briefing	108	48 (52)	92 (99)
No body murder	213	44 (93)	66 (140)
Full report	360	33 (117)	64 (230)
Supplementary	7	29 (2)	29 (2)
Linking report	24	25 (6)	50 (12)
Full report with linking	24	21 (5)	58 (14)
Behavioural assessment	6	18 (1)	67 (4)
Veracity	45	18 (8)	27 (12)

Table 12.6. Type of claim and whether warrant and backing was used

Type of claim	Number of claims	Number of claims with no warrant	Number of claims with no backing
Behavioural	281	150 (53)	251 (89)
Temporal	23	11 (48)	18 (78)
Offender characteristics	305	96 (31)	182 (60)
Geographical	108	27 (25)	50 (46)
Veracity	46	9 (20)	13 (28)
Linking	42	6 (14)	17 (40)

claims relating to the offender's characteristics did not have a warrant, and nearly two out of every three did not have any backing. Due to the nature of the claim, it is unsurprising that a large number of behavioural and temporal claims do not contain any backing. This is often due to what can be described as a 'common sense', almost 'taken for granted' backing; e.g. the claim that 'the offender targeted this building specifically, as it is not likely that a random burglar would have known that the consignment had been delivered on that day'. However, the proportion of offender characteristics and geographical claims that contain warrant and backing was quite low, which is worrying, as it is often these characteristics that are used by the investigation team to prioritise their suspects.

Comparison of the current sample with previous samples

Alison *et al.*'s (2003) sample of 21 offender profiles and Collins' (2002) sample of 26 offender profiles consisted of profiles that could be defined as a full report. Table 12.7, therefore, compares the results from these previous studies and from the contemporary sample, but only for claims made within the full reports. As the table shows, there is a very large positive difference between the contemporary BIA sample and previous expert advice, with the former setting clearer and more transparent boundaries around the claims made and presenting material in a more coherent and evidence-based format. For example, only 4 per cent of claims in the BIA sample had no grounds, backing or warrant, whilst in a previous sample this figure was 82 per cent. The current sample, therefore, contained a greater proportion of each of Toulmin's components. In addition, the current sample contained higher levels of confirmability, in that a higher number of the claims contained in current reports were falsifiable and verifiable than were claims in a previous sample. The claims from the 2005 reports were less likely to be made with great certainty (18 per cent as opposed to a previous sample of 46 per cent), which is encouraging because, in this way, the investigator can measure the weight and significance that can be attached to any inference or conclusion.

Table 12.7. NPIA BIA 2005 (full reports only) with previous sample

Component	BIA 2005 (per cent)	Previous samples (per cent)
Just claim	4	82*
No modality	18	46†
Grounds	98	15.5*
Warrant and backing	36	1.4*
Unverifiable	21	50*
Ambiguous	13	25*
Multiple outs	3	6*
Falsifiable	40	30*

* Alison *et al.* (2003).
† Collins (2002).

Discussion

This examination of the content of contemporary BIA reports has shown that the vast majority contained the information included in the ACPO evaluation check-list. However, due to the potential implications for Senior Investigating Officer's (SIO) and the courts, all reports should contain this information. The date on which the report was provided, details of the materials used to compile the report, and the explicit terms of reference ensure that the courts can assess the impact of a report on an investigation. The inclusion of caveats at the beginning of a report concerning its methodological and legal limitations can assist in ensuring that the enquiry team does not become too optimistic about the profiling advice, and the inclusion of a BIA's background and/or qualifications in a report allows the SIO and the courts to ensure that the BIA has the necessary competence and relevant expertise to provide investigative advice.

The reports contained a large number of claims (805), on average, 17 claims per report. Unlike reports in previous samples (Alison *et al.*, 2003), which in the vast majority of cases solely made a claim (e.g. 'the offender will be aged under 30 years of age'), nearly all of the claims made by the contemporary BIAs also contained grounds. That is, the contemporary reports in the present study referred to the specific details of a case that resulted in the claim being made (e.g. 'the offender will be aged under 30 years of age because this was a murder of a 23-year-old woman'). Nearly two-thirds of the claims contained in contemporary reports contained a warrant, which provided a link between the specific details of the case and the claim (e.g. 'the offender will be under 30 years of age because this was a murder of a 23-year-old woman and the majority of offenders who murder women less than 25 years are themselves less than 30 years old'). However, only one-third of the claims had formal support for this link in the form of empirical studies or databases, this figure increased depending on the type of report and the type of claim being made. These findings may be due to the lack of established relevant literature and appropriate research studies on which

BIAs can draw upon, this issue is something which the NPIA is currently trying to address by carrying out a number of collaborative research projects whose findings the BIAs can then draw upon when writing their reports.

Due to the nature of the report, it is of no surprise that review and briefing reports had a large proportion of claims with no backing, as these reports are summarising a case either before or after a full report is completed. Furthermore, it is also unsurprising that a large proportion of behavioural and temporal claims had no backing because, due to the nature of the claim, this is often due to a 'common sense', almost 'taken for granted' backing. However, the low proportions of claims containing backing in the 'no-body' murder reports and the full reports does need to be addressed because, currently, this figure is only around one-third. Further, the low proportion of offender characteristics and geographical claims that contain backing also needs to be increased, as it is often these characteristics that are used by SIOs to prioritise their suspects. It is important to provide support for a claim by using research studies or established databases, as it allows a clear distinction to be drawn between an individual's opinion and well-documented empirical findings. This allows both the enquiry team and the court to evaluate the certainty and strength of any given claim. Should a report neglect to provide this information, SIOs will be unable to evaluate the certainty with which they can base their suspect prioritisation on the given profile. Indeed, research has suggested that those who use profiling advice may be particularly susceptible to a positive bias in their evaluation of profiling advice, and that this may be due to an increased willingness to accept information from those who are believed to be professionals with specialist knowledge (Kocsis & Hayes, 2004).

However, as the results have shown, the claims made by contemporary BIAs are more transparent and substantive than previous samples. Alison *et al.* (2003) had shown that, in their previous sample of expert opinion, the vast majority of claims gave no explanation as to why a particular claim had been made, they were often ambiguous and half could not be verified post-conviction. In the present 2005 sample, claims had a significantly greater proportion of all Toulmin's components and a greater proportion could be verified post conviction. This is evidence for the increased substantiveness of the claims being made in this current sample. The proportion of claims from the contemporary sample that were made with great certainty, or were ambiguous and vague, was also considerably lower than a previous sample. This provides evidence that this contemporary sample of NPIA reports is more transparent and less open to interpretation by SIOs when compared to a previous sample of non-NPIA reports.

This is an issue of particular importance given the research suggesting that ambiguous profiles may result in 'Barnum effects' in their interpretation (Alison, Smith, & Morgan, 2003). Barnum effects relate to the phenomenon of accepting vague and ambiguous information as specific and can often relate to confirmation biases. For example, where an SIO has a suspect in mind and the profile offers ambiguous information, the SIO could interpret the information to fit the suspect, thus confirming his/her beliefs. Thus, it is particularly important that advice is unambiguous, detailed and that SIOs are able to evaluate the information and its source.

Although this sample contained reports written in 2005 in order to capture the most contemporary dataset, the sample size of 47 is relatively small. Future research should investigate a larger dataset, which would include BIA reports and offender profiles not conducted by the NPIA. However, future research now needs to be conducted into how SIOs interpret the information contained within the reports, as this is a vastly under researched area of study. Decision-making research has shown that many factors such as heuristics, biases, stereotypes, presentation, context and individual differences can potentially influence how individuals interpret information (Baron, 1988; Koehler & Harvey, 2004). The authors of this paper are currently conducting a number of studies to investigate how each of these issues influences the interpretation of BIA reports. Knowledge of these issues will assist the BIAs in writing their reports and will help reduce any potential misinterpretations between themselves and the SIO.

Conclusion

In conclusion, the Toulmin framework has, once again, proved a useful tool for exploring and evaluating the information given in BIA reports, or 'profiles'. The authors do recognize that there may be other approaches which could be used to evaluate profiling advice; however, to date the only framework proposed in the research literature is the Toulmin approach.

While the current evaluation does not give an indication of how *accurate* the profiles actually were in practice, such judgements are only possible if the advice provides unambiguous and verifiable information. Comparison of the present study with earlier work using the Toulminian framework to assess profiles does show evidence of improvement in the constituents of the advice offered. Namely that the contemporary sample of profiles is less ambiguous, with more claims including backing, grounds and warrant, resulting in the SIO being able to determine which claims are speculative statements and which are based on empirical findings. Therefore, with these improvements, we are now closer to the conditions necessary for assessing accuracy and usefulness of behavioural investigative advice.

However, that a proportion of the claims, including those regarding geographical and offender characteristics, were still offered unaccompanied by backing is still worrying and calls for a harsher application of Toulmin's framework in the preparation of such reports. For example, it is offered that ACPO could include the framework components in its existing checklist for evaluating profiling reports and circulate guidelines for the framework's use in practice.

Acknowledgements

This article was supported by a grant provided by The Leverhulme Trust. The authors are grateful to Lee Rainbow and the Behavioural Investigative Advisers at the National Policing Improvement Agency for all their assistance and allowing them access to their files.

Note

1 An existing database containing detailed information about child abduction and homicide investigations.

References

ACPO (2000). Association of Police Officers. *ACPO Crime Committee. Behavioural Science Sub Committee.*

Alison, L., & Canter, D. (1999). Profiling in policy and practice. In D. Canter & L. Alison (Eds), *Profiling in policy and practice. Offender profiling series Vol. II* (pp. 3–19). Aldershot: Ashgate.

Alison, L., McLean, C., & Almond, L. (2007). Profiling suspects. In T. Newburn, T. Williamson, & A. Wright (Eds), *Handbook of criminal investigation* (pp. 493–516). Cullumpton: Willan Publishers.

Alison, L. J., Smith, M. D., & Morgan, K. (2003). Interpreting the accuracy of offender profiles. *Psychology, Crime & Law, 9*(2), 185–195.

Alison, L., Smith, M. D., Eastman, O., & Rainbow, L. (2003). Toulmin's philosophy of argument and its relevance to offender profiling. *Psychology, Crime, & Law, 9*, 173–183.

Baron, J. (1988). *Thinking and deciding.* Cambridge: Cambridge University Press.

Collins, S. (2002). *How certain are offender profilers about the claims they make.* Unpublished Masters Dissertation, University of Liverpool, Liverpool.

Copson, G. (1995). *Coals to Newcastle: Part I. A study of offender profiling.* London: Home Office, Police Research Group.

Kocsis, R. N., & Hayes, A. F. (2004). Believing is seeing? Investigating the perceived accuracy of criminal psychological profiles. *International Journal of Offender Therapy and Comparative Criminology, 48*, 2, 149–160.

Koehler, D., & Harvey, N. (2004). *Handbook of judgment and decision making.* Oxford UK: Blackwell Publishing.

Ormerod, D. (1999). Criminal profiling: Trial by judge and jury, not criminal psychologist. In D. Canter & L. Alison (Eds). *Profiling in policy and practice. Offender profiling series Vol. II* (pp. 207–261). Aldershot: Ashgate.

Pinizzotto, A. J., & Finkel, N. J. (1990). Criminal personality profiling: An outcome and process study. *Law and Human Behavior, 14*, 215–233.

Toulmin, S. (1958). *The uses of argument.* Cambridge University Press.

Conclusions and next steps

Lee Rainbow and Laurence Alison

The original remit of this book was to produce a bundle of papers that already existed in journals in order to provide an updated view on contemporary developments in profiling and behavioural investigative advice. Important though that may be (and there are some examples of already published work here) it quickly became obvious that something more fundamental was missing from the literature that was more relevant to academics and practitioners than merely collating academic 'developments'. The early rumblings of this realization emerged when one of Laurence's PhD students (Susanne Knabe-Nicol) had completed her field research with the Geoprofilers and the Behavioural Investigative Advisers in the UK and Germany. But the realization came into full view when Lee came on board as co-editor.

For all the arguments, controversies, articles and analyses on the worth (or not) of behavioural advice, no one had bothered to actually identify: (i) what advisers actually do; (ii) what Senior Investigating Officers want (and what is possible) from such advice and (iii) how one might set about bringing points (i) and (ii) together. Our conclusions (perhaps recommendations) in this last chapter then focus on the set of challenges we think lie ahead for practitioners and academics. Specifically, these recommendations are set in respect of seeking to answer the question, 'How may we productively develop behavioural investigative advice such that it is both rigorous and operationally relevant?' This requires recognizing the function, process and psychologically relevant issues that are pertinent to advice.

In an effort to examine some of these fundamental issues then we have sought to provide some indications of the following issues:

Identification of what Behavioural Investigative Advisers *actually* do rather than what we might assume they do.

Focus on what is possible within the legislative, practical and operational limits of providing advice within investigations.

Recognize that such advice in not a disparate and disconnected set of elements (linking, geoprofiling, interview advice). Rather, it appears to be a more holistic 'big picture' overview that can inform decision making from a behavioural perspective (amongst all the other aspects of advice). This is to recognize the complex multivariate nature of human behaviour rather than allocating 'separate' bits of behaviour into neat boxes.

The police service regularly makes important decisions that require specialized knowledge across a variety of areas. An SIO cannot possess the required expertise across all areas (firearms, hostage negotiation, and so on) and as such has to draw on multiple sources to help inform decision making. In order to assist in this process professional subgroups are set up to provide unique perspectives and information (Phillips, Mannix, Neale and Gruenfeld, 2004) and to deliver alternative knowledge and viewpoints (Budescu and Rantilla, 2000). The objective is to provide accurate and unbiased decisions (Yaniv, 2004), and increase decision makers' confidence (Van Swol and Sniezek, 2005). There is a tendency for people to weight a message as stronger (Chaiken and Maheswaran, 1994), and to defer to the opinion of another when they are viewed as possessing superior knowledge and expertise in that field (Steginga *et al.*, 2002), thus advisers can play a very important role in decision making.

We have seen how, in light of the Stagg enquiry, a good reputation may be difficult to gain once lost and it is well recognized how quickly subsequent advice can be readily dismissed in the wake of a single catastrophic failure (Yaniv and Kleinberger, 2000). A further critical feature of R-v- Stagg was an apparent failure to recognize advice for what it is and to know that an adviser's role does *not* include selecting options and putting them into action. Option selection, deliberation and cognitive activity directed at implementation, even evaluation of options is really the domain of decision making – not advising. Thus, advisers support decisions but do not (or at least should not) make them. It is worth recognizing as well that many other factors beyond the control of both advisers and decision makers can impact on the success of an outcome (Elliott, 2005), and as such measuring advice quality based solely on outcome is inappropriate and can provide an entirely inaccurate measure of the worth of any given 'bit' of advice.

A more robust method of measuring advice quality should take into consideration at least two other features: (i) the context in which advice was formulated – in other words is it fit for purpose? and (ii) the extent to which the advice recognizes the trade-off between its capacity to transcend different situations (generality) whilst also being sufficiently focused to apply to the situation at hand (specificity).

On the point of 'fit for purpose', if it neither attempts to engage with the 'customer' on need nor operational relevance it is of no value – it can't be used. Further, many inquires are complex, with considerable volumes of seemingly disparate, disconnected or conflicting information. This requires BIAs to be concise, precise and clear in what they are saying, what it is based on and why it is relevant (as we have seen this requires some skill in negotiation and communication). SIOs are responsible for managing the entire incident and so must make sense of inordinate amounts of information. Where lengthy, rambling complexity is present there is a risk that pertinent advice will become swallowed up within less important advice or will be viewed as meaningless, which may lead to subsequent advice being ignored (Wildavsky, 1988).

With regards to the generality–specificity 'dimension', not all problems are clearly covered by policy and guidance, and so it is not always possible to provide advice that complies with the regular protocols. In developing policies within any organization there is a need to strike a balance between generality for guidance to transcend the variety of situations encountered, and also specificity to ensure guidance is adequate to deal with a particular situation (Katz and Kahn, 1978). One example might include a requirement to assess how an unknown offender will respond to a media appeal. Such advice cannot be informed by reference to a strict set of policies, procedures or reference to a clearly demarcated set of research literature. Other examples include questions such as, 'Will this offender escalate in his level of violence?', 'Is this 999 call bogus?', 'Why does this bereaved relative seem so emotionally flat in interview?', 'Why did this victim not seek to save his child in this house fire?', 'Should we use a male or female interviewer?', 'How is this person likely to respond if we arrest their son?', 'Why did the offender not steal the money from the house when it was in plain sight?' and so on. For some of these we could (and should) consult some relevant literature (on bereavement, credibility assessment, rational choice models and so on) but advisers appear to do more than just that. They appear to see the big picture and focus both on the direct question at hand, the known facts of the case and a large variety of other behavioural elements to help inform a well constructed, well considered and comprehensive in-context argument.

Many of the chapters in this book outline the range of apparent ways in which this is done – with respect both to the actual mechanics of the advice (who is contacted, when and how) through to the actual methods utilized (reference to the literature, synthesis of complex multivariate aspects of the offence, consultation) as well as the ways in which different but complementary tacit, experiential and educative knowledge is put into practice (clinical, research, investigative, geographic, criminological) all set against a backcloth of gained domain-specific expertise.

Our argument then is that BIA work is, on the one hand, far less than the media would have us believe (i.e. maverick expert solves crime where previously police have failed) whilst on the other far more than some academic literature has suggested (i.e. Geoprofilers use sophisticated technology to do what students can be trained to do in half an hour). There are of course merits in robust challenges to dramatic claims, and we are not suggesting such problem-oriented endeavours are not critical in moving the field forward, but perhaps it is now time to be a little more optimistic and solution-focused in our objectives and aims.

Our overriding aim is that through greater understanding of the contemporary role of today's select band of professional Behavioural Investigative Advisers, coupled with a stated aspiration and commitment to the highest professional standards possible, a more constructive and collaborative research agenda may be developed. Whilst we recognize that mistakes have been made in the past, and that our predecessors may perhaps have been guilty of enthusiasm over professionalism, such experiences are perhaps inevitable in any emerging discipline and should not continue to represent the stick that beats contemporary efforts into submission. We have a very real belief in the potential of providing behavioural science support to major crime investigations, and this optimism is bolstered by many years of front line experience, hundreds of case consultations, and, significantly, by the policing community. Over the past decade Senior Investigating Officers have gone from blind acceptance of an unproven innovative technique, through suspicion and virtual dismissal, to the more balanced midground of critically and judiciously evaluating the potential such contributions can make within the overall investigative process.

This contemporary policing environment not only safeguards against the excesses and failures of the past, but demands the very evidence-based practice that contemporary BIAs have recognized as critical to the continuing development and professionalization of the discipline. This cannot be achieved by the practitioners alone. The research community has a key role to play in such endeavours, but activity must be focused on solution-oriented research of direct relevance to the practitioners. Historically, BIAs have had to rely on what has been published within disparate research domains (e.g. psychiatry, criminology, environmental psychology, forensic science, medical science, etc.) and tease out the small morsels of relevance to investigative application. What is required is a much more integrated approach where practitioners and academics better understand one another's aims and objectives and produce findings of direct relevance to real-world application. It is acknowledged that many academics will view such bold proclamations as somewhat naive and fanciful, protesting that they have been advocating precisely the same intentions but that such rhetoric is never backed up with access to the masses of relevant data held by the police. This too is changing. The emerging investigative philosophy of a more scientific approach has led to not only the development of larger, centralized and more sophisticated data collection processes, but also a greater willingness to share such data with the academic community.

In addition to the NPIA's broader knowledge and research strategy aimed at improving the way in which the police service create, assure, share and use knowledge in support of practice and decision making, greater access to data held within the ViCLAS (Violent Crime Linkage Analysis System) database within the Serious Crime Analysis Section at the NPIA, together with clear articulation of specific research questions, has began to develop such collaborative activity. It is hoped that such initiatives, viewed in tandem with the evidence provided in this volume of increased transparent participation between practitioners and researchers, will encourage further solution-oriented research and continue to inform future practice.

In many ways, the aim of this book was to lay bare the contemporary practice of behavioural investigative advice and to seek to inform the reader of the continued efforts towards the professionalization of the discipline. We do not claim to have presented such an argument 'beyond reasonable doubt', but hope to have at least sufficiently illuminated some pertinent issues that are worthy of both an academic and practitioner perspective, in order to inform the argument from a more considered 'balance of probabilities' perspective.

Reference

Budescu, D.V. and Rantilla, A. K. (2000) 'Confidence in aggregation of expert opinions', *Acta Psychologica*, 104: 371–398.

Chaiken, S. and Maheswaran, D. (1994) 'Heuristic processing can bias systematic processing: effects of source credibility, argument ambiguity, and task importance on attitude judgment', *Journal of Personality and Social Psychology*, 66(3): 406–473.

Elliott, T. (2005) *Expert decision-making in naturalistic environments: a summary of research*, Australia: DSTO.

Katz, D. and Kahn, R.L. (1978) *The Social Psychology of Organizations* (2nd ed.), New York: Wiley.

Phillips, K.W., Mannix, E.A., Neale, M.A. and Gruenfeld, D.H. (2004) 'Diverse groups and information sharing: The effects of congruent ties', *Journal of Experimental Social Psychology*, 40: 497–510.

Steginga, S.K., Pinnock, C., Gardner, M., Dunn, J. and Gardiner, R.A. (2002) 'Peer support groups for prostate cancer: a snapshot in 2002', *Cancer Forum*, 26 (3): 169–172.

Van Swol, L.M. and Sniezek, J.A. (2005) 'Factors affecting the acceptance of expert advice', *British Journal of Social Psychology*, 44: 443–461.

Wildavsky, A. (1988) *Searching for Safety*, New Brunswick, NJ: Transaction Publishers.

Yaniv, I. (2004) 'The benefit of additional options', *Current Decisions is psychological Science*, 13: 75–78.

Yaniv, I. and Kleinberger, E. (2000) 'Advice taking in decision making: Egocentric discounting and reputation formation', *Organizational Behavior and Human Decision Processes*, 83(2): 260–281.

Index